/= 19-24

Th

Definitive

Christian D. Larson

Collection

6 Volumes
30 Titles

Compiled and Edited
by
David Allen

Volume 1 of 6

Copyright © 2014 by David Allen / Shanon Allen
All rights reserved. No part of this publication may be
reproduced, distributed, or transmitted in any form or by any
means, including photocopying, recording, or other electronic
or mechanical methods, without the prior written permission
of the publisher, except in the case of brief quotations
embodied in critical reviews and certain other
noncommercial uses permitted by copyright law.
Printed in the United States of America

Reprint

First Printing November 2014

ISBN: 978-0-9909643-0-8

Visit Us At **NevilleGoddardBooks.com** for a complete listing
of all our books and **1000's of Free Books to Read online
and download.**

Books include: The Power of I AM 1, 2, 3, The Neville
Goddard Collection, Neville Goddard's Interpretation of
Scripture, The Money Bible, The Creative Power of Thought,
The Secrets, Mysteries & Powers of The Subconscious Mind,
Your Inner Conversations are Creating Your World, The
World is At Your Command - The Very Best of Neville
Goddard, Imagining Creates Reality - 365 Mystical Daily
Quotes, Imagination: The Redemptive Power in Man,
Assumptions Harden Into Facts: The Book, David Allen -
Your Faith Is Your Fortune, Your Unlimited Power

First Printing
Copyright © 2014

Foreword

The Definitive Christian D. Larson Collection is a 6 volume set of 30 titles from one of the most renowned and prolific new thought authors and lecturers of his day. No metaphysical, new thought, law of attraction collection would be complete without Christian D. Larson's books. Before Neville Goddard, before Ernest Holmes, before Joseph Murphy and Napoleon Hill and a host of many of the great authors and teachers of today, there was Christian D. Larson (1874 – 1954) who was credited by Horatio Dresser as being a founder in the New Thought movement.

Christian D. Larson books contain hidden secrets (hidden from the conscious minds of those not prepared to receive them) and treasures that you are unlikely to find anywhere else and if you do it is likely it originated from Christian D. Larson.

David Allen

All Christian D. Larson's books are in the public domain.

* Editors note: Some Christian D. Larson books were originally published without chapter titles. They were later added by other editors of Mr. Larson's works. To my knowledge none of them are copyrighted.

Christian D. Larson Titles
Volume - Original Year Published - Title

Volume	Year	Title
Vol. 1	**1913**	**Brains and How to Get Them**
Vol. 1	**1912**	**Business Psychology**
Vol. 1	**1907**	**How Great Men Succeed**
Vol. 1	**1912**	**How the Mind Works**
Vol. 2	1920	Concentration
Vol. 2	1912	How to Stay Well
Vol. 2	1908	How to Stay Young
Vol. 3	1908	The Great Within
Vol. 3	1912	The Mind Cure
Vol. 3	1912	What is Truth
Vol. 3	1912	Your Forces and How to Use Them
Vol. 4	1916	The Good Side of Christian Science
Vol. 4	1912	The Ideal Made Real
Vol. 4	1910	Mastery of Fate
Vol. 4	1907	Mastery of Self
Vol. 4	1916	My Ideal of Marriage
Vol. 4	1916	Nothing Succeeds Like Success
Vol. 4	1916	Steps in Human Progress
Vol. 5	1918	Healing Yourself
Vol. 5	1912	Just Be Glad
Vol. 5	1940	Leave it to God
Vol. 5	1908	On the Heights
Vol. 5	1910	Perfect Health
Vol. 5	1922	Practical Self-Help
Vol. 5	1912	Scientific Training of Children
Vol. 5	1912	Thinking for Results
Vol. 6	1912	The Hidden Secret
Vol. 6	1916	In Light of the Spirit
Vol. 6	1912	The Pathway of Roses
Vol. 6	1907	Poise and Power

Volume 1

Brains and How to Get Them

Brains and How to Get Them

Table of Contents

Introduction

New Discoveries in Brain Building

When we consider the human brain, together with mental brilliancy, mental power and mental capacity, we find three factors in particular that stand out distinctly; and we also find that the more we have of these three factors, the more brains we possess.

The first factor is the physical cells of the brain; the second factor is the quality of the mind acting through the brain; and the third factor is the actions of the mind itself.

The actions of the mind we may also speak of as mental force; that is, that power in the mind that is distinct both from mental quality and the physical side of the brain; and we always find that the possession of an exceptional degree of this mental force or power, always means mental brilliancy as well as high mental activity.

The fact that these three factors, when highly developed, invariably produce a greater quantity and a higher degree of brains, leads us to inquire how the further development of these factors may be promoted; and we now know that these factors can be developed.

In the past we lived largely in the belief that the increase of talent or ability was something that we might not expect — something that was hardly possible in any case; and therefore we felt it necessary to be content with what ability we might happen to be born with. This however, we do not believe any more, because any number of intensely interesting experiments conducted along these lines have proven conclusively that brains can be developed.

This same fact is being proven every day by a great number of individuals who are constantly building up the mind and its power, through the best methods that they have been able to find in modern psychology. We have all noted how certain people have improved during certain periods of time when they gave attention to the newest principles of mind development; and in many cases such improvement has been remarkable. We may therefore proceed in the conviction that brains can be developed, and that an individual can develop his own brains, not only to a certain degree, but to any degree desired.

Considering the first factor — the cells of the brain — we come face to face with a very interesting fact that has been evolved in recent years through certain laboratory experiments, and this fact is, that the cells of the brain can be increased in number and improved in quality through the mere act of increasing life and power in the various groups of the brain cells. To illustrate, we will suppose that you divide your brain into five or six divisions, and take, say, one-half hour, twice every day, for the purpose of concentrating attention upon those various divisions, for the express purpose of increasing life and energy throughout the brain; you will find, in the course of a few weeks' time, that every part of your brain will be more active than it was before; and you will note a remarkable increase in the power and capacity of the mind as a whole. We all are familiar with the fact that whenever we concentrate attention upon any group of cells, either in the body, or in the brain, we invariably increase life, energy, and nourishment among those cells; and the result must be development.

These experiments in concentration prove that the circulation can be increased anywhere in the human system, at the point of concentration; and we know full well that whenever we increase the circulation, we supply added nourishment as well as added life force. We understand therefore, that by providing the different divisions of the brain with added nourishment and life force, through this process of concentration, we provide those very essentials that nature requires in order to build more cells, as well as develop further the cells already existing in that particular group. This same mode of concentration tends to increase brain activity, and wherever brain activity is increased, there we always find a corresponding improvement in quality, together with finer mental action, deeper mental action, and a more refined mode of mental functioning, which invariably leads to superior thinking.

The development of the brain through this method does not necessarily mean an enlargement of the brain on the whole, for the fact is that the higher development of the brain tends to produce more cells and smaller cells, so that where one crude cell might have existed before, we may produce a dozen or more finer cells; and the law is, that the finer the cells of the brain, the more perfect the brain becomes as an instrument through which ability, talent and genius may be expressed. However, if this process of brain development is continued for a number of years, the entire cranium will have increased in size to some extent. We find in great men and great women who have used their brains and minds extensively all through life, that the measurement of the cranium has increased slightly every ten years; and in some instances we find that the circumference of the cranium has increased one entire inch after the age of sixty. This fact proves conclusively that brain development may be continued far beyond the half century mark; and that ability may be increased remarkably even after the three score and ten has been passed; in fact, the new psychology is proving conclusively that we can increase ability, talent, brain capacity and mental power every year as long as we live, so that any man may become far more brilliant at the age of one hundred than he might have been at any previous time in his life.

When we consider this process of brain development, and the possibility of increasing the number of cells in the brain, we meet a very interesting fact. We will suppose that a certain group of cells in your brain is composed of just one hundred cells. This means that there would be one hundred points of action through which the mind could act in that particular part of the brain; but if you could double that number of cells you would have two hundred points of action through which the mind could be expressed along that line; and in consequence mental capacity and power would exactly double along that particular line of expression. Then suppose that you would promote your development further, and build twelve small, highly refined cells for every one brain cell you previously had; the capacity of the mind would become just exactly twelve times as great as it was before. You would have twelve times as many channels for the expression of talent and genius as you had previously; and the creative power of your mind would be twelve times as large as it was in the past.

It may not be possible for every brain to increase the number of cells to this extent; but every brain can double and treble its number of cells; and a large number, especially those who are faithful, will find it possible to increase the number of brain cells to eight, ten, and twelve times during the course of several years of steady brain development.

This fact brings us face to face with marvelous possibilities; it proves conclusively that there is no need of any one, at any time, being discouraged on account of a lack of ability or lack of opportunity, because even a few months of development of the brain will bring the individual to a place where he will be able to handle and master problems and propositions that he never could have managed before. Besides, this increase of development of the brain will give added ability and power in proportion and we all know very well that however discouraging the present may be, we shall find it possible to take advantage of new and exceptional opportunities the very moment we can add to our ability and power.

In this connection, we must remember that every cell in the brain serves as a channel for mental action. Therefore, the more cells we have in the brain, the more mental actions there will be; and the increase of mental actions means increase of mental capacity, mental power, and also mental creative force.

Mental action, however, does not depend on size, so that a brain cell does not have to be large in order to serve as a perfect channel for mental action. The fact is that the smaller the brain cell is, the more perfect it becomes as a channel for mental action. Therefore, we see the advantage of securing smaller brain cells and more brain cells; and this we may accomplish through the process of brain development, which we shall here outline.

We find that all such development tends to rebuild all the cells of the brain; and in rebuilding those cells, the brain texture is made finer, and the cells themselves smaller and more numerous. The psychology of all of this is very simple, as we shall find the more deeply we study this important subject.

The study of brain development also proves conclusively that the brain or the mind does not wear out. We had that opinion in the past, but it has been discarded as absolutely untrue. The use of the brain does not, in itself, tend to wear upon the brain, for the fact is, that use should constitute, and does constitute exercise; and the more we exercise any faculty or factor, the greater will be the development of that faculty or factor.

The same is true of experience. We have been in the habit of believing that experience will wear on the human system; but the contrary is the truth. Every experience should increase the power of the mind, and the reason why is simple. Every new experience you pass through, should, and naturally does, lead the mind into a new field. It adds a new dominion to the field of consciousness; and our capacity to apply consciousness must increase accordingly. When consciousness acts in a limited field it is limited; but when that field is enlarged consciousness is enlarged in proportion; and the larger the field of consciousness, the larger, the greater and the more brilliant becomes the mind.

Every new experience, every new line of growth, and every new line of mental activity, will naturally add to the powers and the domains of the mind. Thus we secure a larger mental field, and this is one of our principal objects in view. We should always look upon experience in "this way; and if we take this view of experience, we tend to encourage the mind to go farther and farther in the expansion of consciousness, whenever a new experience is entertained or enjoyed. The result will be that every experience will have a tendency to enlarge the mind and add to the field of consciousness.

In building up the cells of the brain, we may consider a few simple methods that have proven themselves most effective through actual experience. This study, however, is very recent, and there are only a few who have undertaken to demonstrate the effectiveness of the principles involved; but we have secured enough facts to substantiate absolutely the science of this new brain development. We may therefore proceed with the full conviction that the results desired will be secured.

The first principle to consider is that of concentration, and the power of concentration to increase life, energy and circulation in any part of the human system where we may choose to concentrate. You can prove this power through various experiments. Concentrate your attention upon your hand, and in a few minutes your hand will become warm. Very soon you will note the veins on the back of the hand beginning to swell, proving conclusively that the circulation there has been increased to a very large extent. Concentrate your attention upon your feet, with a desire to increase the circulation all the way down through your body, and you will soon feel a glowing warmth all over the surface of the skin, and the feet themselves will become quite warm. This method has been found very effective in preventing a cold, in case we should feel such a condition coming on; because it is a well known fact that the increase of the circulation all over the body will tend to open the pores of the skin, and thus enable nature to eliminate those very conditions that are brewing in the system when a cold is threatened.

There are many ailments in the human system that can be prevented or overcome in the same way, because we know very well that the increase of the circulation, with life and energy is all that is necessary to cure a disease, or prevent any ailment, whatever the circumstances may be. We understand therefore that we can, through the process of concentration, increase life, energy and circulation anywhere in the system, and therefore in any group of cells in the brain.

Begin by concentrating attention upon the different parts of the brain; and during the process of concentration try to feel deeply; that is, try to enter into the spirit of this concentration; and express, through your concentration, a very deep desire for the increase of life, energy and action in that group of cells upon which your concentration is directed. It is a positive fact that this method alone will, during a year's time, if practiced every day, increase brain capacity from fifty to three hundred per cent in almost any brain that we might mention.

The mere development of the brain, however, and the cells of the brain, is not all that will follow through this method; for the fact is, that most of us have talents and powers within us that are constantly clamoring for expression, but that cannot find expression, because the brain is not sufficiently developed to act as a proper channel. There are many people in this condition. They feel genius within them, but that genius cannot find expression. They are restless and ambitious, but they do not know what to do with themselves, because the power within them is pent up, so to speak, and is unable to do anything along any definite line. In the minds of these people the brain cells are not attuned to the powers and genius within them, and therefore they accomplish nothing. But if these people would take up this method of concentration upon the brain, they would soon develop the brain sufficiently, and refine the brain sufficiently, to give at least a part of this genius and power within them an opportunity for this expression; and gradually as they continued this development, more and more of the genius within them would find expression, until they would pass from what appeared to be ordinary mental capacity to exceptional genius.

The fact is that there are thousands of people in the world who have exceptional genius within them, but their brains are not fine enough to give this genius an opportunity to come forth and act. All of these people therefore would become highly talented and possessed of genius in actual action, if they would develop their brains; and this simple method of concentration will do far more than we ever dreamed along this particular line.

There are many instances in history where people have been practically of no value mentally, until after forty, fifty or sixty; then suddenly exceptional ability came forth; and this fact can be explained when we know that remarkable genius, if active in the within, will continue to try to express itself and refine the brain, until finally the brain becomes sufficiently developed to give that genius expression; but if we do not assist this genius within, it may take a half a century or more before the brain will, in this indirect way, become fine enough through which genius may act. But we need not wait for this slow and indirect process; in fact, we must not wait; we must proceed at once to build up our brains so that we may give what genius we have full opportunity to work itself out and become a power in life.

In applying this mode of concentration, give a few moments, two or three times every day, to every part of the brain, dividing the brain into eight or ten divisions; and always concentrate with deep feeling, and in a calm, gentle attitude; but be tremendously in earnest. Try to feel the finer life and the finer forces of life as you concentrate and try to enter into the very spirit of the process. The result will be increased brain and mental activity in every instance; and as this process of development is continued, brain development will continue until we may succeed in building up the brain with ten or twelve times as many cells as the brain had before; and also in building up cells that are highly refined, highly cultivated, thereby becoming perfect instruments, through which the highest degree of genius and talent may find expression.

Another exceptional advantage to be gained, through this mode of concentration is this, that the entire brain will come more perfectly under our control so that whenever we want to change mental action, we can bring about that change almost immediately. We are all familiar with the "fact that the average brain responds very slowly to any changed line of thought. It moves and lives in a groove; and where the individual may desire to act along another line for a time, it is almost impossible to do so, because the brain does not respond to the new field of mental action selected. In other words, such brains find it necessary to work at about the same thing every day, and they continue this all through life, a state of affairs which is by no means desirable, as it means a narrow world of nothing beyond mere existence.

However, if we make it a practice to concentrate upon the brain every day, we train the will to gain more and more perfect control of the brain; and we also make the brain itself more responsive to all our desires and intentions. Therefore, whenever we wish to act along another line, or take up some other work, the brain will adapt itself almost immediately to the new demand; and we can proceed with the new line of work with practically no loss of time. This, we realize is of an immense advantage, for we all come to places, every few days, when we are called upon to consider subjects and problems with which we are not dealing constantly; and if we can direct the brain to respond immediately to this new line of mental action, we can take up those problems at once, and deal with them as if we had been working along that line for years.

In this process of brain development, the principal thing to consider is that of making the entire brain active. We know that in the average brain, only about one cell out of every ten is active; and even among very fine brains, fully one-half of the cells are almost totally inactive. Therefore, if we would wake up, so to speak, the whole brain, and make every cell active, we might in that way alone, increase mental activity and brain capacity fully 100 per cent; and in some instances, to a far greater degree.

Here we find the principal reason why most minds are so limited in capacity and endurance. We know that the average mind becomes exhausted very soon and the reason is that the average mind uses only about one-tenth of the cells of the brain. If the mind could use all the cells of the brain instead of only one-tenth, we should have ten times as much brain capacity and endurance as we had before. We realize therefore the tremendous value of this simple method of brain concentration; but in all this work, we must remember that the brain is a very delicate instrument, and responds only to those actions that are deeply calm and tremendously in earnest. We must train ourselves therefore, to feel the deeper, finer mental forces of body, personality and mind; and we must try to get into constant touch with those finer elements that are at work in the deeper subconscious field. Most minds feel this energy to a considerable extent, and most people who are ambitious have moments when these finer energies are felt to the very depth of the soul; and it is at such moments that ambitious minds feel as if they could accomplish anything, and it is certainly true that we can accomplish anything if we learn to apply all the talent and genius and power that we possess. But we must awaken the deeper, finer and more penetrating forces of mind and soul, because these forces are both limitless and invincible.

For practical purposes, it might be suggested that each individual take five or ten minutes every morning for brain concentration; then five or ten minutes more in the middle of the day; and possibly ten or fifteen minutes in the early part of the evening; but whenever we have three or four minutes at any time of the day, it is a splendid practice to become quiet and turn attention upon various parts of the brain, with a desire to promote the increase of life, energy and power. We should go about this process, however, in a very gradual manner, and always be calm and serene, but tremendously in earnest. We should look for results from the very beginning, although we must never permit ourselves to become discouraged, should results fail to appear at once. This system will do the work. It will develop the brain; and all we need do is to persevere to secure the results we desire.

An important fact to remember is, that this mode of brain concentration is not to be used for a short time only. It should be used constantly all through life, because it will not only promote continuous development, but will prevent brain cells from becoming dormant; that is, it will continue to make the whole brain alive; and as long as the whole brain is alive the brain will be young, vigorous, virile and wide awake.

The reason why people lose their memory and their mental brilliancy after they have lived thirty, forty or fifty years, is because they permit so many brain cells to become dormant; but this can be prevented by the simple practice of concentrating upon the entire brain for a few moments every day; and as we proceed with this concentration, we should turn on the full current, and try to increase steadily the natural amount of energy that is generated by the brain and the mind. And one thing is certain, that after we have continued this mode of development for a time, until the brain begins to respond to the will, we shall find a decided increase of power, talent, ability and capacity along every line. We may not notice much increase until the brain begins to respond to the will, and to this process of concentration, but this response will come in a few days or a few weeks to most minds; and after that time most excellent results may be expected in a greater and greater measure.

The second factor is that of quality; and quality consists of any number of elements, the principal ones being mental refinement, high mental activity and complexity of mental activity. To improve the quality, therefore, of the brain and of the mind, the first essential is to refine all our thinking; and the most direct course to pursue in mental refinement is to try to form correct and finer mental conceptions of everything of which we may be thinking. In other words, we should train ourselves to think towards the ideal side of every circumstance, every condition, every factor and every living entity that we may observe or meet in life; in this manner our thinking will become more and more refined, and the quality of mind and brain will improve accordingly.

Another essential in the improvement of quality is to cause the mind to pass from the simple to the complex in all its mental conceptions. To illustrate: If you are thinking of a certain object and have only one general idea of that object, your thinking at that time is very simple. But if you try to consider that object from every imaginable point of view, you will find, that instead of forming one idea of the object, you will form a score or more. Your mental conception therefore of that object will become very large, very extensive and very complex. That object will give you ten, twenty, fifty or possibly one hundred different ideas, instead of one idea which would be the case if you thought of that object in a general way only, and only along a certain line. It is a most excellent practice to make it a point to try to think of every object or subject from as many viewpoints as possible. This will not only give the mind many new ideas, but it will train the mind to act along many new lines, and in addition will improve the quality of the mind in every form and manner.

An important gain in this connection is that of enjoyment. We all have the privilege to enjoy life in as many ways as possible, provided the enjoyment is wholesome and beneficial; and we shall find that the more complex the mind becomes, that is, the more channels there are in the mind, through which we can think and act, the greater will be our enjoyment of everything that we may entertain in life. We will be able to appreciate an immense universe instead of merely a few elements, as before; and we will begin to live in a world that will contain hundreds and even thousands of times as many interesting states or fields of consciousness as we found in the world in which we lived in the past. In brief, our state of existence will become a harp of a thousand strings instead of merely a harp of a few strings, as is the case with the average person.

Our object should always be to enlarge life, to enlarge consciousness, to enlarge the field of the mind, and to multiply the number of channels through which the mind can find action, because the more lines of expression there are, the more talent and genius we can apply in practical life; and we shall find that the practice of making all thinking more complex, that is, learning to see everything from every imaginable viewpoint, will tend directly to produce this enlargement of the mental field; and results will be numerous as well as highly desirable, in every form and manner. The study of mental quality is one that is very large and very deep; and it is a subject that will be considered more thoroughly as we proceed in this study; but for practical purposes the above will be sufficient; and we will therefore proceed to the third factor — the increase of the actions of the mind itself.

Every faculty must have a certain amount of energy and life; and to increase the energy and life of each particular faculty, we must learn, first, that it is what we realize in that faculty that actually finds expression.

We might define the actions of the mind as the inner power of thought, or what might also be called, the thinking of the faculty or the talent that is being employed. To illustrate, take the faculty of music. We shall find that it is large, active and brilliant in proportion to how well the musician can really think music; and to think music, we enter into the spirit of music itself. The mind acts in the world of music, or in the real soul of music instead of simply viewing the element of music from a distance. We shall find it to be a fact, that if we wish to increase mental activity through any talent or faculty, we must think that talent, and think that talent more and more: and we think a talent whenever mind or soul expresses itself through the soul of that talent, forming at the time distinct and definite ideas of the talent itself. Whenever we employ a faculty, we find that a certain force is being expressed through that faculty, and that force consists of thinking what is absolutely in that faculty itself.

To illustrate: When you think music, you do not think of music, but you really think music; and there is a vast difference. You must understand the difference, if you wish to attain genius. When you think invention, you do not think of invention, but you think invention itself. When you think business you do not think of business, but you think business itself; that is, you think through the life and spirit of the business faculty in your possession; and when you think business, your business faculty is acting, not round about the business element, but is acting through the business element; and is consequently producing definite and valuable business ideas. You will find that when you think business according to this definition, your mind will naturally create better business ideas, better business plans and methods than it has ever done in the past, because you are acting in the business faculty itself, in the very spirit, soul and essence of it, and in that part of the mind that has the power to apply itself in the commercial world.

It will be very evident to the student that it is difficult to define in words, what it is to "think" your talent, or to think a faculty. It is something that we must realize through our own experience; but when we attain this realization we shall find that when we make a special effort to enter into a faculty and talent whenever we think of that talent, and at the same time try to think what the talent already is and can do, we are getting down to rock bottom in this immense field.

We should proceed therefore to try to think the ability or talent we possess, or the ability and talent we wish to develop, whatever that ability may be; and by so doing, we will increase the real vital activity of that ability or talent in itself, and thus enter into that indefinable something in the mind that we speak of as native talent or as native genius. It is indefinable; it is real; it is natural; it is inherent; it is second nature. It is an inseparable part of the mind.

We should also make it a point to think of every talent as a growing talent. Think of your faculties and talents as evolving, developing and creating more power. Picture in your mind every talent as being in a process of building. Think of your consciousness as delving deeper and deeper into this vast interior mental process, where talent and genius are created. Think of your whole mind as becoming more and more alive. We know there is something alive in the mind that we call talent. There is a mental power that comes from the depth of the soul; and when the brain begins to respond to that power from within, that power will work itself out through all the cells of the brain, and the result will be that all those cells will become direct channels for a larger, a greater and a stronger expression of all the ability, talent, power or genius that we may arouse within. It is then that the mind becomes a live wire, so to speak; and when the mind becomes a live wire, we shall have no more dormant brain cells and no more inactive forces in our mental world. Every power, faculty and talent we possess will begin to work, and will work constructively as well as effectively along the lines that we have decided upon. The result will be that capacity, power, ability, talent and genius will increase along all lines; and this increase may be continued steadily and uninterruptedly as long as we live.

We must proceed in the conviction that we not only have the power to arouse all the latent capacity and talent within us, but we also have the power to build up and develop that capacity and talent to any degree desired, and for an indefinite period; and here we should remember that the mind has the faculty of rebuilding itself, again and again, on a larger and a larger scale for any length of time. The mind that you have today can double its own power and talent during the present year; and next year this mind that has been doubled, can repeat the process and double once more this larger life and capacity that has been gained. Later, this process can be repeated again and continued indefinitely.

It matters not therefore how small a mind you may have today, you can double the power of that mind again and again as long as you live, until it becomes a prodigious mind, and you become a mental giant. Remarkable possibilities therefore lie before us in this wonderful study; and those who will persevere in the correct application of these principles, will succeed in making real the ideal of these possibilities, steadily and surely in every direction; so therefore no matter how high our ideals may be, or how difficult the undertakings we have in view, those undertakings can be carried out successfully, and every ideal realized. The power to do those things does exist within us; and whenever we want more power than we have now, we need only remember that every human mind has the faculty of rebuilding itself on a larger scale, again and again, for any length of time.

Chapter 1

Building the Brain

Function of the Brain — The brain is to the mind what the piano is to the pianist, or what any instrument of expression is to that which is being expressed. To develop the brain, therefore, to the very highest degree is necessary if the mind is to make full application and tangible use of every power that' may be latent in the great within of the subconscious. The brain as a whole, as well as every cell in the brain, must become perfectly responsive to every action the mind may make, and must possess the capacity to give that action the full volume of power required. The brain must possess the capacity of much work, and must also possess that fineness of quality that is necessary to the highest order of work. In brief, to supply the demands of genius, the brain as well as the mind must be able to furnish both quantity and quality.

Modern Methods — The methods employed in modern education tend in a measure to develop the brain. The practical use of the mind will develop the brain in parts, but such development is both indirect and inadequate. The average mind is much greater than the brain it is trying to use; therefore, it does not accomplish what it has the power to accomplish. To develop the brain even to a slight degree, would in many instances give the mind almost twice as much active capacity and ability as is possessed now, while if such development were promoted thoroughly and in conjunction with further mental development, there would be a decided increase in ability; and in many instances actual genius would appear. In the average brain there are millions of cells that are practically dormant. They are never called into action, and in consequence serve only as obstacles to the efforts of the mind. In fact, in many brains more than half of the cells are not in use. They are constantly being enriched or reconstructed, but they do not serve the mind in any way; and such brain cells as do not permit the expression of the mind will invariably prevent that expression.

Active Brain Cells — The more active brain cells we possess the more mental power we can express. The mental power and ability that is back of the physical brain is limitless, but the cells of the physical brain are only channels through which talent and genius are coming forth. To increase the number of active brain cells, therefore, is one of the chief essentials in the development of genius. When all the cells that now exist in the brain are made active, the mind, if correspondingly developed, will become exceptional in brilliancy and power. But if the mind should so develop that the present number of cells would not be adequate, the number could be increased without changing the regular size of the brain to any extent, although the brain as a whole always becomes a little larger when high development of both brain and mind is taking place. In the crude brain the cells are large and sluggish. In the developed brain the cells are small, refined and very active. In fact, the smaller the brain cell the better it becomes as an instrument of the mind, the reason being that the more closely the cell approaches a point of action, the more perfect the concentration of mental action; and the more perfect the concentration of any action, the greater the power and efficiency of that action. When the brain is well developed all the large sluggish cells will be removed, and the space will be filled with an extra number of small active cells; in consequence a well developed brain has several times as many cells as an undeveloped brain, although the size of the two brains may be the same. And since the cells of the well developed brain will all be alive ready to respond to the mind, we can readily see the advantage of thorough brain development.

The Three Essentials — The brain of the genius is always very fine in the quality of its substance; and this is the first essential. The second essential is an increase in the number of active brain cells. In fact, where we feel real genius we find every brain cell thoroughly alive and in a high state of vibration. The third essential is the awakening of the subconscious life of every brain cell. The brain of the genius is very strong on the subconscious side; and this is one reason why such a brain sometimes gives expression to what seems to be superhuman attainments. Every cell contains a subjective or subconscious life; that is, an inner life that is far greater in power, capacity and efficiency than any phase of life that may exist merely on the surface; and when this subconscious life is fully alive in all the brain cells, we will naturally have a brain that is inexhaustible in capacity and power.

Necessary Elements — There are a number of elements that go to make up genius. One of these is unlimited capacity for work; and this is secured when the subconscious life and power of every cell in the brain becomes alive. Such a brain will not be used up no matter how complex, how intricate or how extensive the actions of the mind may be. It is equal to every occasion that the mind may meet, no matter how difficult, and it can easily hold out until the task is finished. The average brain is used up after a few hours of full mental action; and the reason is found in the fact that its capacity is limited. In such a brain the deep, inexhaustible subconscious life is not awakened, therefore it has but little to draw upon. In the brain of the genius, however, there is any amount of life and power upon which to draw. Every cell is literally alive with unlimited subconscious life, and therefore no matter how great the demands of the mind may be, the brain is fully equal to all of those demands.

Increased Capacity — When the mind is inspired by great ambitions, the desire to do great things in the world becomes stronger and stronger. In consequence, the mind will attempt to obey these desires; in fact, it will have no peace until it does. But if the brain does not have the power and the capacity to work as much and as long as the mind may require in order to carry out these ambitions, failure will inevitably follow. And here we have one reason why so many important undertakings with every opportunity for remarkable success have failed almost from the beginning. The men behind those undertakings had the ambition and the courage to proceed, but they did not have the brain capacity to hold out, the reason being that their brain cells were not alive with the limitless power of the great within. This inexhaustible brain capacity, however, can be developed by anyone, because the subconscious life of every cell is very easily awakened, and the more we draw upon this larger interior life, the easier it becomes to secure more The problem is to take the first step; that is, to enter into conscious touch with the subconscious side of things; and when this is done, we have the key that will unlock all the greater powers that are latent within us.

How to Proceed — To give more life and action to every part of the brain is necessary before real brain development can begin; but to promote this, the three great divisions of the brain must receive special and distinct attention. Each part must be dealt with according to its special function, and every effort to increase the life and action of that part must be animated with the desire to promote the power and efficiency of that function. The function of the fore brain embraces principally the power of intellect, memory and imagination. The mind acts directly upon this part of the brain when it reasons and knows, and also when it creates ideas, forms plans, evolves methods, analyzes laws and principles, understands, comprehends, discriminates, or exercises the elements of insight, perception or discernment. The function of the back brain embraces working capacity, force, determination, push, power, reserve force and kindred elements. The mind draws upon the back brain whenever force is required in the actual doing of things, and acts upon this part of the brain when trying to control, direct and master anything in the physical personality. The function of the top brain embraces aspiration, ambition, consciousness of quality and worth, attainments of superiority, perception of ideals and the realization of higher mental states of conscious existence. The mind acts through the top brain whenever it soars to greater heights, or whenever it builds for greater things anywhere in the physical or mental domain. When the top brain is large and active the finer things of life are readily discerned, but when this part of the brain is small or sluggish nothing is appreciated but that which can be weighed or measured.

Full Development — The combined use of all the different parts of the brain is necessary to secure results along any line. Every effort requires intelligence and imagination as well as power and working capacity. And no effort is worthwhile unless it is prompted by the desire to press on towards the greater, the superior and the ideal. Every part of the brain, therefore, should be well developed. Every part helps every other part, and the best results are secured along any line when all parts of the brain are equally developed. Abnormal development in some parts may give expression to exceptional genius, but such genius is one-sided. It is not properly balanced, and for that reason can never be at its best. When genius is queer, eccentric, peculiar, or addicted to what is called "the artistic temperament" it is not the best developed form of genius; it is not real genius, but the expression of extraordinary powers that are only under partial control; that is, they may be controlled to do great things through a certain faculty, but they are not controlled to act in harmony with all the faculties; and it is only when all the faculties act in harmony that the highest attainments and the greatest achievements become possible.

Real Genius — Where we find real genius we find exceptional capacity for work and remarkable talent for high efficiency. But we do not find such genius to be eccentric, very sensitive or difficult to get along with. The real genius is broad minded and can get along with anybody. He is a master mind and can therefore adapt himself to all kinds of conditions, and can use all kinds of conditions through which to reach the greater goal in view. The real genius is well balanced, and therefore has not simply the power to do great things, but also the power to live a great life. The reason why so many among those who possess certain grades of genius are eccentric or oversensitive, is found in the fact that certain parts of their brains are not sufficiently developed to act in harmony with those better developed parts through which the genius in question is expressed. But when these neglected parts become well developed, those people will not only become well balanced characters and charming personalities, but they will also gain the power to do greater things than ever before.

Building Brain Cells — To develop any part of the brain more energy and more nourishment will be required in that part, and these two essentials may be provided through subjective concentration. When we concentrate subjectively upon any part of the human system we produce more mental action in that part. This increase of mental action will cause more life and energy to be generated in that part. It will also attract surplus energy from other parts of the system because much gathers more; and in brief, will increase the circulation in that part, thus supplying the added nourishment required. When we concentrate upon any part of the brain we promote the building of brain cells. Wherever an increase of energy and nourishment is provided the cell building process will be promoted. And if that concentration is inspired with a strong desire to attain the greater and the superior, the new brain cells will have superior qualities. Accordingly they will become fit instruments for the expression of real genius. The concentration of attention upon every part of the brain will also cause all the inactive cells to become alive, though in order to secure the best results in this respect the mind should try to feel the finer forces of the brain, and the finer activities of those forces while concentration is taking place. So long as concentration is mechanical there are no results, but when the process of concentration works through the finer life forces it becomes a living process, and the desired results will invariably follow.

Special Methods — To build brain cells in any part of the brain, and to cause all of the cells in that part to become alive, concentration should aim to promote the natural functions of that part; that is, when we concentrate upon any part of the brain we should express a strong, deep and persistent desire to do that which that particular part has the natural power to do. When concentrating upon the back brain, be determined. Mentally act in the positive, determined attitude; desire power, and aim to push forward every purpose you have in view. Feel the increase of capacity and try to realize that the energies of the back brain are constantly accumulating, becoming stronger and stronger, until you feel as if you had sufficient power to see anything through. This process of concentration will accomplish three things. The inactive cells of the back brain will become alive. And the more living cells there are in any part of the human system the more power and capacity there will be in that particular part. Secondly, new brain cells will be formed; and as all of these new cells will be alive, there will be further increase in the power and the working capacity of the back brain. And third, the natural function of the back brain will be promoted. You will have more force and more push. You will become more positive and more determined, and your power to see things through to a finish will increase in proportion. In addition, there will be a steady increase of creative energy, and this is very important, because to possess an enormous amount of creative energy is one of the principal secrets of genius. When concentrating upon the fore brain use the imagination extensively. Create mental pictures of every mental state of being that you can imagine. Form plans of all kinds, and try to promote practical methods for every imaginable undertaking in the world. Use the power of analysis thoroughly upon every idea, law or principle that you may encounter in your thinking, and try to form your own original conclusion as to the nature of it all. Try to feel intelligence, and picture mental brilliancy in every cell throughout that part of the brain. But do not permit your thinking to become heavy or laborious. Keep attention in touch with the finer forces of the brain, and have expansion of mind constantly in view. This concentration will do for the fore brain what it was stated the previous exercise would do for the back brain, and in addition it will develop the power to create ideas of merit; and there is no mental power that is more important than this. Everything that man has formed in the visible world was first an idea. And as the best ideas produce the best results in practical life, we realize therefore, that those who develop the power to create better and better ideas will steadily rise in the scale, occupying more important places every year in the world's work. When concentrating upon the top brain aspire to the highest you know. Give full expression to all the powers of your ambition. Desire superiority, and try to feel consciously all the elements of worth that you know to have existence. Live in the ideal. Transcend the world of things and let your mind soar to empyrean heights. Think of everything that is high, noble and great, and desire with all the power of your soul to realize it all. Then know that you can. Have full confidence in yourself. Have faith in all your desires and ambitions. Think that you can. Feel that you can, and inspire that feeling with the loftiest thoughts that you can possibly form in your mind. Concentrate in this manner every day, or several times every day when convenient. A few minutes at a time is sufficient, and if done properly, a year's time will produce improvements that no one at first could believe.

Additional Methods — Another most excellent exercise is to concentrate upon every group of cells in the brain, giving a few seconds to each group, and then picture genius in every cell during the process. What we mentally picture, we create; therefore by daily picturing genius in every brain cell, we will tend to create genius in every brain cell. We thus develop the brain of the genius, and whatever we may wish to attain or accomplish we will then have a brain that can positively do what we wish to have done. To awaken and increase the subconscious life in the brain cells, the following method should be employed: Turn attention upon the back brain and think with deep feeling of the subconscious life that you know permeates every fiber. Continue for a few moments, and try to enter into this finer mental life. Do not be anxious for results, but be calm and well poised, and deeply determined to secure results. In a few moments move attention to the right of the brain and repeat the process. Then move attention to the left of the brain, repeating the process in each case. In each part try to enter into the finer subconscious life, and desire the awakening of this life with the deepest and strongest desire possible. The entire exercise may continue for ten or fifteen minutes, and may be taken once or twice a day.

Important — Pay no attention to the way you feel after the exercise. You may feel drowsy or you may feel mentally exhilarated. In either case keep calm, retain your poise and know that every brain cell in your possession has increased its volume of life and power. Immediately after the exercise relax mind and body. Let your thought pass down through the body so as to distribute equally among all the nerve centers the added life which you have gained. Then proceed to think of something else. The art of concentration, when fairly well mastered, may be exercised at any time. To use spare moments for this work is a most excellent practice, because it will not interfere with the' regular duties, and besides it will make those moments very interesting as well as highly valuable We may promote brain building at any time when engaged in work that is purely mechanical or that does not require direct attention; and in fact, we should try to train ourselves to build the brain at all times, no matter what our work may be. We should train the forces of the mind to pass through certain parts of the brain, so to speak, while doing their work, and we should expect those forces to promote development wherever they are directed to act. The energy employed in thinking should build brain cells and develop mental faculties during the process of thought, no matter what that thought might be. The same should be expected of energy employed in study or in any form of mental work, and all mental energy in action will promote brain and mind development when trained to do so.

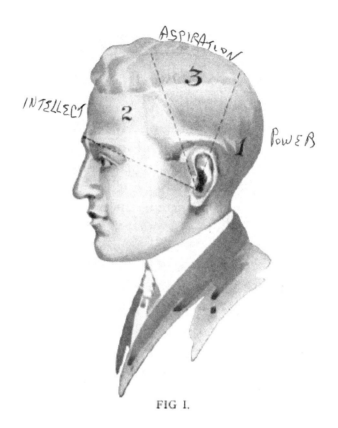

FIG I.

1. Power.   2. Intellect   3. Aspiration

Chapter 2

Making Every Brain Cell Alive

The greater the number of active brain cells, the greater the supply of mental energy; and the more mental energy, the greater the power, the ability and the working capacity of the mind. Every active brain cell generates mental energy. To keep all the cells in action is to accumulate energy; and as much accumulates more, the practice of making alive all the brain cells every day will ere long give the mind far greater capacity and power. In the average brain only one half of the cells are active, and of those that are active only a fraction are thoroughly alive. That ability could be doubled and even trebled in the average mind through a practical system of brain development is therefore evident.

When a majority of the brain cells are dormant the mind is dull, stupid, and even lazy. When the cells in the back brain or in the lower part of the brain are dormant or partly so, a tendency to physical inactivity follows almost invariably. To remove this condition therefore, we must arouse the dormant cells in those parts that are affected. The fact that a person is indolent or stupid does not indicate that there is nothing in him. In fact, he may have remarkable ability along certain lines, but not enough mental energy to put that ability into action. And a lack of mental energy is always due to inaction among the majority of the brain cells. Any person who is inclined to be sluggish in his activity can never do his best. He will accomplish only a fraction of what he has the latent power to accomplish, and will gain very little as far as comfort, happiness and attainment are concerned. An inactive person is never healthy, because there are too many dead cells in his system, and he cannot possibly enjoy life to any degree of satisfaction because his mind is partly in a stupor. His contentment, if he has any, will be the contentment of partial insensibility and not that which comes from having entered into harmony with the life that is alive. There is no real comfort in being sluggish or indolent. The man who takes it easy does not get one-third as much satisfaction from his life and his work as does the one who turns all his energy into his work, and who makes himself the very personification of industry, enterprise and achievement. The happiest man is the one who works with all his power and lives with all his life, but who works and lives in poise. He is also the healthiest man because a live personality is always wholesome and full of vitality.

When the entire personality is not thoroughly alive, waste matter will accumulate in various parts, clogging the blood vessels, obstructing the nerve forces and interfering in general with the normal functions of the system. This waste matter will also cause the tissues to ossify, to harden, to wrinkle up and look old. This is one reason why the man who retires from business and tries to do nothing becomes old very fast. A man, however, does not have to remain in the business world all his life in order to live a long and interesting life, but he must keep his entire system alive and active. And to do this, the first essential is to exercise daily the cells of the brain and the cells of the various nerve centers. The belief that no one can afford to give time or attention to any other part of the mind than that which is employed directly in his vocation, is a mistake, because when the whole of the mind is kept alive and every brain cell is continued in action, the amount of mental energy upon which any faculty may draw will increase to a very great extent. True, those faculties that we use directly in our leading occupations should be developed to a greater degree than the rest of the mind, but the whole of the mind and the whole of the brain should be put to work generating energy. The more energy any faculty may have at its command the greater its capacity for work, and the more thoroughly will its work be done. Every cell in the brain, therefore, should be employed in generating energy, so that the faculties we do employ may have unlimited power upon which to draw. The fact that an increase of mental energy will increase the ability and the working capacity of the mind, and the fact that strong minds, competent minds and able minds are in great demand everywhere makes this subject extremely important.

Another fact that must not be overlooked is that the brain is the instrument of the mind, and must, therefore, be placed in the best possible working condition before the mind can do justice to itself. If every other string in a piano were out of tune, no musician, not even the very best, could produce music through that instrument. But it is just as impossible for the mind to carry on real thinking with a brain wherein a large percentage of the cells are dormant. The fact that so few minds are able to think clearly or produce original thought on any desired subject is due almost entirely to the presence of so many inactive brain cells. Every dormant brain cell is an obstacle to mental action. The energies of thought cannot act upon or act through such cells.. We therefore understand that the presence of such cells will interfere decidedly with the natural action of thinking, and that clear, consecutive, constructive thinking becomes almost impossible where dormant cells are numerous. The fact that the mind may be very active does not prove that all the brain cells are alive, because that activity may be confined almost entirely to certain limited portions of the brain; and the fact that most active brains tire easily proves that the majority of the cells are not doing anything. When all the brain cells are alive and generating energy, there will be so much energy in the brain that the mind will never feel tired, provided of course it works in poise; and the entire brain will naturally become transparent so that the mind can see through every thought, so to speak, and thus think clearly upon every subject. To emphasize this fact, we may add that every dormant cell is like a daub of paint upon a window pane, so therefore, we can realize how the presence of such cells will interfere with clear thought. The belief that every part of brain and mind will be kept in action through an attempt to exercise all the mental faculties at frequent intervals, is not true. First, because no one has the time. To give five minutes of thought in the field of every faculty would require from six to eight hours, something that only a few could do every day. And those few who might have so much time on their hands would naturally have neither the ambition nor the ability to carry out such an extensive regime. Second, to exercise thought in the field of a certain faculty does not necessarily bring into action all the brain cells in that particular part of the brain where the said faculty functions. Ordinary thinking, about faculties, talents, qualities, attributes or definite subjects seldom bring into play other cells than those already in action. Nor does the direct use of the faculty arouse all the cells in the field of action in that faculty. The ordinary use of any part of the mind simply draws upon the energy that is already being generated without doing anything directly to arouse those cells that are dormant. To stir up the dormant brain cells, it will therefore be necessary to employ a different process; in fact, a special process, a process, that will act upon every cell, and that will have the power to arouse that cell into the fullest possible action.

The process that we shall outline for this work need not require more than ten minutes of time each day, although it would be well to give the matter two or three times as much attention, and even that would be possible for anyone, no matter how busy he might be. It has been demonstrated conclusively that you can arouse to action any cells in the system by concentrating attention upon that cell, provided your mind is acting in a state of deep, but highly refined feeling at the time. To awaken a cell, however, it is not necessary to concentrate attention upon that one cell individually. Just as good results may be secured by concentrating upon a large group of cells; and this is especially true when attention aims to move in what may be termed the expansive attitude. To proceed, divide the brain into eight or ten parts, viewing each part as a special group of cells. Then concentrate subjectively for one, two or three minutes upon each group. Take this exercise every day and give it all the interest and enthusiasm that you can possibly arouse in your mind. In a few weeks every cell in your brain will be at work generating energy, and you will discover that the power and the working capacity of your mind will have almost doubled; but this will be only the beginning. If you continue this exercise, and try to make constructive use of all the added power you gain, you will soon come to the conclusion that your ability along any special line can be increased and developed to a remarkable degree. When concentrating in this manner upon each group of brain cells, try to picture mentally all the cells of that group that you can imagine as existing there. This will cause attention to penetrate the entire group through and through, and thus act upon each cell with the full force of thought. The fact that there are millions of cells in the brain need not disturb the imagination in its effort to mentally see them all. The imaging faculty is fully equal to the task. If not at first, it will become so after a little cultivation.

When concentrating upon the brain cells, there should be a strong, deeply felt desire to arouse every cell, but this desire should invariably act in perfect poise, and should never permit the slightest trace of forced action. To establish a full life, a wholesome life, a strong life, a wholly active life and a smooth, calm, harmonious life in every brain cell should be the purpose, and during the process of concentration the mind should be thoroughly determined to carry out this purpose. In many minds certain parts of the brain are very active, while other parts are not. Such minds, therefore, should give most of their attention and concentration to the inactive parts for a while, or until a balanced, thoroughly alive mental action is established in every part of the brain.

The process of concentration should begin at the lower part of the back brain, and should move forward gradually, ending at the upper part of the fore brain. During this concentration all the finer creative energies of the system should be drawn gently, with deep feeling and strong desire, towards the brain. And after the exercise is over, both mind and body should relax completely for a few moments, as this will produce perfect equilibrium. The result of this exercise, if taken daily, will be to eliminate all sluggishness, all stupidity, all dullness and all tendency to indolence or inactivity in any part of the mind, the brain or the nervous system. The mental power will increase remarkably, thinking will become clear and the brain will become such a perfect instrument that the mind can always do justice to itself no matter how highly it may be developed or how great its ambitions may be.

Chapter 3

Principles in Brain Building

The Leading Principle — To increase the size, to improve the quality and to multiply the energies of every faculty, talent or power that exists in the human mind, and to promote in general or in particular the development of ability, talent and genius, the leading principle is to combine the brain, the mind and the soul in every effort made to this end. This, however, is a new idea. No attempt has ever been made in the past to combine these three factors in an orderly and scientific manner for the promotion of any form of development; but we shall find as we proceed that it is this principle that constitutes the real secret of this important work. Many scientists have devoted themselves to the study of the brain. Many metaphysicians have searched for the mysteries of the mind. And others have spent a lifetime trying to fathom the depths of the soul, but no definite effort has been made to combine these three factors for practical results. But this we must do if we are to promote this system of development. And as we carry out this principle we shall find that there is no reason why anyone may not become as much and achieve as much as his loftiest ambitions hold in view. As this principle is applied the weakest mind can be made strong, the dullest mind can be made to improve constantly in activity and brilliancy, and such minds as are already brilliant can be improved to an extent that will in many instances approach the extraordinary.

The Process Simple — We shall understand presently how these exceptional possibilities can be realized. And we shall also find that the process involved is very simple. This, however, is natural, because the greatest things are always the simplest. This is one reason why we fail to find them at once, because there is a tendency in the human mind to look constantly for the complex, laboring under the delusion that the complex alone is great. But now we realize that man can improve himself only as he learns to get down to rock bottom and apply the laws of mental growth in their original simplicity. The obstacle that most of us have met is this, that instead of applying the laws of nature, we have tried instead to apply somebody's interpretation of those laws; but interpretations are usually complex, confusing and misleading, while the laws themselves are sufficiently simple for a child to comprehend and apply.

Important Questions — Proceeding directly to the consideration of this great subject, we will naturally find ourselves asking the following questions: What makes a mind great? Why does one person have ability and another not? What is talent and what does it come from? What is the secret of genius? What is the reason that some minds become so much and achieve so much while others accomplish practically nothing? These are important questions and there must be definite answers to them all; in fact, there must be an inner secret that makes the difference in each case. When we look at a person with a great mind we cannot at first find the secret, and as few are able to look beyond the exterior person, we have remained comparatively in ignorance on this great subject, admittedly one of the greatest of the ages. In most minds the secret of greatness, ability and genius is looked upon as a hidden something that can possibly not be found. But when we analyze man as he really is, and find that he is not simply personal, but mental and spiritual as well, this secret is no longer hidden. We find it to be composed of a few natural laws in orderly application. And we also find that both the understanding and the application of these laws are very simple.

Essentials Required — When we speak of ability in any particular mind, we usually consider only one or two faculties in that mind, as there are but few minds that are really great in more than two things. For this reason, to answer the questions presented above, we must analyze those individual faculties and try to discover why they are so remarkable. When we study such faculties, we find that there are three reasons why they are different from ordinary faculties; and these reasons are, that in all superior faculties we find size, quality and power exceptionally developed and properly combined. So this, therefore, is the simple secret of ability, talent and genius; and being so simple, we can readily understand why it has been overlooked. However, as we proceed in harmony with its natural simplicity, and try to apply it, we find that any one of these three essentials can be developed to almost any degree. And as the combined and harmonious application of the three essentials is a matter that anybody can master, we realize again that there is no reason why we all should not become much and achieve much. In fact, there need be no end to what we can develop and accomplish along any line. The talents we now possess can be developed far beyond anything we have ever imagined or dreamed of. And those greater powers that are still latent in the potential may be brought forth so that man will still accomplish what the race has never imagined possible.

Essentials Explained — Before we proceed further, it will be necessary to know what is really understood by the term size, quality, and power as applied to the faculties and talents of man; and also how those essentials were produced in such minds, as we have made no effort to develop and build through any method whatever. When we meet an exceptional mind we usually come to the conclusion that that mind secured remarkable ability and power without knowing anything about systems of development, and also that ability and genius are for this reason born in those who have them. To the average mind, this conclusion may seem to prove that only those can be able who are born able, and that therefore there can be no use for the ordinary mind in trying to develop added ability. But here we should remember that as it is possible to improve the trees and the flowers as well as all kinds of animals, there necessarily must be some way to improve man both physically, mentally and spiritually, as man needs improvement more than anything else, having greater responsibility, and being at the highest point, so to speak, of the creative powers of nature. We all must admit the logic of such ideas, but we need not depend upon logic. We also have the facts. We have the evidence in the case, and there is nothing more evident than evidence. The human mind as well as all the faculties and powers in man can be developed, and there is nothing to indicate that there is any end to the possibility of such development. We have found the secret, and that it works, is being demonstrated every day. The wise course to pursue, therefore, is to give our whole attention to the application of the laws and the methods involved, so that the best in view may be realized. The size of the faculty is determined by that part of the brain through which the faculty functions. The quality of the faculty comes from the state of the mind, and the power that enables the faculty to do its work comes from the within, and increases as the within is awakened and developed. To give a faculty size, therefore, we must deal with the brain. To give a faculty quality we must deal with the mind, and especially the states of the mind. And to give a faculty power we must deal with the soul, or rather the entire interior realms of life and consciousness. Thus we understand why the brain, the mind and the soul must be combined if we wish to provide the three essentials — size, quality, and power — required in the increase of ability or genius along any line.

FIG. II.

1. The Physical Brain
2. The Metaphysical Brain
3. The Spiritual Brain

Further Explanation — The reason why these three essentials are required can be simply illustrated. The engine must have steam or it will not have the power to do what it is built to do. It may be very large and have enormous capacity, but if there is little or no steam it can do practically nothing. Then the engine may have any amount of steam to draw upon, but if it is very small it cannot use all of this power, and will accordingly accomplish but little. Then again the engine may be large and the steam abundant, but if it is poorly constructed it will not work. In other words, if the engine is to perform its purpose, it must have size, quality and power, and the more it has of these three, the more it can do. It is exactly the same with the human mind, and when we realize this we understand why so many large brains accomplish nothing, why so many fine minds accomplish nothing, and why so many strong minds accomplish nothing. The large brain must have mental quality back of it, and abundance of creative energy from the subconscious. The fine mind must have plenty of power back of it, and a large brain through which to act. The strong soul must have mental quality so as to give its power superior ideas with which to work, and a large brain through which these superior ideas can find full expression.

Increase of Size — It is therefore evident that those who wish to become much and accomplish something of worth must give their attention to the three essentials mentioned, and to give special attention to that essential that is most deficient in development. If you have a large well developed brain, but low mental quality with but little power, give your attention principally to the development of mind and soul. But if you have plenty of energy and ambition with good mental quality, but a poorly developed brain, give your attention to the brain, and have its size increased especially in those parts through which the talent you desire naturally functions. And here we must remember that each faculty functions through a special part of the brain — a fact that is not only important, but that is in perfect harmony with the laws of nature. The function of sight employs the eye while that of hearing employs the ear. The other senses have their own particular channels, and the same is true of the various faculties of the mind. Each individual faculty finds expression through its own part of the brain, and therefore it is necessary that that particular part be well developed if the faculty in question is to function with exceptional ability and power. The increase of size, therefore, in any part of the brain becomes a matter that will require the very best attention we can possibly provide, though the process through which this increase may be brought about is very simply applied. It is a well known fact that any part of the system will grow and develop in size if more nourishment and vitality is supplied; and increased nourishment and vitality can readily be supplied by increasing the circulation in that particular part. This is a fact that has been thoroughly demonstrated, so that we may proceed with the full conviction that as we apply the principle involved we shall positively secure the desired result.

Interesting Experiments — The following experiments will illustrate how nourishment and vitality can be increased in any part of the physical form: Place a dog's paw in a vacuum at stated intervals for some period of time, and that paw will become twice as large as the other one. And the explanation is that the vacuum draws more blood into the paw thus providing additional nourishment and vitality. The same experiment can be applied along a number of other lines, proving the same idea; but here we may enquire how increased circulation can be produced in any part of the brain. We cannot employ mechanical means for such a purpose; therefore, must find another plan. It is admitted that added development will naturally take place wherever there is an increase of nourishment and vitality; and this increase is supplied by an increase of the circulation in that part; but the problem is, how to increase the circulation in any part of the brain. The solution, however, is simple, as the following experiments will illustrate: Place a man upon an oscillating platform, and have him so placed that the body is perfectly balanced, the feet and the head being at equal distance from the floor; then tell him to work out a difficult problem, or tell him to think of something that requires very deep thought. In a few seconds the circulation will increase in the brain sufficiently to cause the head to go down considerable, and even to the floor, as the feet or the other end of the body rises accordingly. Here is an illustration of how the circulation can be increased in the brain simply by carrying out a certain line of thought. Then tell this same man to imagine that he is running a foot race, and in a few seconds the circulation will increase in the feet to such an extent that the feet will become heavier than the head, and go down as the head goes up. This is an experiment that most anyone can try with most interesting results, and it gives tangible evidence to prove that the mind can control the circulation. While the mind was thinking about the deep problem, extra energy and circulation was drawn to the brain; but when that same mind was imagining the running of a foot race, this extra energy and circulation went towards the feet because attention was concentrated upon the feet at the time. Another interesting experiment is to imagine yourself taking a hot foot bath. You will soon find your feet becoming very warm, the veins beginning to swell, indicating that increased circulation has been produced in that part of the body. Here we have the same principle; that is, the power of mind to increase the circulation in any part of the body by concentrating with deep interest upon that particular part. A number of similar experiments can be carried out, proving the same law; and as the law is so simply applied, we find that there is no reason whatever why the increase of the size of any part of the brain may not be produced as we may desire.

Power of Concentration — To apply this law we must understand how to concentrate. If we concentrate simply in an objective sense, we have no effect upon the forces of the system, and the above law will not act. But when we concentrate subjectively, that is, with deep interest and feeling, we find that the forces of the system invariably accumulate at the point of concentration; and where the forces of the system accumulate, an increase in circulation will invariably follow. To explain this matter more fully, we might state that real concentration upon any part of the body causes mind and consciousness to increase activity in that part. Wherever there is an increase of mental activity, the finer life currents will become more active; and where those currents become more active the circulation will increase. This is how the law operates, and it is based entirely upon how deeply the mind feels at the time of concentration, and how deeply interested the attention is in the project we wish to carry out. In other words, it is the concentration that is felt that controls the circulation, because such concentration acts through the finer forces of the system; and the circulation is controlled by those finer forces.

Deep Feeling Necessary — The above may seem to lead us into difficulties, and take away the ease and simplicity that was previously indicated; but we need not be disturbed. This inner consciousness of finer feeling is simply secured, and what is better still, we all have it already. What we wish to make perfectly clear is the fact that you cannot draw additional vitality and nourishment to any part of the brain unless you concentrate your attention upon that part while your mind feels the action of the finer life current. You do not govern functions or activities anywhere in your system until you act through subjective mentality because all physical functions, including the circulation, are controlled by the subconscious mind. Whenever you feel deeply, however, you act directly upon the subconscious, and may, therefore, originate and direct any new subconscious act desired. The principle is to feel deeply whenever you concentrate. Nothing else need be attempted. If you know that you feel deeply whenever you turn your attention to any part of the brain, you will know that there will be an increase of nourishment and vitality in that part, and that the brain cells of that part will be developed and built up accordingly.

Unconscious Development — In answering the question why a great many minds have been developed without the understanding of this law, we need simply state that it is possible to use some of the most important laws of mind and body without really understanding the nature of those laws. In fact, we are doing this all the time. When you wish to succeed in any undertaking, and you concentrate all your efforts upon that purpose, you develop to a certain extent the faculty employed in that undertaking. And the reason is that the concentration that was unconsciously practiced caused the added nourishment and vitality to be supplied to that part of the brain through which the faculty in question was expressed. In other words, you employ unconsciously the same law that we are trying to use consciously and according to exact science. But here we must remember that although the unconscious use of a certain law may produce results, the conscious and intelligent use of that same law will naturally produce far greater results. Therefore, we wish to understand the inside secret of this entire theme, so that we can make the best use of all the principles involved.

The Power of Ambition — In this same connection we learn that ambition is also a channel through which unconscious development is constantly taking place. When you have a strong ambition to realize a certain goal, the force of that ambition naturally tends to build up those faculties that you need in order to reach your goal. And we find that the force of ambition also involves the force of concentration, because we always concentrate upon those things that we are deeply ambitious to realize. We find, therefore, that both the mind and the brain may be built up through the exercise of a strong, determined ambition. But here as elsewhere, we should not be satisfied simply with the unconscious use of the principle involved. If we would, instead of simply being ambitious, proceed to direct the force of ambition upon that part of the brain through which the desired talent naturally functions, we would find that that talent would develop with far greater rapidity than through the old general method of simply being ambitious; in other words, we would have another illustration of the power of concentration and intelligent action.

Illustration — To illustrate this idea further, we will suppose that you are ambitious to become a great musician, but instead of being simply ambitious, you concentrate you mind upon that part of the brain through which the faculty of music functions. The result will be that the power of your ambition will express itself directly in building up your musical faculty, because the additional mental energy that you will provide for that faculty will not only build up the mind in that part, but will also tend to supply additional nourishment and vitality for the corresponding part of the brain. Here we find a new use for that great mental force usually called ambition, especially since it can be employed in the building up of any faculty whatever. We realize that those who will make the right use of this force in building up any faculty, the increased development of which is desired, will naturally secure decided results from the very beginning; and if the process is continued with perseverance, will secure results that will be nothing less than remarkable. In this part of our study we have given special attention to size as previously defined, and have illustrated how size could be secured by building up any part of the brain. Later on, we shall consider quality and power. But we should all remember in pursuing this study that size is of exceptional importance, the fact being that there are very few brains that are sufficiently developed to give the proper expression to the ability and the genius that most of us already possess.

Chapter 4

Practical Methods in Brain Building

Important Faculty — The power of the mind is limitless; that is, the power that is already active in the mind can, as it is directed, reproduce itself in larger and larger quantities. This faculty is latent in every mind, and is employed to some degree by every mind. The more mental power we generate, the greater becomes the mental capacity to generate more. But only as much of the power of the mind can be expressed as the development of the brain will permit. Therefore, the cultivation of the mind and the increase of mental power will not produce an increase in ability, talent and genius unless the brain is developed just as thoroughly as the mind.

The Highly Organized Brain — To develop the brain there are three essentials that must be constantly promoted. First, every brain cell must be made more active; second, the number of brain) cells must be increased; and third, the brain as a whole must be more highly organized. Dormant brain cells obstruct the expression of ability and power, while active brain cells tend to promote that expression. An active brain cell not only permits the expression of mental power, but actually calls forth more and more of that power. The more brain cells you have, the more channels for mental expression you will have, and the greater the number of these channels, the greater your mental capacity. The highly organized brain is superior in quality, and, therefore, can respond readily to the highest forms of genius. The brain that is gross, crude or dense cannot act as an instrument for any form of genius, not even for the simplest forms of practical ability; and the fact that most brains are crude and undeveloped, either as a whole or in parts, explains why extraordinary ability is the exception rather than the rule.

Ability Trebled — Extraordinary ability need not remain the exception, however; there are thousands of minds with ordinary ability that would double and treble their ability by simply taking a thorough course of brain development. They already have the mental power, but their brains are not sufficiently developed to give full expression to that power. And there are other thousands who are not conscious of any talents whatever that would become talented if their brains were sufficiently developed to give full expression to all that is in them. A thorough development of the brain will also reveal what a person is best adapted for, for when every faculty can fully express itself, it is an easy matter to discover which one is the strongest; and if that one is given further development, extraordinary ability will be the result.

More Brain Cells — To know how much you can do through any faculty, is not possible until every cell in the brain is fully alive, and when you do discover what you can do through any special faculty, you can double your ability in that faculty by doubling the subconscious power back of that faculty, and by doubling the number of cells in that part of the brain through which that faculty functions. To double the number of cells in the brain, or in any part of the brain, is possible without increasing the usual size of the cranium, because the cells invariably decrease in size as the structure of the brain is improved in quality. The smaller the cells of the brain the better; and the more active and the more highly organized the brain, the more nearly the brain cell approaches the form of a mere point of expression. And for the same reason, the smaller the cells of the brain, the more easily and the more thoroughly can the mind concentrate upon any special subject.

The Vital Secret — To make every cell alive, the secret is to concentrate attention upon every part of the brain, thinking of the finer substance of the brain at the time, and proceeding with the desire to promote increase in life, energy and power. Turn attention first upon the center (a point midway between the opening of the ears) and think of the finer life and substance that permeates the region of that center. Then, while in that deeper state of thought and feeling, move attention through any part of the brain you like, and toward the surface. This movement should be gradual, and you should try to deeply feel and gently arouse the finer life that permeates the brain cells through which your thought is passing. When your concentration comes to the surface of the brain, move it back again gradually, passing through the same region until you come to the brain center. Take about two minutes for the process of passing concentration from the brain center to any part of the surface of the brain and back again to the center. This exercise may last from ten to twenty minutes and should be taken once a day, but should never be taken immediately after a meal.

Subjective Concentration — When you concentrate upon any part of the brain, do not think of the physical brain, or the physical brain cells, but think of that finer or metaphysical substance that permeates the physical cells. This will hold concentration in the subjective state; and all concentration must be subjective to be effective. All actions of concentration should move smoothly, easily, deeply, and harmoniously; the process should be animated with a deep, calm, self-possessed enthusiasm; be positively, but calmly determined to secure results, and constantly expect results. Think of the brain as a perfect instrument of genius, and hold such a mental picture of the brain in your thought at all times.

The Real Principle — The number of cells in any part of the brain may be increased by concentrating subjectively upon that part. Whenever you concentrate attention upon any group of cells, you cause creative energy to accumulate in that group. Wherever creative energy accumulates, the circulation will increase, and in consequence there will not only be an increase of the power that builds, but also added nourishment with which to build. This is the principle: Concentrate upon any part of the brain, and you bring more energy and more nourishment to that part; and when more energy and more nourishment meet in any place, there will be more cells in that place. Concentration will cause these two essentials to meet wherever you may desire. But the concentration must be subjective; that is, do not concentrate upon the physical part of the brain, but upon that finer life and substance that permeates the physical. If you do not realize the existence of those finer life forces that permeate the physical cells, imagine the existence of finer cells as being within the physical cells, and concentrate upon those finer cells. You will soon begin to realize the finer substance and the finer life that fills or permeates the physical cells, and in the meantime you will have results; you will build the brain; you will develop those parts of the brain wherein you concentrate subjectively and with regularity.

Where to Concentrate — To impress ability in any faculty, concentrate regularly upon any part of the brain through which the faculty in question functions. Every leading faculty employs its own part, or parts, of the brain. Some faculties express themselves through one part only, while other faculties employ several parts. When you know what part of the brain is employed by some special faculty, build up that part; that is, concentrate daily upon that part and aim, not only to increase the number of cells, but also to refine and develop those cells. You will thus give your special faculty a more perfect instrument with which to work, and that faculty will steadily become stronger, more able and more efficient.

Improved Quality — The predominating thought of the mind during any period of concentration will determine the quality of the new cells that are conceived during that period. Therefore, to improve the quality of the brain cells and make the brain structure more highly organized, the quality of thought that is formed in mind during any exercise in concentration should be the highest that can possibly be imagined. When you concentrate upon any part of the brain, think of quality, refinement, worth, superiority, power, ability, talent, genius. Think of all these things in their highest forms and draw upon your imagination for higher and higher forms. Enrich your thinking to the very highest degree possible; this richer, higher, superior thought will permeate the very life and essence of every cell in your brain, and thus you will constantly improve this quality of your entire brain. When you concentrate upon any special part of your brain, use the same method, and in addition, picture in mind the superior genius of that faculty that functions through this special part. Try to impress this picture of superior genius upon every cell in that part of the brain, and try to feel that the spirit of superior genius is alive in every cell. You thus develop both the faculty and that part of the brain through which the faculty functions.

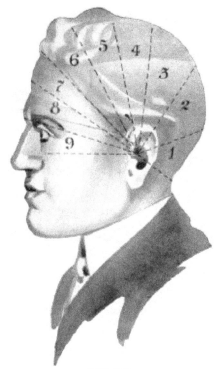

FIG. III.

1. Creative Energy	5. Emotion
2. Love	6. Intuition
3. Individuality	7. Intelligence
4. Interior	8. Application
Understanding	9. Expression

All Around Development — The balanced brain should be the first object in view. No matter what your vocation may be, every part of your brain should be well developed. The balanced brain has always the greatest capacity and the greatest endurance, because those parts that are not employed directly furnish added power to those parts that are employed directly. The balanced brain is also the most practical, having the power both to create ideas and the power to make actual use of those ideas. Compare the shape of your own brain with that of Figure II and you will see at once where the greatest amount of development is required in your own case. But do not give your whole attention to those parts that seem to be small; proceed to develop your whole brain so as to make every cell alive, and aim to improve the quality of your entire brain; give most of your time, however, to those parts that lack in size and activity. If your brain seems to be fairly well balanced, give most of your time to those parts that you employ directly in your daily work and the remainder of your time to the entire brain in general.

Where to Begin — Begin your development of the brain by taking from ten to twenty minutes every day and concentrate for a minute or two on the nine fundamental divisions outlined in Fig. III. Always begin with the region of "creative energy," and close with the region of expression. To increase creative energy is always the first essential in every undertaking; and expression is the final outcome, the climax, the goal in view. When you concentrate upon the region of creative energy, think deeply of accumulation, and try to feel the possession of limitless power. Be in perfect poise and harmony, and realize that your back brain is actually becoming charged with tremendous energy. Be as quiet as possible, try to hold it all in your system, and feel deeply so that the process of concentration will be subjective. When concentration ceases to be subjective, you lose your hold upon energies, and development will be interrupted; but so long as your concentration continues to be subjective, you will hold your energy in your system, you will also awaken more, and every desire for development will promote development.

Individuality — The largest conception of love that you can possibly realize should be deeply felt when you concentrate upon the region of "love." Think of everything that is tender, lovable and sweet; in fact, enter into the very world of immeasurable love; try to feel that you are absolutely at one with everything that is, and that you love with all your heart everything that is. The region of "individuality" is the principal channel of expression for the will; therefore when you concentrate upon the brain cells in this region, proceed to will with all the power of will. This region is also the principal seat of stability, firmness, self-confidence and faith. Accordingly, your desire to express these qualities should be combined with your own concentration. When you concentrate for the development of individuality enter into the spirit of faith; have faith in yourself; have faith in everybody and everything; have faith in your mission in life; have faith in the Supreme and have faith in faith. Be strong and firm; feel through and through that you are yourself — your superior self, and that you can master everything that is in yourself.

Discerning the Within — The inner world of things, as well as the higher side of things, is discerned through "interior understanding." It is also the channel through which the mind acts when we try to discern the ideal, the superior and those elements of true worth that exist within all things, and in the higher life of all things. When you concentrate upon this part of the brain think of the ideal, the higher, the greater, the superior, and try to mentally enter into the soul of your every thought. As you develop interior understanding you will gain the power to understand the metaphysical nature as well as the physical nature of all life, and no one can fully understand life, properly use life, or master life, until he can look at all things both from the metaphysical and the physical points of view.

Feeling the Real — When concentrating upon the region of "emotion" every effort should be made to enter into the most tender feelings of the soul; but all tendencies towards the sentimental should be avoided. Try to feel sympathetic; try to sympathize most keenly with everything and everybody, and try to realize the sublime state of oneness with the higher side of all that is. When trying to develop sympathy do not think of that which is wrong, pitiful or distressing; this will simply develop morbidity, a condition that is frequently mistaken for real sympathy. The true function of sympathy is to place the mind in touch with the real, the true, the sublime and the beautiful; in brief, to feel the touch of life; not false life, imperfect life, or misdirected life, but the life that is life, the life that makes all life truly worthwhile. The more perfectly we develop the finer emotions, the more keenly we can enjoy that something that may well be termed the music of sublime existence, and the more readily can we rise to those lofty heights in consciousness where we can see all things from all points of view. Therefore when we concentrate upon the region of emotion, we should try to enter into the music of sublime existence; we should try to rise to the mountain tops of consciousness; we should try to feel the tender touch of everything that is real, beautiful and true, and we should try to realize that something within us that binds the soul of man to every breathing, living thing in all the vastness of the cosmos.

Function of Intuition — Interior insight, discernment, judgment, decisions and all the finer perceptions of the mind function through that part of the brain termed "intuition." Intuition is indispensable, no matter what our vocation may be, because we are constantly called upon to decide as to what step to take further, or to judge as to the best course to pursue, or to look through this matter or that. It is a faculty, however, that has never been developed, and that is the principal reason why practical minds make so many mistakes, adopt the wrong plans almost at every turn, and so frequently walk right into failure when they could just as easily walk directly into success. The most successful men in the world possess natural intuition to a very great degree, and that is why they usually do the right thing at the right time. They know real opportunities when they see them, and they know when and how to take advantage of those opportunities. But they do not know these things through external evidence; they usually go contrary to external evidence and what is called safe and sane business sense. They follow a "finer business sense." They may not call their superior business judgment intuition, but it is the same thing, and it may be developed to a remarkable degree by anyone. Proceed first to make alive and build up that part of the brain through which this faculty functions. Concentrate for a few minutes upon this region several times a day, and especially just before you are to decide upon some important matter. While concentrating, think of interior insight, try to see through every thought or idea that enters the mind at the time, and desire deeply to see the real truth in everything of which you are conscious. Learn to depend upon your interior insight at all times, whenever you are called upon to judge, select, look through or decide; and the constant use of this faculty in practical life, combined with daily concentration upon this part of the brain, will develop this faculty to almost any degree desired.

Building Intellect — Mental brilliancy and rare mental activity may be developed by concentrating upon the region of "intelligence." Think of pure intellect and picture in mind the highest form of mental brilliancy imaginable when concentrating upon this part of the brain. Also, enter the feeling of mental expansion and limitless intellectual capacity, and try to picture calmness and lucidity in every thought you think. You thus, not only develop and enlarge that part of the brain through which pure intellect functions, but you also become more brilliant; and at the same time your power to think, understand, comprehend and realize is steadily increased. This method, if practiced for a few minutes several times a day, will, in the course of a few years, produce a prodigious intellect. There is no reason, therefore, why anyone should remain in a state of mental inferiority. Rare mental brilliancy and remarkable intellectual capacity are possible to all, but the high places are for those only who will go to work and make their possibilities come true.

Producing Results — Practical application is the art of combining the world of ideas with the world of things; or, rather, the turning of ideas into actual use. The faculty of "intelligence" produces the idea; the faculty of application puts that idea to work. To develop the faculty of application, concentrate upon that part of the brain marked "8" in Fig. II, and think of system, method and scientific application at the time. Impress upon every cell in that part of the brain a deep, positive desire to do things, and you will develop the "knack" of being practical, as well as increase the actual power of application.

The Real Purpose — The great climax of all life, all thought, all effort, is expression. The real purpose of man is to bring forth all that is in him — the whole of himself, and although every force and element in his system is employed, directly or indirectly, in promoting expression, the entire process is governed by the mind acting through a certain part of the brain. This part is the region marked "9" in Fig. II, and therefore as this region is more fully developed, the power to promote expression will increase in proportion. Some faculties employ this part of the brain directly, while all the other faculties employ it indirectly. The singer, the orator, the actor, the artist, the writer and the man who sells things, employ the faculty of expression directly; therefore, all such people should develop this part of the brain to the highest possible degree. But all others should give the faculty of expression thorough attention, because we all must express ourselves if we would be much and do much. When concentrating upon this part of the brain, think of the perfect expression of that which you desire to express more fully. If you are an artist, mentally see the expression of the ideal and the beautiful. If you are a singer, mentally feel the expression of tone. If you are an orator, mentally feel the power of eloquence. If you are a writer, mentally realize the expression, in language, of the ideas that you wish to express in literature. If you talk much, or write much, in a business way, with a view of promoting the sale of your product, mentally see yourself expressing yourself in the most forceful, the most persuasive and the most effective manner imaginable. Imagine yourself expressing yourself as you wish to express yourself, whenever you concentrate upon this part of the brain; and do not fail to draw upon your imagination for the most perfect expression possible. Impress upon your brain cells the greatest thoughts that you can imagine, and you thus train your brain to become a perfect instrument for the expression of those thoughts. In the general development of expression, desire deeply to express the best that is in yourself whenever you concentrate, and try to feel the all that is in yourself coming forth in an ever increasing measure.

Special Rules — It is important to remember that all concentration for brain development should begin at the brain center. First, turn attention upon the brain center;

gently draw, with your thought, all the finer forces of the mind towards this center; then move the action of concentration toward the surface of the brain, thus passing through that region that you wish to develop. Move the action of concentration to and fro from the center of the brain to the surface, but give more attention to those groups of cells that lie near the surface of the brain, as it is these through which the mind functions to the greatest degree.

What to Expect — The time required to secure results through these methods will depend upon present development and how faithfully this process of development is applied. Results will usually begin to appear in a few days, and very marked results within a few weeks. An increase of mental life, mental power and mental capacity will be noted almost from the very beginning, and a decided improvement in practical efficiency will shortly follow. After a few weeks or a few months, you will discover that your general ability is growing, and at times, you will feel the power of genius finding expression through one or more of your faculties. You will then begin to realize that it is only a matter of perseverance in the daily application of these methods, when ability, talent and genius of the highest order will be attained.

When to Exercise — Apply these methods at any time or anywhere whenever you have a few moments to spare. Take twenty minutes once or twice a day, for regular practice if you can; and it is an excellent practice to use spare moments, as they come, for this purpose. Make it a point to concentrate for development upon some part of your brain whenever you have a minute or two. And, if you concentrate properly, you will not only reinvigorate the brain, but you will rest the mind from its regular work. Proper concentration is always subjective; that is, in the field of deeper, finer feeling. Never begin to concentrate until you feel deeply serene, and feel that your mind is acting calmly in those finer elements and forces that permeate the physical cells. To enter this subjective or finer state of thought and feeling, become very quiet for a few moments; breathe deeply but gently, and do not move a muscle; when you inhale, imagine that you are drawing the force of your personality into that finer subconscious life that permeates your personality; and when you exhale, imagine that all the forces of your system are moving down through your personality toward your feet What you imagine you do during this exercise, you very soon will do; then you can master your forces in any way desired by simply thinking of your forces as doing what you wish them to do. During these breathing exercises, turn your attention upon the inner life of your system; try to feel this life, and try to enter mentally into the vast interior world of this life. You will soon realize that there is another world of force within the physical world of force. You are then in the subjective state; you are then in touch with the real power within you — the power that lies beneath every cell, and that can therefore change, reproduce or develop every cell. You may then proceed with your concentration; and this deeper power with which you are in touch will proceed to do whatever your predominant thought may desire at the time.

Chapter 5

Vital Secrets in Brain Building

Remarkable Possibility — The brain is the instrument of the mind or the channel through which the unbounded possibilities of the mind are to find expression. It is therefore of the highest importance that the brain receive the most thorough and the most perfect development possible. The reason for this is readily understood when we learn that the average mind could do two or three times as much if the brain was properly developed, and that the quality of the work done could be improved not less than tenfold in many instances. It is a well known fact that the better the instrument, the better the results, other things being equal, and that no performer can do justice to himself unless his instrument is perfect. But this fact has not been considered in connection with the mind and its instrument. In consequence thereof not one person in ten thousand is giving his mind a fair chance.

Special Exercises Required — That the brain needs development, is admitted by everybody, but there is a current belief that the brain naturally develops as the mind develops, and that to exercise the brain in the mere act of thinking is sufficient to promote this development. This conclusion is based upon the idea that the mind is the unconscious builder of the brain, and that therefore the brain will be at each stage of mental development exactly what the mind requires it to be. But it would be difficult to find a more serious mistake than this. That the mind is the builder of the brain is true in a sense; that is, every change in the brain will be determined by the actions of the mind, and it is the mind that governs the chemical and creative processes that carry on construction and reconstruction. But that function of the mind that governs construction is a distinct function, and is not directly connected with the process of thinking. Thinking in itself does not necessarily develop the brain, nor does ordinary work always develop the muscles of the body. If thinking developed brains and working developed muscle, we should all be marvels of mental capacity and physical power. But the fact that the average person remains undeveloped both in mind and body, no matter how much he thinks or works, proves that special exercises are required for every form of development.

Two Distinctive Processes — To bring a crude, sluggish and perverse brain up to the highest state of action by mere thinking, is just as impossible as it is to bring a discordant piano into perfect tune by mere playing. To play the piano is one thing. To tune a piano or build a more perfect piano is quite another thing. In like manner, the regular creation or thinking of thought and the reconstruction of a more perfect physical brain are two distinct processes, and accordingly require different applications of the mind. It is man who builds the musical instrument, and it is man who employs that instrument to produce music. According to the same analogy, it is the mind that determines what its physical instruments are to be, and it is the mind that acts upon those instruments when thought or expression are to be produced. It is the mind, therefore, that must develop the brain. But the application of the mind in brain development is far different than that of usual thinking.

How Exercise Develops — To apply the mind in brain development, we must eliminate the belief that the use of anything in mind or body necessarily promotes the development of the thing used. It is not use or exercise in itself that develops. It is the extra supply of nourishment and energy that is drawn to the place through use or exercise that alone can promote development. The process of construction in body or brain is not possible without nourishment and creative energy. Therefore, when we increase the supply of these two in any part of the system we cause that part to develop more rapidly. The exercise of the muscle or faculty, however, does not always draw more nourishment and energy to those places where the exercise occurs. If it did, we should have physical giants and mental giants by the millions. And what is important, it is not the exercise itself that draws the circulation or the increased energy to those parts that are being exercised; it is the attitude of the mind that we sometimes enter while body or brain is in action. This is a discovery of exceptional value because when once understood all systems of mental or physical culture will be revolutionized. Instead of systems that produce occasional and accidental results, we shall then have systems that produce definite and positive results in every case. In brief, the idea is that physical or mental exercise does not draw increased circulation and increased energy to the part exercised unless the mind is in a certain attitude at the time; and it is absolutely necessary that increased circulation and increased energy be supplied at the point of exercise if development is to take place.

Subjective Concentration — That attitude of mind that invariably draws nourishment and energy to the part that is exercised is called subjective concentration, and the fact that it is subjective concentration and not exercise, in itself that develops, is a fact that all should understand more perfectly who have greater development for mind or body in view. Whenever any muscle is used, the act attracts attention and the mind will naturally concentrate upon that muscle to a degree. If the concentration is subjective, more nourishment and energy will be drawn to that muscle with development as the result. But if the concentration is not subjective, no added supply of nourishment or energy will be provided. The result will be that the muscle that is being exercised or used will use up the nourishment and energy already there and finally become tired or exhausted. No development, therefore, of that muscle can under the circumstances take place.

Accidental Development — In this connection we may well ask how people have succeeded in developing muscles and faculties before subjective concentration was understood. We know that a large number who have been ignorant of this mode of concentration have improved themselves through various systems. Then how did they do it? The secret is this; whenever you concentrate attention in the attitude of whole-hearted interest, you enter the subjective to a degree and thus concentrate subjectively without being aware of the fact. No matter what system of culture you employ, if you are not interested in the exercise you gain absolutely nothing; but on the other hand, the most perfect system will help you if you are thoroughly interested in the exercise. And the reason is that when you are interested you concentrate subjectively to a degree, and it is through that subjective concentration that you get your results. This idea is well illustrated by the fact that we are always helped the most by those methods that arouse our deepest interest and our most wide-awake attention. By being interested in our work, our studies and our exercises, we have accidentally, so to speak, entered to a degree into subjective moods of concentration, and through such concentration have drawn much nourishment and energy to the parts exercised, thus promoting development in a measure. To depend upon accidental or occasional results, however, will not and should not satisfy those who have greater things in view. We have scientific, exact and unfailing methods for reaching every goal and brain development is no exception. Therefore, we should find the best methods and apply them thoroughly so that every effort we make towards improvements will positively produce results.

Deep Interest — Since more nourishment and more energy are required where development is to take place, and since these two essentials will be provided wherever we concentrate' in the subjective attitude, we understand why subjective concentration is the real secret to brain development as well as all other forms of development. For this reason we should enter the subjective attitude directly before we begin to concentrate, and not depend upon indirect means to produce this necessary attitude. By entering directly into the subjective attitude before we begin our concentration we shall have positive results in every instance, and thus avoid unnecessary delays. But if you feel that you do not clearly understand the idea of the subjective, use the term "deep interest" instead. The two terms mean the same. That is, become deeply interested in that upon which you proceed to concentrate, and train yourself to think, study and work in an attitude of deep feeling. Thus you will concentrate subjectively in the most natural and the most perfect manner, and invariably accomplish what you have in view.

Living Brain Cells — The discovery that the development of brain and body can be promoted thoroughly and rapidly through subjective concentration will prove valuable beyond belief because every brain almost is in such great need of special development. That a fine mind can work properly through a brain that is crude or sluggish is impossible, and yet the majority of brains are very crude in places and so sluggish in parts that hardly any activity is evident. It is a matter of fact that many parts of the average brain are almost entirely dormant — a condition that no one should permit to continue for a moment, because the full capacity of mind can find expression only when every cell in the brain is thoroughly alive. To bring life and full action into every cell, and to cause every cell to continue to be a living cell, attention should be concentrated subjectively upon every part of the brain several times each day. Ten minutes three times a day will produce great improvements within a few months. Then let no one say that he has not the time. The truth is we have not the time to neglect this matter. The possibilities that are within us are marvelous to say the least, but those possibilities cannot express themselves through a brain that is crude, sluggish or undeveloped.

Finer States of Action — To refine the substance of the brain is highly important, because it is only through a refined brain that superior mental qualities can find expression. For this reason a refining process should permeate the entire brain several times every day, or it may be applied in conjunction with regular concentration for development. While concentrating upon the brain, try to perceive or feel the finer elements of the brain that permeate the physical elements. This will draw the entire developing process into a finer state of action, which will tend to refine more and more every cell in the entire brain structure. To comprehend the finer elements of life and to gain conscious power of that something that is within things, beneath things, and above things, is absolutely necessary if we desire to become as much as nature has given us the power to become. But to respond to the life of that finer something, the brain must be so highly developed or refined in its substance and essence that every trace of crudeness and materiality has been removed. A clear understanding of all the finer processes of life and action will aid remarkably in giving this refinement and responsiveness to the brain, because every ascending tendency of the mind will, if applied to the brain, give higher and finer states of action to all the elements and forces of the brain.

Additional Results — When subjective concentration is perfectly understood and thoroughly applied, we shall find that in addition to continuous development of the brain, all undesirable conditions will be removed from the mind. No forms of mental exhaustion, lack of mental energy or mental depression of any kind will ever occur so long as the brain is properly supplied with nourishment and energy; and since subjective concentration if applied daily will provide the brain perfectly with these two essentials, all mental troubles can be brought to an end through the art of this concentration. This is certainly a fact that will mean much, and great will be the gain to those who apply it thoroughly. In addition to subjective concentration upon the brain, a similar concentration should be directed every day upon the body. This will keep the entire system balanced and strong, and will constantly create new avenues for the upbuilding of the entire personality. Every cell in the human person contains the possibility of a new group of cells of a higher order which when formed will supply the requisite channels through which a higher expression of mind and soul may be promoted. The art of cell building in the brain or body is therefore an art we should all cultivate to the very highest degree. When we concentrate daily upon all parts of the brain, every form of mental sluggishness will disappear, and activity will be steadily increased in every cell. But in the increase of life and action in the brain, we must never lose sight of the idea of perfect poise. When we give high, strong, well poised activity to every part of the brain, the mind will secure an instrument through which the greater things we have in view will positively be accomplished.

What Is Needed — In this connection it is well to repeat and emphasize the fact that in the development of ability along any line, there are three principles involved. First, the number of brain cells must be increased in that part of the brain through which the faculty in question functions. Second, the quality of the mind and the faculty must be improved. And third, the power back of the mind must be made much stronger. In other words, we must have size, quality and power, and these must be properly combined if we are to have the best results. Size, however, does not mean quantity alone, because when any part of the brain is made larger, we should also aim to make the substance of that part much finer. The more cells you can build in a given cubic inch of brain matter and the more delicate you can make the structure of those cells, the greater becomes the capacity of that part of the brain. The smaller the cells of the brain, the finer the brain. Common brain matter has large cells, and the structure of such cells is nearly always crude. The higher order of brain matter always has small cells with a fine delicate structure, and their number to each given amount of space is very large. In consequence when we proceed to develop the brain, the brain itself should be made somewhat larger. The cells should be smaller and more numerous, and the brain matter itself should be more delicate as to substance and texture. Very fine brain matter approaches the ethereal in essence and reminds you of the petals of flowers instead of crude clay. In the development of ability, the brain must receive special attention, because it is the vehicle or the instrument or the tool that the mind employs. Not that the tool is more important than the workman, but the tool in most cases has been neglected. We have tried to improve our minds and have succeeded to some extent; but we have given practically no attention to the scientific development of the brain. We have left the brain as it is and have expected the mind to do its best under such circumstances. That only a few in every age have really acquired greatness is therefore a matter that is easily explained.

All Faculties Localized — It has been thoroughly demonstrated that every talent employs one or more distinct parts of the brain, and that the development of these parts of the brain will increase the capacity and the efficiency of the talent. Consequently, when we know what part of the brain each special talent employs, the development of any talent becomes a matter of simplicity, and is placed within easy reach of everyone. As we proceed to take a general view of this idea of localization, we find that the lower half of the forehead is employed by the scientific and the practical functions of mind, and that the development of this part of the brain will increase one's ability to apply in practice what has been learned. The same development will give method, system and the happy application in the world of details. The man whose mind and brain are well developed in this region has the power to do things. He may not always have the best plans or the best methods, but he always produces results. To develop this part of the brain, concentrate attention first upon the brain center, which is a point just midway between the ears; then gradually move attention towards the lower half of the forehead until you concentrate subjectively upon all the brain matter that lies between the brain center and the lower half of the forehead. All the cells that are found in this region are concerned in the function of application. Therefore, when you concentrate, do not simply give your attention to the surface of the brain, but to the whole of that part of the brain that lies between the surface in question and the brain center.

Thought of Expansion — Another very important idea to remember is that all such concentration must contain the thought of expansion, and must be very gentle, though deep and strong. The necessity of finer consciousness while concentration is taking place must never be overlooked. For this reason we should enter into this finer consciousness before we begin. Such concentration upon any part of the brain for promoting development may last ten or fifteen minutes, and may be repeated several times a day. In your work it is a very good plan to concentrate mildly, but constantly upon that part of the brain that you use in your work; thus development will go on steadily while you are engaged in other efforts.

Pure Intellect — The upper half of the forehead is employed by the function of pure intellect. Therefore, if we wish to increase intelligence, the power of reason, understanding and intellectual capabilities in general, that part of the brain should be developed. And again we must bear in mind that it is not simply the surface that should be developed, but all the convolutions that lie between the surface and the brain center. The function of pure intellect occupies all that part of the brain that is found between the brain center and the upper half of the forehead; concentration, therefore, for the development of intellect must be directed upon all the cells found in this region. To help give quality to the intelligence you seek to perfect, try to enter into the real meaning of intelligence while you are concentrating upon this part of the brain. Try to realize as deeply as possible the true significance of intellect, and what it means to reason and understand. You will thus find that results will increase decidedly. At first, you may not gain any considerable insight into the depths of intellect, but by trying to form the most perfect conceptions of intelligence while concentrating in this manner, the brain will actually become more lucid. Your comprehension will enlarge its scope and the intellect will become more brilliant. If you have some deep subject under consideration, and you do not quite succeed in penetrating its depths, you will find the solution coming almost of itself, if you concentrate in this manner upon the upper half of the forehead while that subject is being analyzed. Perplexing problems can be solved in the same way, although the method will have to be carried out properly; that is, all the essentials involved must be given due attention. We find that we can, therefore, in this way make our intellects more brilliant than usual when occasions so demand. And we can, by daily practice, so improve intellect that we may ere long be able to understand perfectly almost any subject that is brought before our attention.

To Develop Individuality — One of the greatest faculties possessed by man is that of individuality, because it gives not only stability to what he is doing, but also causes the individual to be himself, which is highly important. No one can do his best and become all that he is capable of unless he is himself under all circumstances; and this desired trait is invariably brought out through individuality. To develop individuality, you must increase the size and the quality of that part of the brain through which it functions. And this part is illustrated in Fig. II. Individuality includes self-confidence, firmness, stability, faith and the faculty of keeping on. Thousands of fine minds fail because they do not continue right on regardless of what happens. In most instances, however, they cannot help it, because they lack individuality. We all can develop individuality, however, and we must if we wish to succeed in every undertaking for which we are fitted. To develop this faculty, concentrate upon that part of the brain indicated, and animate your concentration with a firm, self-possessed attitude of mind. In brief, as you concentrate, try to feel that you are a strong, masterful individuality, absolute monarch of your own domain. Feel that you have the power to be and do what you want to be and do, and realize that you as an individuality constitute the power that is back of and above everything that transpires in your own life. In addition to this, add faith; that is, have unbounded faith in your own individuality, and believe thoroughly that the purpose you have in view can positively be realized.

Energy and Push — The lower half of the back brain is the seat of energy, and when this is well developed we have what may be called push; that is, we will not give up our efforts because there is too much power back of those efforts.

When individuality is well developed, we continue because we know that we can; and when a great deal of power is added to individuality and self-confidence, nothing can induce us to give up what we feel can be successfully pushed through. A great many people feel conditions of weakness at times, and even pain in the back brain whenever they try to push through something of importance, and the cause is lack of energy. It is therefore well to give this part of the brain attention, before we undertake any kind of work that requires a great deal of energy and perseverance. And when we feel exhaustion in the back brain, we can produce perfect relief almost at once by gently concentrating upon that part while trying at the same time to feel the presence of the finer creative energies. The development of the back brain is promoted in the same way as that of other parts with this exception: During subjective concentration upon the back of the brain, the attitude of mind must contain the thought of greater power, and you must try to feel that creative energies are accumulating more and more where your attention is directed.

Insight and judgment — A faculty of remarkable value is that of insight or real judgment, and its place of expression is found in that part of the forehead where the cranium begins to recede. To develop this part of the brain, that is, all the brain cells that lie between the brain center and the surface of the region indicated, the process is as usual, and the mental attitude should be that of interior insight. In other words, try to exercise the power of interior insight in connection with everything that you may be thinking of while concentrating for the development of this faculty. We all come to places at times where we have to make some important decision, but frequently we are uncertain as to what course to pursue. Thousands have under such circumstances taken the wrong path, and thousands in the midst of many opportunities have selected the least because they have no power of knowing which was the best. Mistakes have been made without number because we did not possess the judgment to know what was right at the time, and a number of similar conditions could be mentioned all arising from the same deficiency. The development, therefore, of judgment, discernment and insight is of more than usual importance. When two opportunities present themselves there ought to be something that could inform us as to the nature of each one. There ought to be a way to know when to do things, when to act, which course to pursue, and what plan to adopt. There ought to be such a way and there is. We have the faculty of judging these things properly. And when this faculty is well developed, our decisions and selections will always be the best. To proceed with the development of this faculty, the following method may be adopted: When you have something to decide, something of great importance, but do not know what decision to make, do not think of the matter for the time being, but proceed instead to give special attention to this faculty of insight. Concentrate subjectively at frequent intervals upon the brain cells involved. Try to increase their number; refine the substance of which they are composed, and try to give the faculty of judgment and decision the most perfect vehicle of expression possible. Continue this for a few hours or a few days if you can put off the decision that long. Then take up the problem and try to see the best way. If the faculty in question is sufficiently awakened, you will know almost at once what course to pursue, and you will lose all desire for other plans. But should you fail to receive a decided answer, let the problem go for a while longer, and proceed to awaken this faculty still further. You will soon bring this faculty up to the desired state of lucidity, and the decision will be made. In addition to this method, carry on regular development every day as you do with all your other faculties.

Improvement of Quality — We gain size in any faculty through the use of subjective concentration, but quality and power are developed in other ways. The first essential in the production of quality consists of forming the highest mental conceptions possible of the faculties themselves as well as every thought or idea that may enter the mind. The term "mental conception" simply means the idea that you form of anything of which you may be thinking. Every idea you form in mind is a mental concept and it serves as a vital factor in the upbuilding of the talent you have under consideration. Metaphysically speaking, every idea is composed of the ideas which you have formed concerning that talent, and every faculty is as large and as perfect as your conscious or interior understanding of the function of that faculty. Therefore, the more perfectly you understand the inner life, the soul, the essence, the true nature, the scope and the possibilities of a talent, the higher will be your mental conceptions of that talent. And the higher these conceptions are the higher will be the quality of the talent itself. To state this matter more simply, we might say that the first law in the improvement of quality among the faculties of the mind, is to have as great and as lofty thoughts as possible at all times. To carry out this idea, we should hold our minds in the loftiest attitude possible whenever we concentrate for the development of any part of the brain. Thus we will develop mental quality at the same time as we develop brain capacity. When we concentrate attention upon the upper half of the forehead, we should hold in mind at the time the highest, the broadest and the deepest conceptions of pure intellect that we can form. The result of this dual process will be increased quality in our intelligence and a more perfect brain through which this improved intellect may be expressed. In promoting development along other lines, the same idea should be applied, and we may thus secure results along several lines through every individual process.

Increase of Power — The first step in the increase of power is to preserve the energies we already possess. There is an enormous amount of energy generated in the average personality, but the larger part of this is usually wasted. Therefore, if we simply prevented this waste, we should, in many instances, have more energy than we could use, no matter along how many lines we wish to promote development. To prevent this waste of energy, all discord must be avoided and perfect poise attained; there must be no anger, no worry, no despondency and no fear; the mind must be composed, the nervous system in harmony and the entire personality in tune with the serenity of the soul. When this has been accomplished, we shall feel a great deal stronger both in mind and body.

Important Fact — We shall realize a decided increase in the force and energy throughout every part of our systems. The personality will feel as if it were charged, so to speak, with energies we never felt before, and we realize that we have come into possession of new and stronger forces than we have ever supposed in the past. When this accumulation of energy is felt, however, we should not become too enthusiastic nor too determined, as such a course may tend to destroy our poise, and thus produce the waste we have tried to avoid. Instead these great moments should be employed in gently directing attention towards those parts of the brain and the mind that we wish to develop. In this way we will give added power to the building up of any particular talent towards which we may be giving our attention; but when our minds become so large that we require more energy than what is being generated in our systems now, we shall find it necessary to secure an additional supply; and this is done by awakening the great within; that is by directing the subconscious to give expression to more and more energy as we may require.

Transmutation — In the increase and use of creative energy, the process of transmutation becomes absolutely necessary; and to transmute any force in the system means to change that force from a lower to a higher state of action; or to change any creative power from its present purpose to some other purpose than we may have in mind. To change any force to a higher or finer state of action, we should enter into the conscious feeling of the finer forces of the system. And this is not difficult as anyone will find after making a few attempts along this line. Through the process of transmutation, all the forces of the system at any time can be changed to different forces, and can be gathered for special work in that part of the system where special development is to take place. The value of transmutation, therefore, is very great, and should receive thorough and constant attention.

Added Lines of Expression — Whenever the creative forces accumulate, the predominating thought held in mind at the time becomes the pattern, and what the creative forces produce will always be similar to the nature of this predominating thought. Therefore, when we concentrate upon any part of the brain for the purpose of development, the thought of development, expansion and growth should receive our first attention. This practice will aid remarkably in the increase of brain cells, and as each brain cell is a channel of expression for the conscious action of that talent that functions through the part in question, we realize its great value. The more brain cells there are in a given place, the more channels of expression will be secured for that talent; and the more channels of expression we provide for a talent, the greater the capacity and power of that talent. To help increase the number of cells in any part of the brain, all the essentials of the talent that function through that part should be held in consciousness during such concentration. And the essentials of a talent are all those different parts of the talent that one can become conscious of by trying to examine that talent from every possible point of view. The more essentials or actions of the talent we are conscious of while we concentrate upon any part of the brain, the more lines of expression we will produce in that part. And since each line of expression tends to create its own cell, provided there is sufficient nourishment and energy in that particular place, the number of brain cells will necessarily increase in proportion to the number of essentials we hold in mind during the process of concentration.

Multiplication of Ideas — In the beginning all that is necessary is to have a clear idea of the nature of the talent you wish to develop, and then hold that clear idea in mind during concentration. As you proceed, this idea will subdivide again and again until it becomes a score of ideas, and each of these ideas will become an essential, that is, a distinct part of the talent and an individual line of action for that talent. You realize, therefore, that to see all the essentials of a talent with the mind's eye, is to dissect that talent and see all its parts as parts, and how they are united to form the one talent. The value of this process is found in the fact that the more parts of the talent you are conscious of while concentrating, the more cells you will create in that part of the brain upon which you concentrate, provided, you hold in mind very clearly the principal ideas of the talent that functions through that particular part. Another gain from the same process is found in the fact that it tends to increase the channels of expression for the talent itself. And the more channels of expression we provide for a talent, the greater that talent becomes.

The Brain Center — When concentrating upon any part of the brain, we should always begin at the brain center; that is, where all the lines meet as indicated in Figure II. We should begin by drawing all the forces of the mind towards this center, and when we feel that consciousness is concentrated, so to speak, at this point, we should turn attention upon that part of the brain we wish to develop. Then we should concentrate upon the entire region from the brain center to the surface of the cranium as it is all the cells within that space that we wish to multiply, refine and develop.

The Metaphysical Side — That part of the brain marked "interior understanding" is employed by the metaphysical side of the mind. Through this region the mind discerns the interior and higher aspects of life, and is therefore of great importance. When this part of the brain lacks in development the mind sees only the surface of things, and the deeper things of life are therefore beyond his understanding. But since the attainment of real worth depends upon our ability to understand the inner and real side of things, this part of the brain must never be neglected. When we concentrate upon this region we should open the mind fully to thought from the depths of consciousness. We should begin by turning all attention away from things and external ideas, and think only of the most perfect ideas that we can form of everything of which we are conscious. It is not necessary to attempt any profound analysis of the abstract, but simply to hold attention upon that perfect something that permeates everything. We should not at this time think of flaws, defects, mistakes or imperfections, but should hold the idea of absolute perfection uppermost in mind. The possibility of absolute perfection is a matter we need not discuss with ourselves because we know that there is such a thing. It is upon our most perfect idea of the perfect that we should turn attention. In the development of this faculty we should remember that there is such a thing as metaphysical consciousness, a consciousness that is distinct from intellectual understanding, and the distinction is this, that the intellectual understanding understands how things are related to each other, while this inner metaphysical understanding understands the things themselves. The intellectual understands phenomena. The interior understands that which produces the phenomena. It is this metaphysical consciousness or understanding that we should seek to realize when we concentrate for the development of this region of the brain. Therefore, all thought must be directed upon the perfect; that is, that something that we discern when metaphysical consciousness begins. The real value of this consciousness will be more fully realized when we come to study special talents, as we shall then find that every talent has a metaphysical foundation, and that to perfect the quality and true worth of that talent we must express more fully the metaphysical nature of that talent. But since we cannot increase the expression of anything until we become conscious of it, we realize that metaphysical consciousness becomes indispensable to those who wish to grow in genuine quality and true worth.

The Use of Emotion — That region of the brain marked "emotion" is the channel of sympathy and every tender feeling of mind or soul. It is through the functions that employ this region that the mind finds unity and at-one-ment with everything that exists; and as the realization of unity and harmony with all things is absolutely necessary to the highest development of mind, this faculty should be well developed. In a great many people the emotional side is more or less perverted, and takes the form of sentimentalism. But this does not come from an over-development of this faculty. On the contrary, it is due to a false conception of the finer things in life, and is therefore caused principally by the lack of intelligence. In concentrating upon this part of the brain, the purpose should be the development of a larger channel for the expression of true sympathy. Everything should occupy the foremost place in mind at the time. But when we think of sympathy, we should think of it as being the essence of the highest unity conceivable, and not as a mere mode of sympathizing with people. When the average person sympathizes, he usually comes down and feels like those with whom he sympathizes; he does not try to realize that finer and higher unity that exists among all things. Therefore he is not in sympathy. He simply imitates the emotions of the other person, and this is a violation of all the laws of man. To feel that deep and high unity that makes all creation one is the purpose of sympathy, and when we feel this sublime unity, we become conscious of the most beautiful and the most tender emotions that the soul can possibly know. Accordingly, the value of such development becomes two-fold; first, the most beautiful qualities of life are brought into expression; and second the mind learns to view all things from that higher state of consciousness where the unity and the harmony of all is discerned. And here we find the secret of knowing the truth, because to know the truth is to see all things from the viewpoint of unity; it is to stand at that place from which all things proceed and to see clearly what they are, where they are going, and what their purpose in life or action happens to be. True sympathy, or the realization of the finer emotion, will tend to bring the mind to this place, because all these high emotions will draw irresistibly upon the mind, thereby leading consciousness up to that place where perfect unity is absolutely real. We all know that the finest emotions of the soul constantly lead us towards higher places. And we also know that the higher we go in consciousness the more perfect becomes our understanding of all things. The value of sympathy, therefore, in its true sense is very great indeed.

The Power of Intuition — The most successful men in the world have had the faculty of intuition developed to a high degree and have thus been able to take advantage of the best opportunities at the proper time. History is full of incidents where men and women have arisen to high places by following the indications of this great faculty. It gives the mind the power to see through things as they are and therefore reveals, not only the facts in the case, but also indicates how to deal with those facts. Intuition may work consciously or unconsciously, but whenever it is well developed it works, and works well. As previously stated, we may develop this faculty by concentrating subjectively at frequent intervals every day upon that part of the brain indicated in Figure II, and we should, during the process of concentration give our attention to the idea of interior insight; that is, we should try to see through things and try to know directly or at first hand without resorting to reason or analysis. In this connection a strong desire for deeper discernment is of the highest value if such desire is expressed persistently whenever we concentrate for development. The development of this faculty can be promoted decidedly by making it a point to have more and more faith in its judgment, and also by depending upon it for judgment in every case that comes up. Like all other things, it develops through use if that use is thorough and continuous. It is a splendid practice to make it a point never to decide upon anything without first getting the highest possible light of intuition on the subject, and also to have perfect faith in your ability to get the real truth in this way. Through this practice you will give more and more energy and life to this faculty. And accordingly it will develop steadily and surely until it becomes sufficiently developed to express its function even to a remarkable degree.

The Most Important Faculty — All the faculties of the mind are important and necessary to each other, but the most important of all is unquestionably that of intellect. This faculty, therefore, should receive our first attention unless it is already well developed. Through the proper concentration upon that part of the brain that is employed by the intellect, remarkable intelligence can possibly be developed, and results will appear at the very beginning. The very first time you concentrate upon that part of the brain with the thought of brilliancy in mind you realize that your mentality becomes clearer and more lucid; you can think better; fine thoughts come more readily, and you can understand things with a clearness that is sometimes remarkable. You do not simply think that the improvement has been realized, however, because in dealing with difficult problems you actually demonstrate that the lucidity of your mind has been decidedly improved. To promote this development we should concentrate attention upon the upper half of the forehead whenever we think or study, as we shall in that way increase the capacity of intelligence at the very time when we are making direct use of it; and we shall accordingly have better results both in our thinking, or study, and in our development. But all such concentration should be easy, and should be associated with the consciousness of the finer creative energies. When you feel the action of these finer forces, you do not have to compel them to work. They work easily, smoothly and harmoniously of their own accord when placed in action. In fact, they act and work as if directed by some superior power; and this is really true because when you awaken the higher powers within you, you are actually bringing into action powers that are superior, powers that have no limitations whatever.

Application and Expression — That region of the brain that is marked "application" is employed by the mind in the doing of things; that is, those faculties that express themselves through this region have the power to use what we understand, and therefore unites intellect with the world of things. When we develop this faculty we shall find that it is just as easy to practice as to theorize, and that every idea of value can be turned to practical use in the tangible world. When trying to develop this faculty, we should hold in mind thoughts of system, method and scientific application. And we should try to feel that we are consciously related to all things in the outer world. Then, to this attitude we should add a strong desire to do things and achieve much, and we shall find ourselves laying the foundation for a power of application that will be a practical power indeed. Through this same region we find the action of the faculty of expression, and though this faculty is employed largely in connection with musical, artistic and literary talents, it is by no means confined to those talents. The power of expression, generally speaking, is used by all faculties and is absolutely necessary to everybody in bringing forth what there is in them. When we develop the power of expression we tend to bring forth our own individuality and make the personality far more powerful than it has been before. And in addition all the talents we employ will express themselves with more thoroughness, efficiency and power. For general purposes we should concentrate upon this part of the brain in the attitude of a strong desire for full expression of mind, soul and personality. And we should try to feel at the time that every power or faculty in our possession is being expressed more and more through its own channel.

Perseverance and Enthusiasm — In all concentration for development we should give the most time to those faculties that we need in our work, and especially to those that are weak and inferior. Our object should be to secure a well developed brain in all respects, and to give special development to those faculties that we use in our vocation. When concentrating upon a certain part of the brain we should think only of that talent or faculty that functions through that part, and we should try to realize as fully as possible the interior or potential nature of that talent. To think of the unlimited possibilities that exist within the talent is of the highest value during concentration, because in this way the richest thought that we are capable of creating will be introduced into the process of development. In all these efforts perseverance and enthusiasm are indispensable. Principles must be applied and to all such application we should give our whole life and soul. The first essential is to understand the principles of mind development. And the second is to persevere in every application, giving so much enthusiasm to all our efforts that every element and force within us is called to action. It is in this way, and in this way alone, that results will be secured, and when we persevere in this manner results will positively be secured. The amount of time that will be required to secure decided results will depend upon our own efforts. To develop ability or genius up to a high state will require years, but in the meantime, we shall be gaining ground steadily. And so long as we are steadily improving we know that we shall finally reach the goal in view, no matter how high or how wonderful that goal may be. Anyone, however, who will faithfully apply the above principles as well as the other principles presented in this study, will realize a decided improvement from the very beginning, and may secure even remarkable results in a few months time. In fact, the majority of those who take up this study should at least double their mental power and ability every year, and a large percentage will positively do far better than this.

Chapter 6

Special Brain Development

The Eight Principal Divisions — That every faculty of the mind functions through one or more distinct parts of the brain is no longer mere theory; it is a fact that leading scientists of the world are demonstrating to be true. And that any part of the brain can be developed through the art of subjective concentration, is also a fact that is being conclusively demonstrated at the present time. It is therefore evident that when we know exactly through what part of the brain each faculty functions, we can increase the power and the efficiency of that faculty to any degree desired, provided we develop the mental faculty itself as well as that part of the brain through which it functions. It is with the development of the brain that we are now concerned, however, because this phase has been entirely neglected by all previous systems of mental training. In Fig. IV we present the eight principal divisions of the brain, although these divisions do not represent the same number of individual faculties. On the contrary, a group of faculties function through each division, but in each case the individual faculties of any one group are so closely related that they can be developed together. Thus time is saved, and a more thorough development is secured.

The Practical Brain — That part of the brain that is marked No. 1 in Fig. IV may be very appropriately termed the practical brain, as it is through this part that the mind functions when direct practical action is being expressed. Whenever you try to be practical your mind begins at once to act upon the practical brain, and when the practical brain is well developed you are naturally of a practical turn of mind. The practical brain should be developed by everybody, and especially by those who are engaged in vocations where

93

system, method and the mastery of details are required. Concentrate subjectively upon this part of the brain for a few minutes several times a day, and whenever you are engaged in the actual doing of things, think of the practical brain; that is, aim to focus the power of thought, attention and application upon this part of the brain, and aim to act through the practical brain whenever you apply yourself practically.

The Mechanical Brain — Every building process and all the faculties of construction function through the mechanical brain (See No. 2, Fig. IV). Engineers, mechanics and builders of every description should develop this part of the brain; and these are the two methods that may be employed. First, use subjective concentration whenever you have a few moments to spare; and second, train your mind to work through the mechanical brain while you are engaged in your special line of constructive work. When you are laying bricks, do not think at random; think of improving your skill; and as you think, try to turn the full power of your thought into the mechanical brain. The power of your mind, instead of being aimlessly scattered, will thus accumulate in the mechanical brain, and will daily strengthen, develop and build up that part of the brain. In the course of time you will become a mechanical genius, and scores of valuable opportunities will be opened for you. If you are building a bridge, digging a tunnel, running an engine or working on some invention, apply the same principle. Train your mind to act directly upon the mechanical brain while you are at work, and deeply desire the active powers of your mind to steadily build up that part of the brain. You will soon become an expert in your line of work, and later on a genius.

The Financial Brain — We all need a very good development of the financial brain (See No. 3, Fig. IV), because the full value of life cannot be gained so long as there is the slightest trace of poverty. When the financial brain is so well developed as to balance properly with all the other leading faculties, the use of those other faculties will result in financial gain; but where the financial brain is weak and small, financial gains will be meager, even though there may be extraordinary ability along other lines. No matter how remarkable your talents may be along any special line, you will not make much money through the use of those talents unless your financial brain is well developed; but if this part of the brain is exceptionally developed, everything you touch will be turned to money. The making of money, however, is not the sole purpose of life; the making of money will not, in itself, produce happiness, nor make living worthwhile, but it is a necessary part of the real purpose of life; therefore everybody should develop the financial brain to a good degree. If you are not directly connected with the financial world, give your financial brain a few moments attention, through subjective concentration, every day; that will prove sufficient. And as you concentrate, think of accumulation, desire accumulation, and try to feel that you are in the process of accumulation. But if you are engaged directly in the financial world, whether in banking, brokerage, financial management, financial promotion or in any form of actual financial work whatever, give your financial brain thorough development. Aim to work through this brain, and use subjective concentration for a few minutes every hour if possible.

The Executive Brain — That part of the brain marked "4" in Fig. IV is employed by the mind in all forms of management. Those who govern, rule, manage, superintend or occupy positions at the head of enterprises, should give special attention to the development of the executive brain. When this part of the brain is large, strong and well developed, we possess what is termed "backbone"; and we have real, substantial "backing" for every purpose, plan or idea that we may wish to carry through. We have force and determination, and have the power as well as the "knack" of guiding the ship of any enterprise through the storms of every obstacle, adversity or difficulty, to a safe landing, at the haven of great success. The true executive governs perfectly without giving anyone the impression that he is trying to rule; he governs, not by personal force, but by superior leadership; he has the power that can rule, therefore does not have to try to rule. The strong man never domineers; it is only weak men who would like to rule that ever domineer; but it is time and energy wasted. Never try to domineer over anything or try to forcefully rule anybody if you would attain superior executive power. To develop the executive brain, try to realize the position and power of true leadership whenever you apply subjective concentration in that part, or apply executive power in daily life. Aim to make the executive brain as large and strong as possible, and whenever you use the executive faculty, try to feel that it is the executive brain that gives the necessary power.

The Volitional Brain — The development of the fifth division of the brain produces will power, personal force, determination, push, perseverance, persistence, self-confidence, firmness and self-control. When the volitional brain is well developed you are no longer a part of the mass; you stand out as a distinct individuality, and you are a special power in the world in which you work and live. The volitional brain, therefore, should be thoroughly developed by every mind that aims to become something more than a mere cog in the industrial machine. The best way to proceed with this development is to concentrate subjectively upon the volitional brain for ten or fifteen minutes every morning. This will give you the power to control more fully your thought, your actions and your circumstances during the day. When you concentrate hold yourself in the attitude of self-control, and deeply will with all the power of will that you possess.

Whenever you are called upon to use exceptional will-power or "stand your ground" against temptations or adverse circumstances, turn your attention upon the volitional brain; that is, think of the volitional brain when you use your will, your determination or your self-control, and you will feel yourself becoming stronger and stronger in personal power and will-power until nothing in the world can cause you to budge in the least from the true position you have taken.

The Aspiring Brain — When the mind aspires toward the ideal, the beautiful, the sublime, the actions of the mind function through that part of the brain designated in the sixth division in Fig. IV. When you "hitch your wagon to a star" you act through the aspiring brain; you do the same when you feel ambitious, or express real desire for higher attainments and greater achievements. It is the aspiring brain that prompts you to advance, to improve yourself, to push to the front, to do great things in the world, to live a life worthwhile; and it is the same brain that keeps you in touch with the greater possibilities that exist in every conceivable field of action. Develop the aspiring brain and you will become ambitions; you will gain a strong desire to rise out of the common; all the tendencies of your mind will begin to move toward greater things; you will discern the ideal; you will begin to have visions of extraordinary attainments and achievements, and you will be inspired with an "upward and onward force" that will give you no peace until you begin to work in earnest to make your lofty dreams come true. So long as the aspiring brain is small and weak, you will have neither the power nor the desire to get above mere, common existence; but when this part of the brain becomes large, strong and thoroughly developed, you will have the power and the desire to reach the top; and to the top you will positively go. To develop this part of the brain two things are necessary. Concentrate subjectively upon the aspiring brain whenever you have a few moments to spare, and during every moment of such concentration, "Hitch your wagon to a star."

The Imaging Brain — This part of the brain (See No. 7, Fig. IV) may be properly termed the "idea factory." It is the imaging brain that creates ideas, that forms plans, that formulates methods and that combines, adjusts and readjusts the various elements that are embraced in whatever the mind may create. To accomplish greater things we must have greater ideas, more extensive plans and more perfect methods. The imaging faculty can furnish all three precisely as we may desire, provided the imaging brain is developed to higher and higher degrees. To proceed, turn your attention upon the imaging brain whenever you use your imagination or whenever you picture anything in your mind. When you are in search of new ideas, look into the imaging brain, and use subjective concentration in arousing this part of the brain to higher and finer activity. Think with the imaging brain whenever you are engaged in forming new plans or formulating new methods, and always aim to express the expansive attitude through that part of the brain. In other words, when you use the imaging or concentrate subjectively upon that part of the brain, think of the imaging faculty as expanding into larger and greater fields of thought. Your mental creative power will thus become greater and greater; you will grasp a much larger world of thought, action and possibility, and the superior ideas and plans desired will soon be secured.

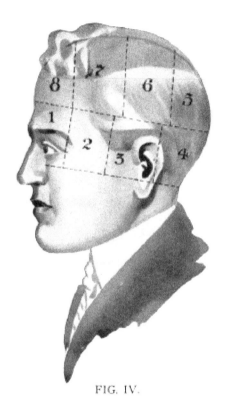

FIG. IV.

1. The Practical Brain   5. The Volitional Brain
2. The Mechanical Brain   6. The Aspiring Brain
3. The Financial Brain   7. The Imaging Brain
4. The Executive Brain   8. The Intellectual Brain

The Intellectual Brain — The eighth division of the brain, as illustrated in Figure IV, is the seat of pure intelligence, reason, judgment, analysis, conception and understanding. Every cell in the brain is animated with intelligence, because intelligence is an attribute of every faculty of the mind, but it is through the intellectual brain that the mind functions when it thinks with that form of intelligence that not only knows, but knows that it knows. Whenever you attempt to understand any particular subject or object, turn your attention upon the intellectual brain, and try to think directly with that part of the brain. Do the same when you reason about anything, when you proceed to analyze anything, or try to find the solution of any problem. Concentrate subjectively upon the intellectual brain for a few minutes several times a day; and while you concentrate, try to see through every thought that comes into your mind at the time. This will increase remarkably your power to know, and will, at the same time, increase the general power of your mental ability. All ability depends, to some degree, upon the power of your intellect; therefore, whatever your work, give special and daily attention to the development of the intellectual brain. As the faculty of pure intellect, reason and understanding is increased in efficiency and power, every other active faculty in the mind will also increase in efficiency and power. It is the intellectual brain that guides the whole brain; and, therefore, intellectual advancement means general advancement; but this general advancement in every part of the brain and the mind will not be satisfactory unless the whole of the brain is developed in proportion. Develop the intellectual brain continuously, no matter what your work; give special and continuous development to that part of the brain that is employed directly in your work; and give general development to your whole brain; this is the perfect rule to follow in order to secure the proper results.

Chapter 7

The Inner Secret

In order to develop any part of the physical system, two essentials are required. The first is more nourishment in that particular part, and the second is an increase in creative energy. The circulation conveys nourishment to all parts of the system, and the nerves transmit the creative energies; therefore, wherever we increase the circulation, additional nourishment will be supplied, and wherever the activity of the nerves is increased or intensified, there creative energy will accumulate. Accordingly, the question will be how to increase the circulation wherever we like, and how to intensify the activity of any desired nerve center. Experiments, however, have demonstrated that this problem is not as difficult as it may seem, because wherever mental attention is concentrated, an increase both in the circulation and in the nerve activity takes place. But this concentration must be in the right mental attitude, and here we come to the inner secret.

It has been discovered that all functions of the personality are under the direct control of what is termed the finer subjective forces, and in order to master any physical function or mental faculty, these finer forces must be employed. Wherever these subjective forces display the greatest activity, there the circulation is the strongest, and there the creative energies naturally accumulate; and these subjective forces will display the greatest activity wherever attention is concentrated during subjective consciousness. The secret, therefore, is to enter subjective consciousness before we begin to concentrate for any desired development; and by subjective consciousness we mean that mental state wherein the finer forces of the system can be felt. But this is not something new or something difficult to attain. We all are

101

more or less on the verge of this consciousness all the time, and most of us enter into it frequently.

When you are thrilled by music that stirs the very soul of your being you are in subjective consciousness, and it is the finer forces or interior vibrations that produce the delightful sensation you feel at the time. When you are inwardly touched by the beauties of nature, you are in this same consciousness; and it is these finer forces that create the lofty thoughts you think during such moments. There are any number of experiences that could be mentioned to illustrate what is meant by subjective consciousness, but the two just mentioned will give anyone the key. And here we must remember that it is this state that we must enter whenever we concentrate for development, either for mind, brain or body; the reason being, that while the mind is in this finer subjective state, the actions of mind will directly control the subjective forces. When the mind is in subjective consciousness, the subjective forces will follow concentration, thus drawing more creative energy and a stronger circulation to that place upon which attention is directed. This is the law, and it is just as unfailing as any law in nature. But how to take the mind into subjective consciousness at any time is of course the problem, although the solution is by no means difficult to find.

When we know what subjective consciousness really is, and remember the sensation we have felt while in such a state at previous times, we can readily transfer the mind to the field of the finer forces by simply desiring to do so, but we must not make a strenuous effort in that direction. To keep the mind upon the ideal and the more refined for a few moments is usually sufficient to awaken subjective consciousness in most instances; and to think of anything that is lofty and sublime, or that touches the soul will invariably produce the same result. In brief, anything that will cause your mind to pass from the mere surface of thought into the finer depths of life may be employed in the beginning to induce this finer state. Possibly few external helps would be better than that of listening for a few moments to sweet, tender, soulful music, and the reading of poetry that really is poetry will usually serve the same purpose. It must be remembered, however, that when we employ external aids in this connection we must make a deep, but gentle effort to enter into sympathetic touch with the soul of that which we employ at the time.

When we gain the mastery of our own consciousness we can enter the subjective state or withdraw from that state at any time as we like. In fact, we can do this just as easily as we can open or close our eyes. This mastery, therefore, should be our great object in view when we are depending upon temporary or external helps. Another method for assisting the mind in producing subjective consciousness is the study of the different planes of vibration with a view of gaining a perfect understanding of the true nature of each individual plane. This is an immense and a most interesting study, and will prove extremely valuable in mental development, for the reason that the mind can consciously enter and consciously act upon any plane that it understands. Therefore, when the mind understands the nature of subjective consciousness, it can enter that state at any time by simply deciding to do so. To gain a better understanding of the various planes of consciousness and the ascending scales of vibrations, the latest discoveries both in physical science and in psychology should be noted with the greatest of care. The Xrays and the Nrays demonstrate conclusively the existence of finer forces and higher vibrations in nature; and the fact that every plane in nature has a corresponding plane in man has been known for a long time. It is also a well known fact that man has a higher sense or consciousness to correspond with every higher force or plane in nature. Therefore the fact that there are higher forces in nature proves that there are higher states of consciousness in man; and it is our privilege to have all of these developed whenever we may so desire.

Many minds look upon the visible physical body as all there is of the body, but chemistry has demonstrated conclusively that within the purely physical body there exists a finer grade of elements, and within this finer grade a still finer grade and so on for a number of grades, the exact number of which has not been determined. The physical body therefore is, strictly speaking, composed of a number of forms, the outermost form being in the lowest grade)of vibration, while the innermost forms being in such a high grade of vibration that they approach what scientists call ethereal elements. Just at this point the subconscious begins and we have a vast interior world, the immensity of which will possibly never be fully demonstrated. It is this interior world that we call "the great within," and it is the source of the boundless possibilities that are latent in man. Whenever we are more or less in touch with this inner or finer realm we are in subjective consciousness, and it is only necessary to touch the subconscious to gain control of the finer forces.

Subjective consciousness deals with a boundless realm and therefore we may expand the mind into this vast realm perpetually, gaining mastery over greater and greater powers as we advance. In usual brain development the mere feeling of these finer forces of the subjective field is all that is necessary to secure results. And those who employ the helps already presented will find no difficulty whatever in reaching this deeper or finer state of feeling. When you are in subjective consciousness during concentration, you can readily feel those finer forces in that part of the brain that you are trying to develop, and you can also feel an increase in the circulation in the same place. The finer creative energies are not always as distinctly felt, but they are always present in abundance where the finer activities are at work. When we begin to gain control of the subjective forces so that we can draw all the creative energies of the system into any part of the brain or body where we desire development, we find we are beginning to master another great process, without doubt one of the greatest processes in the being of man; in other words, what may be truthfully called the inner secret of all human development; and as we advance in the application of the principle of this secret, we shall advance in development in proportion. But as there is no end to the possibilities of this secret, there is necessarily no end to what man may develop in his own mind and soul as he advances in the scientific use of the principle involved.

Chapter 8

The Finer Forces

The consciousness of and the proper direction of the finer forces in mind and personality, is absolutely necessary in all development of brain or mind, and therefore we must learn to know those forces whenever their actions are felt in the system. One of the first signs of the presence of these finer forces is indicated by peculiar warmth in the deeper life of the body, especially when the forces are strong; though it is not necessary that they should produce this warmth nor that they should produce any pronounced physical sensation whatever. It is very important, however, that we learn to distinguish between the finer forces and the other forces in the system because when the finer forces are discerned they may be directed anywhere to promote development. And here we must remember that unless these finer forces are placed in action, no development can possibly take place.

The inner forces are the interior creative energies of the human personality. They are the invisible builders of every force in the body and every state, quality and faculty in the mind. Therefore to promote growth anywhere in the human system, the action of the finer forces in that part must be increased.

When the finer forces are felt or discerned they will readily accumulate wherever attention may be directed; and wherever they accumulate there life, nourishment, vitality, and everything necessary to growth and construction, will accumulate also. To discern the finer forces it is necessary for the mind to enter into the consciousness of those elements that permeate the physical elements; that is, conscious action must act not upon the physical person, but upon the real life that thrills every atom in the person.

During this conscious action no thought whatever must be given to physical matter nor must the mind dwell upon shape or form. When the mind thinks of shape, form, or physical matter during the process of concentration, attention will be directed upon physical matter instead of upon that life that gives animation to matter. The desired results therefore will not be forthcoming. To arouse the finer forces, attention must be concentrated upon those forces; the mind must think of those forces, and consciousness must seek to enter into the very life of those forces. This, however, is not possible while one is thinking of the body or giving attention to its shape and form.

To develop any part of the brain, the cells in that part should be made more refined and more numerous. To accomplish this, more energy, more life and more nourishment will be needed in the part to be developed; and all of these will accumulate where desired if the finer forces are active in the system, and attention is concentrated upon the exact place where development is to take place. During this concentration, however, no thought must be given to the physical brain cells. Attention must be devoted exclusively to the finer elements, the finer forces, the finer life that permeates the finer forces, and the finer life that permeates the physical cells.

Concentrate attention upon the finer forces in any part of the system, and those forces from any part of the system will accumulate at the point of concentration; and whatever you desire to develop at the time, those forces will proceed to develop. When this accumulation of the finer forces or energies is taking place, their presence can sometimes be felt, and they produce a very delicate vibratory sensation. Sometimes these vibrations produce electric thrills, a sensation that is most delightful, and sometimes they cause the personality to feel, as it were, a living magnet, which is true. When the finer forces are highly active, the personality actually becomes a living magnet and gains at the time the creative power of rare genius.

The actions and the vibrations of the finer forces never feel as if they were on the surface, nor even in an external state of physical substance. On the contrary, they always feel as if they were deeply permeating physical substance, giving external power, so to speak, to external shape and form. To try to feel the finer forces, however, is not desirable. Our purpose is to arouse them into high and full action, and whenever they are in action, we shall feel them without trying to do so. When we try to feel those forces, the mind will give its attention to sensation, and sensation is simply effect; but to produce the action of those forces as well as the feeling of their presence in the system, we must act upon those forces themselves; that is, we must act upon the cause, and whenever we produce the desired cause, the desired effect will invariably follow.

Chapter 9

Subjective Concentration

To concentrate upon the finer essence, the finer life of the finer forces in any part of the brain, or in any part of the personality, is termed subjective concentration, and there is no other form of concentration that has any value for any purpose whatever. To accomplish anything in any field of action, concentration is indispensable, but that concentration must be subjective to produce results. And to concentrate subjectively is to act mentally in the conscious feeling of that finer life, essence or force that permeates the objective or physical life.

There are two sides to the human system, the objective and the subjective. The objective is the external, the tangible or the physical side. The subjective is the interior, the finer, or the metaphysical side. The subjective permeates the objective. The metaphysical or the subjective is the cause, or constitutes the realm of cause, and therefore controls the physical, and determines every effect that will be produced in the physical. For this reason, the mind must concentrate upon the metaphysical and produce the desired cause in the metaphysical in order to secure any desired effect or result in the physical. It is the finer metaphysical forces that control the vital forces and the chemical forces in the body, and it is these same forces that are usually termed creative energies. It is these that create and develop, and therefore to promote development, these finer forces must be awakened, directed and properly applied.

To awaken the finer forces of the system, the mind must concentrate attention upon the finer essence or substance that permeates the physical substance of the personality, and this is accomplished by trying to feel the finer forces while the mind is thinking deeply of the subjective or finer life of the system. The principle is this, that the substance of which the body is composed is actually permeated with a much finer substance, just as water permeates a sponge, and that this finer substance or essence is filled with forces that are much finer and far more rapid than the ordinary physical forces. To concentrate subjectively is to direct attention upon this finer essence and these finer forces, and when the mind actually succeeds in acting upon this finer essence the finer forces of the system will be placed in action.

Wherever these forces begin to act, there development will take place. Therefore, to promote development in any part of the brain or in any part of the personality all that is necessary is to concentrate subjectively on that part, and have clearly fixed in mind at the time the degree of development that is desired. To concentrate upon the finer essence of the brain center is to think about the finer substance that permeates the physical brain center, and then turn attention upon that finer substance. In this way the finer forces of the brain will be acted upon, and when these forces are acted upon they will do whatever the mind may desire to have done at the time.

What to think while concentrating subjectively depends upon what one desires to develop, attain or accomplish through such concentration. And this can be determined by applying the principle of scientific thinking. The most important principle in scientific thinking is to think only of that now that you are trying to accomplish now, and turn all the power of thought, life, consciousness and attention upon that one subject. And here we must realize that without scientific thinking concentration is of no value; in fact, it ceases to be concentration; because to try to concentrate upon one subject while thinking of something else is a mere scattering of force. When concentrating upon a certain faculty one should think about the more perfect state of that faculty and also what one desires to accomplish through the use of that faculty. In this connection the constructive use of the imagination will prove highly profitable, because what is imagined in the mind during any process of subjective concentration will be created and developed in the mind. What is imaged in the mind when concentration is not subjective, will not be developed in the mind, because the creative forces, those forces that develop, are not brought into action unless concentration is subjective. To awaken these forces attention must act in the subjective field of consciousness; and this field is simply a field of finer life and action permeating every part of the human system.

To enter mentally into this finer field is not difficult. In fact, when anyone feels deeply, the mind is more or less in the subjective. The same is true when attention enters an attitude of deep, whole-souled interest, a fact that can easily be demonstrated because concentration is always perfect when the interest is absolute; and a finer, stronger life is always felt at such times. Whenever a person concentrates with a deep, living interest, he concentrates subjectively, and if he would analyze the experience he would find that he was not interested in the outer phase of the subject, but actually entered into the real interior life of the subject itself. The simple principle is that when we enter into a subject we concentrate subjectively upon that subject. And when we enter into the finer essence or life of an object, we concentrate subjectively upon that object. The process of subjective concentration, therefore, is easily understood and applied. It is not something special that we have to learn because we are concentrating subjectively more or less all the time, that is, whenever we direct attention upon anything with a deep, living interest. It is a process, however, that should be developed thoroughly and completely mastered as it constitutes the principal secret to all attainment and achievement.

Chapter 10

Principle of Concentration

To do one thing at a time and to give one's whole thought and attention to what is being done now is the principle upon which concentration is based, and nothing worthwhile can be accomplished without concentration. This principle, however, is not confined to definite lines of action, nor does it necessarily mean that the well concentrated mind moves in a groove. On the contrary, the more perfect the power of concentration, the more easily can the mind turn its attention with full force to any subject or object that may be considered. To be able to concentrate well does not simply mean to be able to give one's whole attention to present action; it also means the power to turn one's complete attention upon any new subject or object at will.

In the first place, concentration is a function of the conscious mind only. It is not necessary to concentrate upon that which the subconscious is doing; and all the automatic actions of mind or body are directed by the subconscious; that is, after the subconscious has been given the proper directions, no further concentration along: those lines will be necessary. It is only such actions as have not been given definite tendencies and such modes of thought or effort as require special attention, that need concentration. What is termed mechanical work, therefore, that is, work that can be done without special thought or direction, can be carried on perfectly by the automatic action of the subconscious while the conscious mind may be thinking about something else. But it is not well to carry this practice too far.

To place certain kinds of simple work in the hands of the subconscious while the conscious mind is otherwise engaged may have a tendency to separate the actions of the conscious and the subconscious phases of mind; but this separation must be avoided as it is perfect unity of action between the conscious and the subconscious that we seek to attain, because when this unity becomes perfect, the subconscious will always respond to the directions of the conscious mind. We have discovered that the subconscious can do and will do whatever it is properly impressed or directed to do, but the conscious mind cannot direct the subconscious properly unless there is perfect unity of action between the two.

To think of something else while you are doing mechanical work is permissible to a degree, but it must not be made a general practice. The wisest course is to give your whole attention to what you are doing now whatever that work may be; and if you give soul to that work it will cease to be mechanical. Besides, such a work can be made a channel for a fuller and a larger expression of self. All kinds of work may become channels of expression for the superior powers of mind and soul, and the secret is to give soul to everything that is being done. To give soul to your work is to work in the conscious interest of what you are doing; in brief, to feel that your work is an expression of more and more life, and that expression will steadily increase the power of your entire mind and personality. In other words, you give soul to your work when your whole heart is in your work; when you are thoroughly interested in the work itself and the final result; when you deeply love it and thoroughly enjoy it; and when you give it your very best thoughts, ability and power. In this connection it is important to remember that what you give to your work you give to yourself. The more ability and power you give to your work the more ability and power you develop in yourself. And the more interest you take in your present work the better will your concentration become. To take only a half hearted interest in what we may be doing now is to weaken the power of concentration; in fact, the power of concentration will almost disappear if such a practice is continued.

No one, therefore, can afford to be otherwise than thoroughly interested in the work of the present moment, no matter what the work may be. Occasionally, however, simple tasks may be left to automatic mental action; that is, when we have done those things so many times that their doing has become second nature, so to speak; and we may thus give our conscious attention at the time to other matters. But such a practice should be the exception, never the rule.

A fact of exceptional importance that we shall all discover as we apply the principle of concentration, is that no task can be disagreeable when approached in the attitude of real concentration. The reason why is found in the fact that when we concentrate properly we approach a subject or object from the most interesting point of view; and nothing can be really disagreeable when approached from the most interesting point of view. The value of this fact will increase as we realize the importance of avoiding every attitude of mind that is in any way antagonistic to our work. And as real concentration will perfect all such attitudes, we find what a gain we shall make in every respect when we learn to concentrate in the right way. We concentrate naturally upon that in which we are interested. For this reason the natural method for the development of concentration is always to look for the most interesting points of view; and we should apply this method, no matter what we may be thinking about or what our work may be. Everything has an interesting side, and when we look for it we shall invariably find it. In fact, to look for the interesting side will in itself create interest; and to create interest is to develop concentration. In this connection it is well to remember that no work can possibly be drudgery when entered into in the right frame of mind. And also that all work that is performed in the right frame of mind will open the way to something better. This is a law that never fails, and the right frame of mind in each case consists of the right use of concentration; that is, producing concentration by becoming deeply interested in what we may be thinking of or doing. In other words, to look for the most interesting points of view regardless of what conditions or circumstances may be.

IMPORTANT RULES

1. — In all efforts to develop the brain through subjective concentration always concentrate upon the brain center first, and from that point gradually move attention to the outer surface.

2. — During concentration the mind should be in a well poised, serene attitude, and strongly determined to secure results.

3. — Fifteen or twenty minutes is long enough to practice at a time, and two or three times a day for regular exercise, although it is well to practice for a few minutes every hour if opportunities present themselves.

4. — Never concentrate for brain or mind development immediately after a meal. The digestive functions for about an hour after each meal require a full circulation and all available surplus energy. Therefore, neither the circulation nor additional energy should be drawn elsewhere at that time.

5. — The mind should continue in the attitude of perfect faith during the process of concentration. The more faith you have in the methods you employ the greater your results, because faith invariably awakens higher and more powerful forces.

6. — Affirmations, suggestions and strong positive statements may be combined with the process of concentration. To illustrate; while you are concentrating upon the faculty of intelligence, you may affirm, "My mind is clear, lucid and brilliant," "My mind is alive with exceptional intelligence," "My mind is constantly growing in the capacity to think, understand and create ideas," and statements of a similar nature. Statements to correspond with what you desire each faculty to become may be formulated by yourself, and affirmed as you concentrate for the development of that faculty.

7. — When concentrating, have superiority and worth constantly in mind, and train all the mental tendencies to move towards the higher and the greater.

8. — Never begin concentration until you have permeated the entire system with a refining process, and drawn all the forces of your system into finer states of life and action.

9. — While you are at your work, train your attention to act directly upon and through the faculty that you are using in your work. This will increase the power and the activity of that faculty, thereby developing the faculty at the time, as well as producing better work.

10. — Never be over anxious about results, because you know that results must inevitably follow; then let results come when they are ready. If you proceed in this attitude you will begin to secure results from the very beginning.

11. — It is not always well to try to develop a number of leading talents at the same time. Select one or two that you expect to develop for your life work; then give these fully three-fourths of your attention, and divide the remainder of your time among all other faculties so as to produce a balanced mentality.

12. — It is not necessary to form any mental picture of the brain or the brain cells while you concentrate. In fact, it is best not to do this, as such a practice will tend to draw consciousness away from the subjective into the objective. Do not think of the physical brain itself or of the physical cells, but simply keep in mind those higher and greater qualities that you desire to develop. And hold your attention upon the interior subjective process that is promoting the development. Concentrate your attention upon that part of the brain that you desire to develop, but think only of the finer or metaphysical counterpart of your brain at the time. In other words, give your attention to the finer mental elements that permeate the physical brain. Thus you will awaken those energies and elements that alone have the power to produce the increase in talent and power you desire.

Chapter 11

Development of Business Ability

To become successful in the commercial world, that entire region marked "business ability" in Fig. V. should be developed. Concentrate subjectively upon this region for ten or fifteen minutes every morning before going to work, and repeat the concentration for a few minutes several times during the day. When you concentrate upon this region animate your concentration with a deep, strong desire to make this part of the brain larger, more powerful and more efficient. Be alive and enthusiastic during the concentration, but be fully poised and self-possessed, and positively expect results. It will be noticed that that part of the brain marked "business ability" in Fig. V. includes the first four divisions as indicated in Fig. IV. Therefore in concentrating upon the region of "business ability" it will be well to take these four divisions separately at various times of the day. Take ten or fifteen minutes every day for the development of this region as a whole without any thought as to its divisions. Sometime during the day give a few minutes to the practical brain; at another time during the same day give a few minutes to the mechanical brain and the executive brain. Give most of your attention, however, to that division that seems to be smaller or less efficient than the others.

The practical brain and the financial brain should receive the most thorough development when the individual is engaged in the general business field. But the mechanical brain should always be a close second, as the power to construct, build up, enlarge and develop is absolutely necessary in the working out of a successful business enterprise. When the management of an enterprise demands the greatest amount of attention, the executive brain should receive the most thorough development, while the practical brain should receive the first thought when the working out of details constitutes the principal line of action.

Speaking in general, the manager of an enterprise should constantly develop the executive brain; the general office force should constantly develop the practical brain, so that the ideas of the manager would be actually and efficiently carried out; the financial heads of the concern should constantly develop the financial brain, while everyone connected with the enterprise should give daily attention to the entire region of "business ability." In addition to the development of general business ability, the man who would become a great power in the commercial world, should also develop "originality," the secret of greatness, and "intuition," or finer insight, the power to see through every circumstance and condition, and thus take advantage of the right opportunity at the right time.

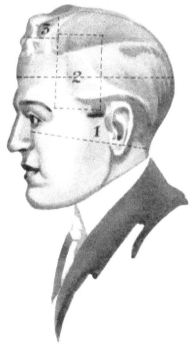

FIG. V.

1. Business Ability
2. Construction and Imagination
3. Intuition

Men and women who occupy stenographic or clerical positions should develop the practical brain in particular, and the entire region of "business ability" in general. Those who are employed in any form of constructive work should give special attention to the mechanical brain and the practical brain. If your clerical position is principally in connection with money, develop the practical brain and the financial brain. Foremen, superintendents and managers in factories should develop the executive brain and the mechanical brain; while those who manage financial institutions, or who superintend the selling of products, should develop the executive brain and the financial brain. The executive brain and the practical brain should be developed by those who manage the detail work of any business concern; and it must be remembered that those who manage or superintend, in any manner whatever, must also develop the volitional brain.

Whenever you concentrate subjectively upon any division of the brain, try to increase the active power of the faculty that functions through that part; and also try to improve the quality of that faculty. This is readily done by combining the proper desires and mental attitudes with the action of concentration. When you concentrate upon the practical brain, desire the power of practical application; think deeply of what it actually means to be practical, and try to evolve perfect system out of every group of thoughts, ideas or plans that may appear in your mind at the time.

When concentrating upon the mechanical brain, deeply desire to construct, invent and build up; try to put together the different parts of your business in every imaginable combination, and try to work out a combination that will be far superior to the present arrangement. You thus develop the constructive brain and the mental faculty of construction at the same time; besides, you may, at any time, invent a combination in your business affairs that will double your success.

When you concentrate upon the financial brain, desire wealth; desire a vast amount of legitimate wealth, and make up your mind to secure it; think deeply of that power in human action that accumulates, that gathers together, that produces increase, and try to feel that the power is becoming stronger and stronger in you. When concentrating upon the executive brain, think constantly of the practical art of management; examine the governing power from every point of view, and analyze as perfectly as possible that faculty in the human mind that is naturally adapted to manage, govern and rule. Deeply desire this faculty, this power, and inspire your desire to govern with the positive conviction that you can. In this manner you not only develop and enlarge the executive brain, but you also bring forth into practical action all the mental qualities that go to make up executive power. In consequence you will constantly gain greater and greater executive power; and if you continue in your development you will, in the course of a reasonable time, be able to manage successfully the most extensive enterprise in the world.

Chapter 12

Accumulation and Increase

The upper half of the brain is devoted to the abstract, to the world of ideas. The lower half of the brain is devoted to the concrete, to the world of things. And since the commercial world deals directly with the concrete, the lower half of the brain must necessarily be well developed if the increase of business ability is desired.

It is usually not difficult to formulate plausible theories concerning what ought to be done, but to apply such theories is quite a different matter; and application invariably demands the ability to apply in the world of things what has been worked out in the world of ideas. Most theories may be good, but not one in a hundred is ever applied, the reason being that there is a decided lack in the power of application among most minds. In the business world it is the man who can do things and who can put ideas into practice that is in the greatest demand. It is such a man who secures the best positions and a princely recompense; and on account of his exceptional worth he deserves all that he receives.

The man who can evolve system in his work, who can formulate methods for the more thorough application of his work, and who can practically apply for actual results all those methods, is never going to fail in his undertakings. And this proves that the power of application has such extreme value that even the man who has no other accomplishment can achieve great things in life if this particular power is highly developed. Though the power of application is of unusual value in every line of work, it has its greatest value in the business world, because in that world results cannot be secured unless the practical element is present in a large measure. The business man should therefore give a great deal of attention to the development of that part of the brain through which the faculty of application naturally functions.

When concentrating upon the faculty of application try to evolve system out of everything that you may be thinking of at the time. And this is very important as there must be system in all action before actual results can be secured. During such concentration, it is best to think principally of the work in which we are now engaged and try to perfect system in that work. In this manner you will apply your efforts in brain building more directly, and accordingly will develop your business ability to a much greater degree and in much less time.

The power of construction is absolutely necessary in the business world; therefore while concentrating for the development of constructive power, think deeply about your work and try to bring the different parts of your work into just such combinations as you desire. In brief, try to think out combinations that you feel will prove superior to every combination along constructive lines that you have worked out before. Thus you develop not only the brain in that particular region, but you also build up the corresponding faculty in the mind — that mental faculty that is applied in all constructive efforts.

You may not adopt all the new combinations that you will evolve in this manner, but you will develop the power of construction in your mind the more you try to evolve superior combinations; and through this practice you will finally evolve some exceptional combination from which the greater results you desire will be secured. It is a well known fact that success in the commercial world depends largely upon the way the business is constructed. Therefore, better and better results will inevitably follow as you increase your power to combine the various parts of your business in such a way as to give the entire enterprise, in which you are interested, the most perfect working system available.

In the world of things we find both the scattering process and the process of accumulation, and when we examine the subject closely we find that each individual has both of these processes in his own hands. He can control things to such an extent that he may positively determine how much is to be scattered in one place and how much is to be accumulated in some other place. In brief, he controls absolutely the disposal of all things and all possessions in his own world. In the majority, however, this faculty has not been developed, and for this reason we find only a small majority who are in possession of abundance, or who have the power to recuperate instantaneously should losses be incurred. But nature is able to give us abundance, and we all can secure abundance if we apply ourselves fully and in harmony with natural law. One of the most important essentials in this connection is the mental power of accumulation, for we must remember that we must be able to accumulate in the mind before we can accumulate in the external world. And as previously stated, this power can be increased more and more for an indefinite period through the proper development of the mind, and through the full development of that part of the brain through which this faculty functions.

To proceed, concentrate for the development of accumulation as outlined elsewhere in this study; and hold in your mind as clearly as possible the idea of accumulation at the time. Realize that you are an individual center, and that you can cause all the rich things in life to gravitate toward yourself as this center. Establish in your mind a deep feeling of what you imagine the process of accumulation to be, and try to feel that the various forces and elements in your system are actually accumulating within you. Hold yourself in a strong attitude of poise, and realize that through this attitude you are holding all things together in your system. Practice these things while concentrating until you realize your own supremacy over things, and feel distinctly the process of accumulation constantly at work in your entire system. The result will be a rapid and steady development of the power of accumulation, not only in your own mind, but in all those faculties whose function it is to gather abundance in the world of things.

It is a fact well known among all minds who have studied these deeper laws, that whenever you establish a certain process in your own system you can establish the same process in your environment. In other words, should you apply this law to the idea of accumulation we would find that you would have gained the power to accumulate possessions in your external world, when you have gained the power to accumulate the richer elements of your own mind. And experience proves that this law is absolutely true. Accordingly, we should seek to attain the consciousness of accumulation and create the accumulating process in our own mental world; that is, we should hold the mind in this consciousness while concentrating for the development of those faculties of the mind that are directly concerned with accumulation; and we will thereby, not only develop the brain in the region of those faculties, but will also develop the mental power to acquire and hold possessions both in the mental world and in the world of things.

Chapter 13

Individual Advancement

Progress and Success — The true meaning of success may be expressed in the one word "progress." You are successful only when you are moving forward, when you are constantly gaining ground in the most comprehensive sense of that term. Therefore, the first essential to those who have success as their goal, is to make individual progress their first and leading aim. And to this aim should be added the constant desire to find better and better methods through which individual progress may be gained.

The Right Vocation — To begin, select the right vocation. In making your selection follow your strongest ambition; that is, if you can do something in that particular field now. Though if this is not always possible, there is another way that may be entered upon temporarily. Accept the best opportunity that you can find under present conditions, and resolve to make good. Then, in the meantime, proceed to improve your whole mind. This will not only enable you to do better work where you are, but it will also make you more familiar with what ability and power you really possess. A great many young men are very ambitious along certain lines, and therefore imagine that their greatest success lies in those lines. But after their entire mentalities become fully alive, they discover that their strongest powers lie in an entirely different direction. Accordingly, their ambitions change; they find their first ambitions to be simply the result of surface action in the mind, while their new ambitions are the result of their real, inherent ability, now awakened to action.

Arouse the Whole Mind — The first ambitions of most young men are "false alarms," due to shallow mental actions produced by some external suggestions. The small boy who wants to be a street car motorman, because that particular work fascinates his boyish notion of responsibility and position, is an illustration. And though those young ideas usually pass away on short notice, still they are frequently followed by other ideas and ambitions equally false and superficial. The necessity, therefore, of waking up the whole mind in order to develop the true ambition and get the proper clue to the correct vocation in each case is most evident. When you accept the best opportunity you can now find, and proceed to develop your whole mind while working in that particular position, you will soon readjust your ambitions, if those ambitions happen to be "false alarms." But if your ambitions actually are genuine, proceeding directly and naturally from your greatest natural ability, the waking up of your whole mind will only tend to make those ambitions stronger and more persistent than ever before.

Your True Ambition — When you find a certain ambition becoming stronger and stronger the more you improve your mind, you may rest assured that that is your true ambition. And if you follow that ambition, you will enter your true vocation. But if you find your ambitions changing as you proceed to build up every part of your mind, you will find it advisable not to follow any special ambition, or select any special vocation until your whole mind is thoroughly aroused, and the strongest faculties determined with a certainty. Wherever you begin in your chosen vocation, you will find it absolutely necessary to promote your own individual progress if you wish to succeed. And by individual progress we mean the constant improvement of your whole self — your mind, your faculties, your powers, your character, your mode of thinking, your conduct, your disposition, your personal life, your personality, your power of application, your habits, your views of life, your personal worth, your ideals — in brief, everything that pertains to your own individual life, thought and action.

Individual Progress — If you are already in the right vocation, individual progress will enable you to meet the ever growing demands of that vocation. And here we must remember that the man who does not improve himself in this age is the man who will be left behind, and later placed "on the shelf." The man who is constantly improving himself will be wanted in the world of action as long as he lives, regardless of his age or the color of his hair. But self-improvement is no hardship; it is a pleasure; in fact, there are few things that help more to make life worthwhile. If you are not in the right vocation, individual progress will soon bring out the best that is in you, so that you will not only know where you belong, but will be competent to go to work where you belong. Then, if you continue this progress and self-improvement, you will constantly advance externally by noting a steady improvement in your conditions. Improve yourself, and your conditions will also improve. This is the law; and it cannot fail when systematically applied. Realize that individual progress must precede individual success, and that individual progress must continue if success is to be permanent. Work unceasingly for the progress and improvement of yourself. Make it a point to build yourself up; and never bring this building process to a standstill. If you are in an uncongenial position, do not try to get out at once; do not force yourself out; but proceed where you are to build yourself up, and improve yourself to such an extent that you become indispensable where you are. You will soon secure a better position, and you will become much stronger and more valuable, on account of the discipline gained by "holding out" under adversity.

Secret of Advancement — Make difficulties and obstacles serve the greater purpose you have in view, and they will, if you enter every position with a view of using the demands of that position for making your whole mind alive. But in this connection do not make the mistake that thousands have who have entered temporary positions. After entering those positions they have failed to improve themselves; instead, they have permitted their minds to retrograde, and therefore have either continued for life in those "temporary" positions, or have been pushed lower still. This accounts for the fact that so many capable and well educated men are now holding inferior positions. They took the best they could find in the beginning, but ignored the necessity of individual progress, and therefore had to continue where they began year after year until they finally gave up hope of ever getting anything better. The mistake of these men must be rigorously avoided at every turn, and every tendency to fall into a "rut" must be stamped out completely. Work for individual progress every minute, and no matter where or how you begin, you will steadily advance in the scale. New and better opportunities will come to you all along the line as you are prepared to accept them. You will prove the fact that better opportunities are always waiting for the better man, and that the better man is invariably the man who makes individual progress his first and greatest aim.

Chapter 14

The Genius of Invention

There are few worlds that hold richer possibilities than the world of invention, and there are few things that are more easily developed than inventive genius. Everything can be improved. Even the most perfect products of the industrial world have defects, and the man whose genius can remove those defects will be most richly rewarded. In the world of new and original inventions there are no limitations whatever. The field is simply inexhaustible because there is no end to the realm of ideas, and invention is simply a new combination of ideas that can be turned to practical use. Another reason why the world of invention is so immense is because inventive genius is not confined to a single field of action. It is, on the contrary, employed in nearly every field of action. A certain grade of inventive genius is absolutely necessary to the writer; another grade is indispensable to the musical composer; still other grades are required by the artist, the mechanic and the skilled worker; while no business man will succeed to any extent unless he has the power of invention developed to a high degree.

The secret of inventive genius is the power to create new ideas, and to produce new combinations of ideas using both old ideas and new ideas as the case may require. The power to combine ideas for practical use is the most important phase in the development of inventive genius at the present time. There are innumerable ideas afloat in the world today that have not been turned to any account; even a few of these if properly combined, and practically applied would revolutionize the industrial world. It is, therefore, not necessary to search for new ideas at the present time while the world is waiting for a genius to tell us how to use the best ideas we already possess.

To proceed with the improvement of any invention a definite plan should be employed, but new inventions, new and original combinations frequently come of themselves while inventive genius is being developed; or they may come when the inventive genius, one may already possess, is aroused to an extraordinary degree by some powerful suggestion or experience that bears directly upon the necessary phases of mind. The first essential in the improvement of the invention is to gain a clear understanding of the principle upon which that invention is based, and the purpose which it is intended to fulfill. If the old invention does not fulfill that purpose with satisfaction, find the reason why. If your objective mind cannot give you your real reason, consult the subconscious. The subconscious can work out the most difficult problems in mathematics while you sleep; then why should it not be able to discover the real cause of imperfections in the invention you desire to improve, and also discover the key to the necessary improvements. The fact is that the subconscious can find out almost anything provided it is properly impressed and directed. And since we all can learn to direct the subconscious in any way desired, we should never permit ourselves to ever use the term impossible.

When you have found the cause of the imperfections of any invention, the proper combinations required to remove those imperfections can be easily made by applying the faculties of imagination and construction, though in this as well as in all other efforts, the subconscious should be brought into the fullest use possible. In its last analysis every improvement is the result of a better mental conception of the workings of the thing to be improved. Therefore, before undertaking to make the proposed improvement, the object under consideration should be analyzed from every possible point of view. In this connection it is highly important to know that there is nothing that will produce so many new combinations of ideas as the practice of looking at every object from every imaginable point of view; and this is especially true when we look at things with an interest that is deeply felt and thoroughly alive. The average person looks at things from a single point of view only; therefore his mental conceptions are one sided. His ideas are incomplete, and such ideas as are required to produce the new combinations or inventions desired are not forthcoming. Those necessary ideas, however, may be gained by taking new points of view, one after the other, until the object under consideration has been viewed and examined in every conceivable manner.

When you have examined something from every viewpoint, you have gained all the ideas of that something that your present mental capacity can comprehend. By combining those ideas, you will have a combination that must necessarily be an improvement upon that which you originally examined, and by turning this new combination to practical use you will have an actual improvement. The simple practice of looking at all things from every imaginable viewpoint will alone develop the power of invention to a remarkable degree, and when this practice is combined with a practical system of development in the art of invention, the attainment of real inventive genius is absolutely certain. The principal faculties to develop in order to gain inventive genius are imagination, construction and intuition. The latter may also be termed insight, discernment, or the power of discovery. To begin, concentrate upon those faculties twice every day, giving about ten minutes to each faculty, and while concentrating upon a certain faculty exercise that faculty in the work which it is being developed to perform. To determine where to concentrate for the development of the brain in this connection see Figure VI. To illustrate, when you concentrate upon that part of the brain through which the imaging faculty is expressed, use the imagination to the fullest extent and use it in picturing the various parts of the invention you desire to perfect. This invention may be a book, a musical composition, a machine, an architectural structure or a group of plans and methods for the promotion of some commercial enterprise. In other words, while you are concentrating upon that part of the brain which is used by the faculty in question, put that faculty to work. You will thereby develop both the brain and the mind at the same time, which is highly important.

To develop the mental faculty alone is not sufficient. You might just as well expect a great musician to do justice to himself on some crude, primitive instrument as to expect a highly developed faculty to express talent or genius through a crude sluggish brain. For the same reason it is not sufficient to develop the brain alone. The brain is the instrument of the mental faculty; therefore when the faculty itself is not developed, there will be nothing in the mind to make full use of the highly developed brain that may have been secured. For this reason the faculty should be exercised whenever attention is concentrated upon that part of the brain through which the faculty naturally functions.

When exercising the imaging faculty during concentration the imagination should be used with some definite purpose in view. We should never permit the imagination to work at random, but should give it something special to work out into a complete mental picture. And here we should remember that the imagination is one of the greatest mental faculties in the mind. In fact, it is so important that no matter how practical or matter of fact your work may be, you will find it absolutely necessary to develop your imagination to the very highest degree if you wish to secure the best results obtainable through that particular work.

FIG. VI.

1. Imagination   2. Construction.   3. Interior Sight

It is imagination that plans the greater enterprise and that supplies the necessary methods for successfully promoting that enterprise. Nothing great was ever done that was not first worked out in the imagination, and no improvement was ever made that was not first conceived and pictured in the imaging faculty. It is the power of imagination that lifts the products of mind above the crude and the ordinary, and that gives real worth to that which has worth. Everything that man has made was born of the imagination. And man has made some things that are truly marvelous, regardless of the fact that imagination has never been systematically cultivated. We can therefore imagine what we may expect when this remarkable faculty is thoroughly cultivated and highly developed.

When concentrating upon the faculty of construction, use that faculty in carrying on a definite building process in your mind, directing attention principally upon those ideas that you wish to combine with a view of procuring a new invention or a new system for practical application in your work. During concentration on this faculty, all the ideas, plans and systems imaginable, in connection with the subject under consideration, should be arranged and rearranged in every conceivable manner until the best arrangement or construction has been secured. This exercise, if practiced during the proper concentration upon the brain, will develop rapidly and thoroughly that faculty that produces new combinations of ideas, and that turns those combinations to practical use; that is, that faculty which can invent, or that is usually defined, when in its highest state of expression, as inventive genius.

When concentrating upon that part of the brain through which the faculty of intuition functions, we should exercise the faculty of insight and discovery, by trying to see through everything that has been brought before our attention. In brief, we should turn our attention upon the hidden parts of those phases of life and work in which we are directly interested, and try to discern the real nature of those parts. We may not discover anything of value at the time, and still we may; but the exercise will positively develop the faculty of insight; and if we continue this development, that faculty will finally discover something, something that may prove of exceptional value. In addition, we should give as much attention as possible to the development of that faculty that is defined as interior understanding, and especially if we desire to employ the power of invention in the fields of art, music or literature. Or, if we wish to devote our genius to mechanics or architecture, we should develop the mechanical brain in addition. While if we wish to apply ourselves principally in the commercial world, we should develop business ability in addition to the other faculties mentioned.

Another essential in the development of inventive genius is the fullest preservation and the proper direction of creative energy. Invention is naturally a creative process in all its phases, and therefore requires more creative energy than almost any other use of the mind. For this reason it is highly important that the faculties of invention be well supplied with such energy. To this end, the development of poise is indispensable, so that all waste of energy may be prevented. And at least fifty hours of sleep should be taken every week so that the subconscious may keep the system well charged with its various creative forces. Try to average from seven to eight hours of sleep in every twenty-four, but if this allowance should be cut short one night on account of important engagements, retire earlier the next night and make it up. This is a rule that should be kept as rigidly as possible, as it will not only aid decidedly in supplying the system with the necessary amount of creative energy, but it will also aid remarkably in preserving good health for mind and body. Lastly, learn to transmute all those energies in the system that are not required for the normal functions, and turn all of that extra energy into the faculties of invention. The more of this energy you can give to those faculties, the greater will be the creative power of your inventive genius, and the greater will be the inventions that will spring from your brain.

IMPORTANT FACTS

When thought and attention are concentrated subjectively upon any group of cells in the brain, those cells will multiply in number, and there will be a decided increase in their efficiency and energy-producing capacity. Accordingly, that mental faculty that functions through those cells, will express greater power and a higher degree of ability. Any part of the brain can be developed to an exceptional degree by this method, but the concentration must be subjective; that is, it must be deep and alive, and must actually feel the real or inner power of its own action.

Every division of the brain is in two corresponding parts, one part appearing upon the right side of the brain and the other on the left; every group of brain cells on the right side has a corresponding group on the left side; therefore, in concentrating for brain development, give attention to both sides, first changing from one to the other, and later, as you become more proficient in the art of subjective concentration, give your attention to both sides at the same time. Always begin all concentration at the brain center, and move the action of your concentrated thought toward the surface of the brain, giving special attention to the cells on the surface, as these are the most important.

Whenever your ambition is aroused, concentrate the force of your ambition upon that part of the brain through which you must work to realize your ambition. That is, if you are ambitious to become a great financier, turn your attention upon the financial brain, or if you are ambitious to become a great inventor, turn your attention upon the mechanical brain and the imaging brain whenever you feel the power of ambition arising within you; or whatever you are ambitious to become, turn the force of your ambition directly upon that part of the brain that must be developed before your ambition can be made true. You thus develop the necessary faculty, and gain the power to do the very thing you desire to do.

To push the development of any one faculty, concentrate subjectively for ten minutes every hour on that part of the brain through which that particular faculty functions. But before you begin, always place your thought in the conscious feeling of the finer forces of your mind. When concentrating upon any part of the brain, picture in your imagination the faculty that functions through that part, and draw a mental picture of that faculty in the largest, highest and most perfect state of development that you can imagine. You thus impress superior mental development upon every brain cell, and gradually every cell will grow into the exact likeness of that superior development.

During subjective concentration the mind should be well poised, deeply calm, but strongly determined to secure results. Act in the feeling of unbounded faith, believe thoroughly and deeply in the process, and you will arouse those finer and greater forces in your system that can make the process a remarkable success. Ten to fifteen minutes is usually long enough for an exercise in brain development; but you may continue for twenty minutes if you feel that you are having exceptional results. Exercises may be taken every hour or two, but never directly after a meal, as a perfect digestion demands that your mind be perfectly quiet for at least an hour after partaking of food. When you concentrate upon any part of the brain, use such good suggestions and affirmations as tend to work in harmony with the development you desire to promote. When you concentrate upon the region of intellect repeat mentally with enthusiastic conviction, "My mind is clear and lucid," "My mind is becoming more and more brilliant," "My mind is growing steadily and surely in the power of genuine understanding," "My intellectual capacity is constantly on the increase," "I AM gaining the power to know, to discern, to comprehend and to realize every fact and every truth that I may desire." Formulate similar suggestions and affirmations as your needs may require, and try to feel that you are moving into those greater things that your affirmations tend to suggest. When you concentrate upon the volitional brain, use suggestions that suggest greater will-power, greater personal force and greater self-control. When you concentrate upon the practical brain use suggestions that suggest the increase of the power of application, the power that does things. In brief, whenever you concentrate use suggestions that will prompt your thought to work with the process of development. You thus cause all your forces to work together in promoting your purpose, and great results will invariably follow.

Chapter 15

The Musical Prodigy

The Power of Music — In the promotion of human culture, refinement and a higher order of life, consciousness and thought, there is no power greater than that of music. It is therefore an art that should be cultivated universally and cultivated to the very highest possible degree. Though all music tends to elevate the mind, it is the music of quality that exercises the greatest power and the most permanent effect. But such music is not as abundant as we would like, the reason being that really great musicians are rare. The number of people who are studying music is very large and is constantly on the increase, but the majority of these are simply learning to apply what talent they already possess. They are not trying to develop talent of music itself. This, however, must be done if real musical genius is to be gained, although it is evident that in order to accomplish this we must have new and superior methods.

Use Plus Development — To learn how to use the talent you possess is one thing, but to develop that talent itself is quite another. The educational systems of today are concerned almost wholly with the former. But the coming systems must concern themselves also with the latter or the many opportunities for superior attainment now at hand will be lost. There are thousands of excellent minds that could develop rare genius if permitted. But most of the systems in vogue do not develop, their object being simply to train. To give these thousands an opportunity to get away from the routine of mere training, and to give expression to the genius that is within them is one of the aims of this study. Not that training is to be neglected, for thorough training is indispensable, but there must also be something more. We must not rest content with simply the training of our talents.

We must also do something definite and effective to enlarge and constantly develop those talents.

Possibilities — To state that anyone who already has considerable musical talent could, through the proper system of development, become a musical prodigy may seem to be far beyond the realm of actual fact. Nevertheless, it is scientifically true. And it is also true that those who have no musical talent whatever, can, if they have a strong desire for musical development, become talented to a considerable degree. And here we must remember that the possibilities of the mind are both limitless and extraordinary, so that if these possibilities are given a fair chance to express themselves there is no reason whatever why genius should not positively appear.

The Three Factors — To develop the musical faculty, the three great factors in all development, the brain, the mind and the soul must receive thorough and scientific attention. The soul, however, should be given the first place, because in music, soul expression is indispensable to high quality. The best music becomes mechanical and, actually ceases to be real music, when the soul is neglected in its expression; and the soul is neglected in too many instances. We find that the lighter forms of music, that music that in itself appeals only to the superficial sentiments, actually becomes superior in its tenderness and sweetness when expressed through someone who has soul; and it is a well known fact that the sweetest music always comes from the sweetest souls, the reason for which will be readily understood.

Brain Development — It has been stated before, and deserves emphasis as well as repetition, that the brain must be thoroughly developed whatever the faculty may be that is to be expressed, because the brain is the instrument of the mind. To neglect the development of the brain is to remain in the ranks of inferiority, no matter how powerful or talented the mind may be; but as the development of the brain has been almost wholly neglected, we must proceed to give this matter most thorough and most enthusiastic attention. That part of the brain through which the musical faculty proper functions is indicated in Figure VII, and it is this region that needs development where musical genius is the object in view. To develop this part of the brain we should concentrate as before upon the brain center, so as to accumulate as much creative energy as possible at that important point; and while concentrating in this manner gently draw the finer forces from all parts of the system towards the brain center. In a few moments energy will flow to this point through all the nerves, because all the nerves meet at the brain center. All the brain convolutions also meet at the same point, and it is therefore the point of accumulation of energy as well as the point from which energy must be directed to that part of the brain that is to be developed.

Abundant Energy — The accumulation of energy at the brain center by this process will not deprive any part of the body of its necessary power, because far more energy is generated throughout the system than is ever used, and most of it is lost on account of never being taken up and applied in any way. There are various ways to prevent this waste or loss, but none of these methods will be of value unless the energy thus preserved is taken control of and practically applied in some part of mind or body. Since fully three-fourths of the energy generated in the average system is lost, we shall, by preventing this loss, secure more than enough for the most extensive system of development that we wish to apply, without depriving any part of the body of its necessary supply. We may proceed, therefore, according to the method indicated, and after a few moments of concentration upon the brain center cause abundant energy to accumulate at that point. This energy should be directed towards that part of the brain through which the musical faculty functions. The first step should be to direct this energy to the right side of the cranium; the second step to cause concentration to be returned to the brain center; the third step to direct this energy to the left side of the cranium; and the fourth step to concentrate upon the brain center again as before. These four steps may occupy one or two minutes each, and when taken, the same process may be repeated several times, and the whole exercise taken two or three times every day.

Exercises in Concentration — All exercises in concentration for brain development should be deeply serene and well poised, but should also be very strong. Force and intensity, however, must not be permitted, because such actions are disturbing, and disturbed actions always prevent growth. But so long as the mind is well poised, the concentration may be very strong and persistent without producing any discord whatever. In all these exercises, we should remember that the object is to produce more cells, smaller cells and finer cells in that part of the brain through which the faculty of music functions; and this is accomplished when the concentration is full, strong, well poised, harmonious and subjective, so that the finer creative energies are supplied in abundance. When taking lessons in music, the pupil should, during practice, concentrate attention as much as possible upon both sides of the forehead as indicated in the Figure. This will not only develop the faculty of music itself, but will also increase the activity of that faculty at the time, which will mean that better results will be secured in the study of music, and each lesson mastered in less time.

Undivided Attention — When the mind is concentrated upon these regions of the brain while you are taking lessons in music, or performing in music, the quality of the music you produce will be far better, though it may be argued that such concentration will divide attention, and take the mind off from the music in a measure. But this is not the case. When you concentrate upon the music you are producing, you should aim to cause your mind to pass through that part of the brain, so to speak, that is employed by the musical faculty. This can be accomplished with a little practice; and in a very short time the one mode of concentration will keep your attention upon the music as well as causing the activity of your mind at the time to act directly upon the proper brain regions as you perform.

Continuous Improvement — The great value of this method is that it not only increases and improves results in the person, but also develops the musical talent itself, so that far greater results may positively be secured in the future. This will insure continuous improvement, and since the possibilities of every talent are unlimited, there is no end to what can be gained through that talent, provided the methods necessary to continuous development and improvement are constantly and faithfully applied.

Feeling in Music — To secure more feeling in your music give special attention to the development of the region of emotion as indicated in Figure III. And this is most important because the more real feeling you can give to your music, the deeper will be the impression produced by your music upon all minds that have the privilege to be present when you perform. For this reason every good musician must be highly developed in the realms of emotion, although in this connection it is necessary to cultivate a well balanced and well poised mind, so that those emotions are always under control, and always full and harmoniously expressed.

Appreciation of the Classical — When the faculty of interior understanding as indicated in Figure III is well developed, you will be able to appreciate classical music. Classical music is, strictly speaking, metaphysical music, and therefore appeals only to those minds that have become conscious of the deeper and the higher realms of thought. This does not mean, however, that those who appreciate classical music will necessarily appreciate the philosophy of metaphysics, as metaphysics is very large, and gives room for a thousand phases, and ten times as many more combinations; but the fact is that classical music comes directly from the realms of superiority and worth, and is therefore appreciated only by those minds that are conscious in a measure of superiority and worth. Such music also awakens in the minds of those who respond a still finer consciousness of the real quality of all things. During a classical performance you invariably withdraw from the superficial side of existence, and dwell more or less in the great depths of mind and soul. And the more highly you are developed in the broader metaphysical consciousness, the more real enjoyment you will secure from classical music. It is therefore well for everybody to enlarge the faculty of interior understanding, and it is absolutely necessary for those who wish to produce classical music. In this connection we must emphasize the fact that no one can become a genius in music without developing most thoroughly the faculty of interior understanding. And for this reason all such methods as have been given in previous lessons for the development of this faculty should be studied and applied with the greatest of care. When we examine classical music, we find that much of it is incomplete, due to the fact that interior consciousness or consciousness of high worth was not in full activity in the mind of the composer during every moment while the production was penned. When the great musicians of today, however, begin to give attention to this matter, and secure a higher state of interior understanding, we shall have classical compositions that will be far superior to anything that the masters of the past have produced.

Consciousness of Harmony — One of the first essentials to higher musical development in the musical world is the consciousness of harmony. The musician should not only live in perfect harmony, but should constantly seek to attain a deeper and a deeper realization of the very principles of harmony. And this being true, we realize that every musician who permits a single feeling of discord in mind or body, places thereby an obstacle in his way both with regard to the expression of music and the further development of the musical faculty. All real music contains the life of harmony to a greater or lesser extent; but how much of this harmony it contains will depend both upon the composition and upon the performer. A performer, however, who has found the world of harmony will express that lofty state even though the music may be lacking in a measure in this respect. To become a great musician, the mind must master the very life of music. To do this, the consciousness of this life must be secured, and it may be secured through the realization of higher and higher states of harmony. We conclude therefore that it is absolutely necessary to be in harmony with one's self, with everything and with everybody if high musical development is to be attained.

Principle of Music — Closely connected with the attitude of harmony is the understanding of the inner principle of music itself, and this is a great essential. But as it is a very deep study, the average mind will necessarily be slow in grasping its full meaning and import. In this connection daily efforts in trying to consciously comprehend music itself will prove of great value. And as such meditations can be enjoyed during spare moments, the results desired can be realized without loss of time. Another essential along this same line is to try to key the mind to finer vibrations of thought, feeling and consciousness. To accomplish this, the study of the law of vibration will be necessary, because it is only when we know the scale of vibrations that we develop the consciousness of grade and qualities. It is an immense field, however, and interesting and fascinating beyond the expectations of the most imaginative. But to those who cannot give the subject thorough attention at present, very good results will be secured by trying to concentrate the actions of the mind upon the highest and the finest grades of thought and feeling that can possibly be imagined. Subjective consciousness will help greatly and the practice of transmuting the finer energies will help still more, so that by combining all these various methods, even though to a slight degree, the mind will soon be keyed to much higher grades of quality and action than before.

To Secure Quality — To dwell constantly in the attitude of superiority and worth is extremely important, because to become a genius quality must be considered; and to secure quality the mind must create only such thoughts as are patterned after that which has quality. It is therefore necessary to hold attention upon the superior side of life, and to live in such close touch with the world of real worth that you can actually feel the superior taking possession of your system. In furthering these efforts, no superficial, common or ordinary states of mind must be permitted. The mind must never dwell on the empty side or on the surface of things, but must be trained to move constantly towards the depths and the heights of the superior within. In addition, it will be necessary to do everything possible to develop a beautiful character and a complete mind of the highest order.

The Soul of Music — As stated before, it is the soul that should receive the first attention in musical development; and by the soul we not only mean the real you, the individuality, but also everything within you that pertains to the lofty, the beautiful and the sublime. All those things that emanate from the ideal side, the finer side, the transcendental side in your life belong to the soul, and these things will give soul to everything you do, provided they are permitted to be expressed. To come into perfect touch with this finer side or those loftier things that we feel at times but cannot define or describe, is the purpose we have in view. It is these things, when expressed, that give soul to music, and it is such music that carries the mind away upon the wings of sublime ecstasy. When we hear such music existence is transformed, life becomes a dream of eternal bliss, and we find ourselves in a higher, more perfect and more beautiful world than we have ever known before. When we soar to those heights we ask for nothing more than simply to live. And the reason why is simple. We have found real life, and whenever we find real life it is sufficient simply to live. When we return to this world again we sometimes wonder if our experience was a mere vision, but we soon conclude that it was real. It must have been real, because we have been changed. We have been immersed, so to speak, in the crystal wonders of real life, and we are decidedly different. Something has been added to our minds, to our feelings and to our thought; and that something keeps watch so that we can never again go down completely to where we were before. There are many ways through which the mind can be awakened to the beauty and the real worth of life, and music that has soul is one of the highest and one of the best of these ways. It is the one way that can touch the greatest number. Therefore, to be able to give soul to your music will not only enable you to become greater in your chosen vocation, but also enable you to become a greater power for good, the equal of which may not be found anywhere.

The Soul In All Things — There are reasons why the soul should be given first place in musical development, and those who will bear this in mind will find their future study of music to be far more successful than it has been in the past. But in order that we may bring ourselves into more perfect touch with this finer something that we speak of as the soul of music, it is necessary to recognize and understand the soul in all things. There is nothing that will aid us more in the beginning along this line than to live in perfect tune with nature, and to try to listen constantly to the music of the spheres. Those who try to learn the spirit of nature's physical forms are usually looked upon by the practical as mere visionaries of no real value to the world, but history proves the fact that the creations of such minds are immortal. It is from such minds that the world has received everything that is worthwhile. We may, therefore, listen to the music of the spheres as much as we like. We may try to live more closely, and ever more closely, to the great spirit of nature, for nothing but good can come from such efforts; and when we employ wisely the inspiration thus received we shall give to the world real life. We shall create something that will never die. We shall write our own names upon the eternal rock of time, and beneath those names nature shall write genius, the highest title she can give to man.

Inspired Music — All real music is in a sense inspired, as it comes into mind when we are on the verge of the cosmic or in touch with the great soul of things. In brief, it is when we hear the symphonies of the vastness of the cosmos that we produce real music. When we hear real music we know where it came from, and we know that it came from the soul that was on the heights. We all long for such music principally because too much of the music we hear is simply "put together." It may pass away time pleasantly, but it does not open the heavens before us, nor awaken the spirit of man. If you would compose real music, therefore, live constantly on the verge of the cosmic. Thus you may do consciously and perfectly what the great souls of the past have done only in part. And here we should remember that there is such a thing as being touched by the spirit. The experience is real. It indicates that your mind is open to revelations, to higher and finer worlds; and this is something that should be encouraged whenever possible, because it is the great secret, or the open way, so to speak, through which man receives everything that is lofty, marvelous, wonderful or sublime. We have not considered these things in the past; but we must consider them now if we would give soul to all our music, and develop our musical faculties to the very highest states of real genius. For here be it remembered that no music is true music unless it has soul.

Soul Expression — Another essential is soul expression, or rather the living of the life of music; that is, the giving of full expression to that finer, higher something that may be described as the music of human existence. The importance of this will be realized when we learn that the more soul we express in our living, the more soul we can give to whatever may be expressed through us either in our thought or in our work. To apply this idea the musician should aim to give soul to every note, and the more soul that is given to every note, the more rapidly will the superior musical faculty develop. The inner meaning of every tone should also be felt, and that feeling should be expressed through every vibration of the personality. Begin by attaining as high and as perfect a consciousness of soul as you possibly can, and aim to express that soul whenever you perform or practice. You will soon discover the real meaning of it all; and when you do, you will know how to express consciously and perfectly the soul of every tone. From that time on your music will begin to attain a quality it never had before. Your progress will be rapid both in your power to perform and in the development of your musical talent. You will not simply produce a succession of concordant sounds, but will begin to produce real music; and it is such music that the world wants. Therefore, whoever can produce such music may look forward to a most brilliant future.

The Subconscious — To employ the best methods known for the training of the subconscious, will be found extremely valuable in musical development as well as in every other form of development. To awaken the great within, and to train the subconscious to respond perfectly to the directions of the conscious — this is one of the greatest secrets in the development of genius along any line. But before the increase of talent from within can be of real value, the brain and the mind must be made perfect channels of transmission and expression; and the soul must be called upon to give quality, superiority and high worth.

FIG. VII.

1. Expression 3. Imagination 5. Memory
2. Tone   4. Intellect   6. Intuition

Leading Essentials — It is therefore necessary to give justice to all the factors involved, and to give special attention to those things that we may lack the most. The methods given for brain development are of special value; and as no practical system for brain development has been presented before, thorough attention must be given to this matter at once. To place the mind in a perfect and harmonious condition is an absolute necessity, because discord cannot produce harmony; and in music especially, harmony is the great principle. The soul must receive special attention, though in the development of that quality called "soul" we shall find it necessary to depend largely upon individual soul consciousness. Since the soul is beyond tangible rules no regular system of rules and methods can be given in this respect. But those who aim to realize higher and higher states of soul consciousness will soon secure the results desired. In addition, we should employ all the helps that we can find from every source, and to employ all these things as thoroughly and as perfectly as we can, for it is in this way that we shall reach the high goal we have in view.

The Spirit of Genius — The most important of all is to train both mind and personality to give full right of way to the spirit of genius, and especially when using the musical faculty in actual performance. Do not try to play or sing. Instead let the spirit of genius play; and let this same spirit sing. How it feels to be touched by the spirit of genius no one can describe, nor is it necessary. Those who will apply this system of development will soon feel this spirit themselves. Then they will know at first hand. They will also know how to give way to the spirit of genius, and give expression more and more to the musical prodigy of the great within. Then remember that there is something wonderful slumbering within you. That something can make you great. That something can make you a prodigy. That something, when fully awakened and fully trained for tangible action, can make you even a greater genius than the world has ever known.

Chapter 16

Talent and Genius in Art

In every vocation possibilities are both great and numerous when genius and talent are employed, and since we all can improve ourselves indefinitely, the greater possibilities of life may be realized more and more by everybody. For this reason no one should think that he must remain in a small insignificant world all his life simply because he is living in such a world now. In every field of action opportunities in an ever increasing number are at hand always waiting and watching to be accepted.

The idea that opportunities come but once is an idea without any foundation whatever, because the fact is that the opportunities that come into your life never take their departure. They continue to remain in a sense until they are accepted when they become a part of the life that receives them. Another fact of equal value is this, that the more opportunities we take advantage of, the more new opportunities we shall meet. It is therefore detrimental to our own interest to keep a single opportunity waiting. And there are many most excellent opportunities waiting for us all this moment, no matter what or where we may be. We shall find this to be absolutely true, because the more familiar we become with the subject the more convinced we become that the opportunities in one field are neither greater nor more numerous than in any other field. Therefore there is, strictly speaking, opportunity for all everywhere.

At present there are few worlds that hold so many opportunities for genius and talent as the world of art. And the reason is that the present age is nearer to the ideal than any other age in history. Thousands of people have recently entered that finer state of consciousness where they can appreciate real art, so therefore the time is ripe for the real artist. When we speak of the real artist, however, we do not mean someone who can simply paint well. Thousands can do that who have not the slightest genius for art. Something more is required besides the ability to place pictures on canvas for the work of the real artist is alive. It has character and soul and is not only a living thing now, but is immortal.

Too much of the good art with which we are familiar has very little character. It may be correct from an artistic standpoint and it may be beautiful. It may also be true to life; that is, true to the life that it pictures, but it does not always inspire that finer, higher something that makes man feel that he is more than a mortal creature.

This, however, real art can do and should do. But the artist himself must inwardly feel those higher qualities before he can express them in his pictures. In this connection we find that laxness whether in mind or character always appears in the product of the individual. When his genius lacks character his work also lacks character. His admirers may rave over his remarkable creations, but something is absent that ought to be there, and on account of that absence the creation fails in its real mission. This is also true in every other vocation. The mind that has both character and ability produces far greater and far more lasting results than the mind that has simply ability alone. It is therefore to everybody's advantage to develop character, no matter what their work may be, and this is especially true of the artist.

The work of the artist appeals to the finer elements in man, and when there is character combined with idealism in his work, the effect of his work will always be increased accordingly. Idealism without character has a tendency to produce idle dreaming, aimless imagination and various forms of sentimentalism that frequently react into morbid moods of depression. But when idealism and character combine, a constructive process begins in the mind, a process with a sound substantial foundation, and a goal as high as perfection itself. For this reason it is highly important to awaken in the mind those elements that tend to combine idealism and character. And there is no one that can awaken those elements to a higher degree than the real artist. And therefore the artist has it in his power to render exceptional service to the human race.

To become a real artist there are a number of faculties and qualities that should be developed, though the three greatest essentials are soul, character and the proper development of the brain. The artistic talents employ several parts of the brain, the first of which is form, or that part of the brain that extends from the brain center to the region between the eyes. The second is construction, occupying the region between the temples. When form and construction are well developed, the faculty of drawing will appear, but if there are no other artistic faculties in evidence this power to draw well will be simply mechanical, and will be of service to those who are employed in mechanics or architecture. The third brain faculty is the perception of color, and is found in or about that region that occupies the outer half of the eyebrow. The fourth is the imaging faculty located directly above construction. And the fifth is the perception of the ideal, the sublime and the beautiful, located directly back of the imaging faculty. To determine the exact location of these faculties see Figure VIII.

To concentrate subjectively upon these various parts of the brain, for three minutes several times every day will, in a few months, begin to show decided results in the development of artistic talent, although these results will be greater when the process of concentration is carried on in the proper mental attitudes. To illustrate, we should aim to analyze and measure shape and form with the mental vision whenever we concentrate upon the region of form; that is, we should take the three dimensions, length, breadth and height and mentally combine them in every shape and form imaginable. This will develop the mental shape of form as well as that part of the brain through which the faculty of form functions. When concentrating upon the region of construction, a similar mental process should be employed though with this difference, that more attention should be given to the size, the form and the shape of the structure in building; that is, instead of simply combining dimensions in the mind, we should try to build up or actually construct according to our highest ideal of form and construction. The faculty of form conceives the exact form and shape of every individual part, while the faculty of construction tries to take all these various parts and build them up into some definite and ideal structure.

FIG. VIII.

1. Expression of Form   4. Imagination
2. Perception of Color   5. Perception of The Beautiful
3. Construction   and Sublime

When concentrating upon the faculty of color we should analyze with the mind all the colors that we know, and try to blend them mentally in every way imaginable. The mental experience that is enjoyed in connection with this practice is beautiful beyond description. During the practice color scenes and panoramas of color will frequently appear before the mental vision. And in many instances they will outrival in gorgeousness everything that the imagination has ever been able to picture. When concentrating upon the imaging faculty try to paint pictures in the mind. Proceed to paint imaginary pictures upon imaginary canvas, and try to make these pictures, not only original, but extraordinary. Do not copy in your imagination something that you have seen, but try to picture something that physical sight has never seen. This will not only develop the imaging faculty, but will also develop originality, which is the secret of greatness. When concentrating upon that faculty through which the beautiful is received, turn attention directly upon the ideal. Try to see and perceive the ideal of everything in your physical world as well as in your mental world. Think about the high, the lofty and the sublime, and try to actually enter into the world of sublimity and grandeur. Also awaken the life and power of aspiration, and try to gain the largest consciousness possible of everything that has real worth and high superiority.

In addition to the above faculties, we should also cultivate the faculties of love and emotion, because this will give sympathy, a quality that is absolutely necessary in all art. The real artist must be in sympathy with nature in general and with human nature in particular, though this sympathy should always seek the finer touch of the more beautiful side of everything. We should never sympathize with the undeveloped conditions of nature nor with the weakness of man; that is, we should not enter into mental contact with those things nor imitate mentally those conditions. Such a sympathy is always unhealthful; and unhealthful states of mind are not conducive to genius. It is not the shortcomings of nature nor the crude side of man that you are to love and admire, but it is the unbounded possibilities that we have the power to unfold and develop that we should select as our ideals, not only in art, but in living.

To understand the laws of harmony and gradation is indispensable to the artist. In addition to what is already being taught on these subjects in art schools, the development of mental harmony should be sought most earnestly. The real artist must convey the spirit of real harmony, and to give this quality to his art he must be conscious of the deeper harmonies of the soul. To this end, therefore, he should seek higher consciousness; that is, that consciousness which reveals the beauty, the serenity and the soul of all things. When a work of art has soul it will forever remain an inspiration, and that which inspires has the power to elevate man to higher states of living. In this connection we should remember that everything we see has a tendency to impress the mind. As these impressions are so are our thoughts, and as our thinking is so are we. Therefore, if we wish to become more than we are, and rise to the subconscious states of a better and a more beautiful life, we should surround ourselves as much as possible with those things that have the power to inspire; and there is nothing that will serve this purpose to a greater degree than works of art that have soul.

Whatever we may be doing, if we feel the soul at the time, we give soul to that which we do; and our work will therefore be classed with that which is superior. In the development of genius, however, many conclude that genius alone is sufficient to produce great ability and promote great achievements. But we have already discovered that this mysterious something that we call soul is just as necessary as genius itself, and in fact must be present before genius becomes real genius. Genius not only does its best work through the avenues of virtue, truth, lofty mindedness and high spiritual qualities, but what is more, genius cannot do itself justice unless those qualities are present to a very high degree. In other words, genius is not genius unless it has soul and character; for without soul and character, genius is but a cheap imitation of its great and wonderful self.

Another essential in the development of ability and genius in art, as well as in the development of all other forms of ability, is to educate the subconscious along proper lines. The subconscious can do anything if properly impressed. This is the law. Therefore the subconscious has the power to bring forth everything that is required for the faculties of art. From this statement we are not to conclude, however, that the direction of the subconscious is all that is necessary. To awaken the subconscious is one essential and an essential that is indispensable, but to train the objective and develop the brain so that the greater subconscious powers can find orderly expression are other essentials equally important. To impress the subconscious along artistic lines, realize clearly in mind what constitutes artistic talent; gain a perfect consciousness of art itself, and try to understand the artistic spirit. In other words, form definite ideas of art and of the art of which you wish to become a master. Then impress those ideas upon your subconscious mind many times every day, being convinced at the time that what you impress upon the subconscious the subconscious will later on express in your mind and faculties. What we give to the subconscious will be returned to us in thirty, sixty or an hundred fold. Therefore, we must impress upon the subconscious the real ideas of art; and when we do we shall receive that power and genius in return that will give us great and even extraordinary talents in the wonderful world of real art.

Chapter 17

Talent and Genius in Literature

The faculties required for literary work depend largely upon the field selected although there are a few faculties that all writers need in common. These are expression, construction and a highly active imaginative intellect. Where there is a desire to write on metaphysical or psychological subjects, interior understanding should be developed in addition to the ones mentioned. And to write well on scientific and practical subjects a thorough development of application is required because this gives one ability to connect principles and laws with the practical world. It also gives system, method and the faculty of turning the abstract into actual use. To become a good writer of fiction, develop the faculties of expression, intellect, intuition, emotion and originality. To these should be added what might be called universal consciousness, or the power to sympathize and enter into harmony with all phases of life.

In this connection it is important to mention that there are several new fields — fields that hold excellent possibilities for those who will prepare themselves for such a work. Ordinary fiction pictures life as it is lived by human nature in its weakness. It is true to life as it is lived by those who really do not know how to live. Therefore, it is largely a picture of flaws, perversions and mistakes. People read such fiction usually for no other reason than to pass time or to be entertained, although a great deal of fiction is read through a morbid desire to devour what is hardly wholesome. It is therefore evident that very little good can come from the reading of ordinary fiction, and to be just to ourselves we cannot afford to do what does not bring good in some way. In addition to the usual fiction we have fiction that is out of the ordinary; that is, that constitutes superior and real literature. Such fiction is highly valuable for the richness of its language, and no one can read such fiction without being decidedly benefited along the lines of higher literature; but such fiction does not as a rule contain anything of direct value concerning the secret of life. Many will contend that it is not the purpose of fiction to teach anything. But the fact is that there is no class of literature that could teach the secrets of life in a more thorough and more convincing manner than fiction. Therefore, fiction that does not aim to be constructive as well as entertaining ignores its greatest opportunity.

To define the new fiction is hardly possible in a brief paragraph, but its object is to picture life as it might be lived by people who have mastered or are trying to master the secrets of life. In other words, it would not deal with ordinary people and their modes of living, but it would deal with the life and the conduct of such people as have taken it upon themselves to attain and achieve the greatest and the highest things that are possible in life. That such fiction could be made more interesting and more fascinating than anything that has ever appeared in print is evident, and if produced by a master mind would constitute a higher form of literature than has ever appeared in the world. The time is now ripe for such fiction, and to those who can produce it, fame and fortune in a large measure are surely in store.

To develop literary genius, the first essential is to develop those faculties of the brain and the mind that are required for such work. These faculties are indicated in Figure IX and full instruction as to their development has been presented in previous chapters. The second essential is to educate the subconscious along literary lines. This is extremely important, because there are few talents that respond as readily to subconscious training as the literary talent. Besides, it is in the subconscious alone that we can find real genius along any line. In the subconscious we find the limitless state of every faculty, talent or power; and we can steadily bring into expression more and more of this capacity, as no limit has been found to its power or possibilities. The real secret of becoming a genius is to awaken and properly train the subconscious mind, though we must not forget that the objective mind and the physical brain must be cultivated in such a way that subconscious genius can find full expression. To bring out the literary genius that may be latent in the subconscious is a process that cannot be perfected in a few weeks, but those who have considerable literary talent may, in a few weeks, realize a remarkable improvement from the application of right methods; and if they will continue indefinitely in the application of these methods, continuous advancement will positively be the result.

Those who may not be talented along literary lines, but who desire to develop such talents, can make their desires true to a very great extent if they will persevere for a year or more in the application of the two essentials mentioned. In this connection it must be remembered that the subconscious contains all the talents in a potential state, and it is our privilege to choose which one we desire to express, develop and apply. If that talent is already expressing itself in a measure it will take less time to increase its subconscious power, but if time, perseverance and the right efforts are combined, any talent desired can be developed to a remarkable degree, whether we have much ability along that line or not at the present time.

The first step is to gain a clear mental conception of what you desire to develop; and this desire should be full and strong at all times, as the subconscious will never respond to half-hearted desires nor divided attentions. When the desired purpose has been clearly pictured in mind, the next essential is to impress this with deep feeling upon every thought. Every thought which has deep feeling enters the subconscious and carries into the subconscious the desire with which it was impressed. As previously stated, the subconscious must be expressed in the present tense; therefore, do not simply desire to become a genius, but desire to bring forth the genius that already exists in the depths of your mind. Never impress the subconscious with the idea that you hope to become this or that. On the contrary, live in the strong, deep conviction that you have those things now, and this is true. A genius is asleep in the subconscious of every mind, and the subconscious is a part of you. It belongs to you. Therefore, you possess now all that is in the subconscious. For this reason it is strictly scientific and absolutely correct to affirm positively that you now have, and that you now are, what you wish to possess or become.

Live in the conviction that you already are a literary genius. Know that it is true, and stamp that conviction upon every thought you think. If necessary use affirmations to establish that conviction. It is always well to use affirmations provided we feel the real truth that is contained in all such statements. These affirmations may be made at any time, but they should without fail be impressed upon the subconscious every night before going to sleep. Take fifteen or twenty minutes every night after you have retired, and impress deep, positive statements upon the subconscious, affirming such ideas as you wish the subconscious to perpetrate and develop. Then go to sleep with the conviction that you now are a literary genius. Statements like these may be employed: "I AM a literary genius;" "I AM a brilliant writer;" "I have strong, clear, lucid mind." "My literary ability is unbounded, and of the highest order;" "I AM complete master of the richness of language;" "I have at my command innumerable ideas;" "I AM original in thought and in expression;" "Well constructed expressions are always ready to flow through my mind;" "I AM alive with my subject and can give it the fullest, the freest and the most perfect expression."

Many other statements of a similar nature can be formulated and employed, though it is not well to use too many. The object is to carry into the depths of the subconscious the idea that there is genius within you, and that this genius is now ready to express itself in rare literary ability. While affirming these statements your attention should be concentrated upon the subconscious side of those parts of the brain that are employed in literary work. Then expect results now; and persevere until results do come, never permitting yourself to become discouraged in the least even though you have to work for months before you secure the desired subconscious response. Through perseverance and the right methods, results positively will come; and when they do come, you will be on the way to a development that will certainly mean much for the future.

Conclusion

Vital Essentials in Brain Building

Moments of Tranquility — In all growth the passive is just as necessary as the active. Moments of action must invariably be followed by moments of repose, and the mode of repose should be selected with the same scientific care as the mode of action. To know how to properly apply a faculty is highly important when certain results are held in view, but it is equally important to know how to rest, relax and amuse that faculty in order to secure those same results. The reposeful attitudes accumulate; the active attitudes take up the new mental material thus secured, and proceed to build more largely. But the amount accumulated during any moment of repose is always larger when the mind expects accumulation during that moment.

When to be Still — Immediately following any form of positive action, physical or mental, the mind should be perfectly still for a few moments. Whether the action be actual work or simply exercise, the same rule should be observed. And also certain periods of tranquility should be taken at frequent intervals, varying from a few moments to a few days, depending upon the circumstances involved. The general purpose of such periods would be rest, recuperation and accumulation; and these are just as necessary to progress, growth or advancement as the periods of exercise, work and action. It is the moments of repose that give the moments of action the necessary material with which to work. This is a law that must receive constant and judicious attention wherever scientific attempts are made in the development of ability, talent and genius. Relaxation — Any action of the mind tends to produce what may be termed the "keyed up" attitude, and this attitude is necessary to the highest state of efficiency. When you are "keyed up," all your faculties are at their best; they are fully aroused, thoroughly alive and are worked up to the most perfect point of practical ability. But when you are through with your work, the "keyed up" attitude should be discontinued for the time being. The majority, however, fail to do this; they sometimes continue in the "keyed up" attitude for hours after they have ceased to work; they even go to sleep in the same attitude, and then wonder why they do not sleep well, why they tire so easily or why their systems are almost constantly on the verge of breakdown. The attitude for work is for work only; when the work is done enter the attitude that is not for work; that is, relax, and give the system the needed opportunity to place itself in proper condition for the next day's work. To relax the system, breathe deeply, easily and quietly, and think of your thought as going towards the feet every time you exhale.

Restful Harmony — The attitude of restful harmony should be entered at frequent intervals every day. A moment or two in this attitude is often the means of doubling the working capacity of the mind for the next hour. The restful attitude accumulates energy, while the harmonious attitude tends to place this new energy in the proper position for efficient action. Harmony always tends to set things right; therefore, the value of combining the feeling of harmony with the attitude of rest, repose or relaxation is readily appreciated. A few moments of restful harmony are especially important immediately after some exercise in brain building or mental development.

Recreation — What kind of recreation to select depends entirely upon your work. The two should always be opposites in nature, tendency and effect. If you are engaged in heavy mental work, choose recreation and amusement that is light, bright and sprightly. But if your work requires but little mental energy, choose recreation that tends to arouse mental energy. A stirring drama would prove highly beneficial to a mind that had been practically a blank during the day; in fact, such recreation might in time arouse enough mental energy to take, him into some position where he could apply the full capacity of his mind. To a mind, however, that had been dealing all day with profound problems, a different form of amusement would be required. If you are stirred up continually by your work, do not select forms of recreation that have the same effect. Hundreds do this; they are in the midst of excitement all day in business; at night they choose some form of amusement that has the same exciting effect. In consequence, life is cut short a half a century or more too soon. Whether in amusement, entertainment, outdoor sports or reading for recreation, aim to select something that produces an effect directly opposite to that produced by your work. Through this practice you will do far better work, and you may add a quarter of a century or more to your life.

Diversion in Concentration — The actions of concentration will be thoroughly effective only when alternated with passive diversions. Concentrate regularly upon your leading purpose, and when you do concentrate, give the subject at hand your undivided attention; but have several interesting diversions to which you can give your passive attention at frequent intervals. To live exclusively for one thing is not to succeed in the largest sense of that term; nor can any mode of concentration produce the results desired unless it is placed at rest occasionally, and the actions of the mind turned, for the time being, in other directions. To cease action in a given line, it is necessary to promote action in a different line; therefore, diversions are necessary. And every action must cease at intervals in order to give that which is acted upon the opportunity to adjust itself to the results of that action.

Imagination in Repose — During moments of repose and relaxation the imagination should be directed to give its attention to that which is quiet and serene. When you are resting the mind, picture scenes of tranquility, and try to enter into that restfulness that such scenes will naturally suggest. The imaging faculty is never completely inactive. So long as you live you will think, and so long as you think you will imagine. Therefore, during serene moments, imagine the serene, and you will give perfect repose to your entire system. The power of the imagination is used extensively in the development of talent and ability; in fact, no development can possibly take place unless imagination is properly incorporated in the process. It is therefore evident that those moments of complete relaxation that should always follow every exercise for development must, to actually produce relaxation, direct the imagination to picture that which is in perfect repose. To relax mind and body is not possible so long as the imagination is picturing something that is not in repose.

Soul Serenity — This is that deeper feeling of calmness and peace that tends to tranquilize the finer forces and the undercurrents of the system. And this is very important, as it is this deep, interior state of poise that makes man a power. Soul serenity should be entered into several times every day; and the result will be that those mental forces that have been aroused through positive exercise in development will become more deeply established in the subconsciousness of the mind. That is, the result of every exercise will take root; it will find deep soil, and will live and grow as a permanent factor in the continual upbuilding of the mind.

Sleep — The mind should be deeply impressed, before going to sleep, with that degree of development that is desired; but before sleep is actually entered, every faculty should be placed in a state of perfect calm. To go to sleep properly is just as important in any form of mental development as any exercise we may take when awake for the promotion of that development. But all that is necessary in securing these results is to think deeply with a strong desire for the development we have in view, and calm the entire mind as we go to sleep. To accomplish this, simply relax, using the method for producing relaxation as stated above.

Recuperative Thinking — During moments of rest and repose, do not think of doing things, but think of enjoying things. The man who is always thinking of doing things may produce the quantity for a time, but the time will be short, and the quality will be absent entirely. The best results are always secured when thoughts of doing things are frequently alternated with thoughts of enjoying things. The simplest, the easiest and the quickest way to recuperate the mind is to think of enjoying things. A few moments of such thoughts are usually sufficient to restore full mental vigor; but those moments must be given over completely to thoughts of enjoyment; the doing of things must be wholly forgotten for the time being, and the mind must give its all to the pleasing picture it has elected to entertain.

Meditation — The practice of tranquil meditation is absolutely necessary in every form of mental development. It is a practice, however, that is rare, and this accounts for the fact that deep, profound, substantial minds are also rare. The many have not discovered the real riches of their own mental domains, and the reason is they have neglected meditation. The purpose of meditation is to "turn over" in the mind every idea that we know we possess. We thus gain new viewpoints, and, in turn, new ideas. Through meditation we become acquainted with the wonderful that is within us. We discover what we are, what we possess, and what we may attempt. When we meditate we take a peaceful tour of investigation through the many realms of our own mind; we are thus brought face to face with many things that are new, and the tour will prove both a recreation and an education. It is always a diversion, and it will never fail to entertain. Meditation will also properly place every new impression that has been received; thus it becomes a building process in the mind, and a factor of absolute necessity. To practice meditation regularly is to become more and more resourceful, because meditation invariably gives depth, to every phase of the mind. The mind that meditates frequently does not live simply on the surface anymore; such a mind is daily becoming enriched with the gold mines of the great within, and is gaining possession of larger and larger interior domains. In consequence it finds more and more upon which to draw, and it will never be at a loss, no matter what the needs or the circumstances may be.

Rest — To give any part of the system rest, we must withdraw attention from that part, and to withdraw attention from any special part we must give the whole of attention to some other part. When the mind needs rest, exercise the body. When the body needs rest, read something of real interest, or listen to soothing music, or think of something that takes attention away from physical existence. Give proper rest to the body, and you will never lose your vitality, your virility or your vigor. Give proper rest to the brain and the mind, and you will never lose your brilliancy no matter how long you may live. But real rest for any special part is not secured by simply trying to cease action. You cease action in one part by becoming vitally interested in some other part. People wear out simply because they do not know how to rest. They are partly active in every part of the system continually. By becoming wholly active in a certain part, you become wholly inactive in all the other parts; and the inactive parts are perfectly rested. Then change about, regularly, giving each part of the system perfect rest for some moments several times every day. This is the art of resting;

and he who rests well will work well and live well; he will also live long and do much that is truly worthwhile.

Business Psychology

Business Psychology

Table of Contents

Foreword

It is not the purpose of this work to present a complete or extensive study of psychology as applied to the business world; the subject is too large; besides, the majority among practical business men prefer a brief and condensed presentation of the best methods that have been evolved through experiments with business psychology. And it is this preference that has been considered in every chapter.

The practical study of business psychology is of recent origin, but enough has been worked out in this vast field to justify the making of almost any claim for its value that psychology itself declares to be within the bounds of the possible. And this is saying a good deal, because thus far neither limit nor end has been found to the possibilities of the psychological side.

The psychological side is invariably the most important side, and everything has a psychological side. The psychological side of the business world is now recognized by all wide-awake business men, and they all admit with pride, that practically all the great improvements that have recently been made, both in the building of business and in the building of more efficient business men, have sprung directly from the study of business psychology. The study of this subject, therefore, is not a novelty; on the contrary, it has become a necessity.

The business man, however, has very little time for extensive or technical study; a work on business psychology therefore should be directly to the point in every respect, and should present the greatest amount of practical information possible in the least space possible. In the following pages a special effort has been made to comply with this requirement; so that where brevity may seem to be too conspicuous, everybody will know the cause.

Special attention has been given to the possibility of evolving an exact business science, a science which when applied would bring success with a certainty; and the aim has been to permeate every page with the spirit of this possibility, which is fast becoming an actuality — first, that success can be realized by all men of push, enterprise and efficiency, and second, that all those factors in the human mind that produce success, when applied, can be developed and perfected to almost any degree imaginable, which means that greater success can be realized in any field, by those who will pay the price, than has ever been realized before.

No attempt has been made to work out some definite system through which the principles of business psychology might be applied in the various fields of the commercial and industrial worlds. For again the subject is too large to be treated exhaustively in a single volume. The object, therefore, has been to present as many ideas and methods as space would permit, giving each reader the privilege to evolve his own system — a course that all progressive business men will prefer. And that the application of these ideas will increase decidedly the success of any man is a fact of which we are positively convinced.

Chapter 1

Laws and Methods that Insure Success

In the past the study of psychology was purely speculative. It had no definite object in view. Its attention was devoted almost exclusively to a general study of mental phenomena, but no thought was given to the possible effect of such phenomena. It did not study the mind itself, nor were attempts made to determine what effect the movements of the mind might have upon the practical side of everyday life. Psychology therefore was something that was more or less intangible, something that was largely theoretical, something that was looked upon as far removed from the field of personal action. For this reason such terms as practical psychology or business psychology could have no significance whatever; but in this respect, as well as in many other respects, things have changed remarkably in recent years.

We now know that all psychology is practical or can be made practical, and that the most important side of everything in the world of practical action is the psychological side. It is therefore evident that there must be a business psychology. In fact, a business psychology is absolutely necessary because it is the psychology of business that makes it possible for the business itself to live, grow and develop. This, however, many business men do not realize, while the majority of those who have come to this realization, do not clearly understand the actual purpose nor the possible power of the psychological element? They know that it is the psychology of the thing, or rather the way in which the psychological side is employed that determines results, but they do not have a clear idea as to how the psychological side can be directed or employed to the best advantage. But as this understanding is absolutely necessary if the desired results are to be secured, with a certainty, it is evident that the need of a business psychology is very great to say the least.

To achieve success in the largest possible measure is the life-long ambition of every wide-awake business man, and therefore he refuses, and justly so, to give his attention to those things through which his success may not be promoted. Though in his enthusiasm to pursue what is usually spoken of as successful business methods, he has overlooked the most important of all; that is, he has practically ignored the psychology of business, not knowing its nature or value. He has instead given his attention almost exclusively to what is usually spoken of as more practical subjects, but here we meet a large question.

What is it that makes a subject practical, and what are the things that really make for success? The average business man is unable to give the answer. In fact, most business men have never thought seriously of this subject. The average business man believes that the principal secrets to success are found in hard work, enterprise, economy, safe investments and an abundance of good luck. But here we may well ask why the great majority of business men do not succeed as well as they might wish, regardless of the fact that they follow all the rules of the captains of business that have gone before.

We also might ask in the same connection why the reason is that such an enormous amount of waste is constantly taking place in nearly every industrial establishment. It is a well-known fact that the waste, both in production and distribution, is enormous, and we know that the business man does not wish it to be so. He is daily losing through such channels, but why does he permit these losses to continue if he is fully convinced that he is in possession of the real secrets of business success? When we note the many mistakes that are made even by the leaders in the commercial world, and how the great majority are almost constantly standing in their own light, we may be pardoned for doubting the idea that modem business has been made a science, and that exact methods have been found for securing success. People who are not in direct contact with the business world are frequently told to imitate modern business methods if they would succeed, and to establish themselves upon the same sound principles if they would achieve something worthwhile. But what are those principles? Who can tell us? It is a fact that the average business man is unable to state definitely what principles he considers to be at the basis of a successful business. Then we may be permitted to ask how modern business can be so very sound, realizing the fact that the majority fail to get more than a bare living out of it, and also that a considerable number of those who achieve great success, as the world measures success, frequently employ methods that are not justifiable.

There are a great many very successful business men who have achieved their success through legitimate means only, but when we analyze the lives of those men we find that they did not succeed through the use of what is usually termed modern business methods. They knew something about the psychology of business or they employed the principal elements of business psychology, possibly without using this term, or without knowing the exact nature of the principles employed.

It is not the purpose here to find fault with business methods, or to criticize anything in any shape or form, but it is a fact that when we thoroughly examine all those methods that are directly connected with modern business, and then at the same time examine closely the nature and the workings of the human mind in all its phases, we invariably come to the conclusion that business as it has been conducted up until recent years has been a hopeless mixture of unscientific schemes and bungling methods. We are speaking, of course, of business in general. There are many noble exceptions, and it is these noble exceptions that give the commercial world what stability it is known to possess. However, when speaking of modern business and modern business methods we do not refer to the progressive business of this age, but to that phase of business that is gradually passing as it is giving away to the coming of business psychology. And we simply mention the methods and the principles of that form of business that is passing, in order to produce a more definite contrast with the new idea of business; that is, a business that will be strictly scientific, or that is, based upon the principles of business psychology.

It is a well-known fact that the commercial world is one of the prime essentials in the promotion of the welfare of man, and therefore it ought to be conducted upon the very best principles possible; and should accordingly employ methods through which the very best results, and only the best results, may be secured; but to make this possible we must go back of effects. We must go back of mere business itself and find the power that is in it all. This power we know to be the mind of man, and the study of mind is called psychology. Therefore the study of the human mind as related to the business world, and as directly applied in the business world, will naturally be termed business psychology.

The mind has many phases; therefore, there are many phases of psychology, in fact, as many kinds as there are individualized uses for the mind; and as the mind is the principal factor in commercial achievements we naturally conclude that a thorough knowledge of such psychology must be indispensable to him who would succeed in business, or who aims to secure the greatest results through his efforts wherever those efforts may be applied.

When we examine what is usually termed success in the commercial world, we come to the conclusion that such success depends directly upon ability, self-confidence, concentration and enterprise. It is with these factors, therefore, that we must begin, as these are fundamental, though there are scores of others that will have to be considered in a complete study of this subject. At the very outset every business man must possess these four essentials if he would be successful in a true and a lasting sense.

But to secure these essentials he must study business psychology; that is, he must study the use of the mind in business. If he already has these essentials he must, in order to secure the best results, understand the use of the mind because a factor is of no value no matter how well it is developed until it is scientifically applied. In either case, therefore, practical psychology becomes indispensable.

In the past, the idea was simply to proceed to use your ability as well as you knew how, without giving any attention whatever to the principles and laws that govern the use of that ability. In brief, the use of talent, or practical ability along any line was continued in some helter-skelter fashion, and when success was secured it was counted good luck. Times, however, have changed. Now we know, that good luck is simply the result of scientific application and that it may be created by man himself, provided he knows how to use himself or apply himself.

The wise business man today does not proceed in any way that happens to be convenient. He insists upon understanding the scientific way so as to get definite results and the desired results from every move he makes. He is not satisfied to simply say that brains and ability will insure success. He knows that a man may have plenty of brains and any amount of ability and never succeed because it is not only an essential to possess those factors that are needed in success — we must also know how to use those factors.

The majority do not know how to use their brains to the best advantage, nor do they know how to use their mental and physical energies. This is proven by the fact that the average person wastes more energy than he applies in his work, and also that most of his faculties are never applied to full capacity. We are all aware of the fact that there are thousands of men and women with fine brains and splendid abilities who go through their work every day, making mistakes at every turn, and who go through life without accomplishing anything really worthwhile. And the cause of this is found in the fact that the science of practical application has not been studied; in other words, those men and women have not become familiar with business psychology.

To have a fine brain is absolutely necessary and a good mind is indispensable, but brain and mind do not control themselves. We must know how to make exact and scientific use of these things if we are to accomplish what we have in view. How to use the mind according to system, law and scientific method — that is what constitutes practical psychology. And the importance of this subject is becoming so great that the day is fast approaching when it will be taught in all universities. In the meantime the man who would succeed according to full capacity must seek this knowledge from every available source, and must never cease his study.

When men and women proceed in life to do their share in science, art, industry or civilization they should have principles upon which to base their work, and such principles as would assure constant advancement. Even though the advancement be slow it is nevertheless true that so long as you understand the principles of advancement and apply those principles you will continue to move forward. And he who continues to move forward is already meeting with success. But in the average mind there is no certainty as to how to proceed in order to move forward continuously. When a man proceeds to dig a ditch he knows that the ditch will continue to grow longer so long as he applies the spade. In his mind there is no doubt as to the outcome of his work. But in the mind of the average business man there is constant doubt. He does not know what the results will be, and therefore his methods are not nearly as scientific as the methods of the man in the ditch. This, however, is not complimentary to the supposed superior intelligence of the business man, though the cause of this uncomplimentary position is found in the fact that the business man does not understand the principles upon which he works. He proceeds usually in a helter-skelter fashion and is not certain as to whether he is building for greater things or is moving toward failure.

The majority today do not know where they will be tomorrow. They do not know whether they will be in poverty or in some unexpected good fortune, and most of them live constantly in a subconscious dread of reverses. Their minds are therefore under a cloud, and no mind can do its best under such conditions. It is evident, therefore, that we must proceed along different lines in the commercial world. We must try to find those principles through which we know success can be attained with a certainty, provided, of course, that we continue to apply those principles with the same enthusiasm as the man applies his strength upon the spade who is working in the ditch.

If we aim to produce great men and women, and to secure the greatest achievements possible from the efforts of such men and women, we must give them methods through which the mind may always be at its best regardless of circumstances or adversity, and methods that will always produce the desired results when applied, regardless of the conditions that may prevail. And to present such methods is the purpose of practical psychology. In fact, practical psychology can give us principles, laws or methods that will positively insure success. Anyone who will apply such methods will move forward. He will advance every year just as certainly as the rising of the sun. So long as he applies the principles of practical psychology he will gain ground steadily, and his success will increase from year to year. In fact, there is one thing that he is positively assured of, and that is success, a continued and constantly increasing success. If his ability is limited, his advancement in the beginning will be slow, but since he can yearly increase his ability, the advancement from year to year will become more rapid in proportion. However, if his ability is very great, his advancement from the beginning will be remarkable and will constantly increase as he continues the further development of that ability. Here we have a solid foundation for sound business, and it is established upon the scientific use of mind and ability according to such requirements as are demanded in the commercial world.

Any man or woman, therefore, who will find the work that is most suitable for the talents possessed, may, through the application of practical psychology be assured of a real, a constant and an ever increasing success. And in this connection it is well to remember that business psychology can also aid the individual in finding that work for which he is best adapted.

Such statements as we must inevitably make when examining the possibilities of practical psychology may seem to be too strong to be based upon absolute fact. But the question is, cannot any mathematical problem be worked out when we know the principles, the laws, and the methods involved? We admit that it can. Then why should not this rule hold everywhere.

Every successful business man in the world has achieved his success through the right use of his mental faculties at the right place and at the right time. We must conclude, therefore, that when we learn to use our talents in the right way, at the right time and in the right place, we shall also have the right results. This everybody will of course admit. But is it always possible to act rightly at the right time and place? This may not always seem possible, but here, as elsewhere, the rule holds that difficult things seem impossible only until we know how. When we know how the most difficult becomes most simple.

The wise man, however, does not stand back and call such things impossible as he does not understand. On the contrary, he comes forward and demands the desired information. If there is anything better to be had he wants it, and such men always get it. The man who has his eyes open, who is always looking for the best that is to be had, that is the man who always gets the best. Accordingly, he steadily rises in the scale, while those who are constantly being frightened by the word "impossible" continue to lag behind, wondering in the meantime why some people have such good luck, and others have not.

The wise man does not require tangible demonstrations to prove a valuable idea. You do not have to show him effects in order to prove the value of the cause. When you give him a good idea he knows that that idea is good, and that if applied will produce good results. Accordingly, he does not wait for somebody else to produce the results. He proceeds to produce those results himself and thereby reaps the benefit of a very valuable principle employed at the psychological moment. Those, however, who wait for somebody else to prove the value of the idea do not take advantage of the psychological moment, and therefore miss a great opportunity.

We see these things taking place every day, and it simply proves that the successful business man must change his tactics and must try to gain a deeper understanding of those laws and principles that underlie results in the commercial world. It is only in this way that he can meet the growing demands of advancement and continue to be up in front, regardless of how rapid the progress of the world may be. And most business men in this age realize this great fact. They realize that something else is needed besides the old methods to insure success in the commercial world. They know that success depends upon the man himself, the mind that the man possesses, and the way the faculties of that mind are employed. They also appreciate the many aids to success that are to be found in knowing how to detect and take advantage of opportunities that are constantly passing by. But beneath all of this they realize that there must be a real science of business, a science that any man can learn, a science which, if faithfully applied, must with a certainty produce results desired in every case. And all that is necessary to add in this connection is that such a science must inevitably be the natural outcome of a thorough study and a thorough application of the principles of practical psychology

Chapter 2

The Four Great Essentials to Business Success

The foundation of success in the business world is found in the proper combination of enterprise, ability, self-confidence and concentration. True, there is a superstructure; there is a lower story and an upper story, and several other stories intervening, all of which we must consider in their proper places.; But the foundation must be considered first, and in doing so our object will be to present the psychological side of all these factors, and prove that the psychological side is not only the principal side, but that a thorough understanding of the psychological side will make success just as certain as the rising of the sun.

When we speak of enterprise the average mind naturally thinks of hustle, push, more work and eternally being at it, but we shall find that this term also involves something else, the understanding of which will be of incalculable value to everybody in the business world. To adopt the rule of more work is necessary, as nothing is accomplished without much work, but simply to resolve to work is not everything in work.

There is an art of working. There is constructive enterprise and destructive enterprise. There is work that promotes your objects and there is work that simply wastes time and energy. In fact, misdirected work is so common that it is met by nearly everybody every hour. If some method, therefore, could be found that would enable every intelligent person to direct his work properly at all times, one of the greatest secrets of success would have been revealed. To strike the nail on the head every time is the purpose of work. But in too many instances the man with the hammer crushes his own thumb.

To define work we may say that it is physical or mental action applied through certain channels for the purpose of producing certain intended results. The work itself is force or energy practically applied, but the results do not depend altogether upon how much energy is employed. Results also depend upon the way the energy is employed. However, that something that directs all energy in work is not to be found in the muscles, nor in the senses, nor even in the ordinary exterior intellect. This something belongs to the very finest elements of the mind and the study of these things constitutes one of the principal fields of the new psychology.

There is, therefore, a psychological side to work, and no work can be done properly without a knowledge of this side. It is a well-known fact that your mental attitude toward your work does just as much for success or failure as the work itself, and also that your states of mind while at work determine largely how much energy you will be able to give to your work. For this reason we realize the importance of the psychological side. To enter into details and present the mental laws involved in this subject will not be necessary, however, but it will be necessary to say that no one can afford to be ignorant of the psychological side of work, because no matter how hard he may work or how much energy he may possess, as long as he does not understand the mental laws involved most of his efforts will be misdirected. The subject, therefore, becomes important and will be given proper attention in the proper place.

Passing to the study of ability we find a theme as large as life itself and containing possibilities too large to be measured. It has been well said that the man with brains can do anything he may set out to do, and can secure practically anything he may wish for. But though this is a great truth it offers no consolation to those who are not in possession of remarkable brains. These people, however, need not be discouraged because brains can be developed. Accordingly, there is no excuse any more for having a small mind, or for being deficient in ability or capacity along any line. These things can all be developed to almost any degree desired, and exceptional improvements secured in a short time. We naturally conclude, therefore, that before every mind lies a path of unlimited possibilities. The average person, however, has not given much attention to the increase of his ability. He has labored under the conviction that no increase was possible and has depended upon the application of what ability he possessed through the channel of hard work. Here, then, is a new field for men and women who desire progress in the world of achievement. To carry out this idea we must not rush headlong with the crowd, expecting to arrive through the lucky application of our present capacity. On the contrary, we must give just as much attention to the increase of our ability as to the practical use of that ability.

At first sight, however, it may seem that success will be interfered with by such a method, as the average person thinks that he needs all of his time for practical work and what ability he has must be put into that work. For this reason he believes that he has neither the time nor the opportunity, but the fact is that every man who wants to can find the necessary time for improvement. That this is a fact will be evident when we realize that the mind will not be tired out after a day's work when we learn to work in the right mental attitude; and also that development will be continuous, even while we are at work, provided we work through right mental actions.

Every man, whether he has been in business for many years or is just beginning, should make it a point to give a certain amount of time and attention every day to the further development of those faculties that are directly involved in his work. More brains must be his leading purpose and his constant desire, and where there is a will there is a way. By adopting this method he may not in the beginning be able to give his work as much attention as he planned, though in most instances he will be able to give it all the attention required. After a short time, however, he will begin to become a greater power in his field of action, and will find himself able to do better work and more work in less time.

In all efforts quality should be sought first, though the average person sets out with his whole attention fixed upon quantity. And here we have one reason why so many fail to accomplish anything of worth.

After you have resolved to give a certain amount of time and attention to the further increase of your personal ability, impress your mind with the fact that the faculties or talents that you employ in your work can be developed indefinitely. Realize this fact so fully that you feel it at all times. To feel inwardly that your ability can be enlarged indefinitely will of itself produce an increase of capacity every moment. And when you apply in conjunction a good system of practical methods the results will be steady and wholly satisfactory.

In this connection it is absolutely necessary to break away from the old habit of being absolute slave to your business; you must always rule your work, and not permit yourself to be ruled by your work under any circumstances. To develop the mind, the mind must not only be free from all conditions and circumstances, but must be the master of them all. And in carrying out this principle we shall find it necessary to possess an abundance of self-confidence, the third essential to real success.

We may have more brains than we can use, but if we have no faith in ourselves we shall accomplish but little. That this is true we all know because we are all acquainted with fine minds who do not believe in themselves and who therefore undertake nothing. Many of these could startle the world if they believed that they could, though where faith and self-confidence are lacking there is no incentive whatever to make any definite attempt along any definite line. Where faith is abundant a little ability will go a long way, and some of the most successful men in the world owe their great results to self-confidence, as their ability is in many instances below the average.

The great power of self-confidence lies in the fact that when you believe that you can do certain things all the power of your being accumulates in those faculties through which the work is to be done. When you thoroughly believe that you can accumulate wealth you draw all the energy of your system into that part of the brain through which the financial faculties function. When you believe with all your mind that you can write a great work of fiction all your literary faculties will become alive with energy, coming in from all parts of mind and personality. The same is true along any line where your self-confidence and your faith in yourself has become very strong. This is why faith is so remarkable, and why self-confidence is indispensable.

True, if you have no ability for the work which you believe you can do, there will be no results for the time being. Energy must have something to work with, even though that something be small. But even though it should be small at first, that faculty will grow with great rapidity when all the forces of your being begin to accumulate there. Therefore, to believe that you can do what you have no ability for, will be useless. Self-confidence alone cannot produce results, but when you know that you have some ability in a certain direction, and everybody has ability in one or more directions, give this ability all the self-confidence you can possibly arouse. Proceed with the full use of that faculty and believe that you can accomplish anything with it. The results will be remarkable. Through such a faith and through such an application this faculty will grow so rapidly that ere long you will be able to do far more than you first expected.

The law is that when we believe we can do certain things all the creative forces in our system will rush into the faculty required to do the thing we have planned. This added power will constantly increase the capacity of that faculty so that in the course of time it will possess remarkable ability. In the average person the various creative forces of his system are scattered all through the system and are mostly thrown away through lack of use; but if all of these energies could be gathered in the one place in the mind it is evident that far more could be accomplished, and this is what happens when self-confidence is strong. The nature of faith and self-confidence is to draw everything along with it into those faculties that are being used for the work at hand. Accordingly, self-confidence converts enemies into friends and uses obstacles as stepping stones. However, to develop faith and self-confidence we must understand the laws of mind and soul, and that involves the study of psychology.

The fourth great essential is that of concentration, and the purpose of concentration is to hold attention upon the work at hand as long as may be required. There are a few minds that can think of one thing and continue to think of one thing for hours and feel no fatigue, but the average mind can keep his attention upon one subject for a moment only, and when he does try to concentrate for some time he becomes mentally exhausted. One reason for this is found in the belief that concentration necessarily involves hard mental work, and that we must force the mind to hold it in a concentrated attitude. This, however, is not the truth.

When concentration is natural no effort at all is required, and in natural concentration you do not try to fix the attention, nor try to hold the mind in place. You simply become interested in your subject or your work. When you are deeply interested in something you naturally concentrate upon that something without making any special effort to do so. And so long as your interest continues your mind will give its whole attention in that direction.

But here the question is how we shall become interested in such things that we care nothing about, for we may be called upon to do things we dislike and the doing of those very things may be stepping stones to what we shall like. But we cannot do that work successfully unless our concentration is good. Thus the problem is how to concentrate upon that which we dislike, or how to become interested in that in which we have no interest. To this problem, however, there is a simple solution.

When we work with a purpose in view we look beyond the mere work. We look upon the work as the path to the coveted goal, and in this light our work means everything to us. Accordingly, we cannot help being deeply interested in it, knowing what we are to find at the end of the journey. When we work simply to make a living and do not use our work as a means to higher attainment, in addition to the making of a livelihood, we may find it difficult to be interested in it. But when we look upon our work as a means to a great end we shall find no difficulty whatever in becoming interested in every step of the way. We shall then enter our work with joy and be animated with a strong desire to do it in the very best way possible. When we proceed in this manner our interest in our work will be constant, and accordingly we will develop natural concentration. Ere long concentration will become highly developed so that we can give our whole mind and all our creative forces to the one thing we are doing now, and for any length of time without feeling the least mental weariness. This is a very simple method, a method that anybody can apply, and if applied faithfully will develop concentration in any mind, even to a remarkable degree.

When these four essentials have been secured or developed the next important step is to attain resourcefulness, and this may, figuratively speaking; be called the first story of the superstructure.

When we examine the average mind we find it to be just so much, and no matter how long you may know that mind you will never see any more in it. New things are not brought to the surface and the mental resources are so limited that you can see them all by looking at the surface of the mind. A person with such a mind has no agreeable surprises in store for anybody. He is what he appears to be, and no more. Such a person, however, will never startle the world with great achievements, nor even live a life satisfactory to himself unless he becomes familiar with the new psychology and applies its principles.

To accomplish much the mind must come into touch with the limitless source of ideas, thoughts and experiences. In other words, we must find that place in consciousness where the elements of construction are stored away in boundless supply; and the resourceful mind has found this place. For this reason the resourceful mind is never at its "wits-ends," it is never at a loss, it is never without a way. Such a mind simply opens itself to the thing needed and it comes. We call such a mind resourceful, but we have not in the past known the secret.

All great minds have this faculty naturally developed, and use it unconsciously; that is, they use it without knowing its true nature and without knowing how to increase its power. We all know such people, and that resourcefulness is one of their strong qualities is common knowledge. But can we all attain the same? The answer is that we can, and the fact is that we must. In these days when so many new things are appearing and so many new possibilities are being revealed, the mind must live very near to the limitless in order to take advantage of everything, as well as to continue in the front ranks.

The art of developing the faculty of resourcefulness takes us deeper into psychology than almost any other study along this particular line, as it is the subconscious mind that must be dealt with. To awaken the great within is the one essential; that is, to expand consciousness so that it can take in at least a part of that immense mental field that lies back of ordinary waking consciousness. Psychologists all admit that the ordinary field of consciousness is but a fraction of the immense field of the subconscious, and though a few minds have succeeded in exploring this region to some extent, it is to the average mind a closed door.

The limitations of most minds is due to the fact that the subconscious has not been explored and developed, while the remarkable resourcefulness we find among a number of the larger minds is caused directly by the awakening of some one or two phases of the great within. When the subconscious begins to act new ideas become very numerous, and in many instances new plans come in such great numbers that you do not really know which one to choose. Sometimes all of them are so good that it is next to impossible to say which one is best. In this experience die mind must be well poised and must stand firmly between the outer and the inner, so as to know how to apply the external needs with the best adapted idea or plan from within. At times minds in this state become so confused from their many ideas that they remain inactive for a time. To overcome this condition we must develop a keen insight and also develop continuity so that we will finish whatever we undertake. However, it is from the great within that all genius, all inspiration, all truth and all remarkable constructive power is evolved. Therefore, we cannot give the subject too much attention if we wish to become much and achieve much.

In practical everyday life we constantly come to places where we do not know what to do next, and accordingly suffer failure because we are not prepared for the emergency; but this could never have happened if the immense inner world had been awakened, and we had been in possession of resourcefulness. In the awakening of the within there are many steps, but the first one is to train the mind to look deeper than the surface no matter what the thought or action may be. This practice will in a very short time begin to produce results, though when results come the mind should be well poised and as clear as crystal in order that it may accept the best ideas as they appear. As in all other things it is practice that makes perfect, and he who proceeds with a view of securing great results will certainly secure them.

When we speak of these inner laws of the mind the very practical man may think that the subject is too transcendental to be of any value in commercial life, but let no one fall into this error. We all know that building capacity, as well as all ideas of value, come from the deeper realms of mind and thought, and since everything follows definite laws, there must also be laws for bringing forth, not only greater capacity and ability, but also as many new ideas, plans, methods and principles as may be required to make the work of any mind highly successful. And as it is these laws with which business psychology is chiefly concerned, it is evident that the man who studies and applies the principles of business psychology will place himself in the most advantageous position that can be found in the commercial world.

2-13-24

Chapter 3

General Rules in Attainment and Achievement

True success is the natural inheritance of every ambitious mind, and to succeed in every undertaking should be the ceaseless aim of every person And this aim cannot be too high. The fact is the majority underrate their ability in nearly every instance, therefore never accomplish much more than one-half of what they might. True success, however, is not measured by mere money, but also by personal worth, ability, real greatness, and the doing of things that are difficult, or of great value to the world.

The successful man has done what others before him could not do. Accordingly, he has made the world richer and better and has become an example for millions to follow. Every man that succeeds becomes a model for the race, and his methods become patterns for many generations. The successful man seeks to become something and to do something, and he does not ignore anything, however trivial it may seem, that may be conducive to his growth and advancement.

In this connection a few general rules may be presented in attainment and achievement, rules that will be found of exceptional value to everyone who has real success in view. But here it must be remembered that the true conception of success is as broad as the powers of man, and that the gains that naturally follow such a success may include everything that has value and worth, everything that heart can wish for, everything that the mind can use.

Of all rules the most fundamental is this, that all true success depends upon yourself. Therefore to make yourself more competent as well as greater in every sense of the term must be the first essential. Improve yourself and aim to gain in knowledge, power and insight every day. Aim to develop a strong mind, a steady and strong personality and a powerful character, as all of these are great essentials.

In this connection, however, the complaint is frequently made that people who work have little time for study or self-improvement, and though this may be true in some cases it is by no means the rule. The fact is that if the average person, especially the younger person, would eliminate useless pleasures and devote that extra time to self-improvement, a change for the better, and in many cases a remarkable change, would be realized in a few years. The young man or young woman who is after real success and true greatness must say farewell to cheap and useless amusements. But this should not be looked upon as a sacrifice, because in truth such a course would mean gain. Look at yourself, therefore, and your habits, then eliminate all those things in your life that are useless, that simply waste time, and you will find abundance of time to give to your own cultivation and advancement.

The old saying, "Let young people have a good time while they are young for it will not last long," is too absurd to remember for a moment. If you live right and constantly improve yourself you will enjoy life every day as long as you live. That young people, therefore, should waste their time on cheap and useless pleasure, and that people of more years should live a dejected and uninteresting life, is an idea that does not belong to this age of wisdom and light.

The new rule is to use your time well while you are young and you will remain young; and what is more, you will be something in the world. The question is not whether we should enjoy ourselves, for we all must have pleasure every day. The question is, shall we continue to live a small, cheap life with nothing but the commonest of pleasures, when we can learn to live a large, rich life that will ever be full to overflowing with the very best that the world can give. This is the question, and every ambitious mind will give the right answer.

One of the first rules, therefore, is to begin today and arrange to carry on a systematic course of self-improvement, embracing as many branches as time and present ability will permit. Another important rule is to associate only with the successful, the industrious and the aspiring. The people we seek as companions have a marked effect upon us. Therefore, if they are pessimistic, believing in nothing but poverty, failure and injustice, you have nothing to gain and much to lose by seeking their association. But there is no reason why we should seek the association of such people. There are any number of great souls in the world so that we can find as many as we may desire for companions.

Above all, have faith in yourself. It is better to overrate than to underrate yourself. Know that you can succeed; thus you will speak and act accordingly. Expect great things of yourself and continue to expect such things until they are realized. Stand upon your own feet, but live closely to minds and souls that have achieved much. Believe that the bright side will prevail, and in the midst of darkness know that better moments are at hand when the sun will shine again.

Draw the bright side of things into your life by a persistent faith in the supreme power of everything that is good; but do not simply desire the bright side of life. Live such a life yourself. The importance of this may be well illustrated by taking two men of equal ability and opportunity, but the one habitually cheerful, while the other habitually morose. In the world of success the former has ten times the chance of the latter. We all seek the sunny soul, both in society and in business. The cheerful man will attract where the sullen man will repel, and in the realms of attainment the power to attract good things is a matter of enormous importance. But cheerfulness has a greater value than this. Cheerfulness is constructive and accumulative. All good things come to the man who is ever bright and happy, for remember that it is sunshine that makes things grow.

Make it a point never to talk or think of failure or adversity. Be determined to succeed, and permit no thought or word to suggest anything else, no matter if things today seem to go wrong. At such times remember the great statement, "This shall also pass away." The fact is that the world is always your friend, even though some parts of it may seem at times to be against you. Though when the world does seem to be against you, remember the reason is that you have not met the world in the right way. Change yourself. Be a friend to everybody — the whole world. Expect everybody to be good to you and desire constantly to be of real service to the entire human race, and you shall find ere long that fate will change. When you believe that everybody is against you, you rub them all the wrong way, so therefore the blame is upon you alone. Know that the true side of mankind is a true friend to every aspiring soul. Then place yourself in touch with the ideal in man. Meet only his better side, and your life, as well as the life of the world, will be made richer thereby.

Make it the rule of your life to think success, to speak success, to breathe success, to attract success, to live success, and to be saturated through and through with absolute faith in your own success. Believe with your whole heart that the whole world is for you, and that nothing is against you. Then you will find that as your faith is, so shall it be.

At the present time there are thousands of people who believe they are in bondage to the present system of competition and they think of themselves as slaves to this system, but they are simply demonstrating the law that he who is for captivity into captivity goes. He who believes that he is a slave to any system will become a slave to that system according to his belief. It is true that the present social and industrial order can be improved, but we are not helping ourselves nor society by acting the role of slaves and weaklings. Society and industry will better themselves as mankind raises himself to a higher level, and every time it passes from the attitude of serfdom to the attitude of mastership will, in a measure, lift up the whole world thereby. When you believe yourself to be a slave to the powers that be you simply forge your own fetters, but when you believe yourself to be a master over yourself, a master over your conditions, a master over your own attainment and achievement, you will gradually gain mastership over all those things, and ere long everything will begin to come your way.

Never live in the attitude of inferiority, and never permit yourself to appear as an inferior being. Both mind and body should be well dressed, especially the mind. If you look common, you will think of yourself as common, and he who thinks of himself as common will become common. To present a good appearance need not involve extra expense. It costs no more to be neat, clean and presentable than to be otherwise, though the gain is very great. The fact is that nothing that has a tendency to make you reckless about yourself or your appearance will awaken mind, character and ability. Give special attention, therefore, to the dressing of the mind. And we all can dress the mind in the most perfect manner imaginable.

To proceed, no thought of inferiority should ever enter the mind. On the contrary, think of yourself as a superior being. Think constantly of greatness that is in you and claim it as your own. Live, think and act as if you were somebody, because you are. All that is great and wonderful is latent in your own soul. Such an attitude, however, need not imply an external display of egotism, for the fact is that he who has found his true greatness will be modest and reserved in his external life; but his internal life will be a life with great power; and in the secret places of his own mind he knows what he is.

In this connection, know that you have a mission in life. Believe positively that your work is important, that the world needs you and that you must do your best. Do not associate mentally, however, with the coldness and heartlessness of the perverted side of live. Continue to live mentally with the better side of man. Associate and work only with those who are upward bound, and think only of the strong and the great. Then remember that adversities to you are but opportunities for demonstrating the greater power that is in you, and as you proceed in this attitude you will always be buoyant with life, joy and power, and the ship of your life will continue to sail on.

To proceed with the fuller application of these ideas it will be necessary to give special attention to the new idea of work, ability, and faith. These are most important factors and where properly combined, failure becomes impossible. How to work, how to apply ability, how to develop greater ability, how to secure faith, and how to use faith — these are problems that demand solution from all minds that would rise in the scale of life. But these solutions are not difficult to find, the fact is they are within easy reach of any mind, and therefore we can state positively that anyone can succeed.

It is a well-known fact that competent men and women are in great demand everywhere, but it is not clear to the average person what it means to be competent, nor is it generally known that practical ability can be developed. According to the old idea the mind with ability might succeed, while the mind without ability would have to be satisfied with what little the limitations of his mind might be able to produce. This idea, however, is not true in any sense of the term and should be eliminated completely.

Any person can improve himself when he knows how, and anyone can learn how. Though you may be wholly incompetent today, next year you may be able to fill a responsible position and be on the way to a great and ever-growing success, for there is nothing to hinder the advancement of anyone after he has learned the secret, and has resolved not to stand in his own way anymore.

To succeed means to move forward, and as all forward movements depend upon constructive efforts all work must be constructive. But work must not simply be constructive, it must be constructive to the very highest degree. And here is where ability becomes indispensable. Too much of the work that is done in the world is a mere waste of time and energy. It is simply taking the haystack from one hill to another without increasing the amount of hay or adding to the welfare of those who do the moving. The amount of waste that is going on in the business world is startling to say the least, though we do not have to look far to find the cause. Lack of ability and insight are invariably the causes, and since the average person has in the past doubted both the existence of insight and the possibility of improvement in himself, we can readily understand why this waste has continued. When we examine the lives of very successful men we find that they had a happy faculty of doing the right thing at the right time; and we also find that this happy faculty combined with considerable ability and a strong desire for work, was the real secret of their great success.

But what is this happy faculty of doing the right thing at the right time? It is simply insight; that is, an extraordinary power of mind to penetrate into the forces, circumstances and conditions of industrial or commercial life. We may call it foresight or we may define it as being long-headed, but whatever our definition may be the faculty remains the same, and we know it is a superior and much-needed faculty. Modern psychology has discovered that this great faculty is faith in practical action, and also that this faculty will steadily develop so long as we exercise continuous faith in conjunction with practical action.

But what is faith? We have been so in the habit of thinking of faith as a mere belief in something that cannot be proven that it will be necessary to employ both persistence and mental discipline to establish in our minds the correct view. Faith is a mental attitude. It does not believe. It knows. It never acts blindly because it can see with a superior mental insight. Faith is the reaching out attitude — an attitude that goes out upon the seeming void with the full conviction that the seeming void is the solid rock. Faith invariably breaks bounds and gives the mind a larger field of action. Then ability follows and informs the mind what to do with the new opportunity. And work completes the circle by doing what ability declares can be done. That these three factors, therefore, when properly combined will constantly acquire new worlds, constantly enlarge the possibility of achievements and constantly convert all fields of action into an ever-increasing success must therefore be evident to every mind.

Work, however, must be constructive; ability must steadily improve and faith must ever become larger and clearer. Constructive work never takes the form of drudgery, and never produces weariness, nor will such work ever do anyone any harm. No one has ever died from work, nor become sick from work. It is worry and wrong thought in general that undermines the system. So long as you get eight hours of sleep every night and live a temperate life, physically, mentally and morally, you can work every hour you are awake and enjoy it; and this is positively true when you have made your work constructive. We do not mean, however, that everybody should work steadily sixteen hours a day. It is not necessary, but if your success depends upon that amount of work in the present, do not be afraid to continue at your work every hour that you are awake. It can do you no harm, and it will be the making of a greater future for you.

Good work, constant work, constructive work, will count in every instance, and especially so when we put all there is in us into our work. Then when our work is guided by ability the results of such work will have still greater worth. And when we dwell in the attitude of faith we will constantly work up to greater and greater things.

The competent mind is the mind that is not only alive with desire for work, but that knows how to work; that can do things without being told, and that is sufficiently original to improve steadily upon the methods employed. And such a mind may be developed in anyone when the new ideas of work, ability and faith are faithfully employed. When we try to increase capacity and improve ability, we find that faith plays a part we did not suspect. It is this phase of faith that will appeal most strongly to the practical mind.

Modern psychology has discovered that the mental attitude called faith awakens new and greater forces in the mind and also increases remarkably the clearness of thought and the lucidity of intellect. The mind that lives and works in faith, as defined by the new psychology, is constantly on the verge of greater power and keener wisdom, and must therefore constantly increase in capacity and improve in ability. This is a fact that has been entirely overlooked, but it demonstrates conclusively that faith is indispensable to him who would achieve greater and greater success. However, when this remarkable value of faith is made known many minds will begin to depend almost entirely upon faith, neglecting ability and worth. But here it must be remembered that faith simply enlarges the mind, thereby producing more mental material; ability is required to employ that material properly, and work is necessary to carry out the plans and demands of ability. These three, therefore, must always combine — work, ability and faith — and when these three do properly combine great success will positively follow.

Chapter 4

The Need of a Powerful Individuality

The facts and experiences of practical life are demonstrating more fully every day that the greatest achievements come always through the strongest individualities. Therefore, in the world of action where success is the purpose, there should be a great demand for information and methods that will promote the development of individuality. And the goal of all such development should be the becoming of yourself; that is, the being of yourself so fully and so thoroughly that neither persons nor environments can exercise influences over you contrary to your own purpose and will.

It is a well known fact that a large percentage of the failures in life come because the individual is not sufficiently himself to hold to his original purpose during trying moments. Thousands who have gone down to defeat would have won great and lasting victories if they had only held on a little longer. Then there is a very large number of failures that come because the controlling individual wavers; that is, influenced by others to change his plans, or influenced by environment or indications to modify his original purpose.

We know that concentration upon that which we are doing, as well as upon our special plans, is absolutely necessary if we are to carry things through to ultimate success of a high order. But no one can concentrate properly while he is being turned this way or that way by persons, environments, conditions or events. Those minds that have produced definite and properly constructed plans, and who can stand by those plans undisturbed until the desired results are secured, are not numerous because the development of individuality has not been promoted to any great extent.

But as all success demands minds of this nature we realize the importance of a powerful individuality in every undertaking. And when we know that each individual is the creator of his own destiny we must naturally conclude, that that individual cannot create a great destiny who is seldom himself. You can create after your own likeness only when you are yourself. When you are under the influence of your environment you are creating a destiny just like your present environment. That is the reason why progress in the average individual has been so slow. In other words, we have created the future after the likeness of the imperfect present because we have been mostly under the influence of our present surroundings.

To see a new world of achievement patterned from something that is far superior to the present and then continue to build up that world in your own life and work — that is one of the secrets not only in securing greater results in our present undertakings, but also in building more nobly for the future. To do this, however, we must be ourselves. We must be so strongly individualized that our own high purpose is safely protected at all times from all counteracting influences from without.

When you enter the world of action your object is to do something different, and to do your work much better than it was ever done before, because that alone can constitute real success; but you cannot do things better in the present unless you become superior to the life of the past. You cannot create something different so long as your creative powers have no other models before them than such imperfections as exist in your present environment. It is certainly evident that if we are to move forward we must give the mind a more perfect group of ideas than those that are gathered from present surroundings; but when we do secure more perfect ideas, plans or methods we cannot stand by them and see them through unless we are sufficiently strong in our own individuality to overcome such inferior influences as may surround us. In brief, we must be strong enough to be ourselves — to stand by the best conceptions that we have formed of ourselves, and of those greater attainments and achievements that we have in view.

The man with new ideas receives very little encouragement from the public or from his associates until he has demonstrated the fact that those ideas are sound and practical. Therefore, while he is making application of his higher views, and carrying out his superior plans, he must depend upon his own strong individuality; otherwise he will fail. But this requirement has not been met by a great many in the past. Any number have appeared with original ideas, superior plans and better methods, all of which would have proved successful if thoroughly worked out; but the individuality necessary to push those things through to ultimate results was not present in every case, therefore we can remember but few in the centuries past who succeeded as fully and as greatly as it was in their power to succeed.

To originate and carry out to completion some great plan that will leave the world richer, and add to the welfare of man, that is real success; but these two essentials are not always found together in the same mind. There are many original thinkers, but they have not the individuality to carry out and push through to the end their original ideas. Then again, others have strong individual qualities and are competent to push through almost anything, but they have no originality, therefore are without the necessary material with which to work. In general, it is one mind that supplies the plans and another that carries them out, and where minds can combine in that way each one concerned will reap his share of just reward and results will be satisfactory.

In too many instances it is the one who carries out the plan who reaps the richest harvest, while the one who discovers the plan secures but a fraction of the final results. There is only a small percentage of the great inventors, discoverers and original thinkers who have received the full financial recompense due them, but no one was to blame but themselves. If they had had the originality to promote their own plans, or to stand firmly upon their own individual prerogatives, while associating with their promoters the results would have been thoroughly in their favor. Illustrations without number could be given to prove these ideas, but this will not be required, as it is clear to everybody that originality and individuality are the two great pillars in the temple of achievement, and that in order to secure the greatest results in any achievement each individual mind should possess these two prime essentials.

Where each individual mind is in possession of only one of these essentials, it will be uphill work to succeed in anything, because it requires a certain amount of individuality or push to secure the proper associates for the carrying out of wonderful ideas; and it requires a certain amount of originality to understand clearly the wonderful ideas of another so as to work them out successfully. For this reason the proper course to pursue is to do one's very best under present circumstances and then go to work at once to develop what is lacking. Let the man who lacks individuality proceed to develop individuality to the very highest possible degree. And let the man who lacks originality learn to become an original thinker, not only in his own field of action, but in as many additional fields as possible.

Resuming our analysis of individuality and its relation to great achievements, we must not omit the fact that the most thorough use of the powers within us is possible only when we are well individualized. It requires power to do things, and the more power we possess the more we shall accomplish, provided that power is well directed. But to direct this power there must be a controlling factor in the mind; that is, the mind must be well individualized. That man who is not himself more than a part of the time does not direct his own powers at all times. When he is not strictly himself he creates in mind something that is foreign to his own purpose in life. The need of individuality, therefore, is again most evident.

Individuality, however, cannot be developed simply through the acceptance of good advice on the subject. Such development is a science and must be studied and applied as other sciences. As individuality develops the creative forces in the mind will accumulate in that part of mentality through which your work is carried out, and will constantly increase the capacity and the efficiency of the faculties that you employ in your work. This is very important and proves conclusively why the talents of the strong individual do not give up until they have accomplished what was planned in the beginning.

Where individuality is not strong there are a number of counter tendencies in the mind, and the faculties that you employ in your vocation do not receive all the energies that are generated. Much of this energy is diverted by those counter tendencies and thus wasted. However, when individuality is well developed you are not only yourself at all times, but you naturally give your whole self to the undertaking at hand. This will cause the mind to concentrate perfectly upon those mental faculties that you employ at present, and according to a well known metaphysical law, whenever the mind concentrates perfectly upon any faculty all the energies of the system pour into that faculty and multiply many times its capacity. That a given faculty can do better work the more power and capacity it has is a fact that anyone will understand, and that the possession of a strong individuality will enable any mind to hold all of this genius and power in the present channel of application must also be perfectly dear. We realize, therefore, the value gained by developing individuality to such an extent that every thought force produced in our systems will always be directed and applied where our work is to be done.

To create your own destiny you must be yourself at all times, and the higher your understanding of yourself the better will be the destiny that you create. To be yourself, however, does not mean that you are to imprison yourself in your own self-consciousness. There is a current idea that individualism leads to selfishness, and that the stronger your individuality becomes the more arrogant, exacting, domineering and tyrannical you become; but there is absolutely no truth to these beliefs. The strong, individualized soul is none of these things, because the stronger you become the weaker will all your faults and defects become. The well developed individual is closer to the human race than anyone else and has a much deeper sympathy. Besides, it is the well developed individual that gives the fullest and best expression to the best that is contained in human nature. When you are well individualized you will not be isolated from others, but will live more closely to the world than ever before, learning from the world as usual, but never controlled by the world. What you learn and receive you employ according to the most perfect methods, in order that greater achievements may follow.

The mind that does things worthwhile is always well rewarded. But what he does also benefits the world. So, therefore, the more you do and the more you accomplish the better off the world will be because you have lived. However, the more we study the subject the more convinced we become that individuality is an attainment we cannot afford to pass by for a moment, but the question is what to do to develop a powerful individuality.

The first step is to turn attention away from the personal self and direct thought more and more upon what is termed the great within. In this connection we must eliminate what is usually called self-consciousness; that is, being too much conscious of the visible personality. So long as we mentally dwell upon the visible side of ourselves we are conscious only of the surface. Accordingly, thought will be ordinary and feeling will be superficial. When you live, so to speak, in the shell, the outer crust, you cannot draw upon the inexhaustible resources from the within. But great minds cannot come from superficial thinking, nor from living on the surface, nor can deep or powerful thinking come from the habit of dwelling mentally upon the visible self. Therefore, if we are to become inwardly strong we must train ourselves to think deeper thought and live more thoroughly in the great depths of life, feeling and consciousness.

To develop individuality and to become inwardly strong mean the same, a fact that may assist many in this great work. We learn after looking closely at the subject that the lack of individuality so prevalent everywhere comes almost entirely from the race habit of superficial thinking, and such thinking continues so long as attention is directed principally upon the surface of life, thought or feeling. The turning of attention upon the depths of thought, life and feeling is absolutely necessary if we are to proceed with the development of individuality. To bring about this deeper form of thinking and to become inwardly strong so as to give thorough development to our individuality is a very simple process when we discover the real principle involved To apply this process proceed as follows:

Take a minute or two every hour and turn all attention upon the depths of your mind. Then desire deeply and persistently to arouse the strongest energies of the great within. This is all that is necessary in the beginning. After a few days of such practice you will begin to feel yourself becoming stronger in your feelings, in your thoughts and in your convictions, and you will also begin to feel something within you that is giving you more courage, more push, more perseverance and a great deal more confidence in yourself.

As you realize these steps in advancement give credit to the new method, and you will thus find that succeeding efforts in applying this method will produce still better results. This fact is based upon the law that the more faith we have in something that is good the more good we will get out of it. As you proceed with this deeper faith you will arouse more of the latent forces, and from day to day you will realize the increase of the new power functioning more and more throughout your entire system. Then you will discover that you are getting backbone, that you are becoming absolutely fearless, and that you positively know that you can carry out your plans.

This, however, is just the beginning. You will soon become deeply interested in the new development and will give the matter more thought with more faith. What will happen henceforth will be of the greatest value to you because the development of individuality has begun. You no longer live in the shell of your being. Your mind is no longer empty or superficial. Your system is being filled up with something that has real worth and you are becoming a real power. You will discover a great change taking place throughout mind and personality. From a state of uncertainty where you did not know how to apply yourself properly, and from a state of where you did not know what the morrow would bring, you have come to a belief where you positively know how to carry out all your plans with the positive assurance of great results. From the tiny acorn that you placed in your mind a short time ago is coming the mighty oak, and from a few thoughts sown in the depths of your mind is coming those remarkable results that you have desired so long.

The beginning may be small, but perseverance in the right direction will accomplish anything. The seed from which will spring this strong individuality is the inner feeling of new power being aroused, and the simple method given above will in every case produce this inner feeling and will do so in a few days. From that foundation you can, if you persevere along the same line, build up an individuality so strong and so powerful that nothing in your life or in your environment can in any way cause you to turn to the right or to the left, or hinder your progress in any form or manner. And when you realize this you will no longer continue with the imperfect methods of the past, but will adopt all the best methods that further study along new lines will reveal to you, so that the greater results and the greater future which you now realize to be in store may be gained with a certainty.

Chapter 5

The Science of Business Success

Every man or woman who enters business life should succeed, and can succeed if the principles that underlie success in the commercial world are scientifically applied. There is a right way of doing things and the use of the right way must inevitably bring success. In the business world there are certain things that have to be done in order to secure results. To know what these things are and to know how to do them, in the largest and most complete sense is the secret. The majority of those who enter the business world do not succeed as well as they should and there is a reason. They do not know the requirements of business success, nor do they know how to supply those requirements. But this information everybody can secure.

To secure certain effects we must apply certain causes, and to this law there are no exceptions. There is no luck anywhere. If we want results we must do the thing that produces those results. If we want business success we must do that which produces business success, and since there are certain lines of actions that always produce success in the business world, it is evident that business can be made an exact science, a science which, when applied will produce the results desired with a certainty. Every man or woman who enters business life in any capacity whatever can succeed, and can steadily advance into greater and greater success by knowing what to do and by knowing how to do it.

In the first place the individual must place himself in the best possible working condition; that is, every factor in his system, physical or mental, that is to be employed in the work he has in view must be so directed that all its energies are given over completely to that particular work. This principle, however, has been almost wholly neglected everywhere in the business world, and for this reason the average person applies less than one-third of his power to his undertaking, the remainder is scattered and consequently lost.

The individual himself is the cause of his own success; therefore how great his success is to be will depend upon how well he applies that which is in himself. This is an idea that we have heard before, but now we must learn how to apply it. It is well enough to tell a man what he ought to do, but it is also necessary to tell him how to do it and this is the purpose of business psychology. Its value, therefore, is far greater than anyone may at first suppose.

To proceed with the placing of the entire mind in the best working condition and to establish a substantial foundation for the application of the science of business, certain lines of action will be found indispensable. To consider these briefly will therefore be necessary before proceeding further in this step.

1. Have a definite object in view, and concentrate your entire attention upon the greatest possible success which you can picture in connection with the purpose you have in mind. Think constantly of this purpose. Live for it, and desire the desired results with a desire so strong, that every atom in your being thrills with its invincible power. So long as you have no definite object in view your forces will be scattered. You will not make any real use of what is in you. You will not apply the cause of your own success. Therefore no effects can follow. To have a number of objects in view and yet be so undecided as not to give yourself to any one of them is equally detrimental. The same is true of the prevalent habit of working at one thing while wishing you had something else to do. Give the very best that is in you to what you are doing in the present and you will secure something larger and better to do in the future. This is a law that never fails. It is as exact and as universal as the law of gravitation. Proceed, therefore, to train all your forces and faculties to work for the object you have selected and be so determined to reach your goal that the force of that determination is positively irresistible.

2. Love the work you have chosen, because you can give your best only to that which you love, and great success can come only when your best — all of your best is given to your work. If you find it difficult to love your present work, think of it as a stepping stone to everything that your heart can wish for; and it is, if entered into with that faith and purpose. The most ordinary occupation can be made a channel to the greatest of deeds and the highest of attainments. Therefore, we do not have to wait for new opportunities. All that is necessary is to make the fullest use of that which is at hand now. However, the only action that is full of the best that is in us, is the action that is inspired and expressed through love, not a love for something past or future, but a love for that which we are doing now.

3. Think that you can, because he who thinks that he can will develop the power that can. When you think that you can do that which you have decided to do your mind will naturally give most of its energies to those faculties that are required in the doing of that which you have decided to do; and by giving extra life and power to those faculties they will develop, thus gaining the necessary ability to do that which you have been thinking that you can do. However, to proceed to think that you can do certain things will not at once give you the necessary ability to do those things, but that ability will immediately begin to develop and will in time become sufficiently developed to enable you to do what you think you can do. But this thinking must not be superficial or egotistical. It must be inspired by a realization of the limitless powers that are latent within you. Think that you can with depth of feeling, a feeling that touches the very soul, and you will awaken those unbounded powers within you that can do what you think you can do. Think that you can do your present work better and you will daily develop more power and ability so that you can do it better. It is therefore possible through this law to promote continuous advancement whatever your work may be.

4. Apply your very best ability in your present work whether your recompense is sufficient or not. A great many competent men and women are underpaid, and there are several reasons, but that person who turns all his ability into his present work will soon have more opportunities for advancement than he can use. To refuse to do any more today than you are paid for today is one of the greatest obstacles to advancement and success, and there are two reasons why. In the first place, you cause a part of your ability to lie dormant which means that that ability will finally disappear, thereby diminishing your capacity and power. If you wish to develop your ability you must use all of your ability to the fullest extent. And, therefore, though you may not be paid in full for your present work, still by giving your best ability to your work you are steadily gaining in that ability so that ere long you will have the power to fill a much larger place. In the second place, by refusing to do any more than you are paid for in the present you announce to the world that you are working simply for pay. You thereby place the stamp of inferiority upon yourself, closing before you the door of progress, because when men of worth, ability and power are wanted the world will not be looking for you.

One thing is certain, however, if you apply your best you will be recompensed in the long run for all the work you do. If you do not receive it all today you will receive it later on and it will be very good when it comes. Absolute justice is the final judge in all these things and this final judgment is constantly taking place, but you will not have to work an eternity for what belongs to you. Give your best every day and the best will constantly be flowing into your own life in greater and greater abundance. In addition, by using all your ability now you will constantly develop that ability, thereby becoming a greater and a greater man. This is very important because in the attainment of a real growing success in any vocation ability is absolutely necessary, and though there are many excellent methods for the development of ability, the greater ability acquired through such methods will not become a permanent possession until it is applied in full effective use.

5. Make yourself indispensable in your present world and you will be called to occupy the highest place in that world. From that place you will soon advance to a larger world where the opportunities will be more numerous, the recompense higher and the work more congenial. It is a fact that as soon as you make yourself indispensable where you are, new and greater opportunities will almost immediately open before you, while, if you so live and work that your place can be refilled in one day's notice you are not in demand anywhere, and your opportunities are both few and insignificant. This being true we not only understand what it is that keeps man down, but we also understand the law through which advancement may be placed within easy reach of everybody.

6. Have the highest goal in view that you can picture in mind, and be, not only determined to reach it, but live in the strong faith that you positively will reach it. To simply aim high is not sufficient. The goal we desire to reach must be so deeply impressed upon the mind that it is a living inspiration to every thought we think. When every thought is inspired with an irresistible desire for greater things, every faculty of the mind will be kept up to the very highest point of efficiency and all the actions of the mind will work for greater things, thereby actually producing greater things. The higher the goal we have in view the greater will be the thoughts we think, provided the mind is animated with a strong, persistent desire to reach that goal. And great thoughts will invariably make a great man. To live in the strong faith that you are daily drawing nearer and nearer to your goal will not only carry you forward positively and steadily, but that faith will arouse those greater powers within you that can carry you forward. And here it is highly important to remember that it takes no more time or effort to work for great things than for small things. And he who works for great things will finally receive everything that he has worked for.

7. Create the elements of success in your own mentality by dwelling constantly in the atmosphere of success, advancement and perpetual increase. This is absolutely necessary, because the powers that make for success must exist m your own mind before you can become successful. So long as your own mind is a failure you cannot succeed in the external world because it is the mind that does things, and we do not gather figs from thistles. The mind is cause. If the effect is to be success the cause must be success; therefore all the elements of success must be created m the mind before success can be secured in the outer life of man. That is, all the actions of the mind must be made successful actions — actions that are inherently and actually constructive and that can produce results. By living in the mental atmosphere of advancement all the faculties of mind will begin to advance. The spirit of growth, attainment and achievement will animate every action and the entire mind will press on to greater things. This will make the mind more competent in every way and a competent mind is a successful mind. By living in the atmosphere of perpetual increase an accumulating process will be established in mentality. This process will increase all the powers and qualities of the mind and thus we shall have more elements that make for success. A mind that is a success in itself will produce success when practically applied in the tangible world, because like causes produce like effects. To establish in the mind therefore the constant thought of success is absolutely necessary to him who would succeed with a certainty in the work he has undertaken.

8. Expect the best, associate with the best and desire the best with all the power of life and soul. Stand for worth and do everything in your power to become more worthy. It is quality that counts and nothing is too good for him to receive who can produce quality. Build for yourself an attractive mind and keep your personal appearance in keeping as far as possible to do so. This is extremely important because a common appearance produces a common feeling, and he who feels common will steadily and surely go down in the scale toward inferiority. Be original, try to do things better than they have ever been done before. Never follow beaten tracks, not even in details. Find a superior method. You can if you make that an aim in everything you do. It is originality that produces greatness and greatness always produces success when practically applied.

Chapter 6

The Three-Fold Basis of Business Success

There are numbers of people in the world who believe that the door of opportunity is closed to the majority and that advancement is possible only to the lucky few. But in this they are wholly mistaken. The fact is the lucky few have made their own luck, and the many can do the same. To be numbered among the favored ones, however, the individual must be competent and must be able to make good, though these requirements are not beyond the reach of the many. Advancement is possible to all and anyone can improve himself when he knows how, and all can learn how.

The fact that the demand for competent men and women is very large everywhere and the fact that anyone may become competent places the future success of any person in his own hands. No individual therefore has anyone but himself to blame if he fails, but he can through his own individual efforts attain the greatest success that is possible to man. To attain a real and permanent success it is only a matter of understanding the principles upon which success is based and applying the laws through which practical results may be secured in one's chosen field of action. And as we are just as familiar with the principles that produce success as we are with mathematical principles there is nothing that can prevent success but the failure to apply those principles.

When these principles are systematically applied, that is, when the use of our faculties and powers is reduced to a science, the application of that science will produce success with a certainty in every individual case. The same causes produce the same effects, no matter who the person may be that applies those causes. We conclude therefore that every person who applies the science of success will positively succeed and every person can learn to apply this science. To begin, we must understand the basis of the science of business success and we find this basis to be three-fold, the first factor of which is work.

Work does things; and every stone in the temple of success is a deed well done. It is therefore evident that the more one works the greater die success will be, provided the work is real work. And we must not forget that there is work and work, the difference between the two being very great. To work does not simply mean to use up energy. To work does not mean to tear down men while they are building up things, for the work of the man should build up the man, as well as those things that the man is building. Too much of the work done has not produced results. It has simply used up energy. The loss of this energy has made man weak and has perpetuated the belief that work is hard on the system, but it is not work that causes the physical body to wear out. The worn out condition met so frequently among men and women is caused by the using up of energy. And between real work and the mere using up of energy there is a vast difference. In fact, there is nothing whatever in common between the two.

To proceed have no fear of hard work. It will not do you any harm, for real work does not produce weakness or weariness. On the contrary, it permanently increases the strength of the entire system. Real work generates energy just as rapidly as it consumes energy, provided the materials from which such energy is generated are supplied in abundance; and such materials may be provided through wholesome food, pure air and eight hours sleep out of every twenty-four. It is mere waste of energy, destructive or non-constructive work and strained or strenuous actions, worry and wrong thinking that cause the mind and body to wear out. But these can all be avoided; therefore, all manner of wear and tear can be completely eliminated from the human system.

The body is permeated with the mind. Every physical action is preceded by a corresponding mental action. It is therefore evident that to work properly the mind must be in the proper attitude; that is, the mind must hold itself in a certain position if all the actions of the personality are to continue in that same position. To illustrate this idea we need simply note the fact that the various faculties and forces of the person will not act in a state of harmony unless the mind holds itself in harmony during the action of those faculties and forces. In like manner, no action of the personality can be fully constructive unless the mind is in a constructive attitude at the time of that action. To state it briefly, the actions of the personality are governed by the attitudes of the mind. And since work is a series of actions, real work becomes possible only when the mind is held exclusively in those attitudes that are directly conducive to real work. This is a fact of extraordinary importance and can easily be demonstrated to be absolutely true, though anyone who is familiar with modern metaphysics will see at once that it is true. Detailed illustrations, therefore, will not be necessary in this connection.

To succeed is to move forward, and back of every forward movement there must necessarily be an abundance of good work. More work is necessary at frequent intervals if great success is to be attained, but no work ought to be hard in the sense that is wearisome or burdensome; and here we must remember that every moment of work should count. What is usually termed hard work is a full and thorough application of our energies, but such work will not be hard on the system so long as the mind is in perfect harmony with itself and its surroundings. We may therefore enter more work with pleasure, knowing that the more we work the more we shall accomplish; and also that such work will not be wearing on the system, but will on the contrary build up the system.

To make everything count that we undertake to do, the mind should continue in a constructive attitude; that is, all work should be entered into with the deep feeling that the work will not only produce things, but will also produce greater power and capacity in the one that works. In other words, make it a point to look upon your work as a continuous cause of physical and mental development and you will not only build up greater and greater success, but such work will also build up your system. Enter your work in this attitude and it will not only make your business a success, but it will make you a success. It will produce a fine man as well as a fine income.

Ability gives worth to things; and real success means the perpetual increase of worth, not only in the man's product but in the man himself. The greater the worth of the product, the greater the price that may he secured as the world wants good things and is willing to pay well to get them; but it is only the mind of ability that can produce good things. Work alone will do things, but the value of those things will depend upon how much ability was applied in the work. It is not a number of ordinary things that constitutes success. Success is the power to produce the extraordinary both in quality and in quantity. And success comes only through the practical application of a mind that is large as well as superior. However, those who do not have such a mind at the present time need not think that success is not in store for them, for ability can be developed even to a remarkable degree; though the first essential is to use thoroughly what ability we already possess.

To work successfully all work must be constructive to the highest possible degree, but it requires ability to so direct one's efforts that every action will do something worthwhile. The mind that lacks ability misdirects the majority of its actions; those actions therefore produce nothing while those actions that can be properly directed, usually fail to produce quality, for the fact is that no action can produce anything of real value unless there is ability m that action. And since success comes only through the production of good things ability becomes indispensable to him who would succeed in the best sense of that term.

To develop your business ability make the fullest use of what ability you now possess and devote as much time as convenient to the further development of that ability. Use your talents now, fully and thoroughly, whether you receive a high salary or not. If you are waiting to use your best talents until you receive a high salary you will never receive such a salary, and your talents will continue to lie dormant. By making the fullest use of the ability you now possess, you not only develop your ability by bringing out the best that is in you, but you prove to those who know you, that you are fully able to fill a larger place; and since competent men and women are in great demand everywhere, you will soon find a larger place waiting for you.

Demonstrate by your work, not by your words, that you are competent and you will have more opportunities for advancement than you can use. If you are in business for yourself the same law will hold without any exceptions whatever. The world wants good things. Therefore, produce them and let the world know what you can produce. You will soon find that your establishment will need enlargement. The world goes where they receive the best service. Supply that service therefore, by making the fullest and best use of your ability. You will find business in. abundance positively coming your way. The development of business ability is a subject that should receive most thorough attention and since scientific methods through which this ability can be developed have been discovered, every moment we give to this matter will positively count. Accordingly, those who are not competent, and who have heretofore been unsuccessful, need not be discouraged. It is just as natural to develop ability along any line as it is to develop muscle.

In addition to the full use of your present ability the mind should be kept in that attitude that is most conducive to the growth of the mind while present ability is being exercised. It is a fact that the proper application of ability will develop that ability during working hours just as the proper use of muscle will increase the size and power of that muscle. To exercise your ability m the proper mental attitude look upon your present work as a means to advancement. Constantly think of your work in this way and impress this thought so deeply upon your mind that whenever you think of your work you think of advancement. Through this attitude you will relate yourself to your work in such a way that everything you do will be used directly in promoting your own success; and what is just as important, when you think of your present work as a means to advancement you animate your work with the spirit of advancement. This will not only push your work, but it will cause you to do far better work, and better work invariably means advancement both in yourself and in your sphere of action.

Faith works up to greater things; and since real success means higher attainments and greater achievements faith becomes absolutely necessary to a truly successful life. It is the truth that no one ever pressed on to greater things without some degree of faith, and it is also the truth that the greatest men have had the largest faith. Faith as employed here, however, is not a belief about something. It is a mental attitude — the reaching out attitude. Faith is that something in man that is constantly breaking bounds, that is ever on the verge of greater things, that is ever working up toward the larger and the greater, and that knows through an interior insight how to use in the present those greater possibilities that are being discerned as the mind looks out toward the future. To be successful to a great degree you must be far sighted; that is, you must have that insight that knows how to do the right thing at the right time, and this insight is produced by the attitude of faith. When you have faith in the greater, your mind will constantly enter into the life and the power of the greater and will consequently gain possession of the greater. It is therefore simple to understand that the mind that works in the attitude of faith must unfailingly work up to greater things.

Faith will increase the clearness of the thought and the brilliancy of the mind because faith takes consciousness into the upper story of the mind where superior intelligence actually does exist. Faith awakens the higher and the mightier forces within us, and expands consciousness in every direction; the mind is thereby enlarged, mental capacity is increased and the essentials to greater ability supplied. Faith brings out the best that one may possess now. The man who has faith in himself therefore will be his best at all times. He will do his best no matter what his occupation may be and he who does his best in his present work will invariably be promoted to a work that is better. The man who has faith in his work will secure the best results from that work. Accordingly, he will pave the way for a greater enterprise; and by having faith in everything and everybody he will dwell mentally with the best that there is in life. This is extremely important because it is the mind that constantly concentrates upon the better and the greater, that will constantly work up to the greater and the better.

From the foregoing it will be clearly evident to all that the three-fold basis of a business science will necessarily be composed of these three factors — work, ability and faith.

Chapter 7

The Seven Factors in Business Success

It has been frequently stated, and wisely, that when the man is made right his work will take care of itself, but the problem with the average person is, how to proceed to make himself right. He may realize that his inability to accomplish as much as he has in mind is due entirely to his own shortcomings, but he does not always know what those shortcomings happen to be; and even though he should know, the question is where to begin to mend after some definite idea has been gained as to what constitutes the law of successful achievement.

Every person knows that self-improvement is the only key to success, but the nature of self-improvement is not clearly understood, and definite methods through which self-improvement may be promoted have not been worked out to a satisfactory degree. The reason why, however, can easily be traced to the fact that the psychology of life, thought and action has heretofore been given but little attention.

When the relationship that naturally exists between the man and his work is closely examined, we find that there are three great essentials to the most thorough expression of the man in his work, and these three are power, ability and originality. When we search for those elements that make man what he is, and that could, through greater development make him more than he is, we find the secret to be personality, character and soul. The man who desires to become more than he is, therefore, and who desires to promote real self-improvement must develop personality, character and soul, while the man who desires to make the best practical use of what he already is must develop power, ability and originality. When these six great factors are thoroughly developed and practically applied through the seventh great factor — system — success must inevitably follow.

To develop personality the man should be trained to think with every nerve and fiber in the entire human system. Every thought should be felt and deeply felt in every atom of one's being. And when this feeling is held in a poised, positive attitude personal growth and power will invariably develop. It is a well known fact that the strong, well poised personality is always selected for the best places in life because such a personality always produces the best impression. Such a personality always carries the stamp of quality and worth, therefore finds little difficulty in forging to the front. In the commercial world few things are more important than confidence; and there is nothing that inspires confidence so quickly and so completely as a well developed personality.

The strong personality feels deeply, is conscious of a great deal of life and power, but this power is always held in poise, and it is much power held in perfect poise that makes the personality what we wish it to be.

The development of character in connection with commercial success has been almost wholly ignored, but the fact is that every person who desires to make the most of himself simply must give character the most thorough development possible. Character is the power that directs all the forces and faculties in their constructive actions. It is character that keeps everything in what may be termed the straight or correct line of action. And it is such actions that produce the greatest results Character prevents the scattering of forces and the misdirection of forces; therefore the more character a person has the fewer will be his mistakes, and the more numerous will be those actions that count for something.

That element of life that we speak of as soul, is that finer something in the nature of man that gives superiority to everything through which it may be expressed. And since self-improvement implies the increase of superiority it is evident that the cause of superiority, that is, soul, becomes indispensable. No person can become superior or develop superiority in any of his talents unless he unfolds that finer something that is called soul whether die unfoldment be conscious or unconscious, though it is the conscious unfoldment and development that counts. The unconscious is always limited and is never certain.

To develop soul the first essential is to realize the meaning of soul and then try to feel the element of soul in every thought and action. To train consciousness to enter more deeply into the finer elements of worth, quality and superiority will aid remarkably in producing this finer feeling of soul, and when one begins to feel soul the constant unfoldment of more and more soul can be promoted with comparative ease.

No person should ever think of himself as inferior or as a mere limited human entity. On the contrary, every thought should be stamped with the realization of that superiority that does exist in the depth of real life, and every action of mind should aspire toward the acquisition of greater worth for every faculty, talent or power that may exist in one's being.

To think constantly of soul will increase the expression of soul, provided one thinks of soul as being the cause of quality and worth. But the right understanding of soul must be given in every thought or that thought will not convey the quality of expression desired. There is no power in the human mind that can promote development along any line as thoroughly as that of direct thinking. But in the average mind thinking is neither direct nor designed. Most thoughts are not animated by any purpose or any degree of quality, therefore convey no particular effect upon the mind. To employ this principle of direct thinking we should animate every thought with a thorough understanding of the quality that we desire to develop and we shall find that every thought we think will tend to develop the quality desired. To develop soul, therefore, the principle is to animate every thought with a deep and thorough understanding of soul, and then to give the feeling of soul to every thought. The result will be that every thought you think will give more soul to you.

The constant and harmonious development of personality, character and soul will promote a self-improvement that actually is improvement. The individual will not only become right, but will become more, and he who becomes more will accomplish more. In the practical application of the personality, the character and the soul that one may possess, the first essential is power, both mental power and personal power. It is power that does things. It is power that makes the ideal real. And it is power that causes our best ideas to become tangible achievements. Therefore to turn the best that is in us to practical account more power must be developed.

To increase one's power the first essential is to prevent the waste of the power already generated in the system. This is accomplished first through poise, and second through the constructive use of all the energies in the system. The principle is to turn every force into some building process. Even physical pleasures should be animated with the desire for attainment, and the forces employed in those pleasures will promote the development of one or more factors in the human system.

The second essential to the increase of power is to impress the desire for more power upon the subconscious side of every atom in one's being. It is the truth that every part of mind and body does contain more power in the potential state. More energy is latent everywhere in the human system than we have ever used or even dreamed of, and all of this energy can be brought out for practical use. To bring out this energy concentrate attention upon every part of the system and make that concentration deeply felt and strong. Impress upon every part of your personality all the power you are conscious of now, and you will thereby arouse the greater power that is latent within you. This method if practiced in conjunction with perfect poise will in a short time largely increase the power and capacity of the mind. And if practiced continuously there is practically no limit to the working capacity that may be secured thereby.

There are many methods for the development of ability that might be presented, but the simplest and most effective is that of the direct power of thought. To apply this method form in the mind as clear an understanding as possible of the real nature of that ability that you wish to develop. Then try to realize through mind picturing the nature of that ability and stamp that picture upon every action of mind. In other words, so think that every thought you think will be created in the exact likeness of the ability you wish to develop. Every thought has creative power, but that power will always create after the likeness of the thought itself. Therefore when every thought you think is an exact image of the faculty you wish to develop, the creative power of every thought will tend to produce or develop that ability. In the average mind, however, this creative power is almost entirely wasted because no thought is given a definite purpose. What one group of thoughts may build up another will tear down, while the majority of the thoughts we think do nothing but scatter their energies the moment they are produced.

When the mind is trained to think always of the most perfect understanding that can be formed of the ability that is to be developed, every thought that is produced will give its creative power to the building up of that ability. And as there will under such conditions be no thoughts to interfere with the building process it can readily be understood that such a method can develop ability even to a remarkable degree.

The development of originality depends upon the practical use of what may be gained from the imagination. To try to formulate practical plans, methods and systems from the many ideas that are constantly presented by the imagination is to continue the development of originality. To apply this principle the products of the imagination should be arranged and rearranged again and again until something practical is evolved, or until original ideas, plans and methods are produced in connection with one's line of work. And in this connection it is well to remember that the more attention we give to the practice of becoming more and more original, the more power and activity we give to the faculty of originality itself. In other words, we develop more and more originality the more we try to be original in all things.

After all the essentials in the building of mind, and the practical application of what is in mind have been provided, there is still another factor that may be added to the seven already mentioned; and this is nothing more or less than interior insight. It is not a separate factor however, in every case as it is more or less combined with several of the other factors mentioned; but it is a faculty that should be highly developed in every case, as it is this faculty that enables the mind to know how to do the right thing at the right time.

It is interior insight that gives foresight, that makes the man long-headed, so to speak, and that enables the mind to discern real opportunities whenever they appear. There are some minds that intuitively know genuine opportunities when they see them. Other minds almost invariably choose circumstances that have no possibilities whatever; and the difference lies in the development of interior insight. There never was a successful man who did not possess this insight to a great degree, whether he was aware of it or not. And there never was a great enterprise that was not engineered more or less by this faculty. Men and women who claim to be very practical may overlook this fact, or may call this insight by some other name, but it is the same insight nevertheless, and no great success is possible without it.

To develop this faculty make it a practice to use your insight, or at any rate to try to use it whenever information of any kind is desired; and train the mind to expect first hand information from this source on every subject. Do not permit the imagination to become too active, however, while this faculty is being employed because the clearest fact is discerned when the mind is acting in the upper story. A high and orderly development of this faculty will be found to be a rare achievement, and every mind that aims at greater things should give this matter not only thorough attention, but all the time that may be required.

Chapter 8

The Use of the Mind in Practical Achievement

Whatever our views of metaphysics may be, materialistic or idealistic, we all realize that it is the use of the mind that determines results in every undertaking. Back of muscle and brain there is mind, and how much the muscles and brains are to accomplish will depend upon how they are used, directed and applied by the mind. The mind is not only the power that controls and directs every action in mentality or personality, but the mind also determines the efficiency of every action.

It is therefore evident that an ignorant use of the mind will cause every action to be a perverted action, a detrimental action or an unsuccessful action, while the intelligent use of the mind will cause every action to produce with a certainty the very results that were originally intended. If an effort fails the cause may invariably be traced to the wrong use of the mind in the direction of that effort. No effort can possibly fail that is properly applied at the right time and place. This is certainly a self-evident fact, and since it is the mind that must make the application, the intelligent use of the mind becomes the one important factor in determining results, be the work purely physical, purely mental, or a blending of the two.

To train the mind to direct properly the various actions of the mentality or the personality, all the forces of mind should be concentrated continuously upon the purpose that is held in view. This will draw all the energies of the mind together into the working line, and as every action is produced by some form of energy it is evident that if all the energies are moving toward the object in view every action will work toward that object. Under such circumstances all the power of mind and body will be turned into the work that is being promoted and as all this power will have to pass through those faculties that are directly employed in that work, those faculties will steadily develop in ability and capacity. This will make you more competent than you ever were before, and the competent mind simply must succeed.

To concentrate all the energy of the mind upon a certain faculty is to develop that faculty. This has been demonstrated conclusively, but when that energy is practically applied in some constructive work while it is accumulating in that faculty, the development will be more rapid and the increased capacity will be permanent. This is what takes place when the mind turns all of its power upon the work it is doing now. Therefore, to use the mind in this way is to make present action directly instrumental in promoting further promotion. Through this law the doing of little things can prepare us for the doing of great things, and invariably will if all the power of mind is focused upon the work of the present moment.

The principal reason why the average person does not advance as he should is found in the fact that he gives only as much of his mental power to his work as may be necessary to do it fairly well. The rest of his power is scattered and wasted through aimless thinking, purposeless imagination, and a dividing and a subdividing of attention. Your present work is the motor-car that is to carry you forward. If you turn your power into the motor you will move forward rapidly, but if the greater part of your power is scattered your progress will t; slow. But it is the mind that directs or misdirects the power that is being generated in the human system. Therefore, whether all the power is to be well directed or not depends upon the use of the mind.

To concentrate the whole of attention upon the purpose that is being promoted becomes an easy matter through steady practice along this line, though it will become easier still if the most interesting viewpoint of this purpose is gained at the outset. We naturally concentrate all of our power upon that in which we are deeply interested, and we can find an interesting viewpoint in everything if we look for it. While we are looking for this interesting viewpoint the mind will unconsciously or subconsciously become interested in the subject Accordingly, we will proceed to concentrate without trying, and that is the best concentration of all.

To dwell mentally upon the idea of success or to keep the greatest imaginable success constantly in view, and to picture oneself upon the path of perpetual increase, these are matters of great importance. To think constantly of perpetual increase is to promote perpetual increase in your own ability and power, provided you are using thoroughly what ability and power you now possess. This is a great law, so great that it merits the constant attention of every aspiring mind. Through this law unlimited success is placed within reach of every person who really wants success, because the perpetual increase of ability and power will, if applied, produce a perpetual increase in attainment, achievement and tangible possessions.

To dwell mentally upon the idea of success and upon the life of success, is to produce the life and the power and the understanding of success in the mind itself. Such a mind will know success, what is conducive to success, and will have the power to push its ideas into successful action. To dwell mentally upon success will also train the mind to use its own faculties more successfully, and it will train those faculties to formulate successful plans, methods, and such systems of application as make for success.

To know what to do with present opportunities is one of the great essentials to attainment and achievement and the mind that dwells constantly in the very life and thought of success will develop that finer judgment that knows the successful side of everything. Such a mind can discern what is practical, and what is not, in every circumstance or possibility that may be considered, because being filled with the very spirit of success, it knows what has success in it and what has not. The mind that can discover successful plans and that knows how to apply them will positively succeed no matter what the circumstances may be. And to think success, work for success, and press on toward greater and greater success, is to open the mind to new methods for promoting success, and new systems for enlarging the range of one's individual success. Success, therefore, in fact, greater and greater success must follow with a certainty.

The mind should see only the successful side of everything, that is, the bright side, the rich side, the growing side, the side of new opportunities and the side of greater possibilities. This attitude of mind will keep all the faculties in the best working condition. The entire mind will be kept at the high water mark of ability, capacity and efficiency; confidence in one's self, in one's associates and in one's work will be complete; faith, that great essential to success will be high and strong, and a most excellent impression will be produced upon all minds with whom we may come in contact. The mind that lives in the upper story, so to speak, not only displays all its faculties and talents to the best advantage, but actually employs all its forces to the best advantage. Such a mind not only makes good now, but impresses everybody with the fact that it can do more just as soon as the opportunity is supplied; and the desired opportunity will not be withheld very long from such a mind.

To complain at any time or under any circumstances is a misuse of the mind. It causes the mind to fall down to its worst. To permit the mind to think of failure or impending trouble is to go down mentally into conditions of failure and trouble. This will cause the mind to become troubled, disturbed, and confused, and such a mind will make any number of mistakes, do nearly everything wrong and be its worst in nearly every sense of the term. To permit hard-luck thought of any description, or to listen to talk of that sort, will produce the same results; the mind will be taken down, and for the time being will become weak and incompetent.

To overcome these tendencies resolve to create your own good luck. Know that you can because it is true that you can. Then eliminate completely every thought, error or suggestion that implies anything to the contrary. The tendency to complain, or to expect hard luck, will almost invariably impress other minds with the belief that you are incompetent; in brief, that you are a failure or that there is something wrong with you. Successful minds, therefore, will have nothing to do with you, and instead of securing the best places in the commercial world you will have to go down and accept something that is ordinary or inferior.

The habit of complaining, or taking the dark view whenever anything goes wrong, will also impress your own mind with failure, and with the belief that you are incompetent. After a while you will begin to think that you do not amount to much, and when such thought begins to take possession of your mind you will soon be counted among those who have failed. If you wish to do greater and greater things you must think that you can, because when you think that you can, you develop the power that can. Thus in the course of time you will actually be able to do the very things that you thought you could do; so therefore it is safe to "hitch your wagon to a star."

To train your mind to work in perfect harmony with the elements and forces of success, try as far as possible to associate only with people who are successful or people who want success, who talk only success and who are living personifications of the very atmosphere of success. Every mental state should be a working power toward greater things and should be animated with the life that has within it the possibilities of greater things. No mental state therefore should be permitted that contemplates the lesser, that drifts toward the lesser, or that has the tendency to be satisfied to work only for the lesser. All thinking should be animated with the spirit of attainment and achievement, and every thought should deeply feel, and persistently feel, the desire to work with all its life and power for the very highest success you have in view.

Stand for the highest worth. Aim to realize greater and greater worth and daily impress upon every part of your mind the highest conception of quality and worth that you can possibly picture. This will develop superiority in every phase of mentality, and the result will be that superior mental power, superior talents and superior ability will inevitably follow. The mind that develops greater worth will gain the ability to produce things that have greater worth. The man with such a mind, therefore, will be worth more in the commercial world, his labor and his brains will command a higher price and his products will be in great demand. By increasing his own mental and personal worth he will increase the worth and the value of his work because the man himself is the cause, his work is the natural effect.

The inferior mind cannot expect to produce high priced products, nor can extraordinary achievements proceed from ordinary talents. He who would do the greater, therefore, must first, become greater; and he can become greater by giving his best ability to his present work and by using his present work through which to express all the worth, all the quality, all the capacity and all the power that he may now possess. In other words, by training his whole mind to apply itself thoroughly to everything he may undertake to do he will develop the whole mind. This will produce the greater mind, and the greater mind will soon have the privilege to do the greater things.

Another essential in turning the whole of the mind and the best there is in the mind into the efforts of today, is to be deeply interested in what you are doing today, and to have a deeply felt love or admiration for that work. This is not sentiment, but an exact scientific principle. The man who works simply for the wages he is to get will always get small wages because such a mind will not improve. In like manner, the man who remains satisfied with a small business, just enough to give him a living, will always continue in a small business, and his living will be cheap and ordinary. The fact is that such people do not turn all the powers of their mind into their work. They simply use enough mind to keep things going; the rest of their powers are wasted.

Make it a point, therefore, when you accept a position, or enter any kind of business, to love it; love it with all the heart and soul that you can arouse; and you will find this an easy matter when you know that your present work is the path to those greater things that your heart may wish for. When you deeply love your work you will naturally concentrate your whole mind upon your work, and you will use all your power in your work. This means better work and a more rapid development of your own ability and talent.

It is the truth that he who loves what he is doing today will be given something better to do tomorrow. He who gives his whole heart and his whole mind to little things will soon have the capacity to take charge of greater things, and he will also have the opportunity. To state it briefly, when you concentrate all your mental and personal power upon your present purpose you will accomplish that purpose because no one can fail who applies his whole mind to his work; and to use the whole mind constantly in everything we do is to develop the whole mind more and more. This means a greater and a greater mind to be followed invariably by still greater success.

Chapter 9

Practical Rules in Business Psychology

1. Have something to give to the world that is worth giving; something that the world wants. Your success depends not only upon your own efforts, but also upon the degree of appreciation that those efforts may have the power to call forth. No matter how good your work may be if it is not appreciated, results will be limited. You will be wasting a large portion of your time and you will benefit no one, not even yourself. To secure appreciation your object must be, not to give that which you think the world ought to want, but to give that which you know the world does want. Make it a point to please others and you will also please yourself. Thousands of brilliant minds fail entirely because they imagine their talents will be degraded if brought down to the wants of the world, but no talent will be brought down so long as it is used in promoting the welfare of others, no matter whether those others be cultured or not. Give your talents and your ability to those who need them, and make your efforts so simple that the largest number possible can appreciate what you are trying to do. Give the largest number what they need and what they want, and make what you give so worthy that everybody will want to take advantage of your service without being persuaded to do so.

2. Be determined to serve the world better in your line than it was ever served before. Whatever you do, know that it can be done better, and know that that better can be done by you. The fact that others have failed must not influence your mind or your conduct in the least. We are not in bondage to the shortcomings of others, nor the failures of the past. What we are determined to do we can do because we have the power. In this connection we must remember that there is no success that is greater than perpetual advancement in one's own ability to do the greater and the better, and there is nothing that gives more contentment or joy. To make the better one's goal and to cause all the energies of being, to work for that goal, is to enter the pathway to real success — the success that is success, and that perpetually reproduces itself in greater and greater success. To be determined to serve the world better than it was ever served before is to improve one's self and one's work in one's present vocation which will ere long open the way to a far more important vocation. He who is positively determined to do the best will positively have the opportunity to do the best.

3. Know that you can do what you want to do because there is no limit to the power that is latent within you. The greatest obstacle to higher attainments and greater achievements is the belief that the power we possess is limited and that the ability we possess is as large now as it ever will be. This obstacle, therefore, must be removed through the realization of the truth in this matter. The truth is that every form of ability can be developed indefinitely and that the powers of mind and soul are inexhaustible. To live in the perfect realization of that truth and to animate every thought and desire with the very spirit of that truth is to promote the development of every form of ability that we may be using now, and also to enlarge perpetually the capacity of mind so that a larger and a larger measure of power will be unfolded, perpetuated and expressed. When you inwardly know that you can do what you want to do, you place yourself in conscious possession of the power that can do what you want to do; and this knowing will steadily grow in mind as every thought is created more and more in the likeness of the truth just mentioned.

4. You will not go down so long as you do not permit your mind to go down. One of the great secrets of success is to keep the mind up even though everything else may seem to go down. If the mind persists in staying up, things will soon change and begin to come up again. This is a law that never fails, and if it was thoroughly applied under every circumstance it would prevent practically every failure in the world. The mind is the master, provided its mastership is exercised; and the way the mind goes everything else will go also. Things will follow very soon, if not at once, provided the mind holds fast to its high ideals and falters not. The mind that dwells constantly upon the bright sides will soon cause all things to leave the world of darkness and begin to create brightness. The mind that aims perpetually to realize higher attainments and greater achievements will cause all things to work together for the promotion of such attainments and achievements. The mind that continues in absolute faith even though every external indication points to certain failure — that mind will cause all things to change in their courses, to cease working for failure and to proceed to produce those very things that the mind believed with faith that it could secure. Permit nothing, therefore, to take the mind down, because if the mind persists in staying up, things will positively take a turn and come up also. Thus the threatening failure will terminate in a still greater success.

5. Know that your life is in your own hands; that you may therefore do with your life whatever you wish to have done. All power comes from life. To increase the expression of life is to increase the expression of everything that has real worth. And in him who has taken the expression of life into his own hands, the expression of life may be increased in any measure desired. When you know that your life is in your own hands you will begin to live the way you want to live, and the energies of your being will begin to work together for the promotion of that which you wish to have promoted; the scattering of forces will cease and all things will move toward the goal you have in view. But so long as your life is not in your own hands it will be more or less in the hands of environment. You will not live, therefore, for your own welfare and advancement, but you will live for every passing idea or notion that the shifting of circumstances may suggest. Real success, however, will be impossible in such a life, because to succeed in any achievement you must live for that achievement. But before you can live for anything definite you must realize that your life is in your own hands, and that you can live for anything by positively deciding to do so. Strictly speaking, it is not necessary to take your life into your own hands, it already is in your own hands. What is necessary is to cease giving it away to every whim or circumstance that may be passing by. Your life is your own. Keep it for yourself, therefore, because it was given to you to be used by you, and by you alone. Nothing else can use your life. Accordingly, when you scatter your life abroad you deprive yourself of that which no one else can use. To apply the truth in this idea, live constantly m the realization of the great truth that your life is your own and that you can turn all of its power into any channel that you may select. Then select the path that leads to real success. Live in that path with all your life, and the goal you have in view will positively be reached.

6. Begin where you are. Do perfectly what you are doing now, but keep the mind open constantly for greater powers and greater opportunities. To dream too much of the future is to neglect the present. And to be indifferent to the lesser while yearning for the greater is to continue to live in the lesser. Be ambitious, be determined to rise in the scale, but use all the force of that determination in perfecting and enlarging the sphere of the present moment. Make the present moment a great cause by turning all your power into the work of the present moment, and from that great cause will come great effects in the coming days. Every vocation, every environment and every circumstance contain possibilities that we may never have known. To work out these greater possibilities is to make the present moment a great beginning of a far greater future, but we cannot enter into the conscious possession of the hidden possibilities that the present moment may contain so long as we give our deep thought to the future and our superficial thought to the present. There is only one place to begin, and that is where we are living and working now. There is only one possibility upon which we can concentrate with success, and that is the possibility that the present moment holds in store.

7. Have great objects in view, but keep them secret. We give our greatest powers to those things that we think of as too sacred to mention. Never speak generally about those things that you wish to accomplish, unless it should be to those who are in perfect harmony with your ideas and plans. And under no circumstances should we speak of our higher ambitions unless the mind be in the upper story at the time. To speak or think of the great things we have in view while the mind is in ordinary or superficial states is to give a measure of inferiority to those things which may lessen results or even produce failure. Before those greater things are given thought, the mind should be elevated to the highest and most sacred places within, that consciousness can possibly realize, because while we are in those loftier states of thought we give immense power to that of which we may be thinking at the time. This is a law of extraordinary importance, and may be applied with remarkable results in any sphere of action. To think of your plans while in ordinary states of mind is to give only ordinary thought to those plans, and nothing can succeed that is not animated by something better than by mere ordinary thought. The same is true when we are doing something of exceptional value. It will be a failure unless we think of it all as being too lofty and too important to be dealt with except in the very highest and strongest states of mind. The higher the action of mind the greater the power of mind. And the more sacred the thought the higher the action of that thought. This is the law, and to those who have great and worthy objects in view this law is positively indispensable.

8. Dwell mentally with the superior, the marvelous and the limitless. Superficial consciousness and every phase of superficial thinking must be entirely avoided or the development of ability will be retarded. Success depends not only upon ability, but upon the constant improvement of ability. And the more closely the mind is brought in touch with the elements of quality and superiority the more rapidly will every faculty develop. To dwell mentally with the superior is to unfold superiority. To dwell mentally with the marvelous is to develop the imagination, the power of originality and to inspire the mind with those ascending tendencies that invariably lead to greatness. And to dwell mentally with the limitless is to place the mind in that position where it can constantly draw upon that power that is limitless. Success, therefore, and great success, must invariably follow.

9. Believe in justice. Establish yourself firmly upon the principle of absolute justice and an exact equivalent, and you will receive what you deserve. Never desire to get something for nothing, as such a desire will decrease your own capacity by retarding the expression of yourself. When you desire to get something for nothing you desire to give nothing in return. You thereby hold back a part of your own ability, which means retarded growth. Have absolute faith in justice and you will secure justice from everybody and under every circumstance. This is a law that cannot fail, for even though it may not prove itself at once, it finally will in every instance bring to every individual what actually belongs to that individual.

10. Your own will come to you provided you live absolutely upon the principle of the exact equivalent, but your own will be only as great as yourself. Therefore, if you wish to increase the quality and the quantity of that which is coming into your life, you must first increase the worth and the power of your own life. By becoming larger than you are you will receive more than you do. Things that are worthwhile will accumulate in your world in proportion to your ability to do that which is worthwhile; that is, when that ability is thoroughly and constantly applied.

11. Real success implies the advancement of the individual himself and the advancement of the world in which the individual may live. It means the building of a greater man and the promotion of greater achievements in the environments of that man. Real success does not simply mean the accumulation of things, but in the development of a personality so strong and so great that it must invariably attract great things, and as many great things as may be necessary to promote the largest and the richest state of existence possible. In the promotion of real success there must be two leading objects in view. The first must be to make yourself greater than you are, and this object must always come first. You are the cause of your own success. Therefore, the greater you are the greater will be your success, because a great cause will invariably produce a great effect. The second object must be to promote higher attainments and greater achievements, and this will naturally be fulfilled when the growing mind is constantly expressed in constructive thought and effective action. The idea is to become much and you will do much; and he who does much will receive much because like invariably attracts like. Causes and effects are always similar and the law works both ways. The very same law that brings disaster will, if reversed, bring us everything that the heart may desire.

12. Air castles are indispensable, but they must be built upon a foundation composed wholly of your own worth. The only air castles that fall are the ones that have nothing but dreams upon which to stand. The man who is positively determined to do what he aims to do, and who will not only give his whole life, but the best that is contained in his life, to the purpose he has in view, may build any number of air castles. They will all stand the test of life, and he will have the pleasure to really dwell in them all in days that are soon to be. He who is determined to make good will shortly have the power to make anything. His ambitions, therefore, cannot be too lofty nor too strong; neither can his castles in the air be too gorgeous. All his dreams will come true because he does not only dream dreams, but actually goes to work and makes those dreams come true. The principle, therefore, is to hitch your wagon to a star; but be sure that the chain is strong. Thus you will scale the heights and there will be no fall.

13. Everything you do will count. Nothing is lost, but whether it is to work for you, or against you, will depend upon what you were working for, when the thing in question was created. However, those adverse forces that are lurking in the mistakes of the past may be transmuted and may be directed to work just as faithfully for you as they previously worked against you. He who is positively determined to do what he is ambitious to do can change everything in his favor, though this determination must be animated with a ceaseless and persistent desire for the realization of the goal in view; and must be literally alive with the spirit of that faith that is faith.

14. Become a strong, positive center in your own world, and constantly improve upon the worth of that center. The law of attraction is the basis of all real success; therefore, the greater the center of attraction which is you, yourself, the greater will be those things that will naturally gravitate into your world. You cannot naturally take what belongs to others, for you can attract only what belongs to yourself, and that alone can belong to you that is an exact equivalent of what you are and what you have done. To become a positive center in your own world harmonize all the elements and forces in your own being by constantly feeling the harmony that exists within you in the real principle of harmony. Develop poise and train all the energies of your mind and body to move towards the limitless within. Realize that you can draw upon the forces that exist all about you and feel the constant accumulation of those forces in your entire system. Through this process you will awaken the greater powers within you and you will thus attract the finer forces from without. You will therefore become a center of great power both in mind and personality; and much does attract more.

15. Being and doing must be the objects in View. To live a great life in the midst of great attainments and great achievements — that is real success. And the beginning of such a success can be made now by using, according to the science of success, every opportunity that may be at hand now. He who makes the best use of what is at hand now will soon have the opportunity to use something better; and since this process may be perpetuated indefinitely there is no end to the greatness of success that is real success. The fundamental principle in the science of real success is the building of greatness in mind tend the use of that greatness in the building of the better, the higher and the superior in the world of man, both in the physical world and in the mental world.

Chapter 10

The New Way of Doing Things

The world admires the man who does things, and therefore imitates as much as possible his mode of thought and action. But to try to do what another is doing will not be productive of results unless the same ability and capacity is secured. Mere external imitation, therefore, is useless; but internal imitation may prove highly profitable, and such an imitation tends to develop the ability and the capacity required. He who would do things worthwhile must develop the power that can do those things, and to develop that power he must do things in the within before he attempts to do things in the without. The doing of things in the within, however, has been almost wholly neglected in our ceaseless endeavor to secure immediate results in the tangible world. And for this reason tangible results that are really worthy have not been as numerous as we should like, while shallow minds have been too numerous.

A fact of importance to consider in this connection is this, that when we concentrate the whole of attention upon the doing of things that can be seen we cause the mind to dwell more and more on the surface until all mental action becomes superficial; and when this condition appears there will not be sufficient depth nor power in the mind to do the things worthwhile. This same condition will appear more or less in the mind of the person whose sole desire is to be practical; that is, he will in time bring the mind so completely out into the objective that consciousness will come out away from everything in mentality that has richness, quality and worth.

When the mind gives the whole of attention to external things it will necessarily fail to give sufficient thought to those inner qualities of mentality that alone can deal intelligently with things. Such a mind therefore will try to do things without possessing the knowledge and the power that can do things. There is such a thing as becoming so completely absorbed in your purpose that you forget to provide yourself with those essentials that alone can fulfill that purpose. In other words, you become so carried away with your desire to overcome the enemy that you forget your ammunition. Nothing worthwhile can be accomplished without mental capacity, and every mode of mental action that tends to keep the mind at work on the surface alone will cause the mind to become shallow.

The mind that can do things is the mind that is trying to do things both in the within and in the without. By acting upon the internal phases and elements of mentality, capacity and power are developed; and by acting upon tangible things that capacity and power are turned to practical use.

When this new method of doing things, that is, acting both in the inner and in the outer worlds is continued, the development of mental capacity as well as practical ability will be steadily promoted. Such a mind, therefore, will not only do things, but will constantly do better things and greater things. That man, however, who neglects to do things in the within while using what power and capacity he may possess in the doing of things in the without will gradually diminish that power and capacity, and his work will accordingly decrease in value. His practical ability will exhaust itself because he has failed to renew and develop the power of that ability; but this failure is found in the great majority. Therefore, instead of the added years bringing added power, increased ability and greater efficiency, the reverse is nearly always the case. Instead of moving forward with the years, the average man gradually deteriorates in mind and efficiency. And the reason why, is found in the fact that the constant development of the great within is neglected.

The man who gives his whole attention to the accumulation of wealth may gain wealth for a while if he originally possessed accumulative ability; but the ceaseless concentration of the mind upon mere things will in the long run cause the inner mentality to become barren, and there will be no further increase in ability or power. This man's power to accumulate wealth, therefore, will diminish; and besides, he will discover that since his real mind is barren he cannot enjoy the wealth he has produced.

Happiness does not come from things, but from the appreciation of things, whether they be physical or metaphysical, real or ideal. Appreciation, however, is a flower that grows only in the garden of the finer mentality; therefore, he who has neglected the finer things in mind and thought has lost capacity for real enjoyment.

The mind that has visions, that dreams, dreams, that lives largely in the ideal and that frequently soars to heights sublime may be looked upon as impractical or worthless, but it is such minds that have given us everything in life that is worthwhile. The mind that explores the wonders and the splendors of the great within, that is, the higher and the finer fields of the mind — it is this mind that discovers music, art, literature and invention; and without these we would still be living in caves. In those same interior realms man finds philosophy, ethics, religion, metaphysics and science, and when he fully understands these he will be able to master himself and place the universe at his feet.

It is evident, therefore, that the path to greatness and the path to the doing of great things invariably leads directly into or through the great within, because it is in the vastness of interior mentality that we find all the limitless possibilities that are latent m man. He who would do things, therefore, that are really worth doing, must place his mind in perfect touch with the finer source of power, capacity and ability. In other words he must try to do things in the within as well as in the without. The possibilities of the within must be awakened and developed, and then practically applied in the field of tangible things.

In this connection, however, we must remember that the mind that acts solely upon the within is no better than the mind that acts solely upon the without. The vision must come first, but the idea that the vision reveals must be applied in real and practical life. When this inner capacity has been gained, or as it is being developed, all the power of that capacity must be utilized constructively in tangible life. What is not turned to use is wasted, and the mind that wastes its power will soon lose its capacity to produce power.

To become proficient in the new way of doing things we should work daily in the two worlds, the inner mental world and the outer practical world; the world of greater possibilities and the world of greater things; the world of ideals and the world of tangible results. There are thousands of minds that have discovered superior ideas in the larger fields of their mentalities, but they have taken no steps toward applying those ideas. And there are thousands with remarkable mental capacity who are making no use whatever of the powers of that capacity. These are minds that have begun to do things in the within, but have not begun to do things in the without. Therefore, no results of any value to anybody are forthcoming.

It is a fact that should be well remembered that no process of development has actually produced development until that power that is being developed can produce tangible results. In other words, no mental attainment is a permanent attainment until it can express itself in actual achievement. On the other hand, no great achievement is possible until the corresponding attainment has been developed, and since attainment constitutes inner mental capacity, power and ability, while achievement constitutes the actual producing of external results, it is evident that the doing of things, both in the within and in the without is absolutely necessary.

Every day should have its visions as well as its tangible deeds. Certain periods should be given every day to the concentration of attention upon the great within with a view of awakening new possibilities of mind and thought. And every day these new possibilities should be worked out in actual use. He who would do things — things worth doing — and who would continue to do greater and greater things, must live a whole life and not simply a half a life. That person, however, who lives only in the practical is living only one-half of his present sphere of existence, though the same is true of him who lives only in the world of visions and dreams.

The life that is full and complete — the life worthwhile — the growing life — is the life that dwells both in the subjective and in the objective; that develops daily the limitless powers of the great within, and that applies those powers every day in the great without. It is such a life that does things that are of real value both to the individual and to the world; it is such a life that has found the new way of doing things, and it is such a life that will ever continue to do greater and greater things.

Chapter 11

How Great Gains Are Realized

Though it may seem paradoxical, nevertheless it is true that the man who works for himself alone is not working for himself alone. For the fact is that the more you are concerned about your own personal gain the less you will accomplish, and the less you accomplish the less you gain. Great gains come through great achievements, but great achievements do not come through the mind that has no higher goal than the working out of a mere personal aim. The man who works for a great idea, even to the extent of forgetting personal gain is doing more to promote personal gain than he could possibly do in any other manner. On the other hand, the man who works for a great idea solely because he knows he will secure personal gain thereby is not working exclusively for his own gain. His own gain may be his original purpose, nevertheless before he goes very far he will find himself promoting the gain of the entire race.

Proceed with a great idea in view and you will do more for yourself than you could do through any other course. But in any case what you are doing for yourself will be insignificant compared with what you are doing for the race. Therefore no person can be called selfish who is promoting a great purpose in the world. Though his personal gain may be large still he is giving more to the world in proportion to his gain than any other person whose purpose in life is of a lesser degree.

The man who carries out a great idea benefits everybody, therefore does not work solely for himself; but the man who has no other aim than to get something for himself does not benefit anyone, not even himself. And the reason why is found in the fact that when you are working solely for yourself you are placing in action only a very small part of yourself.

Work for a great idea and you arouse great ideas in your own mind. Great ideas produce great thoughts and great thoughts produce great men. Therefore the man who thinks great thoughts must necessarily become a greater man, and the simplest way for anyone to form the habit of thinking great thoughts is to work for a great idea. When you work simply for yourself or for your own personal gain your mind will seldom rise above the limitations of the undeveloped personal life; but when you are inspired by some great purpose, some extraordinary project, all your thoughts break bounds; your mind transcends limitations; your consciousness expands in every direction; and you find yourself in a new world, a great world, a wonderful world; dormant powers, faculties and talents become alive, and you discover yourself to be a larger man by far than you ever dreamed yourself to be.

Whatever your present work may be have some great purpose in view. Never permit yourself to settle down to mere prosaic existence. Dream of extraordinary attainments and do all you can both physically and mentally to move forward now toward that superior goal that your visions have revealed to your mind. Never be dissatisfied with temporary conditions in the present and do not resist what appears to be fate, but do follow the light of the greater vision no matter where it may seem to lead. When you are so situated that there seems to be no opportunity for advancement do not imagine that nothing but an ordinary life is in store for you. Have a great idea in view; think of it, dream of it, work for it, live for it. Enter so completely into the superior world of that great idea that all your thoughts become extraordinary thoughts. Gradually you will grow into the likeness of the great thoughts you think, and ere long you will become so large that you will break the shell of your present limitations. Then you will find yourself in a new world where opportunities are so rich and so numerous that you cannot possibly use them all.

There are worlds and worlds of opportunities all about us that are waiting for men and women who are sufficiently competent to take advantage of them. Therefore make yourself a little larger than you are and you will receive a thousand welcomes from those worlds. But first you must begin to think great thoughts, and great thoughts can originate only in that mind that lives for something infinitely larger than the personal self. You cannot bring out the greatness within you, unless your purpose in life is so large, so vast and so immense that all the elements of your being are drawn irresistibly toward the supreme heights of unequalled attainment.

The present may seem to hold nothing in store for you, but that need not concern you in the least. Work for a great idea. If you cannot work for it in the real, work for it in the ideal; but do work for the greatest ideal that you can possibly picture, and work for it every moment of your existence. You will thereby enlarge, expand and develop your mind constantly and ere long you will find yourself in the company of those who have been chosen for greater things. No matter how empty the present may seem to be there is a way out, and to find the way out simply follow the light of some great idea.

To work for a great idea is to work yourself up toward the greater, the larger and the superior in all things, and you will not continue this upward movement very long before you enter the great world of opportunities. Then you may choose what you would do, where you would go and what kind of a life you prefer to live. The drawing power of a great idea is irresistible. Place yourself in the strong current of this power and you will positively move toward greater and better things. To think great thoughts occasionally, however, is not sufficient. Every mind has moments when consciousness soars to empyrean realms, but those moments are not numerous in the average mind, and in most instances they are purely sentimental. They are not inspired by some great purpose or some extraordinary project that we have resolved to carry out; therefore, they do not awaken the greatness that is within us, nor do they call forth the limitless powers that are latent in the superior nature of man.

To produce the results we have in view our great thoughts must be in the majority, and they must be animated with a deep, strong desire to reach the very highest heights that the mind can possibly picture. We are not thinking great thoughts unless we are thinking the greatest thoughts that we can possibly create, and we are not working for a great idea unless we are working for the greatest idea that the most lofty moments of the mind can possibly reveal.

We may now be engaged in a great work, we may now be connected with a great enterprise where opportunities for advancement are very large and try numerous, but that is no reason why we should 4e satisfied to keep our minds in the circumference of that enterprise. In fact, no matter how large the world in which you may be living now, if you wish to expand and develop your mind you must fix your attention upon a still greater world. No matter how large your present opportunities may be, if you wish to become a greater man than you are you must work for a far greater purpose than that which your present opportunities can possibly contain. Wherever you are, in a small world or a large world, have something greater still and you will invariably rise in the scale.

Do not be content to continue as you are, even though you have gained all your wants, because beyond what appears to be everything worthwhile to you, there is more, and this more is for you. When you are working for a great idea, everything that comes to you as a natural product of that great idea is your own, no matter how much it may be. You have not deprived anyone of anything through your efforts. Besides, what you are gaining, others may gain in the same way. The riches of the universe are limitless and any mind that begins to work for greater things will soon work up into greater things, and in the world of greater things there is always abundance. Quantity is unlimited, quality is unsurpassed and perpetual increase is the law. Realizing these facts, do not work simply for yourself. Work also for the greatest idea that your mind can possibly picture. You will thereby scale the heights and in consequence will do more for yourself than you possibly could in any other manner. In addition, you will add immeasurably to the welfare of the world.

In this same connection there is another idea that should be noted and applied with care, and it is the correct idea concerning the minding of one's own business. To succeed in any business, it is necessary to mind that business properly, but no man can mind his own business properly so long as he minds no business save his own. He who knows nothing but his own specialty does not know his own specialty; and he who finds interest in one thing only has too small a mind to know what that one thing really is. The larger and broader your mind the better you can care for your own business, and to broaden your mind, be interested in the progress of all good business. Do not divide your attention, nor scatter your forces, but live in that lofty mental world where you can have a comprehensive view of all things at all times.

The small, narrow, submerged mind can see nothing but his own, therefore fails to do much with his own because every part depends more or less upon the whole. The large mind, however, can grasp the elements of everything that is conducive to growth, advancement and success, and naturally incorporates those elements in his own special work. The man who would succeed in the largest and the best sense must enter into the consciousness of universal success. That is, he must place himself in touch with everything that does succeed, and must enter into the life of that power that is back of every successful enterprise. But he cannot do this unless he takes an active interest in the best and the largest success of everybody.

To take a real interest in the success of everybody is to develop a strong desire for the success of everybody, and the stronger our desire for the success of others the stronger becomes that power that produces success in ourselves. There are few things that are more potent in the awakening of power than that of a strong desire for the results of that power. Therefore a strong and constant desire for the greatest possible success for everybody will naturally develop in ourselves the largest measure of that power that makes for a great success.

When we mind nothing but our own business we call into action only a small part of the mind, but when we take a living interest in all business we call into action practically every part of Ike mind. New power is thus awakened, and if our concentration is good we can turn all of that new power into our special work, thus adding remarkably to our actual working capacity. It is therefore profitable in a certain sense to mind everybody's business, that is, to keep your mind in sympathetic touch with everybody's business. But it is not only profitable, it is the mark of real manhood. To be deeply interested in the welfare of others is an indication of superiority, and to give a great deal of thought to the promotion of the welfare of others is a means toward the development of superiority. The man who minds his own business only is a very small man, and his world is so shallow and contracted that he will gain very little of those things in life that are really worthwhile. Though he may gain riches he will not gain the power to appreciate what riches can procure, which is highly important because we can enjoy only that which we can appreciate; and it is only the large lofty mind that can appreciate the real worth of those things that actually add to the value and joy of life.

In minding the business of others, however, we must not meddle or interfere. Each individual is free to do his own work in his own way, but whenever we can improve the conditions that surround the work of the individual we should count it a privilege to do so. We are our brother's keeper in a certain sense, and we shall find that if all work in harmony trying to promote the welfare of each individual, the whole of the race, as well as each part, will be far better off than when we all work singly, trying to reach our own selfish goal, regardless of what happens to others.

To develop the individual is the supreme purpose, and to give to each individual all that he has earned or produced, no matter how much larger it may be than that of anyone else, is the true principle of justice. But both the development of the individual and his personal gain can be promoted to far greater advantage when he works in harmony with all, trying to add to the welfare of all.

The man who cares only for himself may gain the possession of things, but he will lose those elements of mind and soul through which he can enjoy things, and instead of promoting his progress he will retard it. Selfishness has the tendency to contract; therefore the selfish mind becomes smaller and smaller until its capacity both for work and happiness is reduced to nothing. The man, however, who cares for everybody will live in the universal and will enter into harmony with powers that are limitless. He will thereby not only gain possession of more things and better things, but will also gain the conscious appreciation of the finer elements of things; and it is this consciousness that gives true richness and true happiness to life.

There is no life that is greater or more beautiful than the life that has lived in the universal, that is, in the highest and deepest sympathetic touch with every person, with every enterprise and with every ideal. Such a life will expand and develop all the powers of the mind and make man great indeed; and the great mind will attain much, achieve much, gain much and enjoy much. This universal sympathy, however, must not be sentimental. It must be strong and constructive and must aim, not only to add to the welfare of everybody, but also to gather from every source the very best that we can use in our own individual world. It must be a mutual giving and receiving on the largest possible scale. In that manner everything that comes into life may be as large in quantity as we may desire, and as high in quality as we can appreciate and enjoy. Thus the present moment will be full and complete, and the greatest gains both in thoughts and in things will be realized.

Chapter 12

The Psychological Moment

When all the elements of those circumstances, conditions, forces, environments and opportunities that surround a personal life are about to meet in a favorable climax, we have what is called the psychological moment. It is psychological because the interior powers, the higher powers, the superior powers — in brief, the best powers that are active at the time are on the verge of gaining a decisive victory over limitations and things. At such a moment the mind and soul approach the superior and all the elements and forces concerned are ready to obey. All things pertaining to the exterior have been drawn into the onward current of those things that act from the interior and everything is about to give up its power for the promotion of the predominating purpose.

When all things in your life have come to that state where they can work together for you and bring about a speedy realization of your leading object in view, then you have entered the psychological moment. What to do at such a time is of the utmost importance. If you can properly handle the psychological moment the dreams of your life will come true, but if you cannot, years and years of hard work may be lost, and much of it will have to be done over again.

A psychological moment comes to races, to nations, to armies, to parties, to communities and to every individual person who is alive with some definite purpose in view. To find the cause of the psychological moment is not always possible, but it is usually an effect of much thought and effort along a certain line combined with present powers and such conditions as predominate at the time. The psychological moment can therefore be produced by anyone who knows how and who will take the time. And everybody should learn how, and should take the time, because it is only through the psychological moment that really great things are done at the right time.

When the psychological moment comes the time is ripe for your particular action. The world is ready to appreciate what you intend to do, and all the forces and elements of life are at hand to aid you to a successful issue of the great undertaking you have in mind. To take advantage of the psychological moment is to do things at the right time, when everybody wants you to do it, and when everything wants to help you do it.

The importance of paying attention to the psychological moment is very evident when we know that thousands of great things have been attempted before the race was ready to cooperate. And it was therefore seeds scattered upon stony ground where no results were secured. In like manner, thousands of great things have been attempted while the circumstances, forces and elements were adverse, and these through their adverseness perverted such actions as were applied; those actions, thereby, either became detrimental or were neutralized entirely.

When a great man has acted at the wrong time and has acted in vain, we find that instead of becoming a great light in history he has either been absolutely forgotten or is remembered only with contempt. It may sometimes seem difficult, however, to wait for a great moment, but it is better to wait and then do something of worth than keep on trying at the wrong time and never accomplish anything. But when we speak of waiting for the psychological moment we do not mean that that moment will appear of itself at a certain time to every individual. On the contrary, it is something that we ourselves must create. Therefore, if we have some great purpose in life we should begin at once to create the psychological moment through which that purpose can be brought forward and realized to the very highest degree.

We cannot single handed make the world over, and we cannot at once make the race appreciate our efforts, but we can gradually bring ourselves into such perfect harmony with the world that all will appreciate our efforts in a measure. And we can gradually bring ourselves into such united action with all the elements and forces of life that all of these will come to our aid and work together to promote the purpose we have in view. The wise man will not try to force upon the world what the world cannot now receive. He will do now what can be appreciated now, and in the meantime he will enter into more perfect harmony with the world that all concerned may understand each other better.

The wise man will not undertake difficult things until he realizes that all the circumstances are ready to work with him, because he knows that if the circumstances are not ready to work with him he will fail. Therefore, instead of defying circumstances as so many do, the wise man proceeds to secure the cooperation of his circumstances. He enters into more perfect harmony with the powers that be. He meets half way those conditions that do not understand his purpose. When things will not go his way he goes their way for a while until a better acquaintance is secured; then all things are more than willing to go his way because they have discovered the superiority of his purpose in life.

Before we undertake anything we should prepare the way. We should secure the cooperation of all the elements of life and should secure the appreciation of the world in which we expect to act. In other words we should first create the psychological moment. Sometimes this moment can be produced m a short time, and then again it may take years.

But what is time compared with such deeds as may change the course of the entire race and live for countless periods of time?

To produce the psychological moment, have a strong purpose and keep this purpose uppermost in mind regardless of what may be said or done. Believe that you can carry out that purpose in the fullness of time, and permit nothing to disturb that belief in the least. Hold fast to your belief as if it were life itself, until all thoughts and actions come to recognize that belief as supreme. Whenever any purpose in your life comes to be recognized by your thought as supreme, all thoughts and all actions will begin to work for the promotion of that purpose. Everything in your life will move in the direction of that purpose and will help you work toward the goal in view. And when all your thoughts begin to work for a certain great purpose all your circumstances will begin to move in the same direction, gradually giving more and more power to the good work and steadily becoming more and more favorable.

The stronger you become in your determination to promote that purpose the stronger will be your life and your thought moving in the same direction.

And the more power your personality applies in this direction the sooner will all your circumstances and environments fall into line and turn over all their powers to you. We all know that this is true and we all know why. No further analysis therefore is required, but the fact that such is the case is of enormous importance to us. A strong soul with a powerful mind, living, thinking and working for the promotion of a great and worthy purpose, will soon cause all the elements and forces in his life move toward the great climax. It will not take him long to turn fate, to transform adversities, to change tendencies and thus cause all the powers of his life to work with him and for him. To him the psychological moment will soon come and when it does come he can fulfill his great purpose and cause his cherished dream to come true. It is in this way that great deeds are done, deeds that never die, but that continue as endless inspirations to all the world.

Many minds set out with great aims in life, but they do not continue faithfully. They lose courage and often cease for years to work for those aims; but the psychological moment does not come in this way. It does not come by itself. It is something that we must create. It is the climax of months or years of thought and effort in a certain direction. Therefore, if we permit our high purpose to rest, nothing will be done toward producing the psychological moment for that purpose. The great moment comes when we have marshaled all the powers within us and about us, and brought them all together ready to act at once and in unity in giving their all to the purpose we are just about to fulfill. When all the elements, forces and circumstances in a person's life are brought together and made to act in perfect unity, and at the right time and place, it is evident that nothing can prevent that person from doing something great and very remarkable. The average person seldom acts under favorable circumstances and hardly ever secures the cooperation of all the forces in his life. Great deeds, therefore, cannot be expected through his efforts.

To produce the psychological moment have a great purpose and live constantly for that purpose no matter what may transpire. Bring every thought and action into unity with that purpose as rapidly as you can and steadily direct all the powers of your being to work for the coming of the great day. Circumstances and environments will soon respond to your irresistible determination and will soon go with you turning all their energies upon the one purpose in view.

A resolute determination that cannot be shaken, combined with high aims, abundance of faith and positive actions — these are factors that will bring the psychological moment to anyone and bring it speedily. But we must bear in mind that after we have chosen our purpose we must live, think and work for it constantly, and not fall back for a single moment. When you establish a strong tendency in a certain direction everything in your life will soon establish the same strong tendency and when all these tendencies are speeding forward, aiming at the same goal, the climax will soon come. Then you are in the psychological moment, all things are ready to act upon your word, and through their united action they will be fully able to do that for which they have assembled. The moment may not last long — a few days, a few weeks, or at times a few months. Frequently such moments last but an hour, but in great undertakings that involve many circumstances the time is usually prolonged to several months, or years.

When the moment has come, however, you must act and act properly or the efforts of years will be lost. All things have come your way, not to do something unbeknown to you, but to do something for you. And that something must correspond with the original purpose that brought about the psychological moment. It need not be exactly the same purpose, but it must be a kindred purpose. When the great moment appears you may discover that you can act to better advantage by turning all your energies toward a slightly different plan, but this plan must be in harmony with the original idea or the forces assembled cannot assist you. However, you must act and act in the best manner that you possibly know and this is especially true with regard to the actions of your mind. As you think at this time so will be your interior forces, and as your interior forces are, so are those forces that act in your environment. All things, therefore, have come to follow your word, but without your word or action they can do nothing.

To do the best thing possible at this time have unlimited faith in yourself. Have unlimited faith in everybody that is in any way connected with the purpose in view, and have unlimited faith in all the opportunities, conditions and circumstances that now are with you. View everything from the very highest place you can reach. Be your best. See yourself at your best and think of everything as it is while at its best. Do not criticize anything or anybody. Your object is to get the very best out of this great opportunity and you must not burden the mind with a single adverse thought. If you are not doing your work as well as you wish, or if others are not proving themselves equal to your high ideal give no thought to this deficiency. You will certainly take a long step forward when this moment is finished, and others will do likewise, but every critical thought will act as an obstacle to the greatest result.

Place yourself in the highest and the most harmonious relationship with all things. You must meet everything on the mountain top, because if you are on the heights all your helpers will come up also, and will thus produce that which is rare, worthy and superior. During the psychological moment you are the great master of the situation. As you go so will everything about you go because all things have come to go your way. What you want done that will be done because all things have come to act upon your word. It is therefore of the greatest importance that you occupy a very high place in thought, purpose and action. You must appear at your best, feel your best and recognize your own real superiority.

Your own thoughts become patterns and must therefore be supremely high. Your own actions determine the action of mighty forces and creative powers and must therefore be in harmony with all that k lofty, perfect and true. Do not for a moment lose sight of your purpose, and in the midst of the great moment be more determined than you have ever been before to gain the great goal.

When the psychological moment is approaching many minds make it a practice to relax their efforts, thinking that since things are coming their way the results will be forthcoming without any further personal attention; but this is a serious mistake. Things are coming your way because you have drawn them into your path and they are coming to carry out what you wished to have done when the climax comes. If you leave the field of action the great assembly will have no leader and can therefore do nothing. Accordingly they will soon scatter and you will have lost one of the great opportunities of your life. Thousands of minds have left the field of action at the approach of the great moment, believing that things would come right because indications pointed toward a favorable climax. Thus they lost completely because they did not recognize the psychological side of the moment. And it is the psychological side that is the one most important side.

When this great moment comes all things in your life are brought together to obey your will. And you must be in the very midst of all these things to give the proper word of command. Therefore, when the great climax is approaching have more faith than you ever have had; be more determined than you ever were, and think higher thoughts than you ever thought before. Though you are not to criticize others at the time, still you must bring yourself up to the very highest point of perfection possible. The higher you are in the world of power, superiority and worth the greater will be the results when the expected climax does come. Depend, therefore, upon higher power and relate yourself harmoniously to the Supreme.

Try to feel that you are being filled and surrounded by forces that come direct from the very presence of the Supreme and that it is therefore impossible for you to fail. Do not permit yourself to fall down at any place nor fall short at anything. It is the time for you to attain and achieve as you never did before, and nothing in your personality must stand in the way. While the psychological moment continues, special attention should be given to a pure life, a strong life, an ideal life and a masterful life, and all the qualities and attributes of perfection should be constantly in mind. Live in the upper story, but act upon the tangible world according to the high purpose that you are determined to fulfill. The results will be as you wish. The goal will be gained. Then you can proceed to prepare the way for a still greater psychological moment, and thus in the coming days reach a much higher goal than you have ever known before.

Chapter 13

The Power of Personal Appearance

Among the many things that determine what places in life men and women are to occupy, the power of personal appearance is one of the greatest, and frequently by far the greatest. Although it is ability that counts in the long run provided that ability is applied to the best advantage, still there is a great deal of ability that is so completely hidden back of an unattractive personal appearance that it is never recognized nor given its legitimate opportunity. Where we find exceptional ability we also find exceptions to this rule, but there are thousands and thousands of brilliant minds, and any number of minds not quite as brilliant, that are handicapped constantly and most seriously on account of deficiencies in their personal appearance.

We all know this to be the truth. The subject is therefore worthy of the most thorough attention because no one can afford to permit anything to stand in his way. The best use of the best that we possess must be our purpose and everything necessary to fulfill this purpose should be supplied. The term "personal appearance," however, does not refer simply to dress or manners, though these are important, and everyone should make it a point to be dressed as attractively as possible. But aside from these it is the appearance and the expression of the human face that really determine the final results. To this end the face of the man should be strong and expressive and the face of the woman should be beautiful and expressive.

In the business world the man with the strong face is invariably given the preference. He will be selected for the most responsible positions if he is working for others, and if he is working for himself he will be far more successful than his negative faced neighbor because the public is irresistibly attracted to the man who produces the best and the strongest impression. No matter how able you may be if you do not produce a good impression upon the world your remarkable ability will not serve you as well as it should. On the other hand, when you do produce a good impression, all of your ability will be in demand, and will be called forth to the best advantage, not only to yourself, but to everybody concerned. And since there is nothing that can produce a better impression than a strong, expressive face every man will find it most profitable to develop such qualities or characteristics in his facial expression.

The man with the strong face will forge to the front in his world and the woman with the beautiful face will forge to the front in her world, provided that expressiveness is added to strength and beauty in each case. These are facts. It is therefore of the highest importance to those who wish to press on to greater and better things to understand how personal appearance in this regard can be cultivated to the highest possible degree.

Every man should have, and may have, a strong, expressive face. Every woman should have, and may have, a beautiful, expressive face. The methods for such development are well known so that it is only necessary to understand and apply them.

To improve the form and the expression of the face will require considerable time and attention in most cases, especially where the essentials are still in an undeveloped state. But these essentials can in every case be brought forth, and every person can accordingly develop in his face the qualities and the expression that he may desire. There are a number of men and women, however, whose facial expressions are so near to the strong or the beautiful state of expression that they would only have to be touched up, so to speak, to make them exactly what they ought to be. These people, therefore, can in a very short time, demonstrate conclusively that a decided improvement in facial expression can be secured, while those who may need further development can through the same methods accomplish the same results if sufficient time is supplied.

We meet hundreds of women every day whose faces have an ordinary appearance at first sight, but most of these faces upon closer examination will be found to contain all the essentials to beauty of expression; and though these essentials are so near to the surface as to be almost in evidence, still they are not harmonized and therefore continue to remain ordinary in appearance; they could, however, with a few slight changes be made decidedly attractive. These women fail to produce the favorable impressions that they might produce and consequently are at a disadvantage, both in the social world and in the business world. The places they deserve in the woman's world they do not secure because they do not appear as they really are, and the world usually judges according to appearances. This being true, we must take the world as we find it. And we must not hide what light we may possess nor permit undeveloped or perverse personal appearance to so mince matters for us that our superior qualities seem to produce inferior impressions.

In like manner, we meet hundreds of men every day whose faces are weak in general appearance, and there is nothing expressive about their personalities. We are not favorably impressed by them and usually conclude that they are just ordinary men, no more. But when we look closely at those faces we find remarkable possibilities of strength and power, possibilities so near to the surface that a few slight changes in the expression of the face would make them exceptionally strong. Many of these men are able, but they have not as a rule the opportunity to fully apply their abilities in the positions they now occupy and on account of their weak, negative faces they do not produce the desired impressions when they seek those opportunities elsewhere. In consequence, they continue in small, poorly paid positions when they really have the ability to do far better. We are all personally acquainted with hundreds of men in this very condition, and if we should investigate we should find thousands more.

In the meantime, from every part of the commercial world comes the call for competent men, men who can do things, men who can do greater things, and do them better than they have ever been done before. This being true, do not hide your ability behind a weak, negative face.. Give your power expression so that the world can see what is in you at first sight. The world is too busy to take men on trial or upon anybody's say so, and we must be prepared to meet the world the way we find it. The man who can prove in the least time that he is able to make good will be given the preference in every case. When there are larger places to fill, he will be selected even though there are thousands of applicants all as able as he may be but not prepared to prove at sight what is in them.

The world is constantly looking for good men, therefore if you know that you are one of these, bring your power and your ability into your facial expression. In other words, let the light of your mind shine. The highest places are always given to the most brilliant mind.

There are thousands of men that would be promoted within a month if they would begin today to transform their weak, negative faces into strong, positive faces, and there are thousands of women who would in a short time win the various positions and the affections which they so earnestly desire if they would aim to bring to the surface the charm and the beauty that they actually possess. These are facts — great facts — facts with which we are all familiar. How the man may develop the strong, expressive face and how the woman may develop the beautiful, expressive face will therefore be knowledge of priceless value.

We do know that men with strong faces and women with beautiful faces forge to the front, and we all desire to forge to the front. What is more it is not only our privilege to do so, but to be just and true to ourselves we must do so.

To proceed with the development of the strong, expressive face, begin by eliminating all negative states of mind such as fear, worry, depression, discouragement, lack of self-confidence, lack of push, instability, indifference, inertness and negativeness. Remove these by giving a strong facial expression to poise, determination, positiveness and soul. In other words cultivate the positive qualities and be determined to express them in every fiber of your personality. No forceful expression, however, must be permitted. The proper expression is that expression that inwardly feels great power and that applies that power in perfect poise. When you concentrate a strong, well poised expression through every part of your face think deeply of what you are in ability, capacity and power; that is, place the stamp of your real worth upon every thought you think while this concentration is practiced.

There are few things that will give more strength, more quality and more expressiveness to the expression of the face than to feel the power of real, genuine worth in every cell of the face and to hold that power in strong poise while it is being felt. It is also highly important to give a positive expression to your face at all times, and to give all the quality and worth that you can to that expression. This will not only stamp your face with strength and ability, but it will tend to bring forth more ability from the subconscious mind, and thus develop added ability at the same time. Train your mind to express its very best in every part of your facial expression; that is, express yourself consciously and feelingly in your face so that everybody can see you, the real superior YOU, by looking at your face; because if the world can see you and what is in you in this ready manner you will positively be given the place you deserve.

To permit the mind to express its real worth through the personal appearance of the face in particular and through the entire personality in general, all wrong mental states must be entirely avoided, because all such states misdirect and confuse mental expression thereby producing false and undesirable impressions. The most detrimental of these states are fear, anger and worry and their various modifications. Fear always weakens the face as it is the most negative of all negative states, while anger and worry give the face a hard and ugly appearance. The same is true of all ugly mental states. Think ugly thoughts or permit yourself to feel disagreeable again and again and both beauty and the strength of your face will disappear if you ever had those qualities.

The beautiful face is produced by harmony of mind, sweetness of thought, love, tenderness, mental sunshine, joy, kindness and an inward feeling of the SOUL of the beautiful. Train yourself to feel the beautiful in your own soul and consciousness; then train yourself to express that feeling in your face, and your face will not look ordinary nor unattractive any more. Instead, it will begin to express more and more of the loveliness of that charm that is always irresistible.

To change mental states and mental expressions from the wrong to the right, from the weak to the strong, from the negative to the positive and from the unattractive to the beautiful, is to remove gradually but surely everything that is cheap, ordinary, coarse, common or undeveloped in your facial expression. Your appearance, therefore, will no longer be a cheap edition but will become an edition deluxe, so to speak, and will in time become sufficiently attractive to win the admiration of the most idealistic mind.

That the expression of the face may be remarkably improved through the cultivation of the proper mental states is a fact that everybody will admit. And those who realize the importance of improving personal appearance in all respects will proceed at once with the application of these simple methods. But that the form of the face can be changed or even modified is an idea that will be doubted by many. Doubts, however, on this subject need not be entertained because experiments in physiological psychology have demonstrated that the form of the face can be largely changed, modified and improved. And the law through which this is effected has been called the law of subjective concentration.

The principle of this law is, that when you concentrate the mind upon any part of the body while the mind is in the subjective state, that is, a state of deep feeling, there will be an increase of vitality and nourishment supplied to that part of the body, and development of the cell structures will take place to a degree. That the form of the face, therefore, might be largely modified and improved through this method is evident, and especially since the mind concentrates more readily upon the face than upon any other part of the body. This idea, however, is one that will necessarily involve a great deal of practice, but everybody is advised to test it thoroughly if they feel that for any reason a modification in the form of the face is desired.

However, the application of this idea is by no means necessary to the improvement of personal appearance, because the simple methods presented above, that is, with respect to changing the states of the mind, and by cultivating a positive, expressive attitude at all times, will prove sufficient to produce almost any change that we have in mind in this respect. The principle is, to make the facial expression strong and expressive in the man, and beautiful and expressive in the woman. Because as we already know such facial expressions are of immense advantage, both in the social world and in the business world.

Chapter 14

The Use and Cultivation of Personal Magnetism

We all know that the human personality is more or less charged with magnetic and electrical forces, and it is becoming more and more evident to the students of the psychological side of personal life that those forces have a distinct purpose in promoting the increase of ability and power in man, and that they can be increased indefinitely both in quantity and effectiveness. That man is an electrical battery, so to speak, and that he is more or less a living magnet, is a fact that no intelligent person will any longer dispute. That fact has passed from the world of doubt and has been accepted by the world of science.

It is therefore unnecessary to give time and space trying to prove that there is such a thing as personal magnetism. We all know that such a power does exist in us all and that it is worth a fortune to possess an exceptional degree of this power. What we wish to know, however, is how to use this power properly and how to make it much stronger than it is because we have found its value to be extraordinary to say the least.

In the use and cultivation of this power the first principle to be fully established in the mind is, that personal magnetism can be used upon yourself alone, and that its function is to promote the best possible expression of all the active qualities in your own personality; or in other words, to heighten the effect of everything you may do.

The belief that personal magnetism is intended for the influence of others is absolutely untrue, and what is more, such a thing is impossible. You cannot use this power to any extent m controlling others: it will not work that way. Should you attempt to influence others with this power you will not only fail to exercise any perceptible influence, but you will also lose what personal magnetism you may already possess. If you cannot succeed in life without trying to influence others in promoting your success you do not deserve success; and what you may gain temporarily through force or persuasion is not earned. It is taken, and will not prove of any worth to you in the long run.

When you have something of value to give to the world the world will come and get it without being forced. Everybody is looking for the new, the better and the superior, and you have simply to announce the fact, that is, advertise. You will thus have no difficulty in disposing of your product as rapidly as you can produce it. It is the man who has nothing of value to dispose of who does not succeed. And a few of these have decided to try to force people to come and purchase what they do not want and what may not have any value. And they have imagined that personal magnetism was one of the secrets through which the public could be made to give up their money against their will; but in this they have been very much mistaken, and all who have employed such methods have utterly failed. The underlying secret of success is, first, be of worth, second, do something of worth, and third, create something that has worth. When you have worth the world will want you. You will be in demand. When your work has worth your services will be in such demand that you will have more opportunities than you can take advantage of. And when your products have worth you will have to work to full capacity to supply the demand. These are facts, and being facts all attention and all personal power should be concentrated upon the cultivation of worth in all these respects. And in this connection we shall find personal magnetism to be indispensable.

You may have a great deal of ability, but how much you can accomplish through the use of that ability at the present time will depend upon how well that ability is expressed. The best qualities in our possession can be expressed to advantage, or the reverse. Great ability may appear at its best or at its worst, and the presence or absence of the electrical and magnetic forces of the personality determine which it is to be. The finest mind becomes stupid when emptied of these forces, while even an ordinary mind will become exceptionally brilliant, for the time being, when electrified.

We all know that we can at times bring ourselves up to a place where we are actually superior to our usual selves, and everything we do at such times proves to be a masterpiece. But why should we not be able to bring ourselves up to this superior state at any time when very important work is to be done. The fact is that we can, and no one should permit himself to undertake anything without first placing his entire personality in the best possible working condition. In other words, before your personality is called upon to act, it should be electrified and well charged with those forces that can bring all forces and functions up to their very best state of action. And to possess personal magnetism is to possess an abundance of those forces under conscious control.

To cultivate this fascinating power, the first essential is to fully establish in the mind the true use of this power. You cannot increase a certain power while you are constantly misusing what little of that power you may possess. And in this connection the first fact to be remembered is, that this magnetic energy is to be used upon yourself alone. It is not to be used in persuading others to do something for you, but should be used in making yourself more competent to do something for others. Having fixed this in mind, learn to feel deeply, and learn to live, think and act in poise.

Through the attitude of poise all the forces of the system are converted into what may be called the curve movements, and it is such movements of the electric or vital energies of the system that makes a person fascinating, charming, attractive and efficient The opposite movements, or what may be called the zigzag movements, the broken movements, of the forces within us are weakening, because in such movements force is lost; and in a person without poise nearly all the forces in his system move more or less in a zig zag fashion.

The curve movements of energy are constructive and accumulative, and will constantly charge and recharge the system until the personality actually becomes a living magnet, animated and electrified in every atom. When you are filled with such a power you will give a high polish to everything you do. You will constantly keep yourself up to the very highest point of efficiency, and you will heighten the effect both of your appearance and your actions.

When we speak of curve movements or zigzag movements we do not refer to the physical movements of the body or the muscles. We refer only to the movements of the various electric and magnetic forces that act within the human personality. To have a goodly supply of highly cultivated personal magnetism is to establish curve movements in all the forces of your personality, so therefore in every attempt we make to cultivate this power we should bear this fact in mind.

When the forces of your personality move in the zigzag fashion most of the electricity of your system is lost; that is, it is thrown off at the many sudden turns that your energies make while in that mode of action, and accordingly your system is not electrified. Your personality is thereby kept in a more or less emptied condition, and all your faculties are lowered in power and efficiency.

To develop this power it is not necessary, as a rule, to increase the supply of vital energy in the system in order to secure the desired results. Most of us are already well supplied with personal power, but we waste most of it through anger, fear, worry, nervousness, restlessness, despondency and lack of poise. These states of mind and modes of actions, therefore, must be eliminated and perfect harmony of mind and personality established. To proceed, it is only necessary to take the power we already possess and to train all the forces of the personality to move in curves, to which should be added a deep desire for personal expression. And curve movements in the human system invariably follow the attainment of deep feeling and poise.

Depth of feeling brings consciousness into touch with the finer vibrations of our interior forces and thus enables us to act on that side of our personal power that pertains to the cause realm. And poise causes all those forces to move harmoniously, thereby bringing about the results we desire. The fact is, as soon as perfect poise is established in the system and a deep desire for personal expression is attained the power of personal magnetism will increase every day, provided, of course, that this power is never misused through wrong states of mind.

To be in poise, however, does not simply mean to be quiet. There are a great many people who seem to be quiet who have no poise whatever, and who are utterly devoid of personal power. And this is explained by the fact that poise is a state of mind and personality that we realize when peaceful actions and strong actions are combined. We are in poise when we are full of life and power, and at the same time cause that power to act peacefully and harmoniously.

When you are in poise you can actually feel strong and mighty forces throughout your entire system. You are literally alive with power, but you are also perfectly serene. You feel like a dynamo, but everything in your entire system is under perfect control. There is nothing intense about your actions, for all is harmony and order; but bade of that order there is the consciousness of immense power.

When you are in poise you do not simply feel strength, but you feel strong; and there is a difference. When you feel strength you simply feel power passing through your system, but when you feel strong you feel that you yourself are that power; it is not passing through you, but it is you. When this state is felt and felt serenely you are in poise, and you should watch closely how that state came about. When you find how it came about you have found the secret for gaining this power in yourself at any time, so that you may not only make poise a permanent possession, but you may constantly develop the magnetic powers of your personality to a greater and greater degree.

A number of methods have been given for developing personal magnetism, but few of them are of any value. The only essential is to gain perfect poise; to think, act and feel in harmony; and to desire deeply the full and harmonious expression of all the energies and forces in your personality. In brief, be personally alive and in poise at all times and you will develop more and more of this fascinating power.

Chapter 15

How to Use the Power of Desire

In the practical application of the principles of psychology to the business world, the right use of desire becomes invaluable as the way this power is used determines largely what results are to be secured through any or every effort that is made; and the real truth concerning the great power of desire has been very well expressed in the statement, "We get what we desire and in just the measure of that desire"; and also, "We always get what we wish for if we only wish hard enough." But what it may mean to wish hard enough is the problem; and what it is that truly constitutes real desire is a question that few can answer for themselves.

To the majority a desire is a mere wish for something a wish that may be weak or strong, deep or shallow according to the value of the object desired. But in any case the desire is looked upon as a mere feeling in the mind, nothing more. There are a few, however, who have discovered that there is more in desire than a mere wish for the object desired, and it is these few who get what they wish for. By some, these people are called fortunate, and in a certain sense they certainly are. Those who have learned to get what they wish for are certainly fortunate. Others give them credit for extraordinary ability, which is also true, for though they may not have exceptional mental attainment in every case, still they have ability to use a power that the many know nothing about. By another group they are frequently accused of taking undue advantage of their fellow men, but this does not explain the secret of their success.

The man who has discovered the real power of desire can get what he wants without wronging anybody, and he will get what he wants no matter how adverse the circumstances, how great the obstacles, or how hopeless the aim.

The principle is this, whatever you wish for, wish hard enough and you will get it; but the act of wishing hard is quite different from what the average person may think it is. You do not wish hard enough for anything unless you make that wish thoroughly alive with all the life and power that you can possibly arouse. You do not place in action the real power of desire unless you give your desire soul — the deep, strong invincible power of soul.

When the force of your desire is just as deep as the deepest depths of your interior life, and just as strong as all the power that can possibly be contained in that life, your desire will be realized. In other words, you will get what you wish for when all of you is in your wish. The reason why is simply understood as there is nothing mysterious or supernatural about the process through which these results are obtained. It is only a matter of using all the power you possess instead of a small fraction, and this is certainly important in the business world.

When you make up your mind to reach a certain goal or accomplish something you have in view, results will depend directly upon how well you use the real or inner power of desire. If your determination to succeed is shallow and superficial you will accomplish but little. On the other hand, if that determination is as deep as the depths of your own life you will arouse the deepest forces of your life, and these forces are not only powerful, but are positively irresistible. That you should succeed with such powers at your command is therefore evident When you make up your mind in this deeper, stronger sense you are bringing out into action the strongest and best that is in you. You are deeply in earnest and you feel very deeply on the subject in hand. In consequence, your desire to succeed will actually stir the very depths of your soul. Your whole being will become alive, and when all the power that is in you is alive with the deep, positive desire of invincible determination, there is no adversity or obstacle in existence that you cannot overcome. Make yourself strong enough and great enough and there is nothing in the world that will not change its course in any manner required so as to serve the purpose of your supreme desire. And every person becomes strong enough and great enough when the deepest powers of his soul are aroused. There is more in you than you ever dreamed, and there are times when this more becomes so strong that you feel that you could master the universe. And these deeper feelings are not mistaken. Make yourself as strong as nature has given you the power to become and the universe will make way for any plan or project you may wish to undertake. The secret is to use all the power in your present conscious possession. You may not be required to develop more at the present time, because if you arouse what can be aroused now you will have sufficient for practically anything you may wish to accomplish in the present.

Any person can do what he makes up his mind to do, or get what he wants, when he makes use of all the power he is conscious of; and all that power is invariably aroused when every desire is given soul. Bring out all your power and make your wish alive with all that power. Then you will wish hard enough. And when you wish in this manner you will get what you wish for. To state it differently, you get what you desire and in the full measure of that desire when your desire is crammed with all the life and all the power and all the soul that there is in you.

Failure comes from half-hearted desires accompanied more or less with doubt, or from those desires that are so shallow that they never arouse enough power to overcome a single obstacle. Success demands not only the power to do things, but also the power to surmount every obstacle that may be met, and the power to transform every adversity into a rich and rare opportunity. But such power does not come from shallow thinking and half-heartedness in feeling and desire. He who would gain the power to do what he wants to do must sound the depths of his being. He must learn to draw upon those deeper forces of his mind and soul that alone can give him all the power he may require or demand; but he can do this only by deepening his desire; that is, by giving his desire soul.

Every desire that is felt to the very depths of being touches the vastness and immensity of the great within. And the power of the great within is invincible. The real power of a deep, strong desire comes from the great interior life within us; therefore it is never crude in its actions. It is not mere animal will or the dominating force of physical determination; nor is it necessarily connected in any way with physical might and main. On the contrary, it is one of the most refined among all the forces in the system. It is actual soul force, but soul force is not something that pertains to some other state of existence, for it is the very life of every tangible force in the universe, physical or mental.

When you begin to arouse soul force you begin to draw upon the limitless, and all your faculties and talents will begin to outdo themselves. You are not only bringing out the best that is in you, but you are going farther still. You are going back of present capacity and arousing that something that can give perpetual increase to your capacity. Therefore, it is simply inevitable that you should accomplish what you have in mind and get what you wish for. No one can fail who applies the best that is in him. But back of the best there is more. We all know that there is. We all have had moments when we realized the limitless vastness of the great within.

And when we think of it, something informs us that we can even now bring forth into actual use enough of this superior power to reach any goal we may have in view, or scale any height to which the mind can aspire.

Give the deep, strong, invincible power of soul to every desire and you will awaken those powers within you that can fulfill every desire. Desire greatness with the soul of desire and you arouse the powers of greatness. Those powers are within you. They are positively there. It remains for you to bring them out. And you can if your desires are so deep that they stir the very depths of your inner-most being. Desire changes for the better, and if that desire is as deep as your own life you will produce that change in your own life that is necessary to bring about such changes in your external world as you may have in view. Create the inner cause and the outer effect will inevitably follow. Desire success with the deepest and strongest desire that you can possibly feel, and you will arouse those very powers within you that can produce success. Desire an ideal environment and you awaken those qualities in your own nature which, when applied, can produce or build up that richer and better environment into which you wish to enter. In consequence, you will ere long find yourself in such an environment because like attracts like, and from superior causes come superior effects.

And most important of all, you will, through the use of this law, cause yourself to become what you constantly desire to become. But all your desires in this connection must be deep and strong. They must actually thrill with feeling, life and soul, and must stir into positive action every power that is latent within you. There is enough creative energy and mental building material within you to make you a mental and spiritual giant. Therefore, you need not hesitate to aspire to the very highest state that your mind can possibly picture. It is in you to become what you want to become, and what is in you can be brought out into positive action through the penetrating power of a deep soul desire. Whatever your desire, never fail to give that desire your very life, your whole life and the full power of the deepest strongest, finest life that you can possibly arouse from the inexhaustible depths of your own soul. Do not simply express a wish, express more. And make this more as large, as high and as powerful as you can. Give your wish soul, not simply sentimental soul, but that expression of invincible soul that will press on and on to the goal in view, no matter what the obstacles may be. Make your wish alive and be so thoroughly in earnest that every atom in your being thrills with a positive determination to make that wish come true. But never attempt to use mere mental force.

The soul of desire is far deeper than mind and infinitely more powerful than mind. Try to feel this soul whenever you express the power of desire, and when you do feel it try to feel more and more of the real life of soul. Try to feel the finer elements and the finer forces that exist within all physical life and all mental life. Try to pass in consciousness from the realization of one grade of soul to the realization of deeper, finer and larger grades of soul until you are conscious of the immensity and the vastness of your own supreme within. Then you will know what it means to give the invincible power of soul to every desire. Then you will know why everything must change before the deep, determined power of such a desire. Then you will know why those who possess the secret of real desire invariably scale the heights even though the whole world be against them and every imaginable obstacle in their way.

Chapter 16

How to Use the Power of Will

Among the many important discoveries made in recent times one of the greatest is this: that man has the power to change himself and his environment through the intelligent use of the laws and the powers of his own being; also that he can build health, character and ability to almost any degree desired; that he can remove from his life what is not conducive to his welfare and happiness; that he can gain possession of more and more of that which is conducive to his welfare and happiness; that the possibilities within him have no limitations whatever, and that there is evidently no end to what he can do in the growth and development of himself and the world in which he lives.

The principles of this discovery have been demonstrated by thousands. Results have been secured in every known field of life and human action. Some of these results have been so extraordinary as to appear miraculous, and accordingly, new philosophies and new systems of thought are taking shape and form with these results as cardinal doctrines, while the human world is changing more or less to harmonize with the new conception of man.

We no longer submit to things as they are. We no longer permit our minds to accept adversity in a meek and lowly spirit. We no longer think that we have to give up to what appears to be inevitable, because we have discovered that man holds the destiny of his own life in his own hands. Man is supreme in his own life and in his own world. This is a fact that we now know. He may therefore have his own way in practically everything. He may form his own ideals and make them come true. He may plan his own future and realize everything in general and most things in particular, as expected. He has the intellect to understand the principle and the power to apply the law.

But here we meet a great and perplexing problem. Among the many who have tried to understand the principle and apply the law, thousands have secured the results desired, but other thousands have not. They have either failed wholly or in part to produce those changes in themselves or in their environments for which they have labored so faithfully. They have seemingly done their part and have done it just as well as those who were more successful. Why they should fail may therefore seem difficult to understand, but the real reason is easily comprehended.

There are many powers in man, but there is only one power that has controlling power, and that power is the will. The purpose of the will is to control and direct all the other powers of man; that is, it should direct those powers so as to cause them all to do what we want them to do. Since there is no limit to man's inherent capacity, and since the subconscious cannot be exhausted, neither in quantity of power nor in varieties of power, it is evident that man can do with his life whatever he may desire, provided he can cause all these powers to do what he may wish to have done. And he can.

The controlling power of the will can cause any other power in man to do whatever the will may direct it to do. But this controlling power of the will must be used not simply to control for the sake of exercising control, but for the purpose of turning the other powers in man into those channels of action where the results desired may be produced. When man undertakes to change himself or his environments every power in his system must be directed to so act as to promote that change. And the first power to be so directed is the power of thought.

The mind is creative and its powers can create the change desired when properly directed. This is a fact, however, that is fully recognized by all who have taken up the science and art of applied idealism, and they have almost without exception given their mental powers the direction required. But they have in too many instances neglected to give that same direction to their other powers, and here we find the cause of the failure.

To direct the mind to think and act along scientific and constructive lines is the first essential, but the power of such thought will not produce any change in man until his personality is directed to live and express those elements and factors that are contained within such line of thinking. The idealist wills to think, but does not always will to do. And the reason is that he believes that right action will invariably follow right thought. But this is not always true. Thought never becomes action unless the same will to think also wills to act.

The complete will, that is, the full use of the will, controls both thought and action and must act in both in order to produce results. The creation of a new idea is not necessarily followed by the expression of that idea; because the will that wills to create an idea does not will to express that idea unless so directed by the mind. Some minds naturally combine the will to think, with the will to act, and it is such minds that have such good results both in the science of applied idealism and in practical psychology, frequently with but little effort.

Those minds that fail to secure external changes for the better after they have changed their thought for the better fail because they do not combine naturally die will to think with the will to do. In these minds the will is not fully applied; that is, it may will to think the ideal, but it does not always will to work out the ideal in tangible action. But when the will is so trained that it invariably wills to do what it has willed to think, every change in thought will positively be followed by a corresponding change in external conditions.

Man is as he thinks, but he is not the product of all his thought. The only thought that gives formation to the character, the mentality and the personality of man is the thought that contains the will to express itself. All other thought therefore is useless, and to create thought and not give that thought the will to express itself is to waste both time and energy. The larger part of the thought created in the average mind is of this kind. It takes shape in the mind, but does not contain the will to work itself out into real tangible results.

The path to greater power of mind and personality, therefore, may be found first, in training the mind to think only constructive thought, and second, in giving every thought the will to act. Right thinking will produce right conditions in mind and body, only when the will to act is just as strong and just as deeply felt as the will to think.

Constructive thinking will promote the advancement of man both in attainment and in achievement whenever the desire to work out the ideal is just as positive as the desire to imagine the ideal. And all thinking that pictures the greater and better, and that is animated with a positive desire to attain the greater and the better, is constructive thinking. And all thinking is right that is based upon the principles that the ideal of everything contains the power to become real. But in applying this power it is the will that must be used in every instance whatever the purpose may be.

The power of the will is indispensable whether the action be physical or mental. We can do nothing until we will to do it, and what we wish to have done in any particular sphere of action, we must will to do in that sphere of action. What we wish to have done in the mind we must will to do in the mind. What we wish to have done in the body we must will to do in the body. What we do in one part of the system will not be duplicated in some other part unless we so will it. The power of thought will work itself out in personal life only when we will to convert that power into personal power. The ideal becomes real only when the characteristics of the ideal are acted out in the real.

The secret, therefore, is to act in the real as you feel that you are in the ideal. When you have seen the vision of the soul, will to make it come true in the body. You can. But do not try to will simply with the superficial side of will. It is through the controlling power of the will that you cause your other powers to do what you wish to have done. And this controlling power may be found within what may be termed the soul of the will.

Give soul to your desire to act and the mind will act through the deeper, interior, or actual field of the will. In this way you will consciously apply the controlling power of the will and thus succeed in doing what you will to do. The controlling power of the will is a direct expression of the superior man within, and we must always bear this fact in mind — that there is a larger man within. This interior man is the real YOU, and is infinitely greater and more powerful than your outer personality. And it is upon this interior man that you must depend for results. Whatever you do, expect the interior man to produce results and give the interior man full credit for everything that is thus accomplished. In this manner you become more deeply conscious of the interior powers within you, and therefore can apply them to greater advantage.

The superior man within controls the controlling power of the will, therefore to will to do what we desire to do, we must give the superior man within the right of way. In other words, act as if you were the superior man within and you will feel that you are the superior man within. Then your greater power will act. You will place in action the controlling power of the will whenever you may desire to act, and thus you can readily do whatever you may will to do. Here we should remember that the outer personality has no real will power. You gain possession of real will power only when you begin to feel that you are the greater man within.

That power of will that can calmly, but absolutely, direct all the other powers in your being to do what you wish them to do invariably comes from the depths of your life. When your feeling of life is deep, therefore, and when that depth of life is calm and strong, then it is that you gain that power that contains controlling will power, and then it is that you can work out in tangible life every change for the better that you have produced in the mind. Many minds are so constituted that they naturally give the superior man within the position of supremacy. And it is such minds that secure the greatest results in every field of endeavor. Those minds, therefore, that do not naturally give the superior man the position of supremacy, and do not give the greater powers within full right of way must train themselves to do so. And all minds can.

There are greater powers within you than you have ever expressed before. If you will cause those powers to come forth more and more you will steadily and rapidly advance, no matter what your work may be. If you are so constituted that you naturally give those powers right of way, you will move toward the high places in mind whether you understand those powers or not. You will forge to the front because you can feel something superior within you that prompts you to press on and on, overcoming every obstacle and scaling every height.

You can secure the same results, however, by training your mind to become exactly similar in consciousness and action to those who naturally give the greater powers within the position nature intends them to occupy.

When you proceed to apply the science and art of practical psychology and try to produce changes for the better, both in the mental world and in the physical world, results will depend upon two things, and in the last analysis of these two are one. If the mind naturally gives the greater powers within the right of way, and naturally gives every thought the will to express itself in tangible action, you have combined these two essentials, and results will be forthcoming. When the superior man within is in action, the will to think and the will to act practically become one will, and every mental change is followed by a corresponding physical change. But no mental change can produce a corresponding physical change unless the new mental change contains the will to express itself. And since real will power is inseparably united with the superior man within, in fact, is the expression of the superior man within, it is evident that we must permit this interior man to come forth if we desire superior mental changes to come forth and produce corresponding physical changes.

To be so constituted that the greater man within is naturally given this prominent position is well, provided that tendency is cultivated, but if it is not cultivated we will have results, up to a certain point only, and there will be no further progress. It is not necessary, however, to be so constituted naturally in order to secure great results. The mind can readily be trained to work out into tangible life any new or improved condition that is realized in mind or consciousness. The will to think and the will to act can and must be made one will. And the power of creation and expression can be made so strong that the moment we discern an ideal we can begin to make it real. In this entire study we should always bear in mind the great fact that what comes natural to some can be developed in all, and that the greatest results come, not to those who depend exclusively upon natural talent, but to those who take what they have, be it ever so little, and proceed with further development, never ceasing until they have realized the highest attainments of which they have dreamed.

We all have some will power. Whenever we move a muscle or utter a word we use the controlling power to carry out such actions. We can develop this function further and further until we can cause every power we possess to do what we may wish to have done. And we develop this function whenever we will to act out in the tangible any and every change for the better that we have pictured in the mind. The principle is to will to do whatever you have willed to think; and to will, not from the surface of your mind, but from the deepest depths of your mind. Thus you will become in the real what you desire to be in the ideal; and you will cause the vision of the soul to become a tangible reality.

We all have felt the power of the superior man within. We all have moments when we know that we are greater by far than the visible self ever appeared to be. And those moments can be made not only more numerous, but a constant realization. We can train ourselves to feel more and more of the greatness within and to express more and more of that greatness. We can do this by giving the larger interior man full right of way. We should proceed, therefore, to let the power that is within come forth. We should let it even take full possession of our entire personality. It will never lead us wrong, but will instead prompt us to press on and on regardless of circumstances until we reach the very highest heights we have in view.

Act as if you were this great interior man, think that you are, feel that you are, know that you are; thus you give the greater within you full right of way and the real YOU becomes supreme. Then you discover that it is all you, and that the all of you is great indeed. Henceforth you can proceed to do in larger and larger measure what the modern mind has discovered that man can do; you can change yourself, improve yourself, advance yourself; grow out of any inferior condition into any superior condition; create health, harmony and happiness in abundance; live as you wish to live; become what you desire to become; increase perpetually your capacity to attain and achieve; build character and ability to the highest degree of efficiency and power; and place yourself upon that high pinnacle of being, where you can truthfully say, My life is in my own hands, and what my future is to be, I, myself, have the power to determine.

Chapter 17

The New Meaning of Good Business

The statement is frequently made that it is good business to pursue such and such a course; in other words, that it is profitable in a financial way. And in the minds of many, anything is good business that is profitable financially; but the psychology of industrial life is proving conclusively that the man who is looking for financial profit must not look for financial profit alone. To achieve a real and lasting success the man of business must seek not only to build profit, but he must also seek to build himself. If his business has only financial profit in view the time will come when the business will be larger than the man; and it is the man who is smaller than his business that cannot stand prosperity. Success will turn his head and he will do something to spoil everything. He will thereby lose what he has gained, and being a small man he is very liable to go all to pieces when adversity comes. The large man, however, will not be disturbed by misfortune. He will begin again. He will turn his past experience into capital and will rise higher in the scale of achievement than ever before. But he will not lose his bearings when the greater success arrives. He will grow with the growth of his business and will fully enjoy every step of the way.

A careful study of the industrial world proves conclusively that the majority of the failures in business life are due to the fact that the business man does not as a rule aim to grow with his business. When his sole aim is profit his business will grow for a while, but he will not. Sooner or later he will find himself too small for the further promotion of the enterprise, and when this stage is reached he will either lose his hold upon his business or lose his head. In either case things will begin to go wrong, and failure will follow.

The idea that business is business, regardless of its nature, and that anything is good business that promotes the growth of the business itself, will cause the business man to give his whole attention to methods for producing profit. He will ignore the principles of character and the laws of the mind, and will in consequence deteriorate as a man. His real ability will weaken and his future success, if he has any, will not be the result of business ability, but will be the result of shrewdness. Real ability creates, while shrewdness simply appropriates what others may have created. This, however, is not success, and no man who has respect for his own life, and regard for his future, will ever consider such a method for a moment.

The man who tries to promote his business through questionable methods is harming himself. He is violating the laws of his own mind and is therefore retarding the growth of his own mind. But no person can afford to retard his own growth, because future success as well as happiness depends directly upon the growth of the mind, soul and character. If we wish to live a more successful life, a larger life, a worthier life and a happier life in the days to come we must continue to promote our own growth and personal advancement now.

To picture the next ten, twenty, fifty, seventy-five, or even a hundred years as a period of steady advancement in everything that is worthy, rich, beautiful and ideal is to look forward to a life that is certainly worth living, and such a prospect for the future will naturally fill a person's mind with unbounded gratitude to think that he is alive. But such a future cannot be realized unless a full and constant development of mind, character and soul is promoted now.

To build for greater things in any part of his life man must constantly build himself. Therefore he cannot afford to let anything, not even present financial profit retard his own growth. And financial profit secured through questionable means will retard his growth. In fact, the more profit he secures of this sort the smaller he himself becomes as a man.

There are only two ways through which financial profit can be gained; the one is through business ability practically applied, and the other is through any one or more of the illegitimate methods that are more or less in evidence in the business world. If you have no business ability of your own you cannot create success. Therefore, when a man who has no business ability succeeds, we know that he has appropriated the success that others have created. And the mere consciousness of such a fact will cause the mind of the individual who is guilty to dwarf and deteriorate.

The man who succeeds by appropriating the success of others has been told any number of times by moralists that he is harming his fellow men; but that argument, does not impress itself very deeply on his mind because his answer is that others have the same privilege to do what he is doing. According to his logic there is no wrong in using any method whatever in building up his business so long as others are free to use the same method in building up their business; and with this argument he appears to make a strong case. In fact, he has convinced many of the best minds that business simply is business; that it has laws of its own, laws which have only one object in view, which is to build business; and that whatever is conducive to the building up of business is good and legitimate in business.

There is, however, another side to this argument, and that side deals with the man behind the business. The man behind the business is the cause. The business itself is the effect. Therefore, what is bad for the man is bad in the long run for his business; and what is good for the man is good for his business. When he does something that decreases his ability and power his business will soon feel the effect, and will begin to go down; but when he does something to increase his ability and power, and continues in this course, his business will steadily grow until his success may become remarkable. This fact is self-evident.

We conclude, therefore, that the man who would win success that really is his own success, must aim to build up his mind while he is building up his business. And the building of these two can go together if his business methods are based upon principle, justice and character. But if he is using questionable methods his business will be an obstacle to the growth of his mind, and the reason why is simple. The mind cannot develop unless it is wholesome and works steadily along constructive lines; but no mind can be wholesome nor constructive in its actions that is engaged in an illegitimate enterprise. The mind cannot be straight so long as its work is crooked; and it is only the straight mind that can develop in ability and power, for it is only such a mind that can be in harmony with the laws of growth, development and advancement.

To promote its own development the mind must be true to itself, and just to its own laws. But no mind can be true to itself that is untrue to others. The mind that deals falsely with persons and things is dealing falsely with itself, and the mind that is dealing falsely with itself cannot develop itself. On the contrary, it is gradually destroying itself, and even a casual observation of things and persons about us will prove that this is the truth.

But there is another fact in this connection that is of equal importance. The man who depends upon his own ability to win success is using his own ability; and the more we use the ability we possess the more powerful and highly developed will that ability become. On the other hand, the man who depends upon shrewdness, speculation, games of chance and the like, is not using his business ability. In consequence, that ability will not develop, but will instead decrease in effectiveness and power. His abilities, talents and powers are not called into play; instead they are relegated more and more to the rear, and the man in consequence becomes less and less of a man. His success, if he has any, is not his own success. It was created by others, and justly belongs to the original creators.

The secret of greater and greater success is found in the development of greater and greater ability. And to promote this development it is necessary to use the whole mind constructively and to make the fullest possible use of the ability we already possess. No destructive process therefore must exist in the mind, and no false action whatever must be permitted. The mind must be clean, wholesome, orderly, constructive and aspiring, and every action must aim to build the man while on its way to the building of things.

The man who would develop his ability must be true to himself and true to others. He must act upon principle and must desire the possession of that only that he is creating. He must employ only orderly, constructive and scientific methods because shady methods produce a shady mind, and such a mind will fail. It is therefore evident that no person can afford to establish his business upon any other foundation than that of principle, manhood and character. And it is also evident that the only business that is good business, is that business which tends to build the man while the man is building the business.

How Great Men Succeed

THERE are many essentials to a real permanent success, but there is one essential without which all the others become practically valueless. The man who succeeds is invariably impelled to press on and on by something within him that tells him he can. He may have no name for this something, nor may he give to its presence special attention. Nevertheless, he knows it is there, and it gives him an inner determination that nothing in the world can conquer or destroy. He is inwardly convinced that he will succeed; and this conviction is so powerful and so deeply rooted in the very foundation of his being that it refuses absolutely to be disturbed by any circumstance whatever. In the spirit of this conviction he proceeds with his eye single upon the goal in view, gaining ground steadily and demonstrating every day, through actual results, that his conviction is based upon fact.

But where does this conviction come from? Where do great minds receive this inner determination, the power of which is greater than any obstacle or adversity that can possibly be met in human life? And can anyone get possession of this interior something that simply must press on to victory, no matter what the circumstances may be?

These are questions of vital importance to every mind that longs for greater things, and it is the aim of the following pages to answer them in a manner that will be fully intelligible to all, and thoroughly satisfactory to the most exact.

To attain great success, we must inwardly feel that we can, and we must be inspired by a determination that is not only irresistible, but that is as deep as the fathomless depths of life itself. He can who thinks he can. He who thinks he can will use effectively all his present power and will steadily increase the capacity of that power. He who doubts his power, however, will fail to use it. And herein we discover one of the first causes of failure, as well as one of the greatest laws in achievement.

The less confidence you have in yourself, the less of yourself you will apply in action; while the more confidence you have in yourself, the more of yourself, and all of the powers and faculties you possess, you will use in whatever work you may be engaged.

Some minds naturally feel that they can, and there is a reason why. When we learn why they have this confidence, we may gain the same confidence; and success will come to us as surely as the rays of the rising sun. But other minds of equal, or even greater, ability are confused and depressed with so much doubt that not a single faculty gives expression to more than a fraction of its inherent power. In consequence, they fail where lesser minds reap rich rewards, thus proving conclusively that ability is not the only essential. There must be something back of ability that causes the full power of ability to be pushed to the front. All great men have this something and that is why they succeed; and we must also add that it is the possession of this something that makes them great, though this something is not beyond the many. It can be acquired by all normal minds; and to this rule there is no exception whatever.

Men who accomplish great things do not always have exceptional ability, but there is a power within them that turns all of their ability to the very best account. All that is in them is pushed up, so to speak, to the highest point of action and efficiency. Nothing in their nature is lost. Everything is put to work, and everything works effectively towards the great goal in view.

To possess exceptional ability, however, means great gain, providing the power to apply all of that ability is also present, and such ability not only can be developed, but should be developed. The fact, therefore, that a man does not possess exceptional ability at the present time need not prevent him from attaining exceptional success. By pushing to the front what ability he does possess, he can realize marked success at once, and that something that causes all ability to be pushed to the front can be gained by any mind without delay. Anyone can get that something now and begin a successful life now.

When a man thinks he can he awakens in his mind the power that can; and he thinks that he can because he is conscious of the power that can; that is, he inwardly feels the existence of that power. When you feel that you have the power to do what you wish to do, you cannot possibly doubt any more, nor can you fail when you proceed to use that power.

But how do successful men get this power, and by what means do they come to feel it so distinctly that they positively know they possess it?

To think that you can when you do not feel that you can is hardly possible, and it is only he who thinks he can succeed that does succeed. The man who does not feel within himself the power that can will doubt, and he who doubts that he can will suppress the power that can. Doubt must be removed before success can be gained, but doubt will not disappear until we inwardly feel that we can; that is, until we can actually feel the possession of all the power that is necessary to do what we have undertaken to do. When we know that we have the power, we know it. We know that we can. We are aware of the necessary power within us and this power is so positively determined to succeed that we find neither rest, peace, nor happiness until we proceed to apply it on the largest possible scale.

That something within that causes the full power of ability to be pushed to the front can be awakened and made active in everybody, because we all have it. This something is not a special gift for the few. It is inherent in every mind and is just as natural as life itself. In fact, it is inseparable from life, but thus far there are only a few who have learned to use it. Some of these were born with a natural aptitude in this direction, while others acquired the essential mental attitude later on, and this we all can do now. All minds are built upon the same principle. All minds possess the same possibilities. What one mind has accomplished, all minds can accomplish, and infinitely more.

We are only at the mere beginning of human attainment. Innumerable worlds in the vast mental domains are yet to be explored and conquered. A few know of their existence, but it remains for the future to discover all the wonderful and marvelous possibilities that these worlds may contain. No person, therefore, need doubt the existence of the extraordinary powers within him. We all have those powers, and to be just to ourselves and to the race, we must proceed to use now as many of those powers as we can understand now.

But the most important power is the power of that something that causes all other powers to become alive with all the force, all the ability and all the capacity that is latent within them.

When a man feels within himself that he can, his confidence in himself will express itself in various ways — depending upon whether his mind be crude or highly organized — but in any event, his efforts will produce success. If his mind be crude, or only partly developed, he may become brazen in his efforts and may not always depend upon legitimate push and enterprise; in fact, he may even employ methods that are questionable. When the power that can is aroused he must give it expression in some manner. He simply must proceed to do something, and whether his methods be crude or dignified he will never fail to reach his goal.

The power that can will work for a season through any channel, but it is only through strictly legitimate channels that it will work profitably in the long run, and produce final good as well as the greatest good. Though this power may bring wealth to captains of industry, whether their methods be sound or not, it is only through highly organized minds, where ability and character combine to the highest degree, that this power can produce real success. And it is real success, the working out of a great purpose, and the realization of the results expected through the culmination of that purpose, that all men and women of genuine ambition have in view. Therefore, we shall give no special attention to the misuse of any power or faculty in the human mind. Our prime object will be to learn how every element, force and faculty in our possession can be turned to good account. We know chat success must inevitably follow.

THE man who succeeds is convinced of the fact that he has the necessary power. He knows his power because he is in mental touch with his power. He not only knows that he has it, but he is in actual possession of it. He knows that he can and he has his hands on the power that can. This is the outer rim of his secret, but within this outer rim we find the real secret. Where did he gain his exceptional power and how did he place himself in mental touch with that power?

The first part of this question is answered by the fact that every mind is not only in possession of an enormous amount of available power, but is also in possession of the capacity to perpetually increase the supply of its own available power. The human mind is not only its own dynamo, but is so constructed that it can increase indefinitely the capacity of this dynamo; or, in other words, the energy generated by the present mental dynamo can be used in building additional mental dynamos. The power of man may, therefore, be increased to any degree desired and for any length of time desired. This statement may at first thought appear to be too strong, but it is based upon the most exact scientific research of modem psychology; besides, actual experience as far as we have gone proves the statement itself.

The second part of this question, how great men enter into mental contact with the power within them and thus become charged with that power, is answered by the one word, faith — a word which few understand. Nevertheless, it is one of the greatest words in existence, and it represents the greatest power in existence, a power through which all things become possible.

To have faith in yourself is to enter into the spirit of your life; that is, into the interior depths of your life, and to enter into the spirit of your life is to enter mentally into all the power that is contained in your life. You thus become conscious of the power that is in you. Your mind is placed in mental contact with this power and you become convinced that you have it Your mind is no longer confined to the shallow life on the surface of your being, but is gaining an actual grasp of all that there is in your entire being. You are no longer dependent upon those weak and limited forces that play upon the surface of existence. You are sounding the vast depths of your life and you are beginning to draw upon the inexhaustible forces of those depths.

The small mind is conscious of weak surface forces only. The great mind is conscious of everything on the surface and of the deep, inexhaustible forces within as well. That is the difference. And it is faith that makes this difference. It is faith that places the mind in conscious touch with those great interior depths.

The average man is in possession of simply the outside of his mental world, but the deepening action of real faith will give any mind full possession of all that is contained in this mental world. And when we know the real nature of faith, we shall understand the reason why. When you become conscious of all the power that is in you, your doubt disappears completely. You know that you can. You have aroused the power that can, and this power will not only give you the capacity to succeed, but it will give you the desire to proceed.

When you feel that you can, your desire to prove that you can becomes so immensely strong that nothing can hold you down. It is then that you feel within yourself the expanding power of a deep interior determination, the force of which becomes stronger and stronger until every element in your being is aroused to the white heat of invincible action. The depths of your being are stirred as never before. You feel the positive action of powers within you that you never knew before. Your whole life has become alive. You have discovered yourself — all that is in yourself, and you know that this combined all is great enough to carry through to a most successful termination, any undertaking that you may have in view. You need no longer try to think that you can. You know that you can. You can feel within yourself the unconquerable determination of the power that can.

Success comes inevitably when you feel that success is in you, and you will feel that success is in you when you arouse to action all that is in you. When you feel the interior action of a larger measure of your life you will want to succeed. You will have the ambition, and you will have the power to realize that ambition. It is this interior feeling that you can that produces ambition. And the fact that you have ambition proves that your mind is in touch with the great domains of life and power within you. Therefore, no mind can have an ambition without also having the power to carry through that ambition.

It is the power that can, ceaselessly clamoring for expression, that makes you ambitious to prove that you can. If that power was not alive within you, you could have no desire to use it. You could not know that it was there and you could feel no ambition. You begin to feel a deep, strong desire to do a thing when the power that you can do it is stirring within you, and not before. The power that produces a desire for success and the power that can promote that success is one and the same power.

This is a fact of extraordinary importance, because it proves that your ambition need not remain a mere ambition. Every ambition can be realized. Every ambition contains the power to reach its own goal. If the necessary power was not there, the ambition could not be there. To be ambitious is to be in touch with the greatest power within you. It is the feeling of this power within you that causes you to feel ambitious, and the moment you begin to feel this power you may begin to gain possession of this power. And by turning that power to practical use, you may proceed successfully to do the very thing you have the ambition to do.

When you feel a strong, continued, persistent desire to do a certain thing, you may rest assured that the power to do it has been aroused within you. You may proceed with a positive assurance of success. But you must apply the full force of the power that lies back of your ambition. This, however, the majority fail to do. Therefore, their ambitions are realized only in part, or not at all. But those who do apply the full force of this power invariably succeed. Their dreams come true; their desires are fulfilled; their ideals are made real. They rise steadily and surely, sometimes rapidly, and finally reach the highest places in the scale of achievement. They accomplish great things in every undertaking where they feel they can succeed and their secret is simple.

To understand this secret is to know how great men succeed, and as the secret is so very simple, anyone can understand it perfectly and apply it successfully.

Briefly stated, these are the facts in the case: First, to have the ambition to do a certain thing is to have the power to do it; second, the ambition to do anything can be developed and, in consequence, the power to do anything can be secured. Those who are not ambitious can become ambitious. Those who do not feel the possession of exceptional power can arouse such a power. Those who are not in mental contact with the subconscious world of mental power within them can enter into that contact and thus begin to draw more and more upon the inexhaustible.

To realize any special ambition, it becomes necessary to apply the full force of the power that is back of that ambition, and this can be done by entering positively into the real and inner life of that power. When you enter positively into the real life of a certain power, you make alive the whole of that power. You place in actual use all the power that is back of or within your ambition, and all the power that is in any ambition is sufficiently strong to bring about the realization of that ambition.

To enter positively into the real life of any power, the one great essential is to have real faith in that power. When you have faith in any power that is in you, your mind enters positively into the real interior world of that power; that is, into its vital essence or living force, and thus arouses into positive action everything that exists in the world of that power. This is the nature of real faith. This is how real faith works. It is evident, therefore, that nothing of importance can be accomplished without real faith.

Real faith is not a positive belief, but a positive action of the mind, a deepening action and an awakening action. Real faith is that positive, determined and penetrating action of the mind that enters into the spirit of a power, into the innermost life of a power and makes alive all that is in that power.

Faith goes into everything within the mind and arouses to action the best that is contained in the mind. Faith stirs up every dormant force that is in you and pushes to the front everything of worth that is in that force. Faith can do this because it is a positive action that acts, not on the surface of your being, but through and through the very life and essence of your being.

WHEN you have faith in yourself you enter mentally into all that is in yourself, and you arouse that all. In consequence, you feel greater power within you and thus become ambitious. If you are not sufficiently ambitious, and do not feel impelled by an irresistible something within you to press on and on, regardless of circumstances, to the very highest goal you can possibly picture, proceed to have more and more faith in yourself. Enter mentally into the spirit of every action in your being, into the very soul of every element or force in your system and try to arouse that greater power that you know to exist in the greater depths of your being. Then your life will no longer be shallow. You will no longer feel ordinary, incompetent and insignificant. You will feel that greatness has been awakened in your life, and the fact that there is extraordinary power in man will become to you a positive conviction. You will feel what all great men feel. You will feel that you can, and you will also feel such a strong desire to prove that you can, that you will find neither peace nor happiness until all your new found powers are put to work in the practical world.

To have faith in a certain faculty is to enter into the innermost world of that faculty and arouse all that that faculty may contain. Ambition will then become stronger in that faculty, and to succeed, through the application of the talents of that faculty, will become one of your greatest desires. Have more and more faith in your business ability, and ere long you will develop a stronger desire to succeed in the business world; and remember that back of every deep-seated desire of pronounced ambition, you will find all the power that is necessary to fulfill that desire.

Have faith in the faculties of music, art, literature, invention, or any other group that you may select, and the same results will be secured. Your greatest ambition, as well as your greatest power, will be found in that faculty in which you have the greatest faith. And the reason why is found in the fact that the more faith you have in a faculty, the more power and talent you arouse in that faculty. It is the nature of faith to enter into and arouse. Therefore, whenever you proceed to have faith, desire deeply and positively to enter into and arouse wherever your attention may be directed. You thus develop the real power of faith and as you increase your faith in yourself, you will increase your power, your ability and your working capacity in the same proportion.

There is a certain mental state that may be termed the prime essential in the attainment of success and this state originates invariably in faith — real faith — that deep, positive action of the mind that always tends to enter into and arouse. It is a strong, inner feeling informing you that you have the power to do what you desire to do, and this feeling is produced by the mind entering into all that is in you.

Some minds do this naturally, at least to a degree, and such minds always succeed. But all minds can be trained to enter into all that is in them and arouse that all into positive, practical action. Therefore, success is for everybody. The power of faith, perfectly understood and fully applied, is the secret.

When you have faith in yourself, you enter into the spirit of your being; that is, your mind no longer acts on the surface, but acts through and through everything that exists in your system. Accordingly, everything that is in you is acted upon, aroused and turned to use. And no person can fail to accomplish great things in life who awakens and applies all there is in him.

When you have faith in yourself, you arouse the best that is in you, and it is the best turned to use that produces real success. To have faith is to enter into the very spirit of the best, into the real life of the best. It is the nature of faith to do this. You cannot have faith in that which is useless or inferior. Faith turns attention upon the best only, and it finds the best in everything.

To have faith in everything is to concentrate attention upon the best in everything, and habitually think of the best that is in everything. And the mind develops into the likeness of that which we think of the most. Therefore, in the development of quality, worth and superiority, as well as greater ability and power, faith becomes indispensable.

You cannot have faith in the lesser; it is only the greater in which you can have faith. The moment you begin to have faith, you turn attention upon the greater. Your mind moves toward the greater. You enter mentally into the life and power of the greater, and thus gain possession of the richness of the greater.

To believe in yourself is to believe that there is more in you than you have thus far expressed. You will thus create in your mind a tendency to enter into and arouse this more, and the stronger your faith, the stronger will this tendency become. In consequence, you will enter more deeply and more truly into the more that is in you and arouse a greater and greater measure of this more.

How much of this more you can arouse, develop and turn to use need not concern your thought, nor should you think of any faculty or any power in your system as being limited. No actual limit has been found to any power in man, and as every power in the human system can be used to develop more power, it is evident that no limit ever will be found.

The problem in our present state of development is how to arouse all the power that is now latent within us, and the solution for this problem is faith. The more real faith you have in yourself, the more of your inherent power you arouse in yourself; and as this greater power is applied, your success will be greater in proportion, no matter what your vocation may be.

All great men have faith in themselves. They may not call it faith, but it is the same thing. It is that deep, determined, positive something in mind that tends to enter into and arouse, and that not only believes in greater possibilities, but is also determined to demonstrate those possibilities. All great minds have this something. They are, therefore, in close touch with the great inherent powers within them and are consequently arousing more and more of this power. This is their secret. They may have been born with the tendency to produce such a state of mind, or they may have acquired it in various ways, but it is something that does not come by chance. It comes through exact law and any one can acquire the great secret through the faithful and continuous application of that law. The law is the law of faith. You enter into and arouse all that is in you when you have faith in all that is in you.

Men and women who have succeeded began by having faith in themselves, faith in their talents, faith in the work they undertook to carry through. This faith might have been weak at times, but on the whole it was stronger than their doubts and fears, and accordingly they entered into and aroused at least a measure of the greater power within them. This measure determined their attainments and achievements. Where the measure was small, they gained but a step above the human mass, but where the measure was exceptionally large their lives towered mountains high above all the rest. And as they departed, they left names and deeds that can never die.

The majority of those minds, however, aroused their measure of power without a clear understanding of the law. They succeeded without knowing exactly how their success was attained. They used the law more or less unconsciously without having a full, intelligent control of its principle. They worked somewhat in the dark, but they were impelled by a something within them to press on and on. They obeyed that something and scaled the heights.

How this something was acquired within them in the first place need not concern us. We know it was faith, though we may not know how they originally secured that faith. This we know, however, that any mind can secure such a faith now; and we not only understand the law, but we can control the law through which a greater and a greater measure of power within us can be aroused. Therefore we, all of us, may rise to greater heights of attainment and achievement than has ever been known in the history of the world.

TO develop this something in yourself that tends to enter into the greater power within you and arouse that power, proceed with a deep, positive determination to have faith in yourself and in everything that exists in your life. Have more and more faith in your ability, in your power, in your capacity and in all things connected with the enterprise that you are trying to promote.

Have faith in yourself and you enter into and arouse the best that is in yourself. Have faith in your ability and you increase the power and efficiency of that ability.

To have faith is to enter into the spirit of the real life of that in which you express your faith, and to enter into the real life of any faculty or power, is to act upon all there is in that faculty or power.

When you have faith in anything within you, you act upon the kernel, or the core, or the vital spark of that particular thing. In brief, you act upon the real substance of the thing instead of the outer shell or surface; and this is your purpose. The moment the mind begins to act upon all that is in us, that all will become alive, and will come forth into actual expression in the world of practical use. Any man may succeed if he will only bring out all that is in him. There is enough in any person to give him success, the greatest success, and he may bring out everything that is in him by having faith in everything that is in him. The moment faith begins to animate the mind, every action of the mind will begin to enter into the deeper life of the mind and bring into action the greater power that is latent in the mind. This is the real nature of faith and it is an idea that must not be confounded with those beliefs to the contrary that we may previously have had on the subject.

When your faith in yourself does not cause your mind to enter into and arouse the all that is in yourself, you do not have any real faith. You have simply a superficial imitation. Real faith is a positive mental action that enters into the very spirit of every element and force in your being, and it not only enters into the all that is in you, but it brings that all out into a personal life where you can turn it to practical use. That is the faith that is faith. That is the faith that we all want That is the faith we all can get; and ail minds may succeed when they proceed with such a faith as the very soul of every thought and action.

The reason why is simple. The all that is in you is great enough and powerful enough to give you great success; and to have real faith in yourself, your whole self, is to bring out, into practical action, the all that is in yourself.

When you have faith in yourself, you turn the full force of your thought upon the vast depths of your life, and the full force of that thought begins to act upon all the power that is latent in your life. In consequence, you will become alive with power through and through. You will no longer be a weakling, but will feel yourself becoming a giant both in mind and soul.

To exercise the power of real faith, train your mind to concentrate, at all times, upon the greater life that is within the personal life, and thoroughly believe in that greater life. Try to enter into mental contact with the vast storage batteries of force that exist in the world of that greater life. The greater power of this inner world will soon awaken; then you will feel the coming forth of that something that makes men great.

As you grow in faith, that is, in the conscious feeling of the greater power that is in you, and as you deepen the vital action of that faith, you will arouse more and more of your power. Then you will know that you can. You will know that you can do what you desire to do, and your determination to prove it will become vastly stronger than it ever was before. You will become conscious of all that is in you. You will begin to realize that this all is powerful enough to overcome anything in your life and great enough to accomplish anything that you have planned for your life.

There is enough in any man to give that man unlimited success providing he works in that field for which he is adapted. The problem is to arouse all that is in the mind, the whole mind, conscious and subconscious, and to train that all for practical use.

The solution for the first part of the problem is faith — not mere belief, or a superficial self-confidence, but a strong, living faith — a positive determined, penetrating faith — a faith that actually goes into the greater and places the mind in full possession of the greater.

The solution for the second part is to put all your power to work in that field for which you have a natural aptitude. Go to work where your heart is. Have faith in that work. Have faith in your ability to succeed in that work as no one ever succeeded before. Enter into the spirit o£ that work. Live in the greater life and the greater possibilities of that work and believe that you have the power to make practical everything that is latent in those greater possibilities. Train your mind to work through the spirit of things; that is, give your attention, not to the surface of things, but to that greater world of power and possibility that is within things.

When you have faith in anything, concentrate your mind positively upon the real inner life of that thing; and when you try to have faith, turn your attention upon the real inner life of your understanding of things. To realize that you have faith is to enter into and arouse. Therefore, when you proceed to have faith, try to enter mentally into the greater and arouse the greater that may exist in that in which you have faith. Aim to make every action of faith deeper and stronger, more positive and more penetrating, and ere long you will gain full conscious possession of all the power, all the ability and all the capacity that your mental system may contain.

Do not attempt anything for which you are not naturally adapted. He who works in real faith can succeed to a degree in almost anything, but when he applies that same faith where he has natural ability, his success will be many times as great. If you have no special talent or natural ability, select some vocation that is rich in possibilities and that is open to you now; then give your life to it.

Work in faith. Be determined to succeed. Know that you can. Know that you have the power, and work in the consciousness of the vast interior life of that power. Have faith in every faculty that you apply in that work. Have faith in the purpose of the work and have faith in your ability to succeed in that work. Work in the faith that your ability is becoming greater every day and that you are gaining the power to take advantage of new and greater opportunities every day.

But in all your efforts, do not simply believe in yourself. Direct your mind to enter positively into the deeper life of every faculty and power in your being. Say that you have faith in everything that is in you. Say this a thousand times a day, and every time you say it, turn the full force of your thought upon all that is in you. the best that is in you, the limitless power that is in you. This is how you bring out the best that is in you and when the best that is in you is put to work, your success will be great indeed.

Whatever your purpose may be today, begin where you are and work yourself up into greater things. And begin by having the faith that you can — not a weak, mild faith, but a faith so deep, so positive and so strong, that every atom in your being is fired up to the white heat of unconquerable determination. With such a faith, you can proceed in the conviction that you will succeed; because if you work in such a faith, your success will be as certain as the sunrise of tomorrow.

Work constantly in the determined attitude of a penetrating faith, and failure becomes impossible. You cannot fail so long as you are growing in power, ability and practical efficiency. You cannot fail so long as you are growing in the power of desire to succeed, in the power of ambition to succeed, in the power of the determination to succeed. And all these things become stronger and greater in your life the more real positive faith you have in everything that is contained in your life.

WORK in the living action of a determined faith and obstacles will not be obstacles any more. What previously appeared to be obstacles you will now recognize as opportunities. You will now know that you have the power to transform every obstacle into an opportunity and in doing so you will have the opportunity to arouse and turn to use power that you never used before. Thus you will have no fear of obstacles and difficulties. You know that you can overcome them all, transform them all, and turn everything that is in them all to good account.

You are conscious of the power within you that can overcome anything. Through your faith you are entering into all that is in you; you are awakening all that is in you, and you know that the all in you is greater than any obstacle you can ever meet.

But the all in you does not exist simply on the surface. It exists through and through your entire being, and especially in the greater depths of your being. Therefore, to arouse the all every action of your mind must penetrate the depths, the real interior life force of every atom in your system; and here we find the supreme value of faith.

To inspire the mind with faith is to cause every mental action to enter into those depths and make alive the whole of your life, the whole of your ability, the whole of your capacity, the whole of your power. To live in the spirit of real faith is to place the mind in touch with the deeper life and the power there is latent in all things. You are thus living with greatness in the mental world and you are in constant contact with the "live wire" of universal power.

It is a well known fact that there is a limitless force that pervades all things, an infinite sea, so to speak, of energy and power within which we live and move and have our being. The vital current of this sea may be termed the live wire of the universe, and the problem is to place ourselves in such close contact with this current that we may constantly be charged with its inexhaustible power.

Faith is the secret, because faith enters into the inner life of things, and it is by entering into the inner life, or rather the depths of feeling and consciousness, that we place the mind in contact with this live wire. This wire lies in the depths of existence and great minds invariably touch these depths. That is the secret of their ability and extraordinary power.

But all minds can touch those depths.

Faith is the means of contact and any mind can have faith. Any mind can concentrate upon the greater power within — the all that exists in human life — and develop that deep, positive action of the mind that tends to enter into and arouse.

Have faith in everybody and you cultivate faith in yourself. Have faith in yourself and you will have faith in everything in the universe. And the more faith you have in everything, the more perfect will be your mental contact with the boundless life and the mental power that exists in everything. Believe in the all that is in everybody and make that belief deep, positive and strong. To doubt others is to produce doubt in yourself. But doubt will suppress the power that can, while faith will arouse the power that can.

When things look dark, proceed in the faith that you have the power to turn the tide. Enter into the innermost life of that power and thus you awaken every force that may exist in that power. You will thus become alive with a determination that positively cannot be conquered or destroyed; and that determination will be backed up with sufficient power to do what you are determined to do.

When you have faith in all the power that is in you, all of that power will be placed at your command. This is a positive fact. It is the power back of your determination that produces that determination, and as the cause is always as strong as its effect, the more determined you are to do a certain thing, the more power you will have with which to do it. And through the increase of your faith, this power will increase indefinitely until it becomes strong enough to turn any tide.

Therefore, no matter what your condition may be today, continue to have faith in all the power that is in you. You will become stronger and stronger every day. You will steadily work yourself up to that masterful position where you can control your circumstances and cause everything to turn in your favor.

Have faith. It is the royal path from adversity to prosperity. Faith gives you the power to do what you want to do. Faith can give you all the power you need; all the power you want. This is an exact, scientific fact. Faith connects the mind with all the power that is in you. Faith connects the mind with the limitless power of the universe. The idea therefore that faith can make all things possible is based upon a principle as sound as the very principle of life itself.

You can do anything if you have enough power. Faith will give you more and more power until you have as much as you can possibly require. So long as you increase your faith in yourself, you will increase the power in yourself, and you can increase your faith perpetually.

The deep positive action of real faith will increase your ability and working capacity. When you have faith in your ability, you enter mentally into the real inner life of that ability and you arouse all that is in that ability; but to this all there is no limit. You may awaken more and more power in any faculty and never find any limit to the amount of power that can be awakened.

The more power you develop in any faculty, the greater becomes the capacity of that faculty to develop more power. It is therefore evident that from the day you gain the real secret of faith, your advancement will be continuous, no matter what your work may be, or what may appear to be in your way. And you gain the real secret of faith by training every action of the mind to enter into and arouse the best, the richest, the greatest and the all that is in you.

Have faith in everything upon which you turn your attention and try to enter mentally into the all of that upon which you concentrate. You will soon have the secret. You will soon feel yourself becoming alive with more and more power, and from that day your real success will begin.

The real faith is always calm — deeply calm, but immensely strong. Though the positive, penetrating action of faith can arouse to the very highest pitch of intensity every element and force in your being, the faith itself is never excitable or agitated, never overwrought, never otherwise than calm, poised, masterful and serene. And herein lies the power of faith. It is as deep as the deepest depths of existence, but so calm and masterful in its action that it can control the force of any action. When the attitude of faith becomes agitated and overwrought, it ceases to be faith. It becomes mere shallow emotional intensity, the reaction of which will produce mental weakness and indifference. But shallow emotionalism, no matter how intense, cannot touch the depths of life and power. It cannot arouse the all that is in you, nor place your mind in contact with that inexhaustible energy that flows through the live wire of the universe. But real faith can do this, and that is the reason why he who has real faith will gain sufficient power, ability and capacity to accomplish anything he may have in view.

To promote your success, use all the power and ability you possess. Use all the practical principles you know through which you may increase your usefulness and efficiency. Combine all of these with work, all the work that you can possibly carry through; then add faith. When you add faith, you turn on the current, so to speak — the great invincible current of all the energy that is in you, and the machinery of your mental system will begin to move as you want it to move. The engine that is to carry you to the great goal your ambition is longing to reach, will begin to speed on, and it will continue to speed on until you are within the rich, fascinating city of success — the fair city of your lofty dreams. And remember so long as you are living and working in the deep, invincible spirit of faith, the current will be on; and the engine will continue to speed on so long as the current is on.

Expect all your faculties and powers to do what you want them to do. Expect them all to make good. Constant expectation, if deep and determined, will lead to faith, and faith leads to the continuous enlargement of mind, thought and soul. Continuous, positive expectation, combined with the most thorough application of all the power in your possession, will lead inevitably to the results expected; frequently to far greater results than expected.

When the mind is in touch with the greater depths of interior life and power, and continues to press on toward some lofty goal, all its efforts will become accumulative, and sufficient power will be gained to reach a still higher goal. Those who build well, always build better than they know. But the only minds who are really building well are those who, in their building, are turning to practical use the all that exists within them.

Men who succeed expect to succeed, and this expectation is continuous. They are determined, most positively determined. All their power is focused upon the goal in view, and they have so much faith in themselves and their work that they absolutely refuse to think of fail. In every instance there is an inner power at work and the all within them is alive.

Great men do not succeed through mere surface brains. There is something deeper at work in those brains, and that deeper something is aroused through faith — faith in themselves — faith in their purpose — faith in their ultimate victory.

The great man enters into the spirit of things. He is conscious of the vast, inexhaustible depths of his own interior being. He is in touch with the inner world of real power, and that is how he becomes something more than a mere cog in the wheel of industry. Through the awakening of all that is in him, he becomes not a cog in the wheel, nor even the wheel, but the power that drives the wheel.

You have that power in yourself. Arouse all that is in you and that power will come forth into actual personal possession. Then the great man in you will be placed at the helm, and the great goal you have in view will positively be gained. Expect results. Expect growth. Expect achievement. Expect increase. Expect a real, substantial, ever-growing success. Be determined to secure it and work in the spirit of that determination with all the power of unbounded faith.

The door to the greater will open before you. You will realize your aim. You will reach your goal. You will scale the heights.

IN addition to faith — that deep, penetrating faith that tends to enter into and arouse, we must also have desire — ceaseless, persistent desire. And all great men are actually alive with such a desire. It is this desire that spurs them on towards the loftiest goal they have in view; it is this desire that lays hold upon the greater power aroused by faith, and causes that power to be concentrated upon the purpose they have undertaken to carry through.

That the power of desire is immense when it is thoroughly alive and in earnest, is a fact known to all, and the real truth concerning this power is well expressed in the following statements: "We get what we desire and in the full measure of that desire" and "We always get what we wish for if we only wish hard enough." What it means to wish hard enough, however, is the problem, and what it is that truly constitutes desire, is a question few have answered.

To the many a desire is a mere wish for something, a wish that may be weak or strong, deep or shallow, according to the object desired; but iii any case the desire is looked upon as a mere feeling in the mind; nothing more.

There are a few, however, who have discovered that there is more in desire than a mere wish for the object desired, and it is these few who invariably get what they desire. By some they are called fortunate; and in a certain sense they are, because those who have learned how to get what they desire are certainly fortunate. Others give them credit for extraordinary ability, and this is also true; though they may not have exceptional mental attainments in every case, still they have the ability to use a power that the many know nothing about. By another group they are frequently accused of taking undue advantage of their fellow men, but this does not explain the secret of their success.

The man who has discovered the real power of desire can get what he wants without wronging anybody, and he will get what he wants, no matter how adverse the circumstances, how great the obstacle or how hopeless the aim.

Whatever you wish for, wish hard enough and you will positively get it. But the act of wishing hard is quite different from what we usually suppose.

You do not wish hard enough for anything unless you make that wish thoroughly alive with all the life and power that you can possibly arouse. You do not place in action the real power of desire unless you give your desire soul, the deep, strong, invincible power of soul.

When the force of your desire is just as deep as the deepest depths of your own interior life and just as strong as all the power that can possibly be contained in that life, your desire will be fulfilled. You will get what you wish for when all of you is in your wish. The reason why is simply understood as there is nothing mysterious or supernatural about the process through which results are obtained. It is only a matter of using all the power you possess instead of a small fraction.

When you make up your mind to reach a certain goal or accomplish something you have in view, results will depend upon how you use the inner or real power of desire. If your determination to succeed is shallow or superficial, you will accomplish but little. On the other hand, if that determination is as deep as the depths of your own life you will arouse the deepest force of your life, and those forces are not only powerful — they are positively irresistible, and that you should succeed with such power at your command is most evident.

When you make up your mind in this deep, strong sense, you are bringing into action the strongest and best there is in you. You are deeply in earnest and you feel deeply on the subject. In consequence, your desire to succeed will strengthen every atom in your entire being. Your whole being will become alive and when the power that is in you is alive with the deep, positive desire of invincible determination, there is no adversity or obstacle in existence that you cannot overcome.

Make yourself strong enough and great enough and there is nothing in the world that will not bend its energies in any manner required to serve the purposes of your supreme desire. Even the iron rails of destiny will bend at your command so that you may move in any direction and reach any goal you have in mind. And any person becomes strong enough and great enough when the deepest powers of his soul are aroused.

There is more in you than you ever dreamed, and there are times when this more becomes so strong that you feel as if you could master the universe. And those deeper feelings are not mistaken. Make yourself as strong as nature has given you the power to become and the universe will make way for any plan or project you may wish to undertake.

The secret is to use all the power in your present conscious possession. To develop more may not be necessary for a time. Arouse what can be aroused now and you have sufficient for anything you may wish to accomplish now. Any person can do what he makes up his mind to do and get what he wants when he makes use of all the power that he is conscious of; and all that power is invariably aroused when every desire is given soul.

Bring out all that power and make your wish alive with all that power; then you wish hard enough. That is what it means to wish hard enough, and you will get what you wish for.

YOU get what you desire and in the full measure of that desire when your desire is literally crammed with all the life and all the power and all the soul there is in you. Failure comes from halfhearted desire, honeycombed with doubt, or from those desires that are so shallow that they cannot arouse enough power to overcome a single obstacle.

Success demands not only the power to do things, but also the power to surmount every obstacle that may be met, and the power to transform every adversity into a rich and rare opportunity. But such power does not come from shallow thinking or from half-heartedness in feeling and desire.

He who would get the power to do what he wants to do must sound the depths of his being. He must learn to draw upon those deeper, finer forces of his mind and soul that alone can give him all the power he may demand. And he can do this when he deepens his desire and begins to work in a penetrating, determined faith. Every desire that is felt in the very depths of his being touches the vastness and the immensity of the greater within and the power of the greater within is invincible.

The real power of a deep, strong desire conies from the great interior domains within us. Therefore it is never crude nor uncertain in its action. Its action is not mere animal will or the domineering force of physical determination; nor does it correspond in any way with physical might and main. On the other hand, it is one of the most refined of all the forces of the system. In brief, it is actual soul force. But soul force is not something that pertains to some other state of existence. On the contrary, it is the very life of every tangible force in the universe here and now.

The soul of anything is the kernel, the core, the real substance, the vital spark — in brief, it is the thing itself.

The physical or tangible side of anything is the wire, so to speak, while the soul of that thing is the electrical current. This illustration gives us a more definite idea as to what is meant by the term soul as applied to the force of desire; and thus we can readily understand why desire becomes so much more powerful when it is given soul.

When you arouse the soul force of your system you begin to draw upon the limitless, and all your faculties and talents will begin to outdo themselves. You are not only bringing out the best that is in you, but you are going farther still. You are going back of the present capacity and you are arousing that deeper something in your life that can give perpetual increase to your capacity. Therefore it is but natural that you should accomplish what you have in mind and get what you wish for.

No one can fail who applies the best that is in him, but back of the best there is more. We all know there is. We all have had moments when we realized the limitless vastness of the great within; and whenever we have thought of the realization of those moments, something has convinced us that we can at any time, bring forth into actual use enough Of this superior power to reach any goal we have in view or scale any height to which the mind can aspire.

Give the deep, strong, invincible power of the soul to every desire and you will awaken those greater powers within you that can fulfill every desire; and in addition, you will cause every power in your possession to work for that which you aim to realize.

Desire gives definiteness to the powers we possess. When we have no definite desire, the forces and energies within us will scatter and be lost; but the very moment we begin to desire something with a deep, persistent desire, all our forces and energies will begin to work for the attainment of that something.

The stronger the desire, the more perfectly we concentrate upon that desire, and concentration is one of the chief essentials to greater success.

The stronger your desire along a certain line, the more force and energy you will express along that line, and the more power you express and apply to any action, the greater will be the result gained through that action.

Desire greatness with the soul of desire and you arouse the powers of greatness. Those powers are within you. They are positively there. It remains for you to bring them out, and you can if your desires are so deep that they stir the very depths of your innermost being.

Desire everything to change for the better and if that desire is as deep as your whole life, you will produce such changes in your whole life as are necessary to bring about all other changes you may have in view. Create the inner cause and the outer effect must inevitably follow.

Desire success with the deepest and strongest desire that you can possibly feel and you arouse those very powers within you that can produce success.

Desire an ideal environment and you awaken those qualities in your own nature that can build up that richer and better environment which you wish to enter. In consequence, you will ere long find yourself in such an environment, because like attracts like, and from superior causes come superior effects.

You invariably cause yourself to become what you constantly desire to become; that is, when that desire is so deep and so strong that it actually thrills with feeling, life and soul, and stirs into positive action every power that is latent within you.

There is enough creative energy and mental building material within you to make you a mental and spiritual giant. You therefore, need not hesitate to aspire to the very highest goal your mind can possibly picture. It is in you to become what you want to become, and what is in you can be brought out into positive action through the penetrating power of a deep, soul desire.

Whatever you desire never fail to give that desire your very life, your whole life and the full power of the deepest, strongest, finest life that you can possibly arouse from the Inexhaustible depths of your own soul.

Do not simply express a wish. Express more, and make this more as large, as high and as powerful as you can. Give your wish soul, not mere sentimental soul, but that expression of invincible soul that will press on and on to the goal in view no matter what the obstacles may be. Make your wish alive and be so thoroughly in earnest that every atom in your being thrills with the positive determination to make that wish come true.

Never attempt, however, to use mere mental force. The soul of desire is far deeper than mind and infinitely more powerful than mind. Try to feel this soul whenever you express the power of desire; and when you do feel it, try to feel more and more of the real life of the soul. Try to feel the finer elements and the finer forces that exist within all physical life and all mental life.

Try to deepen and enrich your consciousness from one grade of soul to a deeper, richer grade of soul until you are conscious of the immensity and vastness of your own superior within. Then you will know what it means to give the invincible power of soul to every desire. Then you will know why everything must pass before the deep, determined power of such a desire. Then you will know why those who possess the secret of real desire invariably scale the heights even though the whole world be against them and every imaginable obstacle in the way.

TO secure results in the various fields of action, two methods have been employed. The usual method has been to depend directly upon personal action and to think of personal action as the principal factor in the doing of things.

The other method has been to depend directly upon the power of thought; and where this method has received special attention, personal action has been given a secondary place or looked upon as simply an effect, while the power of thought has been viewed as the one sole cause.

The first or usual method, practically ignores the power of thought as a direct factor in success; while the second method minimizes the value of personal action. Neither method, however, is efficient when employed alone, because whatever man undertakes to do, he will find both personal action and the power of thought necessary to success.

To depend upon personal action alone is to fail to give that personal action the greatest amount of power obtainable. The power of thought is the power that is back of all personal action. Therefore, when the power of thought is not directly employed in connection with the personal action, that action will necessarily be weak.

And to depend upon the power of thought alone is to fail to give that power the proper expression. Nothing tangible can be done without personal action, as no power can produce results unless it acts through personal action.

The average person accomplishes but little as he usually depends almost entirely upon personal action; and as he permits the greater powers of thought to lie dormant, his personal action is naturally weak, limited and inefficient.

The same, however, may be said of the average idealist. He expects to get results through the power of thought alone. He ignores personal action to a degree and therefore does not give practical expression to the power there is in thought. In consequence, that power is scattered and but meager results are secured.

There is a tendency among idealists to act upon the belief that when the thought is right, the action will take care of itself. They also act upon the belief that the power of thought, if sufficiently strong, will produce results in some mysterious manner outside the domain of personal effort; and being true to this belief, they have not tried to combine the power of thought with personal action, not knowing that in the world of results there are two factors instead of one.

That the action will be right when the thought is right, is true only in a certain sense; that is, the action will be right when the right thought becomes action. But the power of thought never becomes action unless it enters personal action. The power of thought becomes action only when the will to do is just as strong as is will to think.

Certain actions of the mind will arouse the power of thought, but it requires entirely different actions of the mind to put that power to work. The average idealist arouses the greater power of his thought, but in too many instances, fails to put that power to work. In other words, he fails to express his power through personal action. It is therefore scattered, and his actual working capacity is made no greater than the capacity of those people who probably never dreamed of the power of thought.

To expect results from the mysterious actions of thought is to enter abnormal states of mind; and to enter such states is to fail. The only channel through which the power of thought can produce tangible results is through the action of the human personality, and the only normal action of thought is that action that is expressed upon or through the personality. Therefore all other action of thought is abnormal and, in consequence, misdirected.

To secure success combine the two great factors. Combine the power of thought with the power of personal action in everything that is undertaken. That is the secret of success, and great men invariably apply this secret Sometimes their application may be unconscious though usually it is more or less conscious. However, whether they fully understand the process or not, they constantly employ the principle, and that is how they reach the goal they have had in view.

To succeed, arouse all the greater powers that are within you and turn those powers into personal action. Put those powers to work. Apply those powers scientifically in connection with everything you do. Do not simply expect your thought to become action, but use your thought — the full force of your thought — IN every action.

Do not permit your thought to scatter. Do not throw out the force of your thought upon some imaginary achievement or possession. Hold all the power of your thought in yourself. Give the full force of your thought to your whole mind and body, to your own muscles, nerves, faculties and talents. Train all the great forces within you to express themselves through you, and through that which you are doing.

Think only of that which you actually intend to do or are doing, and concentrate the full force of your thought upon your present work. Then you will do something worthwhile, and it is the doing of things worthwhile that paves the way for whatever goal we may desire to reach.

To combine the power of thought with personal action recognize the power of thought as a leading factor in everything you do. Direct the full force of your thought into every action and express in every action the power of such states of mind as you know will add to the life, the force, the capacity and the efficiency of that action. Think that you can do what you are proceeding to do, and give your attention positively to what you have undertaken.

Do not simply try to see if you can, but think that you can; and be determined to prove that your thought is right. You thus give added life and power to your action and you double and treble the possibility of success.

Never doubt your capacity or have fear as to results. Believe in your power to carry out your purpose and think constantly of that power as you proceed in your work. Work in the conviction that you can do your work, and combine with your work the practical expression of all the power of mind and thought.

The power of thought produces results according to definite law, and the principal law involved is that law through which mental power tends to increase the power of personal action. And the power of thought invariably does increase the power and efficiency of personal action when properly combined with, and expressed through, that action.

The power of thought can strengthen and develop every mental faculty, improve every personal quality and rebuild the entire man according to a spiritual ideal. But this power must have actual expression, and expression is possible only through personal action.

The average person, when trying to use the power of thought, usually concentrates upon external conditions or upon some vague mental state. His power therefore is mostly scattered. He uses up energy to no purpose and not only fails to advance, but becomes a discouragement to those who are looking for better methods than the world in general can offer.

To use the power of thought in producing success, do not simply think that you are going to succeed. Success comes from the practical application of ability; therefore use your mental power in the development of greater ability, and combine that power with every effort that you make to apply that ability.

The greater the action, the greater the result in whatever the field of action may be; and the more mental power you give to that ability that is expressed in the action, the greater will be the action. To simply think that you will succeed, and permit the power of that thought to scatter wherever your uncontrolled tendencies may lead, is to prepare the way for failure.

When you think success or affirm success, concentrate the full power of your attention upon that ability or talent that you are using in the promotion of success. When you use the power of thought in promoting success, desire to increase your ability and constantly think of the increase of that ability.

If your success depends upon business ability, concentrate all the power of your thought upon business ability. Desire to develop your business ability and think that you can. In this manner your business ability positively will develop, and as it does, greater success must naturally follow.

Constantly will to cause the power of thought to make you more able, more competent, more efficient and more useful, and expect greater success for yourself as you make a greater man of yourself. Great men do this; you will become great by doing the same.

But when you think success and will success, you do not bring about success through some strange, mysterious force. By thinking success, you cause all your faculties to work more successfully. In consequence, ability and efficiency are increased, and you will steadily advance. When all of your faculties work more and more successfully, you, yourself, will work more and more successfully; and that is the secret of success.

The power of thought can remove every form of adversity, but it does not proceed by mysteriously acting upon those conditions that are in the way. On the contrary, it acts upon you alone, and in a manner that is both simple and effectual.

When you properly apply the power of thought in this connection, you give your mind a better insight into adverse conditions, and you secure better ideas as to how to work yourself out. The power of your thought does not directly remove adversity, but makes you so much stronger and so much greater than adversity, that you can remove it yourself through your own determined personal action.

When you are in any difficulty, use the power of your thought in strengthening and elevating your mind. Thus you will not only see how to act, but you can act with greater power; and you must act both with the power of thought and with the power of personal action if you would overcome what is in your way. The problem in overcoming anything is to know how to act, and to have the power to act effectually.

The power of thought, when properly concentrated upon your various mental faculties, will make your entire mind more brilliant. You can, through the use of interior thought force, positive desire, real faith and constructive thinking, work your mind up to a higher level; that is, you can bring your mind up into the upper story of consciousness, so to speak, and while there you may not only form superior ideas, but the very ideas that you need under the circumstances.

You will thus know how to act in order to overcome what is in your way, and by combining the power of your thought with that action, you will act effectually.

Thus adversity will be removed; the difficulty will be overcome; you will work yourself out, and reach the goal you have in view.

WHEN man becomes acquainted with himself, he invariably discovers that he can change himself and his environment through the intelligent use of the laws and powers of his own being; that he can build health, character and ability to any degree desired; that he can remove from his life what is not conducive to his welfare and happiness; that he can gain possession of more and more of that which is conducive to his welfare and happiness; that the possibilities within him have no limitations whatever, and that there is evidently no end to what he can do in the growth and development of himself and the world in which he lives.

The principle of this discovery has been demonstrated by thousands in every age. Results have been secured in every known field of human life and action, and some of these results have been so extraordinary as to almost appear miraculous.

When man makes this discovery, he no longer submits to things as they are. He no longer trains his mind to accept adversity in a meek and lowly spirit. He no longer thinks that it is necessary to give up to what appears to be the inevitable.

He has discovered that man holds his own life in his own hands, and proceeds to act accordingly. Man is supreme in his own life and in his own world. This we know. He may have his own way in everything. He may form his own ideals and make them all come true. He may plan his own future and realize every dream precisely as expected. He has the intellect to understand the principle and the power to apply the law.

But here we meet a problem, and a seeming contradiction of terms. Among those who have tried to understand the principle and apply the law, thousands have secured the results desired, but other thousands have not. They have either failed wholly or in part to produce those changes in themselves or in their environments for which they have labored so faithfully. They have seemingly done their part, and to all appearances have done it just as well as those who were more successful. Why they should fail may therefore seem difficult to understand, but it is simple enough.

There are many powers in man, but there is only one power that has controlling power, and that power is in the will. The purpose of the will is to control or direct all the other powers in man — to so direct those other powers as to cause them all to do what we want them to do. There is no limit to man's inherent capacity; the subconscious cannot be exhausted neither in the quantity of power nor in the varieties of power. It is therefore evident that man can do with his life whatever he may desire, provided he can cause all his power to do whatever he many desire. And he can.

The controlling power of the will can cause any other power in man to do whatever the will may direct it to do. This controlling power of the will, however, must be used not simply to control for the sake of exercising control, but for the purpose of turning the other powers in man into those channels of action where the results desired may be produced.

Great men do this. That is what makes them great, and that is what gives them success. When man undertakes to change himself or his environment every power in his being must be directed to so act as to promote that change; and the first power to be so directed is the power of thought. The mind is creative and its power can create the change desired when properly directed.

This is a fact, however, that is fully recognized by all who have taken up the science and art of applied idealism, and they have, almost without exception given their mental powers the direction required; but they have, in too many instances, neglected to give that same direction to their other powers; and here we find the cause of failure.

To direct the mind to think towards the goal that is to be reached is the first essential, but the power of such thought will not produce any change in man until his personality is directed to live and express the idea conveyed by that thought.

The idealist wills to think, but does not always will to do. The belief that right action will invariably follow right thought is only partly true. Thought never becomes action unless the same will that willed to think also wills to act. The complete will controls both thought and action, and must act in both in order to produce results.

The creation of a new idea is not necessarily followed by the expression of that idea. The will that wills to create a new idea does not will to express that idea unless so directed by the mind. Some minds naturally combine the will to think with the will to act and it is such minds that secure the greatest results, frequently with but little effort.

Those minds that fail to secure external changes for the better after they have changed their thought for the better, fail because they do not naturally combine the will to think with the will to do. In those minds the will is not fully applied; that is, they will to think the ideal, or plan for the desired achievement, but they do not always will to work out those ideals and plans in tangible action. But when the will is so trained that it invariably wills to do whatever it has willed to think, every change in thought will be positively followed by a corresponding change in external conditions.

Man is as he thinks; but he is not always the product of all his thought. The only thought that gives formation to the character, the mentality and the personality of man, is the thought that contains the will to express itself. And the more such thought a man thinks, the greater and more successful he becomes.

All other thought is useless. To create thought and not give that thought the will to express itself is to waste both time and energy. Three-fourths of the thought created in the average mind, however, is of this kind. It takes shape in the mind but does not contain the will to work itself out into real tangible results.

The path to greater power of mind and personality may therefore be found, first, in training the mind to think only constructive thought; and second in giving every thought the will to act.

Eight thinking will produce right conditions in mind and body only when the will to act is just as strong and just as deeply felt as the will to think. Constructive thinking will promote the advancement of man both in attainment and in achievement whenever the desire to work out the ideal is just as strong and just as positive as the desire to imagine the ideal.

All thinking that pictures the greater and the better, and that is animated with a positive desire to attain the greater and the better, is constructive thinking. And all thinking is right that is based upon the principle that the ideal of everything contains the power to become real; that is, that the good that is inherent in everything is infinitely greater and more powerful than any mistake, imperfection or undeveloped condition.

The power of will is indispensable whether the action be physical or mental. We can do nothing until we will to do it, and what we wish to have done in any particular field of action, we must will to do in that field of action. What we wish to have done in the mind, we must will to do in the mind. What we wish to have done in the body we must will to do in the body. What we do in one part of the system will not be duplicated in some other part unless we so will it.

The power of thought will work itself out in personal life only when we will to convert that power into personal power. The ideal becomes real when the characteristics of the ideal are acted out in the real. Act in the real as you feel you are in the ideal. When you have seen the vision of the soul, will to make it come true in the body. You can.

But do not try to will with the mere surface action of the will. It is through the controlling power of the will, the inner, vital action of the will, that you cause your other powers to do what you wish to have done; and this controlling power constitutes the soul of will.

Give soul to your desire to act and the mind will act through the soul of the will; that is, through that force of the will that actually contains real will power. Thus you will consciously apply the controlling power of the will and succeed in doing what you want to do.

WHAT is here designated as real will power is a direct expression of the superior man within. There is a larger man within you. This interior man is the real you and infinitely greater and more powerful than your outer personality; and it is upon this interior man that you must depend for results.

Constantly think of this interior man as the ruling factor in your life and constantly expect this supreme factor in yourself to produce greater and greater results indefinitely. It is the superior man within that exercises real will power — the power that can control. Therefore to will to do what you desire to do, we must give the superior man within the right of way.

Act as if you were the superior man within and you will find that you are the superior man within. All great men do this, some consciously, some unconsciously. This is how their greater power wills to act. This how they place in action the controlling power of the will wherever they may desire to act; and this is how they almost invariably do whatever they will to do.

The visible person has no real will power. You gain possession of real will power when you begin to feel that you are the inner man within. That power of the will that can calmly, but absolutely, direct all the other powers in your being to do what you wish them to do comes from the depths of your life.

When your feeling of life is deep and when that depth of life is calm and strong, then you will gain that power that contains the controlling power. Then you gain what may be termed the indomitable will, and then you gain the power to work out in tangible life every change for the better that you may have planned in your mind.

Many minds are so constituted that they naturally give the superior man within the right of way; and it is such minds that secure the greatest results, not only in the science and art of applied idealism, but in any and every field of endeavor as well.

There are greater powers within you than you have ever expressed. If you will permit those powers to come forth more and more, you will steadily and rapidly advance, no matter what your work may be. If you are so constituted that you naturally give those greater powers the right of way, you will move towards the high places in life whether you understand those greater powers or not. You will forge to the front because you can feel something superior within you that prompts you to press on and on, overcoming every obstacle, and scaling every height.

But if you do not naturally give these greater powers right of way, you must train yourself to do so; and you can. When any mind takes up the science and art of applied idealism and tries to produce changes for the better, either in the mental world or in the physical world, results will depend upon two things; and in the last analysis these two are one.

If the mind naturally gives the greater power within the right of way and naturally gives every thought the will to express itself in tangible action, results will be forthcoming without fail. When the superior man within is in action, the will to think and the will to act become practically one will, and every mental change is invariably followed by a corresponding physical change. But no mental change can produce a corresponding physical change unless the new mental state contains the will to express itself; and since real will power is inseparably united with the superior man within, it is evident that we must permit this interior man to come forth if we desire interior mental changes to come forth.

That greater something within us that constitutes the controlling power of the will must be in action before we can will to do or become whatever we may desire to do or become.

To be so constituted that the greater man within is naturally given right of way is well, providing that tendency is cultivated; but if it is not cultivated, we will have results up to a certain point only, and there will be no further progress.

It is not necessary, however, to be so constituted naturally in order to secure results. The mind can readily be trained to work out into the tangible any new and improved condition. The will to think and the will to act can be made one, and the power of creation and expression can be made so strong that the moment we discern an ideal, it begins to become real.

What comes naturally to some can be developed in all, and the greatest results come not to those who depend upon a natural talent, but to those who take what they have, be it ever so little, and proceed to develop what they have to the highest degree possible.

We all have some will power. Whenever we move a muscle or utter a word, we use the controlling power of will to cause some other power to do what we wish to have done.

We can develop this function more and more until we cause every power we possess to do whatever we may wish to have done; and we develop this function whenever we will to work out in tangible action any and every change for the better that we have pictured in mind.

Will to do whatever you have willed to think; and will, not on the surface of the mind, but will with a ceaseless, determined will from the fathomless depths of your mind. Thus you will become in the real what you have desired to become in the ideal. You will work out your ambition. You will realize your dream, and you will cause the vision of the soul to come true.

We have all felt the power of the superior man within. We have all had moments when we knew that we were greater by far than the visible self had ever appeared to be; and those moments can be made not only more numerous, but an ever present realization.

We can train ourselves to feel more and more of the greatness within, and to express more and more of that greatness. We can do this by giving the larger interior man full right of way.

Let the power that is within you come forth. Let it even take full possession of your entire personality. It will never lead you wrong, but will instead, prompt you to press on and on regardless of circumstances until you reach the very highest heights you have in view.

Act as if you were this great interior man; think that you are; feel that you are; know that you are. Thus you give full expression to the greatest and best that is in you, and as you realize this expression you discover that it is all of you, and that the all of you is great indeed.

Henceforth, you can proceed to do in larger and larger measure what every awakened mind has discovered that man can do. You can change yourself, improve yourself and advance yourself. You can grow out of every unfortunate condition into any superior condition.

You can create health, harmony and happiness in abundance. You can live as you wish to live; become what you desire to become; increase perpetually your capacity to attain and achieve; build character and ability to the highest degree of efficiency and power, and place yourself upon that high pinnacle of being where you can truthfully say that your life is in your own hands and what your future is to be, you, yourself, have the power to determine.

How the Mind Works

How the Mind Works

Table of Contents

Foreword

Everything that is in action must necessarily work through definite laws. And as the mind is in constant action, alternating its actions at almost every turn of thought or feeling, it is evident that a vast number of laws are employed by the mental process. To know how the mind works, therefore, we must know something about these laws.

In the following pages the most important of the mental and metaphysical laws known to date are considered from every possible viewpoint, the principal object being to ascertain their real nature as well as their power and use. In addition, a number of psychological ideas are presented that will throw light both on the inner and the outer workings of the mind.

No effort, however, has been made to delve into the mysteries of the mind; this will be done in another work, the object here being to present the practical side of mental action, and present it in such a way that anyone may learn to use the powers of the mind properly. And at the present stage of psychological study, this is the most important. We want to know how the mind does work so that we may, in all mental work, use the mind in the best, the fullest and the most effective manner.

The fact that we have, in the past, known practically nothing about the real workings of the mind, and also that there are only a few minds, even in the present, that have gained the power to direct and control mental action according to system, design and law, should make the study of this book both interesting and profitable. In fact, we are convinced that all who understand the purpose and the message of this book will become highly enthused over its practical value; and will accordingly gain more from its perusal than tongue can ever tell.

That this number may be very large in the present, and constantly become larger in the future, is our dearest wish in this connection; for when you know that a certain thing is so very true and so very important, you want everybody else, if possible, to gain all that you have gained from the understanding and use of that particular thing.

And this is natural; we all want to share the truth with others; we all want everybody to gain that power through which the richest and the best that life has in store may be realized; and this fact proves that there is far more of the noble in human nature than we have previously believed. However, it is only as we learn to use the mind in harmony with the natural and orderly workings of mental law, that everything that is noble in human nature will find expression.

Chapter 1

The Greatest Power In Man

It is now a demonstrated fact that the powers and the possibilities that are inherent in the mind of man are practically unbounded. And this conclusion is based upon the discovery that no limit can be found to anything in human nature, and that everything in human nature contains a latent capacity for perpetual development. This discovery, and no discovery of greater importance has appeared in any age, gives man a new conception of himself, a conception which when applied will necessarily revolutionize the entire sphere of human thought and action.

To be able to discern the real significance of this new conception will naturally constitute the greatest power in man, and should therefore be given the first thought in all efforts that have advancement, attainment or achievement in view. The purpose of each individual should be not simply to cultivate and apply those possibilities that are now in evidence, but also to develop power to discern and fathom what really exists within him. This power is the greatest power because it prepares the way for the attainment and expression of all other powers. It is the power that unlocks the door to everything that is great and wonderful in man, and must therefore be understood and applied before anything of real value can be accomplished through human thought or action.

The principal reason why the average person remains weak and incompetent is found in the fact that he makes no effort to fathom and understand the depths of his real being. He tries to use what is in action on the surface, but is unconscious of the fact that enormous powers are in existence in the greater depth of his life. These powers are dormant simply because they have not been called into action, and they will continue to lie dormant until man develops his greatest power; that is, the power to discern what really exists within him.

The fundamental cause of failure is found in the belief that what exists on the surface is all there is of man. And the reason why greatness is the rare exception instead of the universal rule can be traced to the same cause. When the mind discovers that its powers are inexhaustible and that its faculties and talents can be developed to the very highest degree imaginable, and to any degree beyond that, the fear of failure will entirely disappear. In its stead will come the conviction that man may attain anything or achieve anything, provided, of course, he works within the natural sphere of universal law. Whatever circumstances may be today such a mind will know that all can be changed; that this condition can be made to pass away, and that the vacancy may be filled with the heart's most cherished desire.

That mind that can discern what exists in the depths of the real life of man does not simply change its views as to what man may attain or achieve, but actually begins to draw upon the inexhaustible power within, and begins at once to develop and apply the greater possibilities that this deeper discernment has revealed. When man can see, feel and understand what exists beneath the surface of his life, the expression of this deeper life begins, because whatever we become conscious of that we invariably bring forth into tangible expression. And since the deeper life contains innumerable possibilities as well as unbounded power, it is evident that when the deeper life is clearly discerned, anything within the human sphere may be attained or achieved.

The idea that there is more and more of man than what appears on the surface should be so constantly and so deeply impressed upon the mind that it becomes a positive conviction, and no thought should be placed in action unless it is based upon this conviction. To live, think and act in the realization of the fact that there is "more of me" should be the constant purpose of every individual. When this is done the more will constantly develop, coming forth in greater and greater measure, giving added power, capacity and life to everything that is in action in the human system.

When the average person fails he either blames circumstances or comes to the conclusion that he was not equal to the occasion. He is therefore tempted to give up, and tries to be content with the lesser. But if he knew that there was more in him than what he had applied in this undertaking he would not give up. He would know that by developing this "more" he positively would succeed where he had previously failed. It is therefore evident that when man gives attention to his greatest power, that is, the power to discern the more that is in him, he will never give up until he does succeed; and in consequence he invariably will succeed.

That individual who knows his power does not judge according to appearances. He never permits himself to believe that this or that cannot be done. He knows that those things can be done because he has discovered the more which really exists within him. He works in the conviction that he must and will succeed because he has the power. And this is the truth. He does have the power. We all have the power.

To live, think and work in the attitude that there is more of you within the great depths of your being, and to know that there is more of you within the great depths of your being, and to know that this "more" is so immense that no limit to its power can be found, will cause the mind to come in closer and closer touch with this greater power. And you will in consequence gain more and more of this power. The mind that lives in this attitude opens the door of consciousness, so to speak, to everything in human life that has real quality and worth. It places itself in that position where it can respond to the best that exists within itself. And modern psychology has discovered that this "best" is extraordinary in quality, limitless in power, and contains possibilities that cannot be numbered.

It is the truth that man is a marvelous being, and the greatest power in man is the power to discern this marvelousness that really does exist within him. It is the law that we steadily develop and bring forth whatever we think of the most. We shall therefore find it highly profitable to think constantly of our deeper nature and to try in every manner and form imaginable to fathom the limitlessness and the inexhaustibleness of these great and marvelous depths.

In practical life this mode of thinking will have the same effect upon the personal mind as that which is secured when placing an ordinary wire in contact with a wire that is charged. The great within is a live wire. When the mind touches the great within it becomes charged with the same immense power. And the mind is more or less in touch with the great within when it lives, thinks, and works in the firm conviction that there is "more of me" so much more that it cannot be measured.

We can receive from the deeper life only that which we recognize, because consciousness is the power between the outer life and the great within; and we open the door only to those things of which we become conscious. The principal reason, therefore, why the average person does not possess greater powers and talents is because he is not conscious of more. And he is not conscious of more because he has not recognized the depths of his real life, and has not tried to fathom the possibilities that are latent within him.

The average person lives on the surface. He thinks that the surface is all there is of him, and therefore does not place himself in touch with the live wire of his great and inexhaustible nature within. He does not exercise his greatest power the power to discern what his whole nature may contain, and therefore does not unlock the door to any of his other powers. This being true, we can readily understand why mortals are weak. They are weak simply because they have chosen weakness. But when they choose power and greatness they shall positively become what they have chosen to become. And we all can choose power and greatness, because it is in us.

We all admit that there is more in man than what is expressed in the average person. We may differ as to how much more, but the more should be developed, expressed and applied. It is unjust both to the individual and to the race to remain in the lesser when it is possible to attain the higher, the richer and the greater. It is right that we all should ascend to the higher and the greater now. And the greatest power in man reveals the fact that we all can.

Chapter 2

The Best Use Of The Mind

We have at the present time a number of metaphysical systems, and though they differ considerably in many respects they all produce practically the same results. We find that no one system is more successful than the others, and yet they are all so remarkably successful that modern metaphysics is rapidly becoming one of the most popular studies of today. The real secret of all these systems is found in their power to draw consciousness more deeply into the realization of the absolute.

The absolute is unconditioned; therefore the more deeply consciousness enters the absolute the less conscious will the mind become of conditions. That is, the mind will be emancipated more and more from conditions as it grows into the realization of that which is unconditioned, or rather above conditions.

Any method that will tend to develop in the mind the consciousness of the absolute will produce emancipation from physical or mental ills, the reason being that there are no ills in the absolute, and it is not possible for the mind to be conscious of ills when it is in the consciousness of that which is absolutely free from ills. In other words, the mind cannot be in darkness, weakness or disease when it is in light, power and health.

Although it is not exact science to state that all is mind, because it can easily be proven that all is not mind; nevertheless, the statement that all is mind has a tendency to resolve consciousness into the allness of infinite mind, that is, the mind of the absolute. This will eliminate from the personal mind the consciousness of personal limitations and thus produce the realization of the absolute, that state of being that is free from conditions. It will also cause the personal mind to function in the consciousness of its unity with the impersonal mind which again is the infinite mind.

In like manner it is not scientific to deny the existence of matter, because matter does exist. Nevertheless the persistent denial of the existence of matter has a tendency to eliminate from mind the consciousness of shape and form, also the limitations and the conditions of shape and form. The result will be a certain degree of emancipation from conditions, and accordingly the ills that may have existed in those conditions will disappear.

The purpose of metaphysical methods is to prevent superficial mental action by deepening thought into the understanding of real action; that is, to prevent bondage to the limitations of form by awakening the consciousness of that limitless life that animates all form, and also to prevent the creation of imperfect conditions by producing in the mind the realization of absolutely perfect states. Any method that will tend to promote these objects in view will prove healthful to a degree in producing personal emancipation from sickness, adversity or want; but if the method is not strictly scientific its value will be very limited, and will prove to be nothing more than a temporary aid in the lesser aspects of life.

In this connection we must remember that no metaphysical method can fully promote the purpose in view unless it recognizes the reality of the whole universe and aims to produce advancement in every individual expression of universal life. However, every method is at first incomplete, therefore not strictly scientific. But to be scientific we must give everything due credit for what it is doing, no matter how limited it may be in its personal power.

To awaken the consciousness of the real, the unconditioned and the absolute, it is not necessary to declare that all is mind, nor is it necessary to deny the existence of matter. On the contrary, such methods should be avoided, because they will prove detrimental to the highest development of the individual if employed for any length of time. And we realize that our purpose is not simply to emancipate man from the ordinary ills of personal life, but also to develop man to the very highest heights of real greatness.

There is a world of absolute reality that exists within and about all things. It permeates all things and surrounds all things. It is an infinite sea in which all things live and move and have their being. It is the source of everything, and being limitless can give limitless life and power to anything. All science recognizes this world of absolute reality, and it is the purpose of metaphysics, that is, the best use of the mind, to gain that understanding that will enable any individual to place himself in perfect conscious touch with that world. This absolute reality is the perfect state of being upon which all individual being is based. Therefore the more perfectly conscious the individual becomes of the absolute, the less imperfection there will be in the life of the individual. And when individual consciousness is completely resolved in absolute consciousness, the cosmic state is realized a state with such marvelous beauty and such indescribable joy that it is worth a thousand ages of pain to come within its gates for just one single moment.

To develop the consciousness of the absolute and to grow steadily into the realization of the reality of perfect being the fundamental essential is to live habitually in the metaphysical attitude. This is a distinct attitude, by far the most desirable attitude of the mind, and comes as a natural result of the mind's discernment of the existence, the reality and the absoluteness of the universal sea of unconditioned life. This attitude is emancipating because it removes the imperfect by resolving the mind into the consciousness of the perfect. It produces the realization of the real and thus floods human life with the light of the real, that light that invariably dispels all darkness, whether it be ignorance, adversity, want, weakness, illusion or evil in any form or condition.

The secret of all metaphysical methods of cure is found in the peculiar power of the metaphysical attitude. To enter this attitude is to resolve mind in the consciousness of the absolute, and since there is no sickness in the absolute it is not possible for any mind to feel sickness while in the consciousness of the absolute. For this reason any method that will cause the mind to enter the metaphysical attitude will give that mind the power to heal physical or mental ailments. However, it is not the method that heals. It is that peculiar power or consciousness that comes when the mind is in the metaphysical attitude. And this power simply implies the elimination of imperfect conditions by resolving consciousness into the perfection of absolute states.

The actions of the mind are back of all personal conditions, therefore when the mind begins to act in the consciousness of absolute states it will express the perfection, the health, the wholeness and the power of those states. And when, the qualities of such states are expressed, imperfect conditions must necessarily disappear. Light and darkness cannot exist in the same place at the same time; neither can health and disease. When the former comes the latter is no more. When the mind is placed in the metaphysical attitude the conscious realization of the more powerful forces of life is gained. This means possession and mastery of those forces, at least in a measure, and the result will be a decided increase in the power, the capacity and the ability of every active faculty of the mind.

It is therefore evident that every person who desires to become much and achieve much should live habitually in the metaphysical attitude, for it is in this attitude that the best use of the mind is secured. The metaphysical attitude is distinct from the psychical attitude, and it is highly important for every person to clearly understand this distinction. Both attitudes will place the mind in touch with the more powerful forces of life, but the metaphysical is based upon the conviction that all power is in itself good, and that the mind naturally controls all power; but the psychical attitude has no definite conviction or purpose regarding the real nature of power. The metaphysical attitude takes hold of those finer powers and applies them constructively; while in the psychical attitude those powers are more or less in a chaotic state. For this reason the psychical attitude is nearly always detrimental, while the metaphysical is never otherwise than highly beneficial.

To approach the universal life of unbounded wisdom and limitless power is usually termed occultism. We find therefore that metaphysics and occultism have the same general purpose, and deal largely with the same elements and powers, but they do not make the same use of those elements and powers, nor are the results identical in any sense whatever. The psychical attitude opens the mind to more power but takes no definite steps in directing that power into constructive channels. If the mind is wholesome and constructive while in the psychical attitude the greater powers thus gained will be beneficial because it will in such a mind be directed properly. But to enter the psychical while there are adverse tendencies, false ideas or perverted desires in mind, is decidedly detrimental because this greater power will at such times be misdirected. And the greater the power the worse will be the consequence when misdirection takes place.

To state it briefly, no mind can safely enter the psychical attitude unless it has a spotless character, a masterful mind, and knows the truth about everything in this present state of existence. But as this requirement is practically beyond everybody, we must conclude that no one can safely enter the psychical state. To enter the psychical attitude is to fill the personality with new forces, some of which will be very strong, and if the mind is not constructive through and through, at the time, some or all of those forces will become destructive.

However, it is not possible to make the mind constructive through and through without entering the metaphysical attitude; that is, the mind is not fit to enter the psychical attitude until it has entered the metaphysical attitude. But as the same powers are secured in the metaphysical attitude, the psychical attitude becomes superfluous. Therefore, to give a single moment of thought or attention to occultism is a waste of time.

When a mind enters the metaphysical attitude it becomes constructive at once, because the metaphysical attitude is naturally a constructive attitude, being based upon the conviction that all things are in themselves good and working together for greater good. All power is good and all power is constructive. All power is beneficial when applied according to its true purpose, but no mind can apply power according to its true purpose until it becomes thoroughly constructive, and no mind can become thoroughly constructive until it enters the metaphysical attitude.

In this attitude all thought and attention is given to that which makes for better things and greater things. The mind is placed in such perfect harmony with the absolute that it naturally follows the law of the absolute, and to follow this law is to be all that you can be. It is therefore the very soul of advancement, attainment and achievement, having nothing but construction in view.

The fact that the practice of occultism produces extraordinary phenomena, either upon the physical plane or in the world of mental imagery gives it an atmosphere of the marvelous, and therefore it becomes extremely fascinating to the senses. Metaphysics, however, does not aim to appeal directly to the senses nor does it produce mere phenomena. On the contrary, metaphysics appeals directly to the superior understanding, and its purpose is to develop worth, greatness and superiority in man.

Those persons who live habitually in the metaphysical attitude have a wholesome, healthful appearance. They are bright, happy, contented, and they look clean. They are thoroughly alive, but in their expression of life there is a deep calmness that indicates extraordinary power and the high attainment of real harmony. We realize, therefore, why it is only in the metaphysical attitude that we can secure the best use of the mind.

The metaphysical attitude is rich in thoughts and ideas of worth. Such ideas are always constructive, and when applied will invariably promote practical and tangible advancement. To entertain pure metaphysical thought is to grow in the power to create higher thought and also to grow in the conscious realization of the real, thereby eliminating imperfect conditions of mind, thought or personality by resolving the mind in the consciousness of the unconditioned.

Metaphysics deals fundamentally with the understanding of the principle of absolute reality, that is, that complete something that underlies all things, permeates all things and surrounds all things: It deals with the all that there is in the world of fact and reality, and we can readily understand that the mind must aim to deal with the all if its use is to be the best. In other words the best use of the mind naturally implies that use of the mind that gives the highest, the largest and the most comprehensive application of everything there is in the mind. And this the metaphysical attitude invariably tends to do.

The understanding of the principle of absolute reality, that is the soul, so to speak, of all that is real, also reveals the great truth that all individual expressions of life have their source in the perfect state of being, and that the growth of the individual mind in the consciousness of this perfect state of being will cause that same perfection of being to be expressed more and more in the personal man. The term "perfection," however, in this sense implies that state of being that is all that it can be now, and that is so much that nothing in the present state of being can be added.

We all seek perfection, that is, that state where the mind realizes in itself those ideals that are discerned as possibilities within itself; and this form of perfection the metaphysical attitude has the power to produce in any mind at any time. In fact to enter the metaphysical attitude is to give higher and higher degrees of this perfection to every power, every faculty, every function and every talent in human life.

There are various methods for producing the metaphysical attitude, but the better way is to give the first attention to the development of a metaphysical sense; that is, to train the mind to think more and more of that state of consciousness wherein the perfection of the real is the one predominating factor. When this sense is awakened each mind will find its own best methods. The majority, however, have this sense and need only to place it in action. To give full action to the metaphysical sense we should aim to discern the absolutely real that is within everything of which the mind can be conscious. We should try to carry out this aim in connection with every process of thought, especially those processes that involve the exercise of the imagination.

Chapter 3

What Determines Mental Action

Every force and faculty in the mind has a tendency to act in a certain way, to move in a certain direction and to produce certain results. It is evident, therefore, that when we control the tendencies of the mind we may determine the actions of the mind and also what results those actions will naturally produce. In addition we may determine whether we are to go forward or backward, towards inferiority or superiority. To control mental tendencies we must control that from which tendencies arise.

Some people are exact externalizations of a single predominating mental state while others form their personalities from a group of mental states. But since every mental state originated in some tiny impression, we understand what may become of us when we permit every impression to follow its natural tendency. Every large object, physical or metaphysical, has a tendency to draw all smaller objects into its own path, and also to make all things in its atmosphere like unto itself. This, however, is partly prevented by counteracting tendencies, though the law is an important one and should be thoroughly understood.

In the metaphysical world the understanding of this law is especially important in the building of character and in the development of talents. If you have good character it means that the strongest tendencies of mind are wholesome, elevating and righteous in their nature, while if your character is weak there is not one elevating tendency that is strong enough to predominate in the world of conduct. A perverted character is always the result of descending tendencies with the ascending tendencies too insignificant to exercise and influence.

The fact that weak characters as well as perverted characters sometimes perform noble acts, and that the finest characters sometimes degrade themselves, is readily explained by the law of mental tendencies. In the first case the better tendencies are permitted occasionally to act without interference, while in the second case we find degrading tendencies arising temporarily, possibly through the influence of suggestion. These adverse tendencies, however, could not have exercised any power over conduct had the strong, ascending tendencies been active. But the strongest tendencies may at times be inactive, and it is at these times that a good man may fall, and the other kind show acts of goodness.

When you think more of the external things of life than that which is within, you create in consciousness a tendency to dwell on the surface. The result is you become superficial in proportion and finally become much inferior to what you were. On the other hand, when you think much of those things that are lofty and profound you create in consciousness a tendency to penetrate the deeper things in life. And the result is you become conscious of a larger world of thought, thereby increasing your mental capacity as well as placing yourself in a position where you may make valuable discoveries or formulate ideas of worth.

When you place questionable pictures before minds that are not established in purity, you create in those minds a tendency to immoral desire, and if those tendencies are continued such desires may become too strong to be controlled, and the victims will seek gratification even at the risk of life. This illustrates how powerful a mental tendency may become and how easily a wrong tendency may be produced when we do not exercise full control over those impressions that may enter the mind.

That man who thinks a great deal about spotless virtue and keeps the idea of virtue constantly before attention will soon create such a strong tendency to virtue that all desires and feelings will actually become virtuous. In consequence it will be simplicity itself for such a person to be virtuous, for when you are virtuous you do not have to try to be. You do not have to resist or fight desires which you do not want because all your desires have become tendencies towards clean and wholesome living. Your energies do not create grosser feelings any more, but have been trained to create vitality, energy, force and power instead.

Here we, should remember that when the predominating tendencies of mind are towards virtue all creative energies will become constructive, and will build up body and mind instead of being dissipated through some desire that is not even normal.

Another illustration of mental tendency and how mental tendency determines mental action is found in the man who is ambitious. Through the efforts of that ambition he is daily training all the tendencies of the mind to act upon the faculties needed to carry out his plans, and he is in consequence building up those faculties with the added force and nourishment thus accumulated. This proves that whenever you resolve to accomplish certain things you will certainly succeed in proportion to your ability. But by resolve we do not mean mere mental spurts. A resolve to be genuine must be constant, and must never waver in the strength of its force and determination. The reason why such a resolve must eventually win is found in the study of mental tendencies; that is, in the realization of the fact that we go as our tendencies go, where we directed them in their first stages.

When we think a great deal about the refined side of life we create tendencies that will cause all the forces within us to recreate everything in our systems according to a more refined pattern. Therefore, to be refined will before long become second nature, provided we keep constantly before our minds the highest idea of refinement that we can mentally picture. This illustrates how the control of mental tendency may absolutely change an individual from the most ordinary state of grossness to the highest state of refinement.

A striking illustration of the power of mental tendency is found in connection with the belief of the average mind that the body decays and grows old. For this reason we find in practically all human personalities a tendency to produce decay and age in the body. And this tendency is actually bringing about decay and old age where there would be no such conditions whatever were the tendency absent. Nature renews your body every few months and there is no natural process of decay in your system. If your system decays, you yourself have created the process of decay, either through mental or physical violation of natural laws, and by permitting those violations to become permanent tendencies.

If there is a process in your system that makes you look older every year, that process is a false one. It is not placed there by nature. You yourself have produced it by perpetuating the tendency to get older, a tendency that invariably arises from the belief that we must get older. The tendency to become weaker in body and mind as the years go by is also a creation of your own. It is not natural to become weaker with the passing of years. On the contrary, it is natural to become stronger the longer you live, and it is just as easy for you to create a tendency to become stronger the longer you live as it is to create the reverse. In like manner you can also create the tendency to become more attractive in personality, more powerful in mind, stronger in character and more beautiful in soul the longer you live.

However, we must eliminate all detrimental tendencies of the mind, and to do so we must find their origin. In many instances we are born with these adverse tendencies although many of them are acquired later in life. Those tendencies with which we are born generally become stronger and stronger, through our own tendency to follow the groove in which we are placed. We find, therefore, that it is always a mistake to live in a groove or to continue year after year to do a certain thing in the same usual way. Our object should be to break bounds constantly and to improve upon everything. Nothing is more important than change, provided every change is a constructive change.

Every impression that we form in the mind is a seed that may grow a tendency. Therefore we should not only eliminate all such impressions as we refuse to cultivate, but we should also prevent inferior and perverse impressions from entering the mind in the first place. To do this, however, we must be constantly on watch so that nothing can enter the mind through our senses which we do not wish to possess and perpetuate.

When we see people growing old, or rather becoming old through the operation of certain false tendencies, the impression of an aging process will stamp itself upon our minds if we permit it. Such impressions contain the tendency to produce the same aging process in us and it usually receives our permission to have its way. Thus we cause the aging process to become stronger and stronger in us the more we see it in others until we soon discover that we are actually creating for ourselves older bodies every year.

The new bodies that nature gives us every year are thus made to look older than the new bodies of the year before, which is a direct violation of natural law. Then we also sing with much feeling about the death and decay that is everywhere about us, and entertain thoughts of a similar nature by the wholesale. But all these indications of death and decay in our environments were not produced by nature. They were produced by false mental tendencies that arose through false belief about life and human nature.

The same is true regarding all other adverse tendencies that may exist in us or in those with whom we associate. When we see the action of those tendencies in others we receive impressions upon our own minds that have it in them to produce the same tendencies in us, which will later bring about the same adverse consequences in us.

Therefore we must not permit our minds to be impressed with anything in our environment that is contrary to what is true in the perfect nature of man. In other words, we must never permit any mental impression that comes from the weak, the adverse or the wrong conditions about us, but we should permit all things that are good and constructive to impress our minds more and more deeply every day.

We have been in the habit of thinking that various things were natural and inevitable because we see them everywhere about us, but when we discover that we have made a great many of these things ourselves and that they are all wrong, and that it is just as easy to make them different, we conclude that it is time to begin all over again. But to begin, we must transform all the tendencies of the mind so that all of them will move in the way we wish to go.

We may wish to enter health, but if there are tendencies to disease in our systems, and especially in the subconscious, our physical bodies will evolve more or less disease every year. Therefore this tendency must be changed to one of health before we can have what we desire in this respect. In other words, every action in the human system must be a health producing action and such will be the case when all the tendencies of the system have perfect health as their goal. The same is true regarding all other desires, tendencies or objects we may have in view.

The first question, therefore, to ask is this: Where am I going? or rather, Where are the tendencies of my mind going? Are those tendencies moving towards sin, sickness, decay, weakness and failure, or are they moving towards the reverse? We must look at ourselves closely and learn whether those tendencies are moving where we wish to go, or moving towards conditions that we know to be wrong or detrimental. And when we find where these tendencies are moving we must proceed to change them if they are wrong, and this we can do by producing right mental tendencies in their stead.

When we look at the tendencies of our mind we can largely determine what our own future is to be, provided we do not change those tendencies later on. Then when we know that our present physical conditions, our present strength, our present ability, our present character, our present attainments and our present achievements are all the consequences of the way our mental tendencies have been moving, and also that we have lived, thought and acted according to those tendencies when we know these things, we shall have found knowledge of priceless value, and by applying that knowledge we can make our own future as we wish it to be.

The question is, whither are we drifting, not physically but mentally, because it is the way we drift mentally that determines both the actions of the mind and the actions of the body. And our mental tendencies answer this question. As they go so do we go.

What we are creating, what we are building, what we are developing these things depend upon how the tendencies of the mind are directed. Therefore the proper course to pursue is to determine where we wish to go, in what direction and when. Then establish in mind what we wish to accomplish and how soon.

Know what you want and what you want to be. Then examine all the tendencies of your mind. All those which are not going the way you want to go must be changed, while all those that are already going your way should be given more and more power.

Then do not waver in your purpose. Never look back, let nothing disturb your plans, and keep your highest aspirations too sacred to be mentioned. You will find that if you will pursue this course you will go where you wish to go, you will achieve what you have planned, and your destiny will be as you desire.

Chapter 4

The Leading Metaphysical Law

Whatever enters the consciousness of man will express itself in the personality of man. This is one of the most important of all the laws of life, and when its immense scope is fully comprehended thousands of perplexing questions will be answered. We shall then know why we are as we are and why all things about us are as they are; and we shall also know how all this can be changed. When we examine the principle upon which this law is based we find that our environments are the results of our actions and our actions are the results of our thoughts. Our physical and mental conditions are the results of our states of mind and our states of mind are the results of our ideas. Our thoughts are mental creations patterned after the impressions that exist in consciousness and our ideas are the mental conceptions that come from our conscious understanding of life. Thus we realize that everything existing both in the mental field and in the personality, as well as in surrounding conditions, have their origin in that which becomes active in human consciousness.

We may define consciousness by stating that it is an attribute of the Ego through which the individual knows what is and what is taking place. Consciousness may usually be divided into three phases, the objective, the subjective and the absolute. Through absolute consciousness the Ego discerns its relationship with the universal that phase of consciousness that is beyond the average mind and need not necessarily be considered in connection with this law. Through subjective consciousness the Ego knows what is taking place within itself, that is, within the vast field of individuality. And through objective consciousness the Ego knows what is taking place in its immediate external world.

Objective consciousness employs the five external senses, while subjective consciousness employs all those finer perceptions which, when grouped together are sometimes spoken of as the sixth sense.

In our study of this law we shall deal principally with subjective consciousness because it is this consciousness that rules over real interior action. The subjective plane is the plane of change and growth so that there can be no change in any part of life until the cause of the desired change has been found or produced in the subjective. What enters objective consciousness will not produce any effect upon the personality unless it also enters subjective consciousness, because it is only what becomes subjective that reproduces itself in the human entity.

In our present state of existence the center of conscious action is largely in the subconscious mind, that is, the interior or finer mental field, and in consequence all the actions of consciousness are directly connected with the subjective. In this connection it is well to state that the terms subjective and subconscious mean practically the same.

Whatever enters consciousness and is deeply felt will impress itself upon the subjective so therefore in order to control the results of this law we must avoid giving deep feelings to such impressions, thoughts, ideas or desires as we do not wish to have reproduced in ourselves. There are many impressions and experiences that enter objective consciousness to a degree, but never become subjective since they are not accompanied with depth of feeling. We may be conscious of such experiences or impressions, but we are not affected by them. For this reason we need not give them our attention, which is well because the majority of the impressions that enter the conscious mind pass off, so to speak, without affecting life in any way.

Whatever actually enters consciousness is always felt by the finer sensibilities of mind, and whatever enters into the finer state of mind is taken up by the creative energies; and impressions are accordingly produced. From these impressions will come similar expressions, and it is such expressions that determine thought, character, conduct and life. To state this law in a slightly different manner we may state that whatever enters subjective consciousness will produce an impression just like itself, and every subjective impression becomes a pattern for thought creation while it lasts.

Therefore whenever an impression is formed in the mind, thoughts will be created just like that impression. And so long as that impression remains in subjective consciousness thought will continue to be formed after its likeness. Then we must remember that every thought created in the mind goes out into the personality, producing vital and chemical effects according to its nature.

Thus we understand the process of the law. First, the impression is formed upon subjective consciousness. Second, the creative energies of the mind will produce thoughts and mental states just like those impressions, and all such thoughts and mental states will express themselves in the personality, producing conditions in the personality similar to their own nature. To illustrate this process from everyday life we may mention several experiences with which we are all familiar.

When you view a very peaceful scene and become wholly absorbed in it your entire being will become perfectly serene almost at once, and this is the reason: The scene was peaceful and produced a peaceful impression upon your mind. This impression entered your subjective consciousness because you became deeply absorbed in the scene. If you had simply viewed the scene in a superficial way you would have felt no change because then the impression would not have entered your subjective mind; but you responded to the impressions that entered the mind through the organ of sight and thus admitted those impressions into the deeper or subjective state. In other words, the scene actually entered into your consciousness, the serenity of it all was impressed upon the subjective; and as explained in the process above, the creative energies of your mind at once began to create thoughts and mental states containing the same serene and peaceful life. These thoughts entered into your entire personality, as all thoughts do after being created, thus conveying the life of peace to every atom in your being.

When you view an exciting scene and are carried away by it you lose your poise and may even become uncontrollable. The reason is you admit confusion into your mind, and according to the law, confusion will be produced in yourself; that is, discord has entered your consciousness and has become the model for the creative processes of the mind. The mental energies will enter such states and create thoughts and mental states that are just as confused as the confusion you saw in the without. And when these confused states go out into the personality, as they do almost at once, your entire nervous system will be upset, disturbed and in a state of inharmony. Thus you have produced the same confusion in your own mind and body that you saw in your environments. However, if you had prevented the confused scenes from entering your mind, you would have been perfectly calm in the midst of it all; but by permitting the excitement to enter your consciousness it was reproduced in yourself, and the discord that entered your consciousness from the without was thereby expressed in your own personality.

There may be indications of threatening failure in your work and you may begin to fear that such failure will come, but so long as you do not feel the inner dread of failure the impression of failure will not enter your consciousness; and accordingly conditions of failure will not be produced in your own mind. But if the fear continues until you actually feel fearful deep down in your heart, the idea of failure has entered your consciousness, and if not prevented will be deeply impressed in the subjective.

When failure is impressed upon your subjective mind, a condition of mental failure will permeate all your faculties, and in consequence they will fail to do their best. And we all know very well that the very moment our faculties begin to go back on us, doing less work and less effective work, we are on the down grade to failure and loss.

Failure means going down to the lesser, and if you have admitted thoughts of failure into your mind you have given your creative energies bad models. These energies will create thoughts and mental states just like those models, no matter what those models may be. If those models are based upon the idea of failure all the thoughts created will contain the failing attitude, or the losing ground attitude. When such thoughts express themselves in the system they will produce weakening conditions and disturbances everywhere in mind and personality. Your faculties will not be able to do their best; they will begin to fail in their work because they are being permeated with a losing ground tendency, and you will make many mistakes on account of the increasing confusion.

The result will be inevitable failure unless you are able to check this tendency or retrace your steps upward before it is too late. We have all noticed that the man on the down grade makes more mistakes than anyone else, and also that his genius or his talents become weaker the further down he goes. The above explains the reason why.

We are all familiar with the folly of judging from appearances and permitting temporary conditions to impress and govern our thinking, the reason being that our object is not to follow the whims of circumstances or the uncertainties of fate, but to carry out our purpose in life regardless of what happens. On the other hand when we do not judge according to external indications, but proceed to impress the subconscious mind with the determination to succeed, we are placing in consciousness an idea that stands for growth, advancement and increase. Immediately the creative energies of mind will proceed to create thoughts and states that have advancing, up building and constructive tendencies. Such thoughts will give push, power, life and added talent to your faculties, and you will very soon begin to do better work; the superior forces will build up your mind, make your mind more brilliant, and add constantly to your capacity.

Thus you will become a success within yourself; that is, your own forces and faculties will begin to work successfully which is the first essential to the gaining of success in the external world. You will be moving forward in your own being and you will be gaining in worth in every respect. The results will be better work, better impressions upon the world, and fewer mistakes. And when the world discovers that there is success in you they will want your service with recompense according to your full worth. When we understand this process of the mind we realize how we can bring upon ourselves almost anything simply through permitting the corresponding impressions to enter consciousness. Therefore we should learn to prevent all such things from entering consciousness as we do not wish to see reproduced in ourselves and expressed through our personality. Then we should learn to impress permanently in consciousness the image and likeness of all those things that we do wish to develop and express.

The workings of this law are very well illustrated in conditions of heath and disease, because when we are constantly thinking about disease and fearing disease we permit the idea of disease to impress itself upon consciousness. In other words, we become more and more conscious of disease, and cause the image of sickness to get a firm foothold in the subjective. The result is that the creative forces of mind will create thoughts, mental states and conditions just like the image of disease, and that which is just like the image of disease actually is a disease. Therefore since every mental state conveys conditions similar to itself to every part of the body, such thoughts will constantly carry diseased conditions into the body, tending thereby to produce the very ailment that we feared, thought of, or impressed upon consciousness in the first place.

Nature may resist these adverse conditions for a while if the body is full of vitality, but when the vital forces run low these sickly mental conditions will have full sway, and the result will be a siege of illness which may be prolonged, and even result in death, which happens thousands of times under just such conditions.

The law, however, works both ways. We can just as easily impress the idea of perfect health upon subjective consciousness and thus give the creative forces a better image as a model for their creative processes. At such times all thoughts and mental states will be wholesome and health producing, and will constantly carry better health, more harmony and greater strength to the body. This is how the law works, and as anyone can understand the process, further details are not required. Briefly stated, the law is this: That everything entering subjective consciousness will impress itself there and become a pattern for the creative energies of the mind. These energies will proceed to create thoughts and conditions just like the impression formed, which will carry their own conditions to every part of the human system.

In this way conditions are produced and expressed in the personality just like the original idea, thought or impression that entered subjective consciousness. Everything that enters the mind through the various senses may also enter subjective consciousness, that is, if deeply felt, and thus produce a permanent impression. In like manner, all our own concepts of things will become impressions, that is, if they are inner convictions. For this reason we must not only watch all those things that enter the mind through the senses, but we must also govern our own thinking so that every mental conception formed will be one of quality, worth, wholeness, health, growth and advancement.

To employ this law properly nothing must be permitted to enter the subjective unless we wish to have it reproduced in ourselves. We should refuse therefore to take into consciousness that which we do not wish to see expressed through mind or body. We should train consciousness to respond only to those external impressions that are desirable; and we should train our own imaging faculties to impress deeply and permanently in consciousness every good thing or desirable quality that we wish to see reproduced in ourselves and expressed through our personality.

Chapter 5

How The Mind Makes The Man

Man gradually grows into the likeness of that which he thinks of the most. This is another important metaphysical law, and is so closely related to the law presented in the preceding chapter that the analysis given for one will naturally explain the process of the other. However, this second law is distinct from the first one in many of its phases, and it is so full of possibility that the understanding of its application opens up a vast world of change and attainment along a number of lines.

We become like the thoughts we think because the creative power of thought is the only creative power that we have within us. And the energies of mind are constantly creating; and what they create now is just like the thoughts we think now. Since every physical condition, every mental state, and every phase of character since all these things are fashioned after our predominating thoughts, and since the capacity of every faculty and the quality of every talent are determined by the thoughts we think, we must naturally conclude that there can be no greater art than the art of correct thinking. In fact, to think is to occupy a position involving far greater responsibility than that of a thousand absolute monarchs. And when we realize this, we will not permit a single thought to take shape and form in our minds without first determining upon the value of that thought.

Why we grow into the likeness of that of which we think the most has been fully explained in the preceding chapter, and it is found in the fact that every impression formed in the mind will reproduce its kind and express its creations throughout the entire system. And though these impressions usually come from without in the first place, still they do not become real impressions until we accept them into our consciousness, or in thought, or in conviction. That is, many minds will think only what is suggested to them by environment, or what they are told to think by those in authority; still it is their own thought that shapes their lives.

Wherever the suggestion may come from, it is your thought about that suggestion that produces the effect.

The analysis of thought presented in the preceding chapter explains how the person is affected by thought, and how thought is always created in the likeness of those ideas, states or impressions that have established themselves in consciousness.

But to carry this analysis to its final goal we must discover why man becomes like his thought and also how he can think thought of a superior nature. And this we discover through the workings of the law now under consideration. In the first place man becomes like his thought because there is no other pattern in his being besides his own thought. The creative forces of his mind and personality always create according to the image and likeness of the strongest and deepest impressions in consciousness, and all such impressions are produced by the process of thinking.

When we use the term "thought," however, we may refer either to the mental model, which is the result of mental conception, or we may refer to that thought which is the result of mental creation. The mental creation is patterned after the mental conception, and the mental conception is the result of our efforts to understand what we are thinking about. Mental conception is conscious and is therefore under our control, while mental creation is subconscious and is therefore beyond our control; but we do not have to control mental creation. Those creations will be just like our mental conceptions; therefore when we form only such mental conceptions as we like we shall have only such mental creations as we like. In consequence when we see mentally that which is superior and can form a true conception of what we see, we give to the creative energies a model that is higher than any we have given them before.

Accordingly the mental creations will be superior.

And here we should remember that these creations are not wholly abstract, but are in most instances as concrete or tangible as the body itself. The creative energies of the human system act both in the mind and in the body, though their central field of action is always in the subjective or inner side of things. In the body these energies constitute the vital forces and the nerve forces of the system, while in the mind they constitute all those energies or powers employed in thought, feeling or mental action of whatever nature.

When we examine these energies we find that they do not simply create conditions after the likeness of the predominating thought, but that they themselves also become just like the predominating thought, which fact illustrates the power exercised by such thoughts as hold the ruling position in our minds. From this fact we conclude that these forces will give vitality to the body that corresponds to the states of the mind. So, that if there is anything wrong in the subjective states of the mind these forces will convey those wrong conditions to the body, the reason being that these forces come from the subjective and cannot be different from the ruling conditions of their source.

The fibers and cells of the body are built up by these energies. Therefore the quality as well as the structures of the cells must correspond with the nature of the creative energies at the time. These energies build cells just like the patterns before them, and the patterns are formed by the subjective conceptions. When that part of the subjective mind that governs cell structures in the body becomes imbued with a more perfect idea of construction the creative energies will build more perfect cells. And when that part of the subjective mind that governs physical shape and form receives a better conception of shape and form, these creative energies will naturally build a body that is more perfect as to shape and form. Every function in the body is governed by a certain part of the subjective mind and the creative energies act through that particular function according to the present state of the subjective mind.

Therefore when more perfect patterns are placed in those parts of the subjective that govern the body, the creative energies will build a more perfect body. And when we know that these creative energies are building us a new body every year, according to the predominating pattern of the subjective, we can see how easily the new body we receive every year can be made more perfect if we will improve the subjective pattern. The creative energies construct brain cells in the same way, the quality being governed by the state of mind. And that part of the brain that is to receive the largest group of cells is determined by the tendencies of the mind.

In the world of talents and faculties the creative energies construct concepts so that every talent is actually composed of all the conceptions that the mind has formed while trying to understand the nature and possibility of that talent. In the formation of character the creative energies do their work in constructing desires, motives, purposes and the like. And in every instance they form these characteristics according to the predominating thought on the subject. In the construction of the spiritual attitudes and higher attainments the process is very similar though in these instances the pattern is gained through faith instead of subjective mentation.

Why man grows into the likeness of that which he thinks of the most becomes perfectly clear when we understand how the creative energies work; that is, that they always create after the likeness of the subjective pattern. And when we learn that the subjective pattern can be changed in any part of mind by thinking a great deal of a higher conception of that particular phase, we have the whole secret. When we think a great deal along any line with a higher conception before us we finally establish that higher conception in the place of the old one. When we hold an idea in mind a long time that idea will become a predominating idea; it will become larger and stronger than the other ideas and will consequently be selected as a model by the creative energies

The next question before us is how to think only of those things that we desire to grow into the likeness of. And this question is answered through the following metaphysical law: Man thinks the most both consciously and unconsciously of that which he loves the best. The simplest way to govern thought is to do so through love.

When we love the lofty and the noble we naturally think a great deal of those qualities without trying to do so, and in consequence we become more noble in thought, character and motives. If we wish to develop the greater and the higher within us we must love everything that contains greatness, and our love must be with the whole heart: that is, every fiber of our being must actually thrill with a passion for that higher something which we desire to develop.

Here we must remember that all intellectual or metaphysical methods for the development of talents or character, or anything of a superior nature within us, will fail unless we passionately love superior attainments. The man who loves honesty, justice and virtue will become honest, just and virtuous; though if he does not naturally love those things no amount of moral training can change his character. Millions of people are praying to become better, more noble and more spiritual, but too many fail to receive answers to such prayers. And the reason why is found in the fact that they do not love as deeply as they should those superior attainments for which they are praying. They may desire those things in a superficial way, but that is not sufficient. Real love alone will avail because such love goes to the very depth of life and touches the very essence of being itself.

When we, as a race, will begin to love the superior and the divine with the same depth that we love gold or material pleasures, we shall become a superior race. When we love divine qualities with the whole heart we shall think a great deal of such qualities and the more we will try to understand the inner nature of those qualities. The higher this understanding becomes the higher will our conception of the divine and the spiritual become. And the higher those conceptions are the higher will be our thoughts. And since the outer man is fashioned after the ruling thoughts of his mind, we shall in this way steadily rise in the scale of life until we become in mind and personality like those higher thoughts we have learned to think. In other words, we shall manifest in the without more and more of the divinity that is within. And that such a process would in time transform humanity into a superior race anyone can readily understand.

Love, however, is not mere sentiment, nor is it ordinary emotionalism. Love also has quality. There is ordinary love and there are the higher forms of quality. Therefore, the love with which we love must be developed into greater worth if we are to penetrate the realms of worth through our love.

The reason why we naturally think the most about what we like the best is found in the fact that there can be no division in love. When you actually love something that something will receive your undivided attention. And as all your thought goes where your attention is directed you will in this manner give all your thought both consciously and unconsciously to that which you love. This we all know from our own personal experience, and we shall find that everybody has had the same experience, thus proving universally the absoluteness of this law.

We have all seen people become beautiful in countenance and character after they had begun to love some high and noble purpose. And we can find thousands who have become more and more common because they have continued to love the ordinary. By living the ordinary they naturally became like the ordinary thus their mental actions became inferior, and both mind and personality became inferior in proportion. The elements of the body may be in a low state of action and express grossness, or they may be in a high state of action and express refinement; and the state of the mind determines what those actions are to be, whether they are to be crude or refined. The low, common mind invariably gives sluggish or crude actions to the system, and in such a person the physical form looks very much like ordinary clay. But a lofty mind, a mind that is living in the ideal and the beautiful, and in the realization of the marvelous possibilities of mind, gives highly refined actions to the body; and such a body will naturally be superior in fineness, quality and substance. It is therefore true that there are people who are made of a finer clay; not because they have come from so called noble ancestors, but because their thoughts have become beautiful, lofty and high.

The attitude of love towards all that is superior should be cultivated with the greatest enthusiasm, and the love itself should also be made superior as we advance in the realization of true worth. It is in this way that we shall find the true path and the simple path to high thinking, noble thinking and right thinking. And man grows into the likeness, steadily and surely, of that which he thinks of the most.

Since we think the most of what we love the best we should love passionately all that is beautiful and sublime; we should love all that is lofty and ideal; we should love the true side, the superior side and the genuine side in all persons and in all things. But we should never think of the inferior at any time. We should love the perfect, the divine and the spiritual in every soul in existence, and give the whole heart to the love of the sublime qualities of the Supreme. Thus we shall find that body, mind and soul will respond to the perfect thought that we thus form while living on the mental heights. Gradually we shall find all the elements of our nature changing for the better, becoming more and more like those sublime states of mind of which we are so vividly conscious while on the heights.

Chapter 6

How Mental Pictures Become Realities

Every thought is patterned after the mental image that predominates at the time the thought is created. This is another great metaphysical law and its importance is found in the fact that thoughts are things, that every thought produces an effect on mind and body, and that the effect is always similar to the cause. According to these facts we can therefore produce any effect desired upon mind or body by producing the necessary thought or mental state, so that when we have learned to control our thinking we can control practically everything else in life, because in the last analysis it is thinking that constitutes the one great cause in the life of the individual.

To control thinking, however, we must understand the process of thought creation. To think is to create thought, and to control thinking is to create any thought we like at any time and under any circumstance. When we analyze the process of thinking we find three factors involved; that is, the pattern, the mental substance and the creative energy. The pattern is always the deepest impression, the clearest image, or the predominating idea.

The quality of the mental substance improves with the quality of the mind; and the quantity increases with the expansion of consciousness, while the creative energies grow stronger the less energy we lose and the more we awaken the greater powers from within.

When an idea or image is impressed upon the mind the mental energies will proceed to create thought just like that image; and will continue while that image occupies a permanent position in consciousness. When the mind is very active a great deal of thought is created every second, though the amount varies with the activity of the mind. It is therefore more detrimental for an active mind to think wrong thought than for a mind that is dull or stupid; proving the fact that responsibility always increases as we rise in the scale. It is the function of the creative energies of the mind to create thought that is just like every image impressed upon mind and to continue to create thought in the likeness of that image while it lasts. The creative energies do this of their own accord and we cannot stop them. But we can make them weak or strong, or give them better patterns.

Mind is an art gallery of many pictures, but only the most prominent are selected for models in thought creation. Only those pictures that are sufficiently distinct to be seen by consciousness without special effort are brought before the creative energies as patterns. We thus find that the art of controlling one's thinking and the power to determine what kind of thought is to be created is acquired largely through the training of the mind to impress deeply only such mental pictures as are desired as models for thinking. The law, however, is very simple because as the picture in the mind happens to be at this moment so will also be the thoughts created at this moment, and the mental pictures are in each case the ideas and impressions that we permit in mind.

Whatever enters the mind through the senses can impress the mind, and the result will be a picture or mental image that will become a pattern for the creative energies. What takes shape and form in your mind through your own interior thinking will also impress the mind and become an image or pattern. It is therefore possible through this law to determine what kind of thoughts you are to create by impressing your mind with your own ideas regardless of what environment may suggest to you through your senses,

And it is by exercising this power that you place the destiny of body, mind and soul absolutely in your own hands.

As we proceed with this process we find another vital law that may be stated as follows: What we constantly picture upon the mind we shall eventually realize in actual life. This law may be spoken of as a twin sister to the one stated above as they are found to work together in almost every process of thought creation and thought expression.

The one declares that all thought is patterned after the predominating mental pictures while the other declares that the entire external life of man is being daily recreated in the likeness of those mental pictures. The fact is, as the mental tendencies are, so is thought; as thought is, so is character; and it is the combined action of character, ability and purpose that determines what we are to attain or accomplish, or what is to happen to us.

Through the law of attraction we naturally meet in the external world what corresponds to our own internal world, that is, to what we are in ourselves. The self constitutes the magnet, and like attracts like. This self who constitutes the magnet is composed of all the active forces, desires, tendencies, motives, states and thoughts that are at work in mind or personality. When we look at everything that is alive throughout our whole being and put all those things together we have what may be termed our present active self. And this self invariably attracts in the external world such conditions as correspond to its own nature. This self and all its parts in the person correspond to the thoughts that we have been creating in mind. In fact the nature of the self is actually composed of thought, mental states and mental activities. We realize, therefore, that when we change our thought, the nature of the self will change, and this change will be good or otherwise depending upon the change of thought.

Your external life is the exact counterpart of this active self. This self is the exact likeness of your thought, and your thoughts are patterned after the pictures that are impressed upon your mind. Therefore we understand that whatever is pictured in the mind will be realized in external life. And the reason why is not only simply explained but can be proven along strictly scientific lines. However, to determine through the law of mind picturing what our external life is to be, every process of mind picturing which we desire to carry out must be continued for a sufficient length of time to give the creative processes the opportunity to make over the whole self.

When a certain picture is formed in the mind thought will be created in the likeness of that picture. This thought goes out and permeates the entire self and changes the self to a degree. But as a rule it takes some time to change the entire self; therefore we must continue to hold the desired picture in mind until the whole self has been entirely made over and has become just like the ideal picture. And you can easily discern when the self has been wholly changed because as soon as the self is changed everything in your life changes. Then a new self will attract new people, new conditions, new environments, new opportunities and new states of being. It is evident therefore that so long as there is no change in the outer life we may know that the self has not been changed. However, the changing process may be going on, but the new has not as yet become stronger than the old, and for the time being things continue as they were.

When the self has been changed to such an extent that the new becomes positive and the old negative we will begin to attract new things. We may therefore begin to attract new and better things for some time before the entire self has been completely changed. When we are changing only a part of the self that part will begin to attract the new while those parts of the self that have not been changed will continue to attract the old as usual. This explains why some people continue to attract trouble and adversity for a while after they have begun to live a larger and a better life.

In promoting the art of mind picturing we must not change ideas or plans at too frequent intervals for such changes will neutralize what has been gained thus far and here is the place where a great many people fail. The average person who wishes to change his life for the better does not hold on to his ideals long enough; that is, he does not give them a fair chance to work themselves out and bring the expected results.

When he does not receive results as soon as he expects he changes his plans and produces new pictures upon the mind. Thus he begins all over again, losing what he had built up through previous plans; but before long becomes discouraged once more, so tries still other ideas or methods. When our ideals are the highest we know we do not have to change them. They cannot be improved upon until we have so entirely recreated ourselves that we can live in a superior state of consciousness. It is therefore highly important to determine positively upon the ideals that we wish to realize, and to hold on to those ideals until they are realized regardless of what may happen in the meantime.

However, we must not infer that we can realize in the external the correspondence of every picture that we hold in mind, because the majority of the mental pictures that we form are so constituted that they can be worked out in practical action. We must therefore distinguish between such ideals, as can be made practical now and those that are simply temporary dreams, having no connection with real life here and now.

To be realized a mental picture must be constant, but only such pictures can be constant as are sufficiently elaborate to involve a complete transformation in yourself, and that are so high that they can act as an inspiration until all your present ideals are realized. When we form such pictures in the mind and continue to hold on to them until they are externally realized we shall certainly obtain the desired realization. At such times we can proceed with the perfect faith that what we have pictured will become true in actual life in days to come, and those days will not be far away. But to use this law the mind must never waver; it must hitch its wagon to a star and never cut the traces.

In scientific mind picturing it is not necessary to go into minor details, though we must not be too general. The idea is to picture all the essentials, that is, all those parts that are distinct or individualized. But we need not include such things as are naturally attracted by the essentials. In other words, apply the law, and that which will naturally come through the application of that law, will be realized.

If you wish to realize a more perfect body it is not necessary to picture the exact physical appearance of that body. You may not know at present what a perfect body should look like. Therefore picture only the quality of perfection in every part of the physical form and those qualities will develop and express themselves more and more throughout your personality. And if you wish to enter a different environment do not give your thought to some special locality, nor to persons and things that would necessarily be included in such an environment. Persons come and go and things are generally the way we wish them to be.

To proceed realize what constitutes an ideal environment and hold that picture in your mind. In analyzing an ideal environment we would find it to contain harmony, beauty, love, peace, joy, desirable opportunities, advantages, ideal friends, wholesome conditions and an abundance of the best of everything that the welfare of human life may require. Therefore we should picture those things and continue to hold them in mind with the faith that we will soon find an environment containing all those things in the highest degree of perfection. Gradually we shall find more and more of them coming into our life until we shall find an environment that comes up in every respect to our ideal.

The law of mind picturing will also be found effective in changing physical conditions. Any physical malady must eventually disappear if we continue to hold in mind a perfect picture of health and wholeness. Many have eliminated chronic ailments in a few weeks and even in a few days by this method, and all would succeed if they never pictured disease but perfect health only. In the field of achievement we will find the same facts to hold good. Whenever we fear that we shall not succeed we bring forth the wrong picture thus the wrong thoughts are created and wrong conditions are produced; in consequence the very thing we feared comes upon us. When we are positively determined to succeed, however, we picture the idea of success and attainment upon the mind, and. according to the law, success will be realized in external life.

Mental and spiritual attainments respond remarkably to mind picturing, principally because all true mind picturing draws consciousness up into the world of superiority. The same is true in the field of talent. If there is any talent that you wish to develop draw mental pictures of yourself in full possession of that talent and you will comply with the requirements of the steady growth of that talent. This method alone will accomplish much, but when it is associated with our processes of development the results desired will surely be remarkable.

In the building of character, mind picturing is of exceptional importance. If you continue to associate only with impure minds and continue to think only of deeds of darkness you will picture only the wrong upon your mind. Thus your thoughts will become wrong and wrong thoughts lead to wrong actions. The contrary, however, is also true. So therefore if we wish to perfect our conduct we must impress upon the mind only such ideas as will inspire us with desires and aims for greater and higher things.

We all admit that character can be influenced most decidedly by mind pictures, but everybody may not be ready to accept the idea that ability, attainment, achievement, environment and destiny can be affected in the same way. However, it is only a full analysis of the law of mind picturing that is necessary to prove this also to be an exact scientific fact. It is the way we think that determines the quality of the mind, and it is the quality of the mind that determines what our ability, mental capacity and mental force is to be. And we can readily understand that the improvement of ability will naturally be followed by increase in attainment and achievement as well as a greater control over fate and destiny.

Man is constantly increasing his ability, is making his own future and is making that future brighter and greater every day. Therefore, if mind pictures can affect mental quality, mental power and mental ability they can also affect environment and achievement, and in brief, the entire external life of man. In looking for evidence for the fact that mental pictures can affect ability, simply compare results from efforts that are inspired by high ideals and efforts that are inspired by low ideals, and you have all the evidence you need.

When your mind is filled with pictures of superiority you will think superior thoughts, thoughts that have more quality, power and worth, and such thoughts cannot fail to give power, quality and worth to your talents and faculties. We also find that tendencies, desires and motives originate largely from mental pictures and we also know that these factors exercise an enormous power in life. The active self of man is so dominated by desires and tendencies that it is absolutely impossible to change the self until tendencies and desires are changed. But tendencies and desires as well as motives cannot be changed without changing the mental pictures a fact of extreme importance.

Through scientific mind picturing you can create or eliminate any kind of desire; you can produce or remove any tendency that you like. All that is necessary is to impress upon the mind the perfect picture of a desire or tendency that you wish and then continue to hold that picture in the mind until you have results. A mental picture, however, is not necessarily something that you can see in the same way as you see external, tangible things. It is an impression or idea or concept and is seen only by the understanding. In order to hold a mental picture constantly in mind keep all the essentials of that picture before your attention; that is, try to be conscious of the real nature of those powers and possibilities that are represented by the picture. In other words, enter into the very nature of those qualities which that picture represents.

The mind is very large. It is therefore possible to form mental pictures of as many ideals as we like, but at first it is best to choose only a few. Begin by picturing a perfect body, an able mind, a strong character and a beautiful soul; after that an ideal interior life and an ideal external environment. Thus you have the foundation of a great life, a rich life and a wonderful life. Keep these pictures constantly before your mind in fact, train yourself to actually live for those pictures. And you will find all things in your life changing daily to become more and more like those pictures. In the course of time you will realize in actual life the exact likeness of those pictures; that is, what you have constantly pictured upon your mind you will realize in actual life. Then you can form new and more beautiful pictures to be realized in like manner as you build for a still greater future.

Chapter 7

The Increase Of Mental Power

All mental actions that consciously move towards the within tend to increase the capacity, the power and the quality of mind. The majority of mental actions in the average mind, however, move towards the surface, and this is one reason why advancing years bring mental inferiority as the converse of this law is also true. That is, that all mental actions that move towards the surface will decrease the power of mind.

According to the law of growth the more we use a faculty the larger and stronger and more perfect it should become, provided it is used properly. Therefore continuous use in itself should invariably bring increase. However, the use of anything may follow the lines of destruction as well as construction. For this reason we must train all mental actions along constructive lines. And we find all constructive action tends to deepen mental action; in other words, tends to move towards the within.

The value of the increase of mental power is clearly evident along all lines. Everything must increase in the life of him who is perpetually increasing his own personal power. We know that a large mind creates more extensively than a small one.

The creations of a highly developed mind are more worthy than the creations of an inferior mind, and the achievements of anyone are in proportion to that one's capacity and power. Therefore when we begin to increase the value of life everything pertaining to life as well as everything coming into life will increase also. Perpetual development in ourselves means perpetual increase of everything of worth required in our sphere of existence. This is the law; but so long as mental actions move towards the surface, mentality is diminished; therefore the opposite process must be established.

By training all mental actions to move constantly towards the within we increase perpetually the capacity, the power and the quality of mind and the reason why is very simple. When mental actions move towards the surface consciousness will be centered upon the surface of things and will therefore picture in mind the lesser and inferior side of things. Those mental energies that serve as patterns for the creative energies will in consequence be formed in the likeness of the smaller. And the result is that the mind will be created according to the lesser and more inferior conception of itself.

On the other hand, when all the actions of mind move toward the great within, the eye of the mind will concentrate upon the world of greater possibilities. The conception of things will in such a mental state constantly increase because attention at such times is concerned only with that which is larger and superior. Thus the mental energies will be directed towards the idea of superiority, and the creative energies will naturally rebuild the mind gradually and steadily upon a larger and more perfect scale.

This is all very simple and anyone who will examine the workings of his own mind will find it to be absolutely true. We understand therefore how each individual has in his own hands the power to create for himself a greater mind, a more perfect personality, a richer life and a more desirable destiny.

In all methods for mental development this law must be wisely considered for no matter how perfect the method may be, if the mental actions move towards the surface, no results will be gained. While on the other hand, if the mental actions move towards the within results will positively be gained even though the methods be inferior. Nearly all minds in the past that continued to develop through life did so without system, but gained increase through aspiration, or rather concentration upon the greater possibilities of life, which in turn caused mental actions to move towards the within.

When your attention is turned upon the inner and the larger phases of life your mind will begin to turn its actions upon the great within. Accordingly all mental tendencies will begin to move toward superiority, and all the building forces in your life will have superiority as their goal. That you should constantly rise in the scale when thinking and acting in this manner is therefore evident. Remarkable results have been gained and can be gained simply through aspiration, but if a complete system of the best methods are employed in conjunction with the fundamental law, these results will naturally increase to a very great degree. For this reason all things that are conducive to the growth of the mind should be employed in harmony so that the increase of mental power may be gained in the largest possible measure.

To train the mental actions to move towards the within we should concentrate attention upon the greater possibilities of life, and think as deeply and as much as we can upon those possibilities. In fact we should train the mind to look towards the within at all times and view with great expectations those superior states that before long will be attained. In addition all tendencies of life should be trained to move towards the higher and the larger and every thought should have an ascending spirit.

When you feel that you are becoming too much concerned with the superficial, turn attention at once upon the depths of existence. And when you feel that you have fallen down temporarily into the world of inferiority use every effort at your command to rise again towards the heights. The leading purpose should be to train all the forces, desires, tendencies and actions in life to move upward and onward at all times. This will cause the greater powers and possibilities within to be awakened, which will be followed by the perpetual increase of the capacity, the power and the quality of the mind. And with this increase comes also the increase of everything else in life that is required for our highest welfare.

When this increase of power begins it will naturally be felt in various parts of mind, and in order to know how to make the best possible use of this increase, as well as of the power we already possess, we should remember the great law, that whatever you feel that you can do, that you have the power to do. There are many methods through which we can determine what the mind really can do and what work we may be able to carry out successfully, but this particular law is the best guide of all, provided it is properly understood. And it is extremely important to discover what we are able to do because the majority are not in their true spheres of action.

To be in your true sphere of action means better work, greater results and more abundant good both to yourself and to others with whom you are associated. It also means that you can be at your best at all times and he who is at his best at all times is on the way to perpetual growth and perpetual increase.

To do your best work and your true work you must employ the largest and the strongest faculty that you possess. But to learn what this faculty actually is, this is the problem. This problem can be solved, however, if we live in compliance with the law just mentioned. The power that we possess is always felt, therefore when you feel that you can do a certain thing it means that there is sufficient power in that particular faculty that is required. But a faculty must be large before it can contain enough power to be consciously felt. Consequently the fact that you feel power in a certain faculty proves conclusively that that faculty is large, and is possessed of considerable ability.

From this point on, the question to decide is, where you feel the greatest amount of power because where you feel the most power there you will find the greatest ability. This is conclusive, but here another question arises, that is, if the feeling of the average person is always reliable. The answer is that it is not. But it can be made so with a little training.

All psychologists have come to the conclusion that there is but one sense, the sense of feeling and that all other senses, both in the external and the internal are but modifications of this one sense. It is also admitted that the sense of feeling can be cultivated along scores of lines where it is now wholly inactive, and that there is no perceptible limit to its development along any line. This being true we shall go to the very foundation of all the senses, and all the modes of discerning things, when we take the sense of feeling for our guide in the selection of that work for which we have the greatest talent and power.

To train the sense of feeling in detecting the exact place in mind where, the greatest power resides, the first step is to make this sense normal, which is highly important because the average person has so many artificial desires, and permits the mind to be stimulated by every successful venture that is heard of.

There are a great many people who become aroused with ambition to enter the literary world whenever they learn of remarkable success attained in that world. Thus their energies are temporarily turned upon the literary faculties and they feel considerable power in that part of the mind. This they think is sufficient evidence that they have literary talent and make attempts to get results in such work; but they soon find that the inspiration in that direction did not last and they are compelled to try something else.

Then these people may learn of remarkable success in the business world. They become enthused over the possibilities of commercial ventures and turn their energies in that direction. But they soon find that their commercial faculties are not large enough to carry out their ambitions along this line. In consequence they turn their attention to the next venture that looks promising. There are thousands of minds who are constantly affected in this way, drifting from one thing to another. They imagine that because someone is succeeding in a certain work they may also succeed in that work, provided they have inclinations along that line. They also imagine that they are the very ones to enter every particular field where the demand for great service and great ability is required. The reason is their minds are controlled by appearances and what they feel as the result of the switching of energy here and there from one faculty to another. Such people therefore cannot rely upon the sense of feeling in any line of action because it is seldom normal.

To produce a normal sense of feeling for the purpose in question we should never pay any attention to what others have done or are doing because the success of others proves nothing as far as we are concerned. We must not look at the power of another man's brain, but try to find what there is in our own brains. We should never permit the enthusiasm of others to intoxicate our own minds. We should let others be enthused in their way and we should let them concentrate upon what work they like. But we should not imitate others either in thought, enthusiasm or feeling.

The course to pursue is to watch yourself closely for some weeks or months and try to discover in what faculty you feel the most power. If you feel the greatest power in a certain faculty and in that one only, you may choose that faculty without further examination and give it all your force, energy, ambition and desire, realizing that the application of that faculty will bring the greatest results that you could attain in your life.

But if there are several other faculties that seem to be equally strong, wait and watch more closely until you finally discover the seat of the greatest power. When two or more seem to be equally strong, and continue thus under the most rigid self-examination, choose the one that you can use to the best advantage now, and turn all your power for attainment and achievement in that direction.

When there is prolonged uncertainty as to where the greatest amount of power is expressed try to increase the power of every part of your mind by directing the subconscious to express more power from within. The value of this is found in the fact that the greatest amount of power always goes to the largest faculty so that an increase of power will in every case reveal the existence of the leading talent or faculty in your possession.

After you have made the sense of feeling normal so that you can feel the state of your mind as it really is, you can always depend upon the law that whatever you feel that you can do you have the power to do. And you may proceed to act along that line knowing that you will succeed, no matter how difficult the undertaking may seem to be. It is the presence of great power in a certain faculty that makes you feel that you can do things by using that faculty. Therefore when you can feel what faculty is the largest and strongest you know positively what you can do, what you can accomplish and what you should undertake. True, a great deal of training of that strongest faculty may be required, but since the talent, the ability, and the power are there the results must follow when the practical application is made.

Chapter 8

The Within And The Without

It has been stated that the average person is nine-tenths environment; that is, nine-tenths of his thoughts, ideas, desires and motives are suggested by environment, or created in the likeness of what he has come in contact with in the outer life; and this is largely true. He is therefore almost wholly patterned after the things that make up his surroundings, and instead of being himself is a reflection of his circumstances. That such a person can master himself and control his destiny is out of the question because we cannot control external things so long as we are almost entirely in the control of those things.

When we analyze this phase of human life we find that the multitudes float with the stream like dead logs; therefore can never go where they wish nor accomplish what they wish. However, no life is complete until we can have things the way we like; that is, until we can consciously change ourselves and our environments according to those higher views of life that we are constantly receiving as we promote our progress. For this reason we must find some way that will lead us out from the control of environment if we wish to live a complete life and a life really worth living.

To proceed we find the law to be that anything in the without that is permitted to impress its likeness upon the mind will influence character, conduct, thought, action and living. And when you give such impressions full right of way they will actually control your life, the reason for which has been explained in preceding chapters. To avoid this influence from environment therefore, we must refuse to receive impressions from without that we do not desire. But since the greater part of these impressions come unconsciously the question will be how to avoid them. This question, however, is answered through the understanding of the law of receptivity.

It is natural for the mind to receive impressions from the without. It is also necessary. That is what the senses are for. But it is not natural to absorb through the senses all sorts of impressions from everything with which we may come in contact. When such impressions are absorbed without discrimination and without our cognizance of the fact we have a mental state called unconscious receptivity, and this state is produced by a weak character.

But here we must remember that a weak character is not necessarily a bad character; because when you are very weak you may not even be able to do mischief. To be really bad you must be strong because a bad character is a strong mind misdirected, while a weak character is a negative sort of goodness, a goodness that means well but is wholly incompetent. What is called character is that quality of mind that discriminates, selects, chooses and holds in possession what has been selected.

Character therefore has two functions. The one selects the right and the other holds the mind in the right. When character is absent or so completely negative that it is almost wholly inactive it is not possible for, the mind to select the right or to hold the right. Such a mind will absorb nearly everything that environment may suggest and will therefore be a reflection of the present sphere of existence. Most minds have some character and therefore have a few ideas and motives of their own; they accordingly eliminate some of the undesirable impressions that may try to gain entrance to the mind. But we are all aware of the fact that the average person is entirely too much under the influence of those things that surround him. The majority are affected to a large extent by surroundings, climatic conditions and atmospheres in general, though it is a sign of weakness to be influenced in this manner. The coming and going of events and the opinions of others also play a very large part in molding the thought of most minds. But no mind should be modified by such influences unless he accepts those modifications by personal choice.

Every mind should be able to be himself, no matter what happens or fails to happen, and every mind should be able to think his own thought regardless of anyone's opinion on the subject. This, however, requires a strong character; that is, the ability to make your own selections and the power to stand by that which you have selected. The attitude of receptivity has frequently been looked upon as a weakness, but it is the lack of character in this connection that constitutes the weakness. Receptivity in itself is indispensable. There are any number of illustrations to prove this fact. The mind that is not receptive to the finer things of life, such as music, art, love, the beauties of nature and so on, has not begun to live. Without the attitude of receptivity, however, no one can respond to anything.

But here we must remember that in becoming receptive we should train ourselves to respond only to such things as we consciously select. The most receptive mind has the greatest opportunities for enjoyment as well as for the increase of wisdom. But this receptivity must be guided, and character alone can do this. Receptivity must be employed consciously only, and unconscious receptivity must be entirely avoided.

The mind must be able to use consciously that to which it wishes to respond, and must also be able to respond perfectly when the choice is made. When such an attainment is secured you will always be yourself, you will never be influenced by anything but your own thought and you will get many times as much enjoyment out of those things of life that you are able to appreciate. And the path to such an attainment is a strong, highly developed character.

Continuing this study of man, and man's relations to his surroundings, we meet a metaphysical law of extreme importance, and it may be stated as follows: Man's welfare depends upon what he does in the within and how he relates himself to the without. The related to everything in life; and what is more it is absolutely necessary.

When true harmony is absent full expression is prevented, and since it is the bringing forth of the best alone that can give us the best, we find that the full expression of what is in us becomes indispensable to our highest welfare.

What we do in the within makes us what we are. And how we are related to the without determines what we are to receive from the world. When we do much in the within we become much, and the more we can accomplish and attain, or create, in our sphere of action. When we are properly related to the world we receive the very best from the world, that is, the best that we can appropriate, appreciate and use now. We can all understand therefore why man's welfare depends upon what he does in the within and how he relates himself to the without. However, to promote constructive action in the within we must learn to apply the law of growth in every part of the human mind, and we find that all growth and development is preceded by the expansion of consciousness. To expand consciousness therefore becomes one of the great essentials in everything that may pertain to perfect advancement and higher welfare.

Mental growth involves three stages unfoldment, development and cultivation; and in each stage new fields of action are appropriated. Whenever anything in the life of an individual is enlarged a new field of activity has been entered. Unfoldment is the bringing out into a larger sphere that which previously occupied a smaller sphere.

Development is the multiplying of modes of action. And cultivation is the perfecting of those channels or vehicles through which the various modes of action may find expression. The term development is usually employed to cover the entire process because it merges with unfoldment on the subjective side and with cultivation on the objective side. Therefore when used by itself the entire process of growth is implied.

Since development in any sphere cannot take place until consciousness has been expanded in that sphere no process or system of development is complete until provided with practical methods for promoting such expansion. This being true we see how inadequate modern systems of training must be; and accordingly it is not difficult to find numerous reasons why the race is not more highly developed. However, any process of development will expand consciousness in a measure, provided the desire for expansion is held in mind when such a process is employed. But this desire must be present and must be very strong.

To try to feel the life of all life, or rather to place mind in conscious contact with all existence, will also promote the same purpose to a degree because in this attitude the mind actually transcends present limitations. In fact all limitations are eliminated in this way and the mind is set free to enter new regions whenever it may desire. This method, however, must be employed with wisdom and perfect self-control. There are many minds who have recently set themselves free from all limitations of consciousness through the exercise of universal sympathy; but not all have gained anything thereby. A few have been afraid to venture beyond what they already felt to be substantial, while others have roamed here and there and everywhere on the borderland of the unknown, wasting their energies in search of pastures green. They have had no definite aim except to find the new, and therefore have accomplished nothing. For the fact is that to find the new is not all that is necessary. When we find the new we must stop there awhile and get out of it what it may contain.

As a rule the imagination runs wild after limitations of consciousness have been removed, and only fragmentary impressions are gained whenever a slight pause for observation may be taken when in the midst of these new fields. The result is, ideas and conclusions that have no foundation whatever, or opinions that seemed plausible to the one that produced them, but wholly devoid of truth, in fact mere freaks of aimless creative power. And it is a well-known fact that such creations are entirely too numerous in the mental world at the present time. Imagination is a splendid servant, but as a master it will invariably lead you into chaos. And in the expansion of consciousness imagination is liable to take the lead unless controlled, because at such times it becomes intensely active.

To control the imagination at such times we should not permit it to do anything but construct the more perfect mental images according to such principles of life as have proven themselves to be scientifically true. The imagination should never be permitted to roam aimlessly. Whenever employed it should be put to work on something definite that you are resolved to perfect or work out.

Do not accept every new mental image as an exact truth, for a truth is usually represented by a large group of mental images. But such images cannot properly group themselves until the mind gets down to sound, rational and analytical thinking. It can therefore be stated as a fact that no mind really understands new ideas until its thinking concerning those ideas has been reduced to a system.

In order to expand consciousness in any sphere, after the limitations of that sphere have been eliminated, the imagination must be controlled and the feeling of real life intensified. A highly active imagination, however, must be avoided because new ideas created by an act of the imagination does not necessarily indicate the expansion of consciousness because an active imagination is not always deep. It usually skims the surface or acts on the borderland of new fields and generally acts in the most haphazard manner. It is the quiet orderly imagination combined with deep feeling that indicates expansion of consciousness, and that actually creates new ideas that are really true as well as of actual worth.

When we proceed to expand consciousness we find that consciousness will not enter the new field until the faculty of interior insight has established the reality of that field. In other words, we must discern that the larger mental world is real before consciousness will proceed to work itself out into that larger world. For this reason we realize that all great minds must of necessity have interior insight, or that something within them that reveals the fact that the larger field is also solid ground.

The man who attempts great undertakings usually does so because he feels within him that success will crown his efforts. Something has told him that he can move out upon the beyond of present thought and action without any fear whatever. To the senses the new realms may look empty, and to venture on may appear to be nothing more than a wild leap into the fathomless abyss of utter destruction; but interior insight takes a different view. This superior sight can see further and knows that the seeming void of the larger conscious field is actually solid rock. It also knows that this seeming void is rich with possibilities, many of which can be worked out in practical life now.

Interior insight may be defined as faith taking shape and form for practical action.

Faith itself is a mental state that dwells constantly on the borderland of the unknown, while interior insight is a mental faculty the function of which is to examine things at a long range. Farsightedness among practical men of affairs is the same thing, and is one of the chief secrets of success in all-important undertakings. Interior insight may be called the telescope of the human mind, and the more perfectly it is developed the better you understand the greater possibilities as well as the difficulties that lie before you.

It is therefore evident that when you have this insight you will know not only how to proceed, but also how to deal with those things that you know you will meet in your advancement toward greater achievements. When equipped with a well developed faculty of this kind you will know what to do to make all personal actions work together for the speedy realization of the greater things in store. In other words, you can plan ahead to advantage and you can turn all effort, thought and attention in the right direction. Many a time we fail to see the great opportunities that are almost within reach and instead of working up to them as we should if we saw them, we turn our efforts into channels that have practically nothing for us. Millions of mistakes of this kind have been made, but all of them could have been avoided through the use of interior insight.

According to the fact under consideration this insight must establish the reality of a new field before consciousness will naturally expand in that direction; that is, it must prove to the mind that the new field is substantial and full of possibilities. The development of interior insight is therefore absolutely necessary to the promotion of all other kinds of development and without it neither great attainments nor great achievements are possible. But with it there is no mental field, however large or marvelous, that the mind may not finally enter, explore, acquire and possess.

Chapter 9

Finding Your Place In Life

According to the natural workings of things, man gravitates towards those environments that are the exact counterparts of his own active nature. This is invariably the law. However, those who are living in undesirable environments may not take pleasure in accepting the idea presented in this law. It is more agreeable to place the blame elsewhere. But the fact that your surroundings are ordinary does not necessarily prove that you are an inferior person, although it does prove that you have not brought forth into full action the superior qualities that you may possess.

Here we should remember that it is the active nature that determines the surroundings in which we are to be placed, and the active nature in most persons is a mixture of conflicting forces, many of which are constantly neutralizing each other, or disturbing each other, thus preventing the more desirable of those forces to produce such results as they have the power to produce.

In addition, we must remember the fact that a disturbed nature always attracts inferiority or is drawn into disagreeable conditions. When the active forces in your nature conflict and neutralize each other your nature becomes like a leaf in the whirlwind, and you may become a victim of all the unpleasant conditions you meet.

There are a number of people with high and strong powers who never meet anything but the dark side of things and the reason is that their active forces are in conflict. One desire goes this way and another that way. Some intentions are constructive while others move at random. Their objects in life are constantly being changed and what they build up one day is taken down the next. Thus we understand why such people fail to build for themselves such environments or surroundings as they have the power to build, and also why they are found in situations that are inferior to the best that may exist in their own nature.

If the average mind should look closely at his own nature and ask himself if all the forces of his being are moving constructively and harmoniously towards his one great goal, he would find that they are not. He would discover far more conflict in his own mind and consciousness than he expected, and he would have to admit that his surroundings are the exact counterpart of those things that are active in his own self.

There is one exception, however, to this rule, an exception that must be considered before we proceed further, and this exception is found in misdirected sympathy. We frequently find excellent people in environments where we know they do not belong. At first we may fail to discover the reason, and in failing to do this we may conclude that there is nothing in the idea that people attract their own environments, or are drawn into environments similar to themselves. But a close examination of these cases will reverse this conclusion. There are many people who remain where they are, and frequently in most undesirable environments, not because they belong there, but because their sympathy keeps them there. They do not wish to break away for fear others may suffer. We all know of many such cases, and when we look into this subject closely we find that misdirected sympathy is one of the greatest obstacles to the proper adjustment of persons with their true surroundings.

If it were not for misdirected sympathy several million people would today be living in far better environments, environments that would be directly suited to their present natures and needs. But to break loose from old associations and accept new opportunities may at times seem unkind. However, we must remember that we are living for the whole race, and not only for a few friends. And also that we can render the best service to the race, including our present friends, by being perfectly true to ourselves; that is, by living and working where we actually belong.

Sentimentalism and abnormal feelings have kept down thousands of fine minds, and compelled many a human flower to wither among weeds; but this is always wrong. The entire race is kept back in a measure whenever a single worthy person is held down. Therefore we must seek to avoid such a circumstance whenever we can. Each individual must be permitted to be true to himself; and it is wrong for us to shed tears when a friend finds it necessary to go elsewhere to promote his progress.

You may be living today in uncongenial or unpleasant environments, or your work may call you where you know you do not belong; and there are several causes. You may be held where you are on account of misdirected sympathy. If so, give reason a chance to prove to you that you are wronging everybody by staying where you are. You cannot do the right thing for yourself nor for anyone else unless you are at your best, and to do your best you must be where you belong.

Then you may be held where you are because you have no definite purpose in life, and if so, decide upon a purpose, proceeding at once to train all the forces of your being to work for that purpose and that alone. Gradually you will work away from your present surroundings and doors will open through which you may pass to better things. There is nothing that will take you into better environments more quickly than to have a fixed and high purpose, and to marshal all the powers of mind and soul to work together for the promotion of that purpose. And since this is something that all can do, there is no reason whatever why a single person should live in surroundings that are inferior to himself.

Then there is another reason, possibly the most important of all. You may be held where you are because your good qualities are negative and have neither working capacity nor practical application. If the better side of you is negative and if such adverse tendencies as you may have inherited are positive and active, you are making for yourself a world that is anything but ideal. In this case it is not the best that is in you, but the worst that is in you that determines what kind of surroundings you are to receive, build up or attract. However, when your better side becomes strong and positive; when your good intentions are filled with living power, and when you turn all the forces of your being into the promotion of larger and higher aims, there is going to be a great change. You will soon begin to build for the better, you will begin to gravitate towards better environments and you will meet everywhere more congenial conditions.

But in this connection one of the great essentials is that all the forces of your better nature be in harmony and trained to work together for those better environments that you have in view. It is not what you are negatively, inherently or potentially that determines your present conditions in life. It is what you use and how that something is used. There are people with small minds and insignificant abilities that are now living in most desirable environments simply because the active forces of their nature work together for a definite object constantly in view. Then there are others with splendid minds and remarkable talents that are living in the midst of failure and distress simply because they did not make constructive use of the powers they possessed; in other words, the better elements in their nature were not in harmony and therefore could not produce results.

It is strict adherence to the quiet, steady, orderly and constant forward movement that will bring you to the goal in view, and even when your forces are so weak that you have to move slowly. But when you are endowed with extraordinary capabilities you will through this process rise rapidly, and finally attain everything you have had in view. A man may not be strictly honest or moral; nevertheless, if he has ability and employs his faculties constructively and harmoniously, he will build for himself a superior environment. And through his power to achieve the greater things he will be attracted towards opportunities that will promote still further the improvement of his environment. But it must be remembered that if this man were honest, moral and true his power would be still greater, and he would enjoy far better the richness and beauties of his delightful surroundings.

There is a belief among many that honest people ought to have the best that life can give, but the mere state of being honest is not sufficient. The best man in the world will be a failure if he does not employ his ability constructively, because it is doing things that counts. And to do things the powers we possess must work in harmony and work with a definite object in view.

In this connection we must not forget that the mind that is pure, honest and just can accomplish far more with a given ability than one who does not have these virtues. Virtues do not create but they do have the power to give proper direction to the process of creation. It is constructive ability that does things. Character simply guides the doing so that the product may be of the highest order and the greatest worth. That the person, therefore, who has character only and no constructive ability will accomplish very little in the world and will have to submit to the inconsistencies of fate.

The course to pursue is to combine ability with character, and to turn all powers and talents towards the attainment of some definite goal. When we take this course we are going to rise out of our present conditions and enter steadily and surely into the better and the superior. It is your active nature that counts. You may have a score of good qualities, but if those qualities are not active they will contribute nothing to the building up of your environment or your destiny. Therefore the more development, the more power and superiority that you can express through your active nature, the greater will be the results in the external world.

But all the qualities of your active nature must have worth and must work together. Superior qualities working at variance with each other will take you down into inferior environments, while inferior qualities if constructive and united in action will take you into better environments than you may be living in now. The whole problem therefore is to express your best in action, and to train the active powers and qualities in your being to work in perfect harmony; that is, to work together for the same purpose and in the same attitude.

Conflicting tendencies of mind have given poverty, distress and misfortune to many of great ability and superior goodness, while properly united tendencies have given success to many a man who was neither able nor true. However, nature is just. We receive according to what we have accomplished; not according to what we have tried to do, but what we actually have done; or in other words, not according to what there is in us, but according to how much of what is in us we applied in a thorough and practical manner.

We will receive material success and delightful exterior surroundings if we have worked properly for those things. But if we have neglected to work for the finer things of life we will receive nothing that has permanent value in human existence, and we will not have the capacity to enjoy our ideal surroundings. For this reason the wise man works for all that is beautiful and true, both in the material sense and in a higher sense.

Accordingly he will receive riches both in the without and in the within; thereby gaining the privilege to live the full life, the complete life and the life that is really worth living. You may conclude therefore that if things are not right in your world you are to blame. Accept the blame and resolve to take things into your own hands and make them right. This you can positively do because your environment will be exactly what your active nature is, and you can change your active nature as you may desire.

Chapter 10

When All Things Work For Good

In analyzing the workings of the mind there is no subject of more importance than that of the relation of good and evil. Concerning evil there are many doctrines, some of which declare that it is a real and permanent power battling with the good, while others declare that it is nothing, or simply the absence of good. Then between these two extreme beliefs almost any number of other beliefs may be found. To prove that evil is an actual principle personified in some form is not only difficult, but also impossible. On the other hand, to prove to the world that evil is nothing is by no means simplicity itself. Nevertheless, this doctrine comes very nearly being the truth.

However, it is not our purpose to analyze the nature of evil in this connection. That is a subject so large that separate attention would be required. Our object here is to make clear what we wish to bring out in connection with a most important law, viz., that when we give conscious recognition to the existence of an evil we tend to increase its power and multiply its effects. And in dealing with this law it will be necessary to define briefly what evil actually is, or rather what the new psychology has found it to be.

To say that evil is the absence of the good is not sufficiently explicit; while to say that evil, is undeveloped good is simply to play upon words. The process of development is continuous; therefore the fully developed of today is undeveloped in comparison with the possibilities of tomorrow. So that according to that idea the good of today would be evil in the light of tomorrow which is by no means a scientific idea. The truth in this connection is that when we employ the undeveloped just as if it were developed we produce what we call evil, and it is this fact that has given rise to the belief that evil is undeveloped good.

When we look closely at those things that are called evil we find that in every case force has been employed contrary to the natural laws involved. It will therefore be correct to say that evil is misdirected good, or that it is the improper use of a power that is in itself good. In fact, all powers, forces and elements are good in themselves because all that is real is good. Everything is created for a good purpose and is actually good, but it is possible to employ it for a purpose that is not in accord with those laws under which we live at the present moment. And here is where evil may arise.

Every act is good, proper and useful when performed in its own sphere of action, but when performed outside of its own sphere it is not good. It produces conditions that we call evil. This being true the fact that every act has its own sphere of action is one of the greatest facts in the universe. We can do only such things at such times that harmonize with the laws that obtain at the time and under the circumstance. And it is absolutely necessary to the persistence of the universe that such laws be absolute, because if they were not the universe would be chaos.

To simplify the subject we may state that evil is a condition produced by an act that is performed outside of its natural sphere, and that the power and effects of that condition depend upon how much life the mind throws into that particular act. It is a well known fact that the mind gives its life to those actions and conditions upon which consciousness is directed, and consciousness is always directed where reality is supposed to exist. Therefore when we give conscious recognition to the existence of an evil we give more life and power to those conditions that we call evil, and in consequence make them much worse than they were.

This is very simple because the more attention you give to anything the more life and power you add to that particular thing, be it good or evil. Accordingly it is unwise to give attention or recognition to evil under any circumstance.

However, the question is how we can prevent giving conscious attention to the evil and the wrong. When evil seems so very real how can we avoid giving conscious recognition to its existence? The answer is that we must get a better understanding of the real nature of evil and the real nature of good, because when this understanding is gained we can train the mind to act correctly in this connection. When we know that evil is not a thing, not a principle, not a reality, but simply a certain temporary and mistaken use of reality; and when we know that the use of that reality has its origin in our own minds, our attention will at once be transferred from the unpleasant condition surrounding the evil, and be directed instead upon our own inner mental domain. Thus consciousness will be withdrawn from the condition called evil and will become concerned with the change of mental action. Accordingly the power of the evil will at once be diminished. Actual experience in life has demonstrated the fact a number of times that pain or even a severe disease will disappear instantaneously when consciousness is fully and completely taken into another sphere or thought or action.

This proves that an evil condition can live only so long as we give it life, and we give it life only so long as we consciously admit or recognize its existence. When an evil condition is felt, attention should at once be directed upon the opposite good that exists in the inner world of perfection. This action of the mind will take consciousness away from the unpleasant condition and will cause all the faculties of the mind to work in realizing the absolutely good.

When we proceed to trace all perverted action to its inner mental source consciousness will follow, leaving evil behind, and coming to give its life to the change of the said source that proves itself simply to be a misunderstanding of things. Then if the desire of the heart is to change the source of that action, or in other words, to gain a correct understanding of things, the new and the ideal image of the good will appear in the mind, and according to laws previously presented a change for the better will follow at once.

To illustrate, we will take a depressed condition of mind or body and proceed to remove it by this method. First, we will picture clearly upon the mind the perfect image of harmony so that we can almost see harmony with the mind. Second, we will prove to ourselves through reason that this depressed condition is not a thing, but the temporary result of valuable power misdirected. And since this power is misdirected by our own mind, our own mind must contain the origin of that misdirection. Then we will turn attention upon our own inner mentality with a view of removing the source of perversion, establishing a state of harmony; and while thus directing attention upon the inner mentality we will hold the mind in such an attitude that it is moving directly upon the image of perfect harmony.

The result will be that consciousness will become so absorbed in creating the new state of harmony that it will withdraw completely from the outer evil condition. This outer condition will in consequence disappear as it is deprived of life, while the new state of harmony will be firmly established by receiving all the attention and all the life. In other words, when consciousness leaves the condition of evil, evil has nothing further to live on, and will disappear; and as consciousness enters the condition of harmony and good in the within those conditions will receive all the life that consciousness has to give, and will accordingly grow and develop until they become sufficiently strong to take possession of the entire human system.

This is a simple process that works perfectly and that can be employed successfully in removing any undesirable condition from mind or body. However, before we begin we must picture clearly upon the mind the image of the perfect state that we seek to realize and develop, and proceed as above in the elimination of the wrong through the creation of the right. A perfect understanding of the law under consideration will aid remarkably in turning our attention as required because there is nothing that can change the mind so readily as the reasoning process involved in a clear understanding of the subject at hand.

To realize fully that life and power always go wherever consciousness goes, is extremely important and also that consciousness can be directed anywhere by becoming thoroughly interested wherever we wish it to go. In applying these methods people who feel deeply always have the best results because deep feeling tends to produce deep interest in those conditions into which we wish to direct attention.

Closely connected with this process we find a most important metaphysical law that may be stated as follows: All things work together for good to him who desires only the good. And as it is possible for anyone to desire the good and the good only we realize that it is possible for anyone to cause all things to work together for good in his life. This law proves that the way to better things is not nearly as difficult as we have supposed it to be, and also that the straight and narrow path is by no means a path that the few alone can enter.

The doctrine of the straight and narrow path has been misinterpreted as it does not refer to something that is so extremely difficult to pass through, nor is it a path that leads directly away from everything that is pleasant in life. Neither is it so narrow that we can pass through it only when we have given up everything else in life. The belief that everything in life must be left out if we wish to take this path is not only absurd, but is the very opposite to the real truth. The path that leads into life, the full life, the complete life, the beautiful life is straight because it is established upon law. When you take this path you begin to use all the laws of life properly and will therefore gain all the good things that life has the power to give.

Here we must remember that a law is not a cruel something, the function of which is simply to punish. A law is a path that leads to greater and better things. Therefore to follow a law is to move directly towards the better and the greater. When we live according to a law we are constantly receiving the greater riches that lie in that path, and when we live according to all the laws of life we receive everything good that life can give. However, when we violate law we go outside of the path, where there is nothing to be gained and nothing to live for. In fact, we step out of everything that pertains to life and thus enter chaos, the result of which is pain, loss and retrogression.

It is not the law that gives us punishment when we go astray. When we go astray we deprive ourselves of the good things of life by going away from that path where those good things are to be found. And when we are deprived of the good, the good is absent; and the absence of the good means evil, the entering into of which means punishment.

The path that leads into life is narrow because it gives room only for your own individuality, and only for the true self. You cannot be a double self, one part good and the other not, when you enter this path. There is only room for the true self. Neither can you lean on someone else. There is not room for anyone upon which to lean, as the path is for yourself alone. On this path you must live your own life and give all others freedom to live their own life.

Life is given us to be lived, and to live life we must live to ourselves according to our own light and our own individual needs. The path to life is the path to better things; in other words, it is, the advancing path and is therefore not a dismal, disagreeable or difficult path. On the contrary, it is the very opposite and is found by seeking the good and the good only. So long as we have only the good in mind we will be on this path.

We will live according to the laws of life and will receive only good things because the laws of life can give only good things. But when we begin to desire what is not good we are at once drawn out of the path. Thus we will be deprived of the essentials of life, and instead we will enter into emptiness, weakness, perversion, confusion and all kinds of disaster.

When all our desires are directed upon the attainment of the highest good our creative powers will proceed to create and rebuild everything within us and about us, thus causing all things to become better. Everything in life will improve. We will be in more perfect harmony with our surroundings and will attract more agreeable persons, circumstances and events. We will become creators of the good. Everything that we do will produce good and everything that we attempt will result in good. We will meet all persons and environments on the better side, and will in consequence receive the best things that such persons and environments have the power to give. Every change that we make will be an open door to greater good because we are moving towards the good and the good only as every change is being made.

Here it is very important to remember that when we desire only the good we are always moving towards greater good, and must without fail realize the greater good in the near future. If we pass through a few unpleasant experiences while we are waiting we must not pay attention to such seeming inconsistencies. The fact that all will be well when we reach the goal in view should so fully occupy our minds that we will not be disturbed by any defect that may be found in the way over which we must for the present pass.

To desire the good, however, does not mean to desire mere self-satisfaction. It is the universal good that must be held in mind, the greatest good for everybody. And this must not only be held in mind but deeply desired with the whole heart and soul. The proper course is to desire only the highest good and then turn all the life and power we possess into that desire. In fact we should make that desire far stronger than all other desires and we should live in it constantly.

As you proceed in this manner all the laws of the mind will work with you in promoting the realization of the good that you have in view and will gradually eliminate the results of past mistakes. Should the personal self tend to make new mistakes or take missteps, thereby leading your plans out of the true path, something will occur to prevent you from doing this before it is too late. The laws of your being will cause something to come in your way and thus turn your life in another direction, that is, in a new direction where the highest good you have in view may be finally realized.

When you have set your heart and soul upon the attainment of the good and the good only, the predominating powers in your being will work only for good, and a lesser powers will, one after the other, be taken into the same positive current so that before long all things in your life will work together for good. We may not understand at first how these powers operate, but we shall soon find that the results we had in view are being realized more and more. And as this realization is gained we shall come positively to the conclusion that all things do work together for good when we desire the good and the good alone.

Chapter 11

With What Measure Ye Mete

He who gives much receives much. This we all know, but the question is what it means to give. When we speak of giving we usually think of charity and poverty; and believing that the latter is inevitable we conclude that the former must be an exalted virtue; but poverty is not inevitable. It is not a part of life's plan. It is simply a mistake. Therefore charity cannot be otherwise than a temporal remedy. Such remedies, however, though good and necessary, do not always constitute virtues because virtue is permanent and is a part of a continuous advancement in man.

He who gives in charity does not receive anything in return unless he also gives himself. It is therefore not the giving of things that brings reward, but the giving of life. But to give much life one must possess much life, and to possess much life one must live a large measure of life. According to the law, life is measured out to us with the same measure that we employ in the measuring of our own existence. In other words, we will receive only as much life as our own measure can hold; but it is not only life that is measured out to us in this way. Everything that pertains to life is measured in a similar way.

We conclude, therefore, that he who sets out a large measure to be filled will receive a large measure full, and that he who gives himself simply offers his own life for further enrichment. He who gives much of himself will be abundantly enriched because he places in life a large measure of himself to be filled. He who gives things may lose all that is given. But he who gives himself, the best that is in himself, loses nothing. Instead he gains a larger and a richer self. He who gives himself to the race gives life and life can supply all needs.

To have an abundance of life is to have the power to help yourself and to recreate your own world according to your highest desires. The gift of life is therefore the highest gift. It is also the largest gift because it includes all gifts. He who gives life does not give to relieve poverty, but to build strong souls, and when strong souls appear poverty disappears of itself. To give one's life is to express in thought, word or action everything of worth that one may possess in mind or soul; that is, everything that one may live for. And how much we live for depends upon how largely the life is measured in our understanding. When we measure life largely, life will give us a large measure of itself.

When we blend consciousness with the universal we will receive universal consciousness in return.

When we think only of the boundless, our thought will be limited no more. When we take a larger measure of our talents the wisdom that fills the universe will also fill that larger measure. When we take a large measure of man and have faith in the superior side of every mind, every mind will give to us as much as our measure of that mind can hold. Realizing these great facts we should dwell constantly in the world of greater possibilities.

We should expect much, work for much, live for much, have faith in much, and we shall find that as much will come to us as we have thought, lived and worked for. We should never limit anything nor anyone. The measure of all things should be as large as our conscious comprehension and we should refuse to be contented with anything except that which is constantly enlarging its measure. Accordingly we should live for great things and press on. Thus the greater and the greater will surely be measured out in return. This is the law and it cannot fail.

Very few, however, apply this law and that is the reason why the majority accomplish so little. They undertake so little and they never reach the high places because they nearly always aim at the low ones. Many minds that aim high for a while lose their lofty aspirations later on because they fail to reach the mountaintop the first week or the first year. Others again aspire to the high things though at the same time think of themselves as limited, insignificant and even worse. But if we would become, great we must blend all though with greatness and measure ourselves with that measure that is large enough to contain all the greatness we can possibly conceive of.

He who expands consciousness so as to measure things largely gains capacity, while he who takes a small view of everything remains incompetent. We do not get power, growth or ability by trying to cram a small mind, but by trying to expand the mind. And to expand the mind we must take the largest possible view of all things. We must live with the limitless and blend all thought with infinite thought. When the senses declare you cannot do this, reply by saying, it is in me to do it; therefore I can.

While the person is working with the limitations of the present, the mind should transcend those limitations and constantly take larger measures of both life and attainment. And as soon as this larger measure is taken the larger will begin to appear until even the person is called upon to enter a larger work with increased remuneration. Make yourself worthy and greater worth will come to you. Take a larger measure of your own capacity, your own ability, your own worth. Expect more of yourself. Have more faith in yourself and that something that supplies everybody will completely fill your measure.

It is the law that no matter how large your measure will be it will be filled. And your measure of things is as large as your conscious realization of those things. Therefore to take a larger and a larger measure of anything is to expand consciousness beyond the present understanding of that particular thing. Therefore all that we are conscious of is but a partial expression of something that is in itself limitless because everything in existence is limitless. Therefore by gaining a larger consciousness of those partial expressions we will become conscious of a larger expression. And a larger expression of those things will appear through us, which means that our own life has been enlarged and enriched. This is all perfectly simple and proves conclusively why the boundless measures out to each individual only as much as the measure of that individual can hold.

But since there is nothing to hold consciousness in bounds except our own limited view, and since we can take a larger view of anything whenever we choose, it is in our power to increase the measure of anything in our own life or in our own sphere of existence. Perpetual increase and perpetual expansion of consciousness go hand in hand in the life of man. The former is produced by the latter and the latter is produced by man himself. We conclude, therefore, that anyone can make his life as large as he wishes it to be, and can bring into his life as much of everything as he may desire.

In considering this great subject we must give due attention to the process of growth. And in this connection we must remember that the desire for growth and the effort to promote growth must be constant. This law, however, is frequently neglected as it is the tendency of nearly every person to lean back, fold arms and suspend all desire and every effort whenever a victory has been won, or an onward step taken. But we can never afford to stop or to suspend action at any time and what is more it is impossible to suspend action.

We cannot stop living, therefore we cannot stop thinking, and so long as we think, some part of our being will act. And that part should act with some definite goal in view. When you leave the field of action to rest, so to speak, you permit that part of your being that does act to act aimlessly, and aimless actions always produce perversions, false states and detrimental conditions. It is the conviction of every thorough student of life that aimless action is the fundamental cause of all the ills that appear in life. And aimless action is caused by the attempt to stop all action when we try to rest. However, the fact that action will go on perpetually in some part of our system proves that the individual Ego should be constantly at hand to guide that action.

The Ego does not need any rest, nor need it ever suspend activity, because rest simply means recuperation, and it is those organs that receive and use up energy that require recuperation. The Ego does not create and does not employ energy, but simply governs the distribution and use of energy. So that the real you should always be active in some sense, and should always desire the promotion of growth as well as carry out the promotion of growth, regardless of how many special parts of your system have suspended action for the time being.

When we understand the real purpose of rest we perceive clearly why the governing conscious Ego requires no rest whatever, and also why it does require ceaseless conscious action. To prevent aimless action the Ego should guide action on the mental or spiritual plane whenever rest demands suspension of activity on the physical plane. It has been demonstrated conclusively that the body rests most perfectly when some constructive action takes place in mind or soul, and it is for this reason that the first day of the week has been consecrated to the spiritual life. By giving this day entirely to higher thought, and the contemplation of the finer things of life, the body and the mind will recuperate so perfectly that you can do more work and far better work during the coming week than ever before; although not simply because you have properly rested mind and body, but also because you have through your higher devotions awakened new life, more life and a number of higher, stronger powers.

The principle that the body rests most perfectly when consciousness is actively at work on some higher plane is a principle that should receive the most thorough attention, and every person should adopt some system of living by which this principle could be carried out completely in every detail. Such a system of living would prolong the life of the body, increase the power of the mind and remarkably unfold the soul.

The metaphysical law under consideration is based upon this principle. Therefore to live according to this principle, this law must be constantly employed; that is, the desire for growth and effort to promote growth must be constant. In addition, the desire for growth must be constructive because no action is constructive unless it is prompted by the desire for growth. And every effort to promote growth must be constant, because efforts that do not aim at growth are destructive, while suspended efforts cause aimless action. To carry out this law transfer your desire for growth from one faculty to another, and from one plane to another, as conditions may demand, or as your work may require, but never suspend that desire.

When you feel that a certain faculty, through which you have been acting, needs recuperation withdraw action from that faculty and begin to act through another faculty, expressing through this other faculty all the desire for growth that you can possibly create. Or, when you feel that the physical plane needs recuperation act upon the mental. When both mental and physical planes require recuperation enter the spiritual and express there your desire for soul unfoldment. Then whenever you express your desire for growth do something to promote that growth use what methods you possess and gradually you will evolve better and more effective methods.

As you apply all these ideas, consciousness will constantly expand, development will be constantly taking place in some part of your being, and you will be improving in some way every minute. In addition, you will prevent all aimless action and all retarded growth. Every part of the system will receive proper rest and recuperation whenever required, and this will mean complete emancipation because all ills come from aimless action, retarded growth and their consequences. It will also mean greater achievements and higher attainments because all the faculties will improve steadily and surely, and the entire system will be at its best under every circumstance.

Chapter 12

Finding Material For Mind Building

To live is to move forward but there can be no forward movement without new experience. Therefore in all advancement, in all progress, in all attainment, in all achievement, and in the living of life itself experience is indispensable. Experience being necessary to the promotion of advancement as well as to the increase of the value and the welfare of life, it becomes necessarily a permanent and continuous cause in the world of every individual, and as like causes produce like effects, both in quality and in quantity, experience should be sought and selected with the greatest possible care.

It is also highly important that we seek an abundance of experience because so long as the cause has quality it cannot be too extensive in quantity. Experience is the material from which character and mentality are constructed. Therefore the richer and more abundant our experience, the stronger and more perfect will our character and mentality become. Everything has its purpose and the real purpose of experience is to awaken new forces, new states, new phases of consciousness, and to originate new actions in the various parts of being.

To unfold and bring forth what is latent in the being of man is the principal object of experience. And it is well to remember that without experience no latent quality or power can ever be aroused and expressed. The power of experience to bring forth what is latent and to originate the new gives cause to enjoyment and happiness, as well as progress, and since experience is the only cause of enjoyment, it follows that what the enjoyment is to be in the life of any individual will depend directly upon what experience that individual will select.

The average mind makes no effort to select experience wisely, therefore fails to promote the real purpose of experience; and failing in this he also fails to awaken and develop those things in himself that can produce the most desirable of all experience, that is, the consciousness of a perpetual increase of all that has real worth in life.

The more experience the better, provided it is rich, constructive and wholesome, though no person should seek experience for the mere sake of passing through experience. The belief that experience itself builds life is not true, nor is there any truth in the doctrine that all kinds of experience, good and otherwise, are necessary to the full development of life. It is only a certain kind of experience that can add to the welfare of life and promote the purpose of life. Therefore to understand the psychology of experience and how experience is connected with the workings of mind is a matter of exceptional importance.

The daily purpose of each individual should be to seek the richest experience possible in order that the best material possible may be provided in the building of himself. To this end he should place himself in daily contact with the best that is moving in the world, and the more of this the better. Such a practice will develop the mind, perfect the character, refine and repolish the personality, and increase perpetually the health and the wholeness of the body. It will also tend directly towards the promotion of a long and happy life.

The mind should be wide-awake to everything in its sphere of existence that can give expression to superior action, and seek to gain the richest possible experience by coming in contact with that action. To place one's self in mental contact with the best that is in action in the world is to originate similar actions within one's own mentality. These will arouse the superior forces that are latent in the deeper mentality and before long a superior mental life will have been evolved.

The more experience that the mind can gain by coming in contact with the best things that are alive in the world the larger, the broader and the more perfect will the mind become. It is therefore evident that the recluse must necessarily have a small mind whether he lives in the world or apart from the world. To live a life of seclusion is to eliminate experience to the smallest degree possible and thereby cause the mind to become so small that only a mere fraction of its power and intellect can be in conscious action. In consequence such a person can never be his best in anything, not even in a single isolated talent, nor can his ideas as a whole have any practical value, being based wholly upon one-sided opinions.

In this connection it is most important to understand that the philosophy of the hermit is useless in practical life. And the same is true of moral or physical views as formulated by those who live in seclusion. Such ideas may look well in theory and they may be accepted by millions of people, but nothing outside of mere intellectual satisfaction will be gained. Intellectual satisfaction, however, when not directly associated with physical, mental and moral progress is detrimental; the reason being that it produces a phase of mental contentment that culminates in mental inactivity.

The only intellectual satisfaction that is normal and that can be beneficial, is that satisfaction which comes from the consciousness of continuous advancement. Any other satisfaction means mental inaction, and mental inaction leads to death invariably, not only in the intellectual but also in body, mind and character.

Those who live in the world and who are daily required to meet the problems of the world should seek guidance and instruction when necessary only from those superior minds that have had experience in the world. Those who live apart from the world do not appreciate the conditions that exist in the world. They have not been awakened to the real nature of those conditions. Therefore the solution that they may offer for the problem which may arise from such conditions can be of no practical value. He alone really knows who has had experience, though experience is not the whole of knowledge. It is only a small part, but that part is indispensable.

Minds that live only for themselves or for a selected few only, will also become narrow in mentality and dwarfed in character. Such living invariably results in retrogression because too many of the elements of life, both physical and metaphysical, are compelled through the lack of experience to remain inactive. The entire mentality and the entire personality should be active, and to promote such activity the entire individual life should be entirely filled with rich, wholesome and intellectual experience.

In brief we should live while we live and not simply exist. The lives of young people in particular should be well provided with an abundance of wholesome amusements and of every imaginable variety, though this practice should not cease with the coming of the thirties. We should all enjoy this life to the fullest extent so long as we remain in this life, though not simply because it is the privilege of us all to enjoy every moment to the fullest extent, but also because there are few things that are more conducive to wholesome experience than that of wholesome, enjoyment. We gradually grow into the likeness of that which we enjoy. An abundance of wholesome amusement therefore will invariably produce a wholesome nature. And by enjoying the greatest possible number of the best things we shall naturally and steadily develop the best that is latent within us.

Every experience that we pass through awakens something within us that was not active before, and this something will in turn impress upon the subconscious the nature of the thought that was created during the experience. In fact the nature of the experience will determine what is to be awakened in the conscious mind and what is to be impressed upon the subconscious. And since subconscious impressions determine the character, the mentality and, the personal nature of man, it is of the highest importance that only such experiences be selected as are rich, constructive and wholesome.

What is awakened in the mind of man is awakened by experience alone. For this reason no change in the mind can take place, unless preceded by some experience whether that experience be tangible or imaginary. And what is awakened in the mind of man determines first what he is to think, and second what he is to do and to be. These facts prove conclusively that experience is the material from which character and mentality are constructed. And therefore experience should receive the most thorough consideration during every period of life, and especially during the first twenty-four years of personal existence.

The experience that a person passes through during this early period will determine to a very great extent what is to be accomplished in later years; the reason being that the early tendencies are the strongest as a rule, be they good or otherwise. We are not inferring, however, that man cannot change his nature, his character, his mentality, his habits, his desires or his tendencies at any time, because he can.

But time and energy can be put to better use in later life than to that of overcoming the results of mistakes that could have been avoided if the proper mental tendencies had been produced early in life.

We should take advantage of favorable periods when we have them, and we should create such periods when we do not have them. This we can do, but when they come of themselves, as they do in the early years of personal existence, everything possible should be done to make these periods become a permanent power in our favor.

To permit the young mind or any mind to pass through experiences that are unwholesome or adverse is to cause tendencies to be produced that will work against him all his life, that is, if those tendencies are not removed later on, and they usually are not. But to limit the supply of experience at this period or at any period is equally detrimental. That person who enters the twenties in the consciousness of an abundance of rich experience is prepared for his career, and if he has a fair degree of ability he will succeed from the very beginning. He is ripe, so to speak, for his work. His mind has found normal action in nearly all of its phases and. he will make but few mistakes of any consequence. It is totally different, however, with that person who has entered the twenties in what may be called the green state. Even though his mind may be highly active he will accomplish but little, because being as yet unconscious of his real nature, his real capacity and his true state of normal action, he will misdirect most of his energies and they will be used up before his success can begin.

The mind that lacks experience does not know its own power, its own possibilities, its own desires nor its own natural sphere of action. It has not found its bearings, and even though it may have remarkable ability it will invariably misplace that ability, and will in consequence fail utterly where lesser minds, with an abundance of wholesome experience to begin with, have nearly everything their own way.

It is therefore evident that the practice still prevalent in thousands of homes of compelling young people to be ignorant of what is going on in the world is most detrimental to the future welfare of those people. Such a practice has caused many a young mind to be a complete failure until he was thirty-five or more, though if he had received an abundance of wholesome experience early in life he could easily have entered into real success more than ten years before. An abundance of rich experience secured early in life will awaken the best that is in the person. He will thus become acquainted with himself and will know what to do with himself. He will also know what to do with others and how to apply himself in the outer world.

However, we must remember in this connection that it is not necessary for anyone to do wrong or to mix with the wrongs of the world in order to gain experience. The fact is that such experience is not experience simply a misuse of mind, thought and action. The proper kind of experience is just as necessary to the young mind as the proper kind of education, and parents should in no way eliminate the opportunities of their children to gain experience of value and worth. But they should not let their children loose, so to speak, without paying any attention to the kind of experience that children seek to enjoy. To pass through experience that is neither rich nor wholesome is to cause tendencies, desires, habits and traits to be formed that are adverse to everything worthwhile that the person may try to do. The results of such experience will have to be removed before real living and real achievement can begin.

All young minds should be given the freedom to enjoy every imaginable form of enjoyment that can be found, provided such enjoyments are wholesome. And here we should remember that those young people who stay at home ignorant of the world are not any better in character than those who go out to enjoy the best that is living and moving in the world. And as to mental power they are much weaker than those who have come in contact with the movements of life and thought in all its phases. Moral purity does not come from keeping the mind in a state of inaction, nor does goodness come from the absence of desire. The best way to make the mind pure and the character strong is to give the person so much rich and wholesome experience that he will not care for that which is inferior or perverted. No normal mind will care for the lesser after he has gained possession of the greater. And those minds that are not normal do not need ethics, they need a physician.

An abundance of wholesome and most interesting enjoyment may be found anywhere, and the supply will increase with the demand. It is possible for any person to go out and come in contact with the world without going wrong, and the experience is invaluable, not only in a practical way but also in a way that touches the very cause of everything that has worth in the being of man. The more constructive experience that a person passes through the larger will the mind become and the more substantial will everything become that is active in his nature. An abundance of rich experience will invariably be followed by a larger subconscious life and this will add remarkably to the power and capacity of every talent and faculty. Such experience will also tend to give every force in the system the proper direction and thus prevent the waste of energy.

The more experience we seek the better, provided that experience is sought for the purpose of awakening the larger and the better that is latent within us. And since experience in some form is absolutely necessary to the promotion of this awakening, the art of securing experience becomes a fine art, in fact one of the finest and most important in the world.

Every experience produces a subjective impression and when a number of such impressions of the highest order are secured there is not only a feeling of completeness and satisfaction that is beyond price, but the entire individuality gains a marked degree of superiority and worth. An abundance of rich experience will also give a substantial foundation to the mind, a foundation that no circumstance, however trying, will be able to disturb. And so long as the foundation of the mind is secure the various elements and forces of the system will be able to perform their functions well, no matter what temporary conditions may be.

One of the greatest secrets of success in any undertaking, or in any vocation in life, is found in the possession of a mental foundation so strong and so substantial that it is never disturbed under any circumstance. And as the right kind of experience will tend to build such a mental foundation, we realize the extreme value of the subject under consideration.

To feel that you have received your share of the good things that have come your way is one of the rare joys of life. And this feeling comes invariably from the subjective memory of rich and abundant experience. This feeling produces the consciousness of mental wealth and without it life is not complete; but with it any person can pass through physical poverty and not feel poor in the least. While the mind that has had little or no experience is poverty stricken, no matter how extensive external possessions may be. Such a mind is practically empty, it finds no satisfaction in life and is incapable of turning its energies into constructive action. In brief, it flows with the stream and is almost completely in the hands of fate.

Experience, however, in the true sense is not synonymous with hardship. And to pass through trials and tribulations does not necessarily mean to gain experience. Occasionally it does, but as a rule it does not, and real experience awakens new life. It gives new points of view and enlarges the mental world. Instead of crushing individuality as hardships sometimes does it strengthens individuality, and makes the man more powerful both in mind and character than ever before.

To enjoy real experience, therefore, is not simply to pass through certain mental or physical conditions, but it is to gain something of permanent value while passing through those conditions. Experience of this kind may sometimes be gained through mistakes; that is, when the mistake causes the mind to seek the other way; otherwise the mistake does not produce experience of value, and nothing is gained. However, it is not necessary to make mistakes or to go wrong in order to gain valuable experience. Neither is hardship, pain nor adversity necessary to growth, progress and advancement.

The most valuable experience comes, not through mistakes, but through the mind's sympathetic contact with the best that is alive in the world. Such experiences, however, may not be had for nothing. But to employ a small percentage of one's earnings in procuring such experiences is to make a most excellent investment. The bank of rich and wholesome experience pays a very large interest. It will be profitable, therefore, for everybody to deposit as much as can be spared every week in this great bank. To keep in constant touch with the best that is living and moving in the world will give new ideas, new mental life, greater ambition, greater mental power, increased ability and capacity, and will in consequence increase the earning capacity of the individual. It will also increase the joy of living and make every individual life more thoroughly worthwhile.

The good things in the world, however, should not be sought for mere pastime. They should invariably be sought for the purpose of gaining conscious possession of the richness that they may contain. This will increase immeasurably the enjoyment of the experience, and will cause the experience to add directly to the power, the quality, the worth and the value of life. It will make living more and more worthwhile, and nothing is worth more.

Chapter 13

Building The Superior Mind

According to the conclusions of experimental psychology the possibilities that are latent in the soul of man are both limitless and numberless. It is evident therefore that when we learn to draw on the abundance of the great within we can readily build within ourselves all the elements of a superior mind. In applying this idea, however, the first essential is to recognize the fact that every effort to build for greater things must act directly upon the soul, because the soul is the only source of that which is expressed or that which may be expressed in the human personality.

In trying to build the superior in mind, life and character two methods have been employed. The first has been based upon the belief that man is naturally imperfect in every part of his being and that advancement may be promoted only by improving upon his imperfect qualities. The other method, which is the new method, is based upon the principle that man contains within himself all the qualities of superiority in a perfect state and that advancement is promoted, not by trying to improve upon his imperfections, but by trying to bring forth into personal expression more and more of the many perfect qualities that already exist within him.

The first method is necessarily a failure. And the reason why the race has improved so slowly is because this method has been used almost exclusively. A few, however, have in all ages, consciously or unconsciously used the second method, and it is through the efforts of these, that the advancement that we have made has been brought about. That the first method must be a failure is clearly understood when we realize that nothing can be evolved unless it is involved, and that it is impossible for man to bring forth the more perfect unless the more perfect already exists in a potential state within him.

This principle is well illustrated by the fact that we cannot produce light by acting upon darkness, nor produce perfection by trying to improve upon such things as do not have the possibilities of perfection. We cannot develop quality, worth or superiority in ourselves unless those elements which go to make up qualities of worth and superiority already exist within us. Development means the bringing out of that which is already within. But if there is nothing in the within no development will take place, no matter how faithfully we may apply ourselves. Thus we realize that before development along any line can be promoted, we must recognize the fact that we already possess within us all those elements that may be needed for the promotion of that development even to the highest possible degree. In other words, we must recognize the fact that all the possibilities of perfection already exist within us, and that we are therefore in reality perfect through and through as far as our real or interior nature is concerned.

Those who employ the first method do not recognize the greater possibilities within and therefore they do not try to bring forth what is already within them. They simply try to improve the imperfect in their personal nature by acting upon the imperfect. But we cannot fill an empty space by simply acting upon emptiness. We must bring something into that empty state if we wish fullness to take place. The imperfect lacks something; that is the reason why it is imperfect. And that something must be supplied from some other source before improvement or change for the better can be brought about. That something, however, that is lacking may be found in the great within because the great within contains everything that man may require to produce perfection in any part of his mind, character or personality.

The possibilities of the within are limitless and numberless. Of this fact we have any amount of evidence. Therefore by adopting the second method for building the superior in the human mind it is evident that any individual may steadily rise in the scale until he finally reaches the high goal of attainment that he may have in view.

To proceed, realize that the source of perfection and the source of all the elements of quality and worth exist already within you. Then by becoming more deeply conscious of these superior qualities that you possess within yourself those qualities will be expressed more and more, because the law is, that whatever we become conscious of within ourselves that we shall naturally express through mind and personality.

If you wish to improve any faculty or talent realize that the interior foundation of that faculty is perfect as well as limitless, and that you can make that faculty as remarkable as you wish by unfolding the perfection and the limitless power that is back of, beneath, or within that faculty. There is nothing to be gained by trying to patch up, so to speak, the imperfections of the exterior side of mind or personality through the application of some superficial or artificial method, though this is practically all that modern systems of mind building have attempted to do.

When we examine the results of those systems we realize how futile such methods necessarily are in this connection. However, when we proceed to enlarge the actual capacity of a faculty by drawing upon the interior and limitless source of that faculty we secure something with which to work. And by employing a scientific system of objective training in addition to the perpetual enlargement of a faculty from within, we build up not only a powerful faculty, but we learn to apply all of its power and talent in practical use.

The same methods will hold in the building of any part of the mind or the whole of the mind. And it is such methods through which we may secure not only satisfactory results in the present, but a perpetual increase of results for an indefinite period. Before we can employ these methods, however, we must recognize the fact that the real man within is already perfect and limitless and that the subconscious root of every talent or faculty is also perfect and limitless.

Therefore our object must not be to perfect our external selves by trying to improve upon our external selves regardless of what we may possess within us, but our object must be to bring forth into expression an ever increasing abundance of the power, the quality and the worth that is already latent within us. We must live, think and act with this great purpose uppermost in mind regardless of circumstances. In fact, everything we do must be done with the desire to bring forth more of the wonderful that is within us. And it is in this way that we may build the superior mind.

Those who have gone beneath the surface of mere existence and have familiarized themselves with real life know that the personal man is as he thinks. Therefore to perfect the personal man thought must be more perfect. But here we must remember that thought is created in the likeness of our own conception of ourselves. Therefore, so long as we think that we are imperfect in every part of body, mind and soul it is natural that our thought will be imperfect, and the personal man will accordingly in body, mind and character continue to be imperfect.

The law is that thought is the cause of every state or condition that appears in mind, character or personality. Thus we realize that so long as we think of ourselves as imperfect we will create imperfect thoughts; and imperfect thought will produce nothing else but imperfect conditions and states in every part of our being.

However, when man discovers that he himself in the real and in the soul state of his existence is absolutely perfect, he will think of himself as perfect, that is, he will not consider himself as an imperfect personality, but constantly think of himself as an individuality possessed of all the elements, powers and qualities of the highest state of perfection. Accordingly his thought will be perfect as far as he has developed this higher conception of himself. And since the personal man is in his nature the result of thought, more and more perfection will accordingly be expressed in every part of the personal man.

As man grows in the understanding of his own interior perfection his thought of himself will be higher and higher, better and better, more and more perfect. His mind, body and character will in consequence improve in proportion. And since there is no limit to the latent possibilities of perfection any individual can by attaining a larger and deeper conscious realization of the perfect qualities within develop himself perpetually, because whatever we become conscious of within ourselves that we naturally express through the life of the personality.

The art of building the superior in the human mind as well as in personality and character is therefore based upon the discovery that the real interior man is not only perfect in all his latent elements and qualities, but is actually a marvelous being; in fact is within himself limitless in power, having superior qualities that are actually numberless.

To unfold these possibilities and gradually bring out into expression more and more of the marvelous man within, we must become more and more conscious of this power and worth and perfection that exists within us. And this consciousness may be attained by thinking constantly with deep feeling of this interior perfection; and also by actually living for the one purpose of unfolding more and more of this interior perfection.

In brief, the principle is this: The superior already exists within us. When we become conscious of the superior we will, according to a leading metaphysical law, express the superior; and what we express in mind or personality becomes a permanent part of the personal man. Mind building, therefore, is based upon the bringing out of the greatness that is within, and in learning to apply in practical life that power which naturally comes forth, through mind and personality, as this interior greatness is unfolded.

Chapter 14

The Secret Of The Master Mind

The mind that masters himself creates his own ideas, thoughts and desires through the original use of his own imaging faculty, while the mind that does not master himself forms his thoughts and desires after the likeness of impressions received through the senses; and is therefore controlled by the conditions from which those impressions come, because as we think so we act and live. Accordingly the master mind is a mind that thinks what he wants to think regardless of what circumstances, environments or associations may suggest.

The average mind desires what the world desires without any definite thought as to its own highest welfare or greatest need, the reason being that a strong tendency to do likewise or to imitate is always produced in the mind when desires are formed in the likeness of impressions that are suggested by external conditions. It is therefore evident that a person who permits himself to be affected by suggestion will invariably form artificial desires. And to follow such desires is to be misled in every instance. The master mind, however, desires only that which is conducive to real life here and now and in the selection of those desires is never influenced in the least by the desires of the world.

The power of desire is one of the greatest of all powers in the human system. It is therefore highly important that every desire be normal and created for the welfare of the individual himself. But no desire is normal that is formed through the direct influence of suggestions. Such desires are always abnormal and cause the individual to be misplaced.

This explains why a very large number of people are misplaced. They do not occupy those places wherein they may be their best and accomplish the most. They are working at a disadvantage and are living a life that is far inferior to what they are intended to live, and because of abnormal desires. They have imitated the desires of others without consulting their own present need. They have formed the desire to do what others are doing, permitting their minds to be influenced by suggestions and impressions from the world, forgetting what their present state makes them capable of doing now. Thus, by living the lives, the habits, the actions and the desires of others they are led into a life not their own; in other words, they are misplaced.

The master mind is never misplaced because he does not live to do what others are doing, but what he himself wants to do now, and he wants to do only that which is conducive to real life, a life worthwhile, a life that steadily works up to the very highest goal in view.

The average mind requires a change of environment before he can change his thought. He has to go somewhere or bring into his presence something that will suggest a new line of thinking and feeling. The master mind, however, can change his thought whenever he may so desire. A change of scene is not necessary because the master mind is not controlled by external conditions or circumstances. A change of scene will not produce a change of thought in his mind unless he so elects for the master mind changes his thoughts, ideas, or desires by imaging upon the mind the exact likeness of those new ideas, new thoughts, or new desires that have been selected.

The secret of the master mind is found wholly in the intelligent use of the imaging faculty, for man is as he thinks, and his thoughts are patterned after the predominating mental images, whether those images are impressions suggested from without or impressions formed by the mind through original thinking. When any individual permits his thoughts or desires to be formed in the likeness of impressions received from without he will be more or less controlled by environment. He will be largely in the hands of circumstances and fate, but when he proceeds to transform into an original idea every impression received from without and incorporates that idea into a new mental image he will use environment as a servant, thereby placing fate in his own hands.

Every object that is seen will produce an impression upon the mind according to the degree of mental susceptibility. He will, in consequence, be a reflection of the world in which he lives. He will think, speak and act as his surroundings may suggest. He will flow with the stream of his circumstances and he will be more or less of an automaton instead of a well individualized character.

However, every person who permits himself to be largely and continually affected by suggestions is more or less of an automaton, and accordingly is more or less in the hands of fate. So, therefore, in order to reverse matters and place fate in his own hands he must proceed to make intelligent use of suggestions instead of blindly following such desires and thoughts as his surroundings may suggest.

We are all surrounded constantly by suggestions of every description, because everything has the power to suggest something to us, provided we are susceptible. But there is a vast difference between permitting ourselves to be susceptible to all sorts of suggestions and by training ourselves to use intelligently all those impressions that suggestions may convey. The average student of suggestion not only ignores this difference, but encourages susceptibility to suggestion by constantly emphasizing the belief that it is suggestion that controls the world.

But if it is really true that suggestion does control the world, we want to learn how to so use suggestion that its indiscriminate control of the human mind may decrease steadily. For the human mind must not be controlled by anything, and this we can accomplish, not by teaching people how to use suggestion for the purpose of affecting their minds, but in using every impression conveyed by suggestion in the reconstruction of our own minds.

Suggestion is a part of life because everything has the power to suggest and all minds are open to impressions. Suggestion, therefore, is a necessary factor, and a permanent factor in our midst. But the problem is to train ourselves to make intelligent use of the impressions received, instead of blindly following the desires produced by such impressions, as the majority do.

To carry out this idea never permit the objects discerned by the senses to reproduce themselves in your mind against your will. Form your own ideas about what you see, hear or feel and try to make those ideas superior to what was suggested by the objects discerned. When you see evil do not form ideas or mental impressions that are similar to that evil. And do not think of the evil as bad, but try to understand the forces that are back of all evil, forces that are good in themselves though misdirected in their present state.

By trying to understand the nature that is back of evil or adversity you will not form bad ideas, and therefore will feel no bad effects from experiences that may seem undesirable. At the same time you will think your own thought about the experience, thereby developing the power of the master mind.

Surround yourself as far as possible with those things that suggest the superior, but do not permit such suggestions to determine your thought about the superior. The superior impressions that are suggested by superior environments should be used by yourself in forming still more superior thought. For if you wish to be a master mind your thought must always be higher than the thought your environment may suggest, no matter how ideal that environment may be.

Every impression that enters the mind through the senses should be worked out and should be made to serve the mind in its fullest capacity. In this way the original impression will not reproduce itself in the mind, but will become instrumental in giving the mind a number of new and superior ideas. To work out an impression try to see through its own nature; that is, look at it from every conceivable point of view while trying to discern its causes, tendencies, possibilities and probable effects.

Use your imaging faculty in determining what you want to think or do, what you are to desire and what your tendencies are to be. Know what you want, then image those things upon the mind at all times. This will develop the power to think what you want to think. And he who can think what he wants to think can be what he wants to be.

In this connection it is most important to realize that the principal reason why the average person has not realized his ideals is because he has not learned to think what he wants to think. He is too much affected by the suggestions that are all about him. He imitates his environment too much, following desires and tendencies that are not his own, and therefore he is misled and misplaced.

Chapter 15

The Power Of Mind Over Body

It is through the law of vibration that the mind exercises its power over the body. And through this law every action of the mind produces a chemical effect in the body, that is, an effect that actually takes place in the substance of the physical form. The process of this law is readily understood when we find that every mental action is a vibration, and passes through every atom in the body, modifying both the general conditions and the chemical conditions of every group of cells.

A chemical change in the body is produced by a change in the vibrations of the different elements of the body because every element is what it is by virtue of the rate of vibrations of its atoms. Everything in the universe is what it is because of its rate of vibration; therefore, anything may be changed in nature and quality by changing the rate of its vibrations.

When we change the vibrations of ice it becomes water. When we change the vibrations of water it becomes steam. When we change the vibrations of ordinary earth in one or more ways it becomes green grass, roses, trees or waving fields of grain, depending upon the changes that are made. Nature is constantly changing the vibrations of her elements thus producing all sorts of forms, colors and appearances.

This being true the problem is to use this power intelligently and thus not only secure desirable results, or results as desired, but also to secure superior results to anything we have secured before.

When we analyze this law of vibration we find that every unpleasant condition that man has felt in his body has come from a false change in the vibrations of some of the elements in his body. And we also find that every agreeable condition has come from a true change in those vibrations, that is, a change towards the better. Here we should remember that every change in the vibrations of the human system that takes us down, so to speak into the lesser grade is a false change and will produce unnatural or detrimental effects, while every change that is an ascending change in the scale is beneficial.

To apply this law intelligently it is necessary to know what chemical changes each particular mental action has the power to produce, and also how we may so regulate mental actions that all changes in the vibrations of our system may be changes along the line of the ascending scale. This, however, leads us into a vast and most fascinating subject; but on account of its vastness we can only mention it here, which is all that is necessary in this connection, as our object for the present is simply to give the reason why every mental action produces a chemical change in the body.

Since every element in the body is what it is because it vibrates at a certain rate; since every mental action is a vibration; since every vibration that comes from an inner plane can modify vibrations that act upon an outer plane; and since all vibrations are within the physical plane of action, we understand perfectly why every mental action will tend to produce a chemical change in the body. Although it is also true that two different grades of vibration on the same plane, or in the same sphere of action, may modify each other, still they do so only when the one is much stronger than the other.

All mental vibrations act more deeply in chemical life than the physical vibrations; therefore the former can entirely change the latter, no matter how strong the latter may seem to be. And this is how the mind exercises power over the body. Some mental vibrations, however, are almost as near to the surface as the physical ones and for that reason produce but slight changes, changes that are sometimes imperceptible.

Knowing this we understand why the power of mind over body becomes greater in proportion to the depth of consciousness and feeling that we enter into during any process of thought.

Therefore when we promote such changes in the body as we may desire or decide upon we must cultivate deeper consciousness, or what may be called subjective consciousness. This is extremely important because we can eliminate practically any physical disease or undesired physical condition by producing the necessary chemical change in those physical elements where that particular condition resides at the time. This is how medicine aims to cure and it does cure whenever it produces the necessary chemical change. But it fails so frequently in this respect that it cannot be depended upon under all circumstances.

Mental vibrations, however, when deep or subjective can in every case produce the necessary chemical change in the elements concerned. And the desired vibrations are invariably produced by positive, constructive and wholesome mental actions, provided those actions are deeply felt. Thus we realize that the power of mind acting through the law of vibration can, by changing or modifying the vibrations of the different elements in the body, produce almost any change desired in the physical conditions of the body.

What we wish to emphasize in this connection are the facts that every mental action is a vibration; that it permeates every atom of the body; that it comes up from the deeper chemical life, thereby working beneath the elements and forces of the physical body; and that according to a chemical law can modify and change the vibrations of those elements and forces to almost any extent within the sphere of natural law.

To modify the vibrations of the physical elements is to produce a chemical change in the body. But whether this change will be desirable or undesirable depends upon the nature of the mental action that produces the change. Therefore by entertaining and perpetuating only such mental actions as tend to produce desirable changes, or the changes we want in the body, we can secure practically any physical change desired; and we may thereby exercise the power of mind over body to an extent that will have practically no limitation within the natural workings of the human domain.

Chapter 16

The Power Of Mind Over Destiny

The destiny of every individual is being created hourly by himself, and that something that determines what he is to create at any particular period in time is the sum total of his ideals. The future of the person is not preordained by some external power, nor is fate controlled by some strange and mysterious force that master minds can alone comprehend and apply. It is our ideals that control and determine our fate. And we all have our ideals, whether we be aware of the fact or not.

To have ideals is not simply to have dreams or visions of that which lies beyond the attainment of the person, nor is idealism a system of ideas that the practical mind would not have the privilege to entertain. To have ideals is to have definite objects in view, be those objects very high, very low or anywhere between those extremes. The ideals of any mind are simply the wants, the desires and the aims of that mind, and as every normal mind will invariably live, think and work for that which is wanted by his present state of existence, it is evident that every mind must necessarily follow his ideals both consciously and unconsciously.

However, when those ideals are low or inferior the individual will naturally work for the ordinary and the inferior, and the products of his mind will correspond in quality to that for which he is working. Thus inferior causes will spring up everywhere in his life and inferior effects will inevitably follow. But when those ideals are high and superior he will work for the superior; he will develop superiority in himself and he will give superiority to everything that he may produce. Accordingly every action that he originates in his life will become a superior cause and will be followed by a superior effect.

The destiny of every individual is determined by what he is and by what he is doing. And what any individual is to be or do is determined by what he is living for, thinking for, or working for, be those objects great or small, superior or inferior. Man is not being made by some outside force, nor is the fate of man the result of causes outside of himself. Man is making himself as well as his future with what he is working for and in all his efforts he invariably follows his ideals.

It is therefore evident that he who lives, thinks and works for the superior becomes superior while he who works for less becomes less. And also that any individual may become more, achieve more and be more by entertaining superior ideals.

To entertain superior ideals is not to dream of the impossible, but to enter into mental contact with those greater possibilities that we are not able to discern. And to have the power to discern an ideal indicates that we have the power to realize that ideal. For the fact is we do not become conscious of greater possibilities until we have developed sufficient capacity to work out those possibilities into practical tangible results.

Therefore when we discern the greater we are ready to attain and achieve the greater, but before we can proceed to do what we are ready to do we must adopt superior ideals, and live up to those ideals according to our full capacity and power.

When our ideals are superior we shall think constantly of the superior because as our ideals are, so is our thinking.

And to thing constantly of the superior is to grow steadily into the likeness of the superior. Thus all the forces of the mind will move toward the superior. All things in the life of the individual will work together with greater and greater goals in view, and continuous advancement on a larger and broader scale must inevitably follow.

To entertain superior ideals is not simply to desire some larger personal attainment, nor is it to dwell mentally in some belief that is different from the usual beliefs of the world. To entertain superior ideals is simply to think the best thought about everything and to try to improve upon that thought every day. Superior idealism therefore is not mere dreaming of the great and beautiful. It is also the actual living in mental harmony with the very best we know in all things, in all persons, in all circumstances and in all expressions of life. To live in mental harmony with the best we can find anywhere is to create the best in our own mentalities and personalities.

And as we grow steadily into the likeness of that which we think of the most we will in this manner increase our power, capacity and worth, and in consequence be able to create a better future and a more worthy destiny. For it is the law under every circumstance that the man who becomes much will achieve much, and great attainments are invariably followed by a greater future.

To think of anything that is less than the best or to dwell mentally with the inferior is to neutralize the effect of those superior ideals that we have begun to entertain. It is therefore absolutely necessary to entertain superior ideals only, and to cease all recognition of inferiority or imperfection if we want to secure the best results along these lines.

In this connection we find the reason why the majority fail to secure any tangible results from higher ideals, for the fact is they entertain too many lower ideals at the same time. They may aim high, they may adore the beautiful, they may desire the perfect, they may live for the better and they may work for the greater, but they do not think their best thoughts about everything; therefore the house in their case is divided against itself and cannot stand.

Superior idealism, however, contains no thought that is less than the best, and it entertains no desire that has not greater worth in view. Such idealism does not recognize the power of evil in anything or in anybody. It may know that adverse conditions do exist, but it gives the matter no conscious thought whatever. And to pursue this course is absolutely necessary if we would create a better future. For it is not possible to think the best thought about everything while the mind gives conscious attention to adversity and imperfection.

The true idealist therefore gives conscious recognition only to the power of good. And he lives in the conviction that all things in his life are working together for good. But this conviction is not mere sentiment with him because he knows that all things will work together for good when we recognize only the good, think only the good, desire only the good, expect only the good and live only for the good.

To apply the principle of superior idealism in all things, that is, to live, think and work only for the highest ideals that we can comprehend means advancement in all things. To follow the superior ideal is to move towards the higher, the greater and the superior. And no one can continue very long in that mode of living, thinking and acting without creating for himself a new world, a better environment and a fairer destiny. We understand therefore that in order to create a better future we must begin now to select a better group of ideals, for it is our ideals that constitute the cause of the future we expect to create. And as the cause is so will also be the effect.

Chapter 17

The XRay Power Of The Mind

There are many things that the human mind can do and all of them are remarkable when viewed from the highest pinnacle of consciousness; but one of the greatest and most wonderful is the power of mind to see through things; that is, to cause the rays of its insight and discernment to pass through the problems of life just as the Xray passes through opaque and tangible substances. This power is latent in every mind and is active to a considerable degree in many minds; and on account of the extreme value of this power its development should be promoted in every possible manner.

When this power is highly developed practically all mistakes can be avoided. The right thing can be done at the right time, and every opportunity can be taken advantage of when the psychological moment is at hand; and in addition that finer perception of life will be gained through which consciousness may expand into larger and larger fields until the mind goes beyond all limitations and lives in the spirit of the universal.

We are all surrounded by possibilities that can never be measured, possibilities that, if employed even in a limited degree, would make life many times as rich and beautiful as it is now. The average person, however, does not see these many larger and greater ways of adding to the value and worth of existence. In other words, he cannot see through the circumstances of his life and thus take possession of the more substantial elements of growth, attainment and realization. Therefore life with him continues to remain a very ordinary matter.

He may know that there are better things in store and that there is something just beyond his present conception of life that could change his life completely if he could only lay hold upon it; still here is where he fails. He is in the dark. He cannot see how to proceed in gaining those greater and better things that life must contain. There is something in the way of his vision, a cloud, a veil, or an obstacle of some kind that hides the path to better things. And he cannot see through the obstacle. For this reason he remains where he is, wondering why he has not the power to reach what he is absolutely certain could be reached.

Millions of minds complain, "If we could only have things cleared up." This is the problem everywhere. Therefore, if they could all see their way clear what might they not accomplish both for themselves and others. But as a rule they do not see their way clear. Occasional glimpses of light appear when the real path to all good things seems to reveal itself, but before they are ready to take this path another cloud comes in the way and they have no idea what to do next. This is the experience of the average person along these lines.

And there seems to be no hope for the average person of ever passing from the lesser to the greater. The reason seems to be that when everything looks bright and the way is clear for greater results, desirable changes, more happiness and a larger life, something invariably happens to confuse things again, and the way to pastures green has for the time being been closed up once more. However, there is a way out of all sorts of conditions and everybody can find this way. Though it is a fact well to remember that every individual must always see this way for himself.

To proceed, everybody must develop the power to see through things. In fact, see through all things, or in other words learn to use the Xray of what may be termed superior degrees of intelligence. Every mind has this Xray, this higher power to penetrate and see through the difficult and the confused. And there is no condition, no circumstance, no obstacle, no mystery through which this ray cannot penetrate.

Therefore, when we employ this Xray of the mind we clear up everything, we see exactly where we are going, where we ought to go and where we should not go. So that to live constantly in the light of these finer grades of intelligence is to live in the cleared up atmosphere perpetually, no matter where our sphere of activity may be.

That those minds who live in the lower atmosphere of thought cannot see clearly where they are going is quite natural. Because in the first place these lower atmospheres of life are usually dense, being surcharged with the confused thought of the world; and in the second place, those who live in these lower grades do not employ the higher and finer rays of mental light.

We all know that the lower vibrations of physical light cannot pass through objects that are opaque. And we have also learned that the lower rays of mental light cannot pass through conditions and circumstances that are confused with discord and materiality. But it has been demonstrated that the higher rays of physical light can pass through almost any physical object. In like manner the higher rays of intelligence or mental light can see through almost anything in the mental world. And, therefore, the one who employs these higher rays of his mind will have the power to see through all things in his life.

However, when we speak of higher grades of intelligence as being the power that can see through things we must not infer that such intelligence is too high to be gained by the average individual. For the fact is that we all have this higher intelligence or finer rays of mental light active within us at all times. The secret is simply to learn how to apply these finer rays of mental light; thus we shall all be able to exercise the power to see through things.

The difference between the lower and the higher rays of light is found almost wholly in the attitude of the mind. That is, it is materiality on the one hand and spirituality on the other hand. By materiality we mean the attitude of mind that looks down; an attitude that is absorbed wholly in things; that dwells on the surface, and that lives exclusively for the body, not being consciously interested in anything but the body.

By spirituality we mean that attitude of the mind that gives an upward look to every thought, every desire, every motive, every feeling and every action of the entire being of man. But this upward look is not an attitude that looks for the invisible, nor an attitude that dreams of the glories of another sphere of existence. It is an attitude that simply looks for the greater possibilities that exist everywhere now, and for the beauty and the truth that crowns the whole world.

The mind that is material or that lives exclusively in the world of things is more or less in the clouds of confusion, therefore employs the lesser rays of intelligence, those rays that do not have the power to see through things. Such a mind, therefore, can never be in a cleared-up mental atmosphere. At times those minds that have been conscious of higher grades of mentality and that have seen the superiority and the brilliancy of this higher intelligence within them, may fall down temporarily into materiality, and for the time being they may lose sight completely of the higher consciousness of truth which they previously gained. Thus they frequently forget every principle in higher experience that once was so vivid, and while in this state of depression they generally conclude that all is sin, sorrow and human weakness after all; that is, it seems so to such a mind, because at such a time it is only the discord of the world and the results of mistakes that are discerned.

While in this submerged state the mind cannot see the splendors that are immediately beyond, and he cannot feel the supreme joy that higher realms have in store. Accordingly he comes to the conclusion that all is trouble and pain; he feels nothing else, knows nothing else and has temporarily forgotten the light and the joy that be knew while in higher realms of consciousness. The wise man who wrote the proverbs was in this lower mentality when he declared that all is vanity and vexation of spirit. And he spoke the truth about that lower world, that is, that material state that is composed wholly of the mistakes of man.

That material state, however, is not the only world that there is. There are other and finer worlds in the mind of man worlds where vanity does not exist and where nothing vexes the spirit. It is these higher and finer worlds of the mind that we must train ourselves to love, if we wish to see through things and thus learn to understand things as they really are. Then we shall find that the wrong is insignificant compared with the immensity of the right and the good.

When we look at things from a worldly or materialistic point of view, things do not appear very well, nor are things always very well in that particular state. They are frequently wrong and misdirected. But when we learn to see through things and see all things as they are we change our minds. Then we discover other worlds and other and higher stories to the mansion in which we live. The cellar is usually dark and damp, but how much better we find it further up. And yet when the average person is in the cellar of his mind he imagines that it is the only place there is and that there is neither light, comfort nor joy in the world. But why should we ever enter the cellar of the mind, and why should we permit a dark damp cellar to exist in our minds at all? There is no need of it in human life, for it is simply the sum total of our mistakes, and does not represent the real mansion of existence in any sense of the term.

The whole of the being of man should be illumined and every atom should be filled with harmony, comfort, joy and life. When the mind that had fallen down comes up again it realizes how absurd it was to forget all the truth and all the joy of real existence simply because there were a few clouds for a little time. However, after a few such experiences the mind learns to interpret the experience of the cellar and does not consider it real any more, but on the contrary makes haste to prevent that experience as well as all other descending attitudes in the future.

The mind that has never experienced the higher phases of consciousness does not know how to proceed to prevent the more adverse experiences of ordinary existence, and therefore will remain among the dense fogs of confusion more or less until taught how to rise into the finer grades of mental light. To proceed in rising above these undesirable conditions the first step to take is to make harmony, happiness and brightness of spirit the great objects in view. Even when we simply think of these states we elevate the mind in a measure, and whenever the mind is elevated to some extent we find that finer light comes into our world of intelligence; that is, the higher rays of mentality begin to express themselves and many things begin to clear up.

In this connection it is well to remember that our brightest ideas come while we are on the mountaintop of intellectual activity, and also that we can find the correct answer to almost any problem that may appear in personal life if we only go up in mind as high as we possibly can reach at the time. While the mind is up in those finer grades of intellect the most abstract principles are comprehended with almost no mental effort, and the path to greater things becomes as clear as the midday sun.

It is therefore a great and valuable accomplishment to be able to go up in the mind as high as one may wish. For to bring superior intelligence into constant use is to live in the world of absolute light itself, the reason being that this intelligence actually does possess Xray power of penetration in the mental world. There is nothing that this ray cannot see through, and there nothing is hidden that it cannot reveal to light.

Again we must remember, however, that it is not necessary to attain an enormous amount of wisdom and knowledge in order to gain the power to see through things in this way, because every stage of development that exists has the power to see through everything that may appear in that particular stage. Every individual in his present state has the power to see through everything in that state, that is, a finer grade of a mental light that belongs to that particular state and it has the Xray power of penetration in its own sphere. Accordingly he can learn to see through everything where he is without becoming a mental giant, or without acquiring wisdom which belongs exclusively to higher states of mental attainment.

The idea is to live in the upper story of your mental world whatever that world may be now, because by entering the upper story of your mental world you enter that state of your present intelligence that can see through everything that pertains to your present world. In order to enter the upper story of the mind the whole of life should be concentrated so to speak, upon the most superior states of existence that we can conceive of. This will cause the mind to become ascending in its attitude and the power of the ascending mind is immense. Such a mind will steadily grow upward and onward towards higher and finer grades of intellect, wisdom and mental light, and gradually this power to see through things will be gained. In addition everything will be turned to greater use and better use, and thus be made more conducive to a life of beauty, richness and joy.

However, when we proceed to consecrate a life to the superior in this manner we do not leave the world of things. We simply turn the life and the power of all things towards the higher, the larger and the better. We thereby cause the world of things to move steadily towards superior states of life and action. As we enter more and more into this upper realm of thought, light and understanding we should employ this penetrating power of finer intelligence in connection with every move we make. For it is the constant use and the true use of a power that develops that power. Therefore, we should do nothing without first turning on the Xray of the mind. In other words, we should view every circumstance from the standpoint of a clearer perception before any decision is made, and we should seek to secure the very highest viewpoint under every circumstance. This will not only give the mind a better understanding of how to proceed, but the faculty of finer discernment will be developed constantly, and our growth in wisdom and intellectual brilliancy will in time become remarkable.

In this connection we should remember that nearly all the missteps that are taken in the average life are the results of the mind's failure to penetrate the surface of things and conditions so as to see the real nature of the factors at work. But the lower mental rays, that is, that phase of intelligence that we use while in the lower story of the mind, do not possess.

Chapter 18

When Mind Is Broad And Deep

It has become a virtue to be broadminded, but there are times when certain virtues become so extreme in their actions that they cease to contain any virtue. In like manner it is possible for the mind to become so broad that it contains practically nothing of value being too superficial in its effort to cover the whole field to possess a single idea of merit.

To be progressive in thought is another admirable trait in the eyes of the modern world, but there are not a few of our advanced thinkers who advance so rapidly, according to their own conception of advancement, that their own minds are literally left behind; that is, they become so absorbed in the act of moving forward that no attention is given to that power that alone can produce advancement. In consequence their remarkable progress is in the imagination only.

Here it is well to remember that all is not thought that comes from the mind or that is produced in the mind. For the mere fact that we are thinking does not prove that we are creating thought. A large percentage of the products of the average mind is but heaps of intellectual debris accumulated in one place today and moved to another place in the mind tomorrow. In brief, too much of our modern thinking is simply a moving of useless mental material from one side of consciousness to another. However, in promoting the right use of the mind this practice is something that must be avoided absolutely for the mind cannot work to advantage under such conditions.

Thought that really is thought is the product of design and purpose, and is invariably the result of systematic efforts to work out principles. Accordingly such thought contains the power to serve certain definite objects in view.

We should therefore realize that the object is not to see how much we can hold in the mind, but how much we can actually possess or use. Therefore, if we learn to live, think and act correctly under all sorts of circumstances we must learn to employ the Xray of the mind; that is, that light of the mind that we are conscious of when living in the upper story of the mind; and it is when we are in that light that we can see through all things but how much we can take care of in side of every belief, every system, every idea and every experience this is genuine broad mindedness.

In considering this subject we must remember that what we accept becomes a part of ourselves. Therefore it is a most serious mistake to take into the mind everything that may come along. The fact is we cannot possibly exercise too much care in selecting our ideas, although we must not go to the other extreme and become so particular that we remain dissatisfied with everything. There is a happy medium in this connection that everyone can establish by training the mind to penetrate everything for the purpose of understanding the principles that underlie everything.

It has been well stated that we gradually grow into the likeness of that which we admire the most and think of the most. And it is true that we nearly always have special admiration for that which we constantly defend, whether we have fully accepted the same as true or not. The mind that is willing to accept almost anything for the sake of being broad will also be ready to defend almost anything to justify that position.

Therefore to defend all theories the past has advanced, is to reproduce our minds more or less in the likeness of all those theories. But since those theories contradict each other at almost every turn, many of them being illusions, we can readily imagine the result. In fact, the mind will, under such circumstances, be divided against itself and will be incapable of doing its work according to principle and law.

A confused mind is the greatest obstacle to real progress and the attempt to take in every new idea as true because it is new will invariably confuse the mind, and what is more such a practice will so derange judgment that after a while the mind will not be able to discriminate intelligently between the right and the wrong in any sphere of life.

In this connection we must remember that among the new ideas that are springing up in the world the larger number are either half-truths or illusions. And the reason why so many of these ideas are accepted as true is because real broad mindedness, that is, that attitude of mind that does not embrace everything but attempts to penetrate everything, is an art yet to be acquired by the majority. The average mind is ready to take in and hold almost any belief or idea if it happens to produce an impression that is favorable to his present condition of life, but there are few who are training their minds to penetrate everything for the purpose of understanding everything. For this reason a mass of ideas are accepted that contain neither virtue, truth nor power.

The attitude of tolerance is closely connected with broad mindedness and is usually considered an exceptional virtue. But again we are liable to be misled because there are two kinds of tolerance; the one holds a passive charity for everything without trying to find out the truth about anything; while the other enters into friendly relation with all things in order that the good and true that may exist in those things can be found.

The attitude of tolerance, however, is always valuable, in so far as it eliminates the spirit of criticism, because the spirit of criticism can never find the truth. But the spirit of friendly research always does find the truth. For this reason the penetrating mind must be kind, gentle and sympathetic. If it is not, the very elements that are to be examined will be scattered and misplaced. Besides it is the substance of things that contains the truth, and to enter into this substance the mind must be in sympathetic touch with the life and the soul of that which it seeks to understand.

That attitude of tolerance that is passive, is either indifferent, or will soon become indifferent; and mental indifference leads to stagnation, which in turn makes the mind so inactive that it is completely controlled by every condition or environment with which it may come in contact. Such a tolerance, therefore, must be avoided and avoided absolutely.

True tolerance refrains from criticism at all times but that is only one side of its nature. The other side enters into the closest mental contact with all things and penetrates to the very depths of the principles upon which these things are based. In this way the mind readily discovers those ideas and beliefs that constitute the true expressions of principles, and also discovers those that are mere perversions.

However, the tolerant mind does not condemn the perversions. It forgets them entirely by giving added life and attention to the true expressions, and thereby proceeds to give full and positive action to all those ideas and powers of which it has gained possession by being broad as well as deep.

Chapter 19

The Greatest Mind Of All

In order that we may rise in the scale of life the mind must fix attention upon the ideal. And the ideal may be defined as that possible something that is above and beyond present realization. To become more and accomplish more we must transcend the lesser and enter the greater. But there can be no transcending action unless there is a higher goal toward which all the elements within us are moving; and there can be no higher goal unless there is a clear discernment of the ideal.

The more distinctly the mind discerns the ideal, and the more frequently the ideal is brought directly before the actions of attention the more will the mind think of the ideal; and the mind invariably moves towards that which we think of the most. The man with no ideals will think constantly of that which is beneath the ideal, or rather that which is the opposite of the ideal; that is, he will think the most of that which is low, inferior and unworthy. In consequence he will drift more and more into the life of nothingness, emptiness, inferiority and want. He will steadily go down into the lesser until he wants for everything, both on the mental and physical planes.

The man, however, who has high ideals will think the most of the greater things in life, and accordingly will advance perpetually into the possession of everything that has greatness, superiority and high worth. The wise men of the past declared that the nation with no visions would perish. And the cause of this fact is simple. When we are not going up we are going down. To live is to be in action and there is no standstill in action. To continue to go down is to finally perish. Therefore to prevent such an end we must continue to go up. But we cannot continue to go up towards the higher unless we have constant visions of the higher. We cannot move mentally or physically towards that which we do not see. Nor can we desire that of which we have never been conscious.

In like manner the individual who has no ideals and no visions of greater things will continue to go down until his life becomes mere emptiness. Thus everything in his nature that has worth will perish, and finally he will have nothing to live for. When he discovers himself he will find that there are but two courses to pursue: To continue to live in the vale of tears he has made for himself; or to ascend towards the heights of emancipation, those heights which can be reached only by following the lofty vision.

It is the visions of greater things that arouse the mind to greater action. It is higher ideals that inspire man to create more nobly in the real, and it is the touch of things sublime that awakens in human nature that beautiful something that makes life truly worth living. Without ideals no person will ever attain greatness, neither will there be any improvement in the world. But every person who has ideals, and who lives to realize his ideals, will positively attain greatness, and will positively improve everything, both in his life and in his environment.

It must be clearly evident to all minds who understand the true functions of the ideal that the life of man will be worthless unless inspired by the ideal, and also that everything that is worthwhile in human existence comes directly from man's effort to rise towards the ideal. Such men, therefore, who are constantly placing high ideals before the world in a manner that will attract the attention of the world it is such men who invariably have the greatest mind of all.

The majority have not the power to discern the ideal clearly without having their attention aroused by the vivid description of some lucid mind that already does see the ideal. But when their attention is aroused and the ideal is made clear to their minds, they will begin at once to rise in the scale. That individual, therefore, who is constantly placing high ideals before the minds of the many is causing the many to rise towards the more worthy and the more beautiful in life. In consequence he is not only doing great things himself, but he is causing thousands of others to do great things. He is not only awakening the superior powers in his own nature, but he is also awakening those powers in the natures of vast multitudes. His mind, therefore, is doing work that is great indeed.

However, to place ideals before the minds of others, it is not necessary to make that particular purpose a profession, nor is it sufficient to reveal idealism in the mere form of written or spoken words. Actions speak louder than words and the man who does things exercises a far greater power for good than the man who simply says things. The ideal can be made a vital and a ruling element in every vocation. And all men and women can reveal the ideal through their work without giving voice to a single word concerning any particular system of idealism.

But it is not necessary to be silent concerning those sublime visions that daily appear before the mind, although it is well to remember that we always secure the best results when we do a great deal more than we say. The man who makes his work an inspiration to greater things will invariably do greater and greater work and he will also cause thousands of others to do greater work. He will make his own ideals practical and tangible, and will make the ideal intelligible to the majority. For though it is true that great words inspire the few, it requires great deeds to inspire the many.

The man who makes his own life worthwhile will cause thousands of others to make their lives worthwhile. In consequence the value and happiness that he will add to the sum total of human existence cannot possibly be measured. He is placing great and living ideals before the world and must therefore be counted among those who possess the greatest mind in the world.

The man who performs a great work has achieved greatness, but his work is the work of one man only. That man, however, who places high ideals before the minds of the many, thereby awakening the greatness that is latent within the many, causes a greater work to be performed by each one of the many; thus he gives origin to a thousand great deeds, where the former gives origin to a few only. That he is greater in exact proportion is therefore a fact that cannot be disputed. For this reason we must conclude that the greatest mind of all is invariably that mind that can inspire the greatest number to live, think and work for the vision.

To awaken the greatness that is latent in man is to awaken the cause of everything that has real worth in the world. Such work, therefore, is the greatest of all great work and it is a work that lies within the power of everybody. For we all can awaken the greatness that is latent in other minds by placing high ideals before those minds.

The great soul lives in the world of superior visions and aims to make those visions real by training all the powers of mind and personality to move towards those visions. And here it is highly important to realize that when the powers of mind and personality steadily move towards the ideal they will create the ideal more and more in the present, thereby making the ideal real in the present.

To live where there is neither improvement nor advancement is to live a life that is utterly worthless. But improvement and advancement are not possible without ideals. We must have visions of the better before we can make things better. And before we can make things better we must discern the greater before we can rise out of the lesser.

To advance is to move towards something that is beyond the present; but there can be no advancement until that something is discerned. And as everything that is beyond the present is ideal, the mind must necessarily have idealism before any advancement can possibly take place.

Everything that is added to the value of life has been produced because someone had ideals; because someone revealed those ideals; and because someone tried to make those ideals real. It is therefore evident that when lofty ideals are constantly placed before the mind of the whole world we may add immeasurably to the value of life, and in every manner conceivable.

The same law through which we may increase that which is desired in life we may apply for the elimination of that which is not desired. And to remove what is not desired the secret is to press on towards the ideal. The ideal contains what is desired, and to enter that which is desired is to rise out of that which is not desired. Through the application of this law we eliminate the usual method of resistance, which is highly important, because when we antagonize the wrong or that which is not desired we give life to the wrong, thereby adding to its power. For the fact is we always give power to that which we resist or antagonize. In consequence we will, through such a method, either perpetuate the wrong or remove one wrong by placing another in its place.

However, no wrong was ever righted in the world until the race ignored that wrong and began to rise into the corresponding right. And to enter into this rising attitude is to become an idealist. It is the idealist who reforms the world. And the greatest reformer is invariably that man whose conception of the ideal is so clear that his entire mind is illumined by a brilliant light of superior worlds. His thought, his life, his word, his action in brief, everything connected with his existence, gives the same vivid description of the ideal made real. And every person with whom he may come in contact will be inspired to live on those same superior heights of sublime existence.

Chapter 20

When Mind Is On The Heights

When the great soul transcends the world of things it invariably begins to dream of that which is greater, finer, more perfect; more beautiful and more sublime than what the life of present experience has been able to produce. But those dreams are not mere dreams; they are actually glimpses of what is possible or what may be near at hand; that is, prophetic visions of what is to be. The dreams of the small soul are usually temporary creations of an unguided, imagination. But the dreams of the great soul are flashes of light emanating from the realms of supreme light, revealing secrets that man shall someday be able to make his own.

What the great soul discerns in his visions and dreams is nothing less than that greater life and those greater things into the possession of which he is being prepared to enter. But if we would gain those greater things which are in store we must proceed to claim our own, and not simply continue to dream. The prophetic vision of the great soul does not reveal what will come to pass of its own accord, but what such a soul is now competent to bring to pass, provided he will use the powers that are in his possession now. In brief, a prophetic vision does not reveal something that is coming to you, but reveals something that you now have the power to bring to yourself if you will.

The soul that can transcend the world of passing things and dream of the world of better things is now in possession of the necessary power to make his dreams come true. For the fact is, we cannot discern the ideal until we have the power to make it real, nor can the mind arise into worlds sublime until it has gained the power to make its own life sublime. Therefore the soul that can look into the mystic future and discern a more beautiful life is prepared for such a life, has found the secret path to such a life, has the power to create such a life, though not merely in ages to come, but now. For what we see in our visions today we have the power to bring to pass in the present. This is indeed a great truth, and than this, nothing could possibly bring greater joy to the soul of man.

If we can see better days while our minds are, on the heights we can rest assured that we have the power to create better days. But we must proceed to use that power if we would enter into the pastures green that are before us. The law is that what we see in the ideal we must work for in the actual, for it is in this way alone that our dreams can come true without fail.

The dreams of the great soul always appear when the mind is on the heights. And it is such dreams alone that can contain the prophetic vision. What we dream of while on the low lands of life has no value. The fact is that if we would know the next step; if we would know what today can bring forth; if we would know what is best now; if we would know what we are able to attain and achieve now; if we would know those greater things that are now in store for us, we must rise to the mountain top of the soul's transcendent existence. It is there, and there alone, that these things are made known.

And every mind can at times ascend to those sublime heights. The great soul can readily rise to these mountaintops; in brief, such a soul has no other visions than those that appear on the mountaintops. Therefore the dreams of the great soul are not mere dreams; they are positive indications of what can be done, of what will be done; they are glimpses of the splendors of a greater day.

The soul that can rise to the mountaintops and see the splendor of greater things can indeed rejoice with great joy for such a soul is not destined for an ordinary life.

Greater things are at hand and a wonderful future will positively be realized. But such a future, with its richer possibilities and its more worthy attainments, will not come back to us where we now stand. We must move forward and work for what we have seen in the vision. That which is greater does not come back to that which is lesser. We must press on into the life of the greater if we would realize such a life. And if we dreamed the dreams of the great soul those dreams will indicate that we can. What we have seen on the heights reveals what we can do if we will. We have gained the power; the gates are ajar, and in the beautiful somewhere our own is waiting.

CPSIA information can be obtained
at www.ICGtesting.com
Printed in the USA
BVHW040753020323
659475BV00001B/47